PC Hardware Tuning
& Acceleration

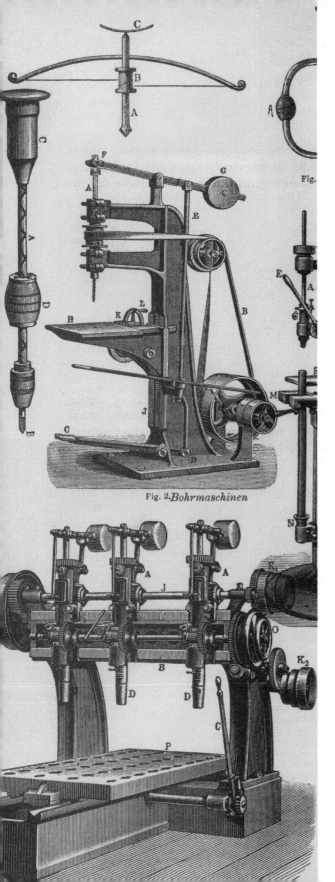

Fig. 2.*Bohrmaschinen*

PC
HARDWARE
TUNING
& ACCELERATION

VICTOR RUDOMETOV
EVGENY RUDOMETOV

A-LIST, LLC
295 East Swedesford Rd.
PMB #285
Wayne, PA 19087
702-977-5377 (FAX)
mail@alistpublishing.com
http://www.alistpublishing.com

This book is printed on acid-free paper.

PC Hardware Tuning & Acceleration
By Victor Rudometov, Evgeny Rudometov

ISBN 1-931769-23-0

Printed in the United States of America

04 05 7 6 5 4 3 2 1

A-LIST, LLC, titles are available for site license or bulk purchase by institutions, user groups, corporations, etc.

Book Editor: Julie Laing

Contents

Chapter 1

From the Industrial Era to the Information Age

Recent advances in technology have rapidly pushed humanity from an industrial age to a period that can be characterized mainly as informational. Computers gradually have become cheaper and more readily available. Their power and functional capabilities increase at a rapid pace. All these factors allow them to be used in practically every field of human activity. However, efficient usage of modern computers requires both advanced infrastructure and a certain level of user skill. These elements are essential to making the most of the high potential of computer hardware.

The advent of calculating devices during the industrial age was a logical stage of evolution: Science, technology, and industry require a high processing speed of intensive information flows. At first, the problem was alleviated by the creation of data-processing centers. These were based on sophisticated information-processing centers, which were very powerful (for that time) and, consequently, rather expensive. These centers were serviced, maintained, and supported by numerous highly qualified professionals. Recall the dinosaur machines of the 1960s and 1970s, known as mainframes: A typical mainframe was capable of processing 100,000 to 2 million simple 32-bit register-to-register operations per second. The amount of Random Access Memory (RAM) installed on such machines varied from several hundred kilobytes to several megabytes. Although such parameters are laughable today, they were impressive at that time.

A data-processing revolution took place about two decades ago, with the arrival of personal computers oriented toward individuals. The user-friendly interface (both hardware and software) of PCs significantly lowered the level of user knowledge and skill from that required by previous-generation computers.

Fig. 1.1. First IBM PC, developed in 1981

Fig. 1.2. Contemporary PC equipped with a wireless keyboard

Personal computers are created with relatively cheap components. The central element of the PC is the processor. The first microprocessor was designed and manufactured by Intel engineers, and this historic event began an era of cheap microprocessors. This first processor was named Intel 4004. Parameters of this key component were relatively modest: a clock frequency of 108 kHz, 0.06 MIPS (millions of instructions per second, or 60,000 operations per second), 2,300 transistors, 10 micrometer (μm) technology, a 4-bit bus, and 640-byte addressable memory. Still, it was the first chip used for arithmetical operations, and the computing power of this processor exceeded that of the ENIAC, the world's first electronic computer. The Intel 4004 microprocessor was officially released on Nov. 15, 1971.

Fig. 1.3. First processor released by Intel

Fig. 1.4. Intel Celeron 2 GHz processor

Since that time, processors have become much more powerful and sophisticated. The number of transistors has increased thousands of times, the clock frequency has grown significantly, and the potential capabilities of the processors have been extended dramatically.

Table 1.1. Number of Transistors in Intel Processors

Processor	Year of release	Number of transistors
4004	1971	2,250
8008	1972	2,500
8080	1974	5,000
8086	1978	29,000
286	1982	120,000
386	1985	275,000
486DX	1989	1,180,000
Pentium	1993	3,100,000
Pentium II	1997	7,500,000
Pentium III	1999	24,000,000
Pentium 4 (Willamette)	2000	42,000,000
Pentium 4 (Northwood)	2001	55,000,000

Processors with different architecture and power have been the basis for several generations of computers. This allowed for the creation of a variety of computers; it also provided a foundation for transition from centralized to decentralized information processing. Within a short period, billions of computers have been manufactured, ensuring the possibility of decentralized data processing. This factor made possible the wide use of an enormous number of computers in practically all spheres of human activity. As a result, the working style of millions of people has changed dramatically. Even more importantly, the development priorities of contemporary society have changed. Information has become an object of labor, as well as an important and valuable product. In the industrial societies of economically advanced countries, about 90% of total profits are related to information processing, accumulation, and sales. The efficiency of these activities strongly depends on the functional capabilities of computers, which, in turn, are dependent on the advancement of technology, information infrastructure, and the computer literacy of the population. These factors have top priority in the evolution of contemporary society and have attracted close attention from its members.

Processors comprising a billion transistors are expected to be released in 2007. As Intel Chief Executive Craig Barrett mentioned in a report at an Intel Developer Forum (IDF) session, within 15 years, advances in semiconductor technology are expected to enable processor architects to implement products with parameters that include the following:

- ❏ CPU clock frequency of 30 GHz
- ❏ 1 trillion instructions per second
- ❏ 2 billion transistors
- ❏ Transistor size of 10 nanometers (0.01 micrometers)

 Note

IDF is the largest technological conference for leading developers in which representatives of the mass media participate. IDF sessions are held several times each year in countries around the world. At these sessions, leading manufacturers discuss new and emerging technologies and products in the electronic industry. Traditionally, spring and autumn sessions take place in California. Other sessions often are held outside the United States.

Technological advances in the field of computing allow continual performance improvement and extend the functional capabilities of contemporary computers. However, the transition from centralized to decentralized data processing, accompanied by steady growth in the number of individuals involved in the process, has given birth to numerous problems — many unknown until recently. Some problems arose with the personalization of computers. This is reflected in the name of the most popular class of computers — personal computer, or PC. Availability, relatively low prices, and individual usage of these devices necessitate personal maintenance of computers. At the same time, the choice and the initial configuration of a particular computer are determined at the time of purchase. Final tuning of hardware and software is accomplished either by third-party specialists or by computer users themselves.

Such an approach ensures an optimal set of system software and application programs. This, in turn, allows efficient solutions to tasks and customization of the interface according to the individual preferences of the computer owner, or *end user*. However, the personalization of computers compels end users to have some technical background and to constantly improve their computer skills. Without this, it is impossible to optimally tune both hardware and software.

Overall performance, stability, and reliability of the system mainly depend on the quality of hardware customization and software fine-tuning. It is expedient to repeat the procedure of fine-tuning on different computer subsystems when new types of problems need to be solved or after the computer hardware and software have been upgraded.

Using the appropriate customization and running some utilities can compensate for negative changes to certain parameters in the course of long-term operation. These changes are usually related to the natural degradation of electronic components over time. To improve performance, it is useful to periodically upgrade device drivers and their Basic Input/Output System (BIOS).

Operations such as scanning and defragmenting hard drives must be performed regularly. Ignoring these operations results in performance degradation, and, in the worst case, data loss. It is necessary to track all news related to software patches and to upgrades of operating systems and third-party software.

The computer, which currently comprises millions of transistors distributed over hundreds of chips, has become a sophisticated system. It probably is the most sophisticated device designed by human beings. Like any complicated device, the computer has many hidden capabilities. Knowing and rationally using these hidden features of computer components allows them to be implemented to their fullest potential. This allows for the improvement of performance and the extension of the functional capabilities of hardware and software tools.

Thus, humanity has entered an age of informational civilization, which evolves according to its own laws and rules and has its own dead-ends, dangers, advantages, and interesting new capabilities.

Chapter 2

Philosophy of Hardware Overclocking

The complexity of system programs and application software is steadily increasing. Each individual can choose, purchase, and fine-tune a computer. Some time later, the PC user inevitably encounters performance problems when attempting to complete new tasks. After resources for improving computer performance by optimization have been exhausted, the user must take a more radical approach, such as purchasing a new computer, upgrading the existing one, or even using overclocked modes.

Computer performance and its functionality strongly depend on the parameters of the components in computer system and on their coordinated operation. It is not sufficient to choose a computer and determine its hardware components and software configuration. A computer must be fine-tuned and customized if you want to achieve maximum performance from its components and maximum efficiency from its functional capabilities. Furthermore, like any complicated device, a contemporary computer needs maintenance and service, and its software and hardware components must be used correctly.

If you ignore these requirements, an expensive contemporary computer will operate less efficiently than earlier and significantly cheaper models that have been optimally tuned.

Solving the Problem of Limited Resources

Even the newest computer that has been carefully selected and is regularly serviced cannot keep pace with constantly growing requirements. Sooner or later, you will face problems caused by inadequate performance for solving tasks. When there are no more resources for increasing the performance by optimizing computer hardware and software, radical measures must be employed.

Some people solve the problem of insufficient performance by purchasing a new computer; others try to upgrade an existing one. Both approaches involve financial expense, which can be significant. In addition, insufficient performance can occur on relatively new and workable computers, even those purchased less than a year ago!

Most PC users feel frustrated by this situation, and they search for ways to complete tasks while retaining the existing computer. Some people invent new methods and algorithms that allow them to solve problems with limited resources. Other people simply reduce the range of tasks they solve using a computer. They often abandon contemporary operating systems with convenient but resource-consuming interfaces. They prefer more economic but less advanced operating systems of previous generations. A computer with such limited resources often runs simple, obsolete programs that efficiently complete a limited range of unsophisticated tasks.

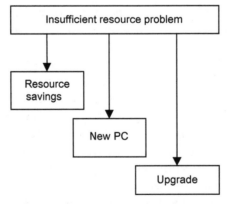

Fig. 2.1. Traditional solution to the problem of limited resources

A community of a different type of computer users balances cost with the rapid rate of technological advancement. People from this community often replace existing hardware, and in most cases, they are prepared to purchase a new computer.

Still, they have a clear understanding of the disadvantages of this approach, and many try to find an alternative. Such people realize the necessity of financial investment. They purchase the required devices and/or the newest computer hardware, then get rid of the existing equipment. Later, they either call experts or, if they have the required experience and qualifications, proceed through the steps that upgrade their computers. In the course of such multistep upgrades, they gradually replace obsolete components with high-performance ones that provide broader functional capabilities.

However, some serious problems often prevent people from upgrading such computers. These problems are mainly related to further technological advances and to improvements of the architecture and quality of the components. The fast progress of silicon manufacturing technologies often fails to provide backward compatibility or compatibility with standards, interfaces, or architectural solutions. These factors regularly become an obstacle to upgrading computers.

Evolution of Technologies and Components

Computing technologies are evolving, and new hardware and software appear constantly. Therefore, the lifetime of computer hardware components shortens constantly. As new components with higher performance and better quality appear on the market, it becomes economically unjustifiable to work with obsolete prototypes. This happens despite advances in manufacturing technology, reliability improvements, and the mean time between failures (MTBF).

Table 2.1. Evolution of Intel Manufacturing Processes

Process name	P854	P856	P858	Px60	P1262	P1264
Implementation (year)	1995	1997	1999	2001	2003	2005*
Lithography (nanometers)	350	250	180	130	90	65
Gate length (nanometers)	350	200	130	<70	<50	<35

* anticipated

Currently, the average maximum lifetime of processors, video adapters, and hard disks is five years. However, most people try to replace these components while they still are usable and operating satisfactorily. Typical computer users replace components after two or three years. However, the high reliability of computer components makes it possible to use them for more than ten years.

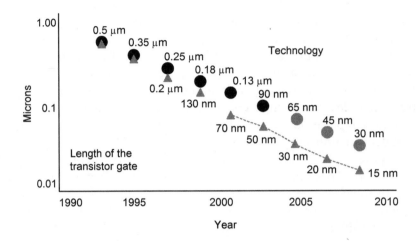

Fig. 2.2. Forecast for the evolution of Intel's semiconductor technology

These estimates also apply to central processing units (CPUs). Despite their complexity, these components are capable of working ten years or more. Still, significant changes, often referred to as *new architecture,* are introduced into the core of CPUs every three or four years. Standards for processor slots, via which CPUs are installed on motherboards, change even more frequently. Newer and more advanced processor models manufactured within the same line of products are usually released every few months. These newer models often are incompatible with the platforms designed for their predecessors, even if the processor-slot type is preserved. For example, Intel Pentium processors with MMX technology were designed, like earlier models of Intel Pentium, for the Socket 7 slot. However, in contrast to their predecessors, PMMX processors required motherboards that provided two levels of a processor's core voltage. This means that newer processors based on the P5 architecture required platform replacement. A similar situation took place with the arrival of processors created using 130-nanometer technology. Like their predecessors — Intel Pentium III processors based on 180-nanometer technology — they had P6 architecture. However, despite retaining the same type of socket — Socket 370, generally manufactured in those days — the newer processors needed a change of core voltage as well as the release of new chipsets. Once again, this meant that new motherboards were required.

Similar situations even took place for high-tech products. The evolution of CPU architecture and the form factors for Intel Pentium 4 processors also initiated corrections and changes to the PC platforms that supported these processors. Changes in power supply became traditional; they took place not only with changes to core architecture, but also with the migration from 180-nanometer to 130-nanometer technology. Form factors of the released models also changed. The Socket 423 standard, introduced for the earliest models of these processors, lasted only one year. After that, it was replaced by the incompatible Socket 478, which, as usual, required newly designed and manufactured motherboards and power supply units (i.e., a complete replacement of the PC platform).

Table 2.2. Evolution of Intel Processor Architecture for Desktop PCs

Processor	Slots	Year of release
8086	—	1978
286	—	1982
386	—	1985
486DX	Socket 1/Socket 2/Socket 3/ Socket 6	1989
Pentium/Pentium with MMX technology	Socket 4/Socket 5/Socket 7	1993
Pentium II/Pentium III	Slot 1/Socket 370	1997
Pentium 4 (Willamette/ Northwood/Prescott)	Socket 473/Socket 478/Socket T (Socket 775)	2000

Advances in computing technologies have changed other components, such as video adapters. Within a short time interval, the video subsystem of the PC has cycled through the following interfaces: Industry Standard Architecture (ISA), Video Local Bus (VLB), Peripheral Component Interconnect (PCI), and Accelerated Graphics Port (AGP). These interfaces have several types of specifications, which set standards for a range of specialized video adapters. For example, the AGP video adapters that dominate today's market have evolved over several generations: AGP 1X, AGP 2X, AGP 4X, and AGP 8X. They differ not only in performance, but also in the requirements of their electric, logical, and design interfaces, which makes video-adapter compatibility impossible. A new, advanced, and promising interface, PCI Express (at development time, it was known as 3GIO), also requires new designs for video adapters and motherboards.

As a result of this interface evolution, platforms change every two or three years, keeping pace with the release of new lines of video adapters that support more advanced interfaces.

Table 2.3. Evolution of Video Adapters

Video adapter	Throughput (MB/sec)	Year of release
ISA	8	1984
VLB	100–133	1992
PCI	133	1993
AGP	266	1997
AGP 2X	533	1998
AGP 4X	1,066	1999
AGP 8X	2,100	2002
PCI Express	2,100+	2004*

* anticipated

The situation with RAM is no less dramatic. RAM also is subject to constant changes of types, interfaces, and form factors. During the relatively short time that has elapsed since the arrival of the first PCs, several mutually incompatible types of RAM have appeared.

Table 2.4. Evolution of RAM

RAM type	Year of release
FPM DRAM	1992
EDO DRAM	1994
SDRAM (SDR SDRAM)	1997
DRDRAM	1999
DDR SDRAM	2001
DDR II SDRAM	2004*

* anticipated

Each RAM type had several versions with different frequency and timing parameters. For example, Single Data Rate (SDR) Synchronous Dynamic Random Access Memory (SDRAM), usually referred to as just SDRAM, has modules corresponding to PC66, PC100, and PC133 specifications. (The digits in the specification names designate their maximum operating clock frequencies: 66 MHz, 100 MHz, and 133 MHz.) Double Data Rate (DDR) SDRAM contains modules designed to operate at frequencies of 100 MHz, 133 MHz, 166 MHz, and 200 MHz. DDR SDRAM ensures a data rate twice that of SDR SDRAM, even at the same frequencies. DDR SDRAM modules are intended to operate at 2.5 V, SDR SDRAM at 3.3 V, and Extended Data Output (EDO) SDRAM at 3.3 V or 5 V. Compatibility is complicated by different form factors for modules released at different stages of microprocessor evolution. Examples of common form factors of the RAM module include Single In-line Pin Package (SIPP), Single In-line Memory Module (SIMM), Dual In-line Memory Module (DIMM), and the RIMM memory module. (RIMM often is referred to incorrectly, with "R" standing for "Rambus." However, the term RIMM is not an acronym; it has been trademarked.) Each form factor has several variants with different sizes and different numbers of pins.

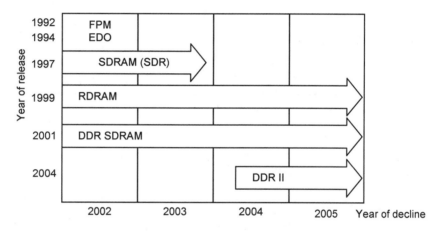

Fig. 2.3. Forecast for the evolution of RAM

It should not be necessary to prove that these differences result in the incompatibility of memory modules.

Other components, such as hard disks, also evolve at a rapid rate. During the last few years, hard-disk capacity usually doubled every 9 to 12 months. The MTBF declared by manufacturers often exceeds 500,000 hours.

In contrast to processors, video adapters, and RAM, new hard-disk models retain compatibility with earlier models for a long time. For example, ATA100 (100 MB/sec) disks can be connected to ATA66 (66 MB/sec) and even to ATA33 (33 MB/sec) controllers. However, with such connections, you cannot get the maximum speed potential. Furthermore, it is impossible to achieve the full compatibility of Advanced Technology Attachment (ATA) devices with controllers implementing Serial ATA150 (150 MB/sec) and Serial ATA300 (300 MB/sec) interfaces. The same relates to the compatibility between Serial ATA150 devices and parallel interface ATA100/66/33 controllers.

Table 2.5. Evolution of the ATA Interface

Bus	Throughput (MB/sec)	Year of release
ATA16	16.7	1996
ATA33	33.3	1997
ATA66	66.7	1999
ATA100	100	2000
ATA133	133	2001
Serial ATA150	150	2002
Serial ATA300	300	2004*
Serial ATA600	600	2007*

* anticipated

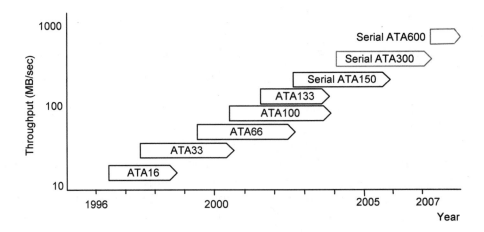

Fig. 2.4. Forecast for the evolution of the ATA interface

The data provided in this chapter prove that the rapid progress of semiconductor technologies and of the architecture of computer components doesn't allow standards, interfaces, and form factors to be retained for long periods of time.

Table 2.6. Lifetime of Architectures, Standards, and Components

Components	Period (years)
Processors	3–4
Video adapters	2–3
RAM	2–3
Hard disks	1–2

Under such conditions, after several years of operation, it becomes impossible to upgrade a computer system by simply replacing obsolete components.

Last Resort for Performance Improvement

Besides purchasing a new computer or optimizing hardware and software, there is another way to improve computer performance. This approach prolongs the lifetime of a usable machine that rapidly becomes obsolete. Furthermore, it often gives a "second life" to a computer that hardly can be classified as "modern." This approach uses special methods of enhancing performance. The underlying idea of these methods is to exploit some computer components in forced modes to get the most out of their hidden reserves. As a rule, this significantly improves the speed of each component, increasing overall system performance. One of the most common methods of achieving a forced mode of operation is to increase the clock frequency beyond the level recommended by the manufacturer. That's why these methods are generally known as *overclocking*.

The possibility of overclocking is the consequence of manufacturing principles. It is impossible to ensure that a factory will produce identical processors. A similar situation exists for video adapters and RAM chips. Therefore, to guarantee that the manufactured components satisfy the declared requirements, manufacturers have to provide some performance reserve. This is especially true with the implementation of new technologies and architectures, whose initial performance barely differs from that of earlier products of the line. This hidden performance reserve usually can be implemented via forced modes such as overclocking.

Note that forced modes sometimes are achieved at the expense of component stability and, consequently, overall system reliability. In addition, forced modes usually decrease the MTBF parameter. In many cases, this is acceptable. Taking into account the duration of expedient usage of computer components, a possible decrease of reliability and the MTBF (for example, from 10 or 20 years to 5 years) often is justified. The system would remain usable until it became obsolete. In addition, as previously shown, upgrades become problematic after a certain amount of time. However, if overclocking procedures are used expertly, system crashes and hang-ups will be rare, and they seldom will produce fatal results.

The use of forced modes for server components is not recommended. Furthermore, the use of such modes should be prohibited in computer systems that manage potentially dangerous or critically important tasks at nuclear power stations, chemical industries, rocket launching facilities, hospitals, etc. In these areas, computer failures potentially are more dangerous than in homes or offices.

Concepts, Principles, and Stages of Overclocking

Forced modes extend the lifetime of obsolete computers that can't be upgraded because of the reasons given in this chapter. Recently, however, this method of performance enhancement became popular even among the users of brand-new PCs. The cases in which such users ask someone to overclock a computer before its purchase are not rare. Experienced PC users prefer to overclock newly purchased computers at home, carefully choosing optimal modes, and then carefully testing all subsystems at all overclocking stages.

Thus, improvement of overall system performance is one of the main goals of overclocking. Overclocking is popular not only because of the natural desire, characteristic of most advanced PC users, to improve the computer architecture. The main reason behind its adoption lies in the field of economics. The overclocking procedure achieves relatively high performance for relatively little financial cost. For example, performance gain for processors might increase 20% to 30%. With extreme overclocking modes (which are more risky), performance may improve 50% or more. Proceeding the similar way, the performance of RAM, a video adapter, and even a hard disk can be improved significantly. An overclocked computer automatically moves into a higher category. Lower-level components often compete successfully with more powerful and expensive products. The most important fact here is that this goal can be achieved without additional financial investment. Processor overclocking alone can save you several hundred dollars. You can compensate for decreased reliability by observing several recommendations and taking some simple steps. By following these recommendations, you can work successfully with an overclocked system for a long time.

Note that the popularity of overclocking has a negative effect on the economical interests of manufacturers. Most aren't willing to lose even a small part of their profits. Apart from this, some individuals use overclocking capabilities to gain illegal profits. For example, such individuals may fake a trademark; supply fraudulent components, including processors and memory chips; then sell them as more advanced and more expensive components. Some small companies go further: They manufacture ready-to-use systems based on overclocked components and sell them without informing their customers about the overclocking.

To counteract potential fraud and protect their commercial interests, most leading manufacturers introduce features into their modules mainly aimed at preventing fraudulent distribution and limiting performance improvement, making it difficult to use overclocked modes of operation.

Despite these efforts by brand-name manufacturers, overclocking popularity gradually has increased. The arrival of appropriate motherboards and chipsets, as well as the release of specialized software, serves as a catalyst to this process. The contemporary market consists of a variety of specialized tools that maintain optimal temperature modes for computer components. This simplifies the process of setting overclocked modes and of testing the system in various modes of operation.

However, improving system performance by using overclocking mustn't be considered only from the economical point of view. The newest units and components often operate in overclocked modes, even though the initial performance of these components is high. Current silicon-manufacturing technologies allow performance to be increased much higher than the level declared by manufacturers. In addition, most advanced PC users have a natural desire to predict the evolution of computer components. Hence, they have a goal beyond financial savings: Use forced modes to investigate the architecture of different elements and forecast the development of current technologies.

The investigation of forced modes and the development of recommendations interest not only addicted individuals (also known as overclocking fans), but also many serious companies all over the world. Such research work even may be sponsored by leading manufacturers. (The cooperation between KryoTech and AMD, mentioned in some publications, is an illustrative example. As a result of this research work, AMD processors in an extremely overclocked mode reached the barrier of 1 GHz long before the release of processors for which this clock frequency was routine.)

The interest in the overclocking problems manifested by some manufacturers can be easily explained. This research work helps them improve the architecture and enhance the performance of their products. Apart from this, it allows them to accumulate valuable statistical information on malfunctions and failures, which helps them develop efficient hardware and software tools that improve reliability. Finally, the ability of computer hardware components to retain stability in over-clocked modes serves as excellent promotional material for products. Some companies use the experience and technologies accumulated by overclockers in their manufacturing process and attempted to supply high-performance hardware. For example, Compaq was supplying high-end server platforms based on tech-nologies developed by KryoTech for the extreme cooling of AMD Athlon and similar processors operating at clock frequencies that exceeded recommended val-ues 1.5 to 2 times.

The results of cooperation and research conducted by famous and respectable companies have stimulated the growth of an army of enthusiasts. Most of them view extreme overclocking as a kind of sport.

As the number of overclocking fans grows, the number of Web sites dedicated to this topic increases. These sites consider various aspects of overclocking prob-lems that might arise, and provide useful recommendations.

The materials provided in this book attempt to explain overclocking topics systematically and produce both general and specific recommendations for tuning and overclocking the main elements of a computer.

Chapter 3

Moderate and Extreme Overclocking Modes

Modern computer components have significant hidden performance reserves provided by contemporary manufacturing technologies. These hidden reserves can be used to improve performance considerably. This can be achieved via forced modes — either moderate overclocking with partial implementation of reserves, or an extreme variant that gets the most out of potential reserves of computer-hardware components.

The problem of using computer components (particularly processors) in forced modes has been avidly discussed in recent years. Many publications and Web sites (some references will be provided in the appropriate sections of this book) have been dedicated to this topic.

Overclocking procedures are aimed at enhancing the functional capabilities of computers, the most important goal being performance gain. Note that numerous methods allow you to achieve this goal. These methods include hardware tuning for a specific configuration, as well as fine-tuning of the operating system and application software. Optimization of the chosen operating system holds a special place among these operations. Regular maintenance procedures are also important. All of these operations are aimed at achieving the maximum possible performance of the computer.

Further reserves for performance improvement are related to implementation of the overclocking potential, which often remains hidden from end users.

The measures that implement this hidden potential include special operating modes of computer components and the usage of special software tools such as accelerators and drivers. Besides this, newer versions of BIOS codes can be useful. Versions developed for powerful high-performance devices also may be suitable.

Overclocked modes with the optimal choice of external and internal clock frequencies are the most important means implementing hidden reserves. This ensures the possibility of achieving maximum performance of computer hardware.

Motherboard manufacturers, trying to attract potential users, not only support overclocking capabilities, but also promote and popularize features that support the possibility of using such modes. Some manufacturers even supply software products with their motherboards that simplify the implementation of overclocked modes. As a result, the overclocker community has grown. Even official overclocking contests have become a common event.

Different people have different views of the overclocking problem. Some users are not excited by this aspect. Others consider themselves the principal opponents of overclocking, based on the well-grounded opinion that performance gain that results from overclocking has a negative effect on the overall stability and reliability of a system's components. The third category of users contains the overclocking fans. Each party has strong arguments and deserves respect; therefore, each user must make his or her own choice.

Nevertheless, things aren't that simple as they might seem at first glance. Overclocking isn't a panacea for performance improvement. It cannot help you to turn your Intel Pentium III into an Intel Pentium 4.

There are two types of overclocking. These differ in both method and goal.

The first type is known as *extreme overclocking*, or overclocking for its own sake. When choosing this approach, extremely high results can be achieved. However, practical work in such modes might be impossible, because both overclocked systems and their operating conditions are usually exotic. This may remind you of Formula One cars: They race at nearly aerospace speeds and they are unsuitable for driving under normal conditions. Such extreme overclocking is usually incompatible with stable operation of processors; therefore, it is of little or no interest to ordinary PC users. Some people even consider extreme overclocking to be a kind of extreme sport. Extreme overclocking normally requires cryogenic cooling via liquid gases. Such experiments are usually conducted to report specific records. Under current conditions, extreme overclocking can be considered research work, which contributes to contemporary scientific knowledge.

Another type of overclocking is achieved without a negative effect on overall system stability. *Moderate overclocking* is the optimal compromise between high performance and excellent reliability. This sort of overclocking interests the vast majority of users. For this reason, it is the main topic of this book. This type of overclocking also can be used for scientific evaluation of the capabilities of semiconductor technologies and the architecture of specific computer-hardware components. Such evaluation can be used to predict future development.

Growth Problems and Hidden Reserves

When overclocking is discussed, it usually relates to the processor, and often to the memory modules. Most individuals define overclocking as a forced increase of the clock frequency. As a result of such operations, computer performance improves considerably. If you purchase a system equipped with Intel Pentium 4, operating at a frequency of 1.6 GHz, and with DDR266 memory modules (DDR SDRAM operating at 266 MHz), you could use straightforward manipulations to make it operate as Intel Pentium 4 with a frequency of 2.4 GHz equipped with DDR333 memory modules. Detailed instructions on performing these procedures will be covered later in this book. Here, a general understanding will be given of the *CPU clock frequency* specified in the product names of various processors (such as Intel).

CPU clock frequency, usually expressed in gigahertz, determines the time interval, also known as *clock*, during which the processor executes a specific number of instructions. If a processor has a clock frequency of 1 GHz, then 1 clock equals 1 nanosecond (nsec). If a processor has a clock frequency of 2 GHz, 1 clock is half the length of that from the previous processor; therefore, it equals 0.5 nsec. Consequently, the processor is capable of executing the same number of instructions twice as fast (if both processors execute the same number of instructions per clock). Based on these facts, the performance of the second processor is twice that of the first processor. In practice, however, this conclusion is not quite right.

At this point, the term *processor performance* should be clarified. From the end user's point of view, processor performance is the time required to execute a specific set of commands that make up the program code. The smaller this time interval, the greater the performance of the processor installed in a specific system. This means that performance can be considered the number of commands executed per clock multiplied by the CPU clock frequency:

Performance = (Commands per clock) × (Clock frequency)

The number of commands executed per clock depends both on the program being executed and on the processor architecture (i.e., which set of commands can be processed and how this job is done). At the processor level, each command is converted into a set of several machine instructions or elementary commands. The efficiency of this transform depends both on the processor architecture and on the code optimization for specific processor architecture. Besides this, depending on the processor architecture, elementary commands can be executed in parallel.

These considerations make it clear that it would be incorrect to compare the performance of processors that have different architecture if that comparison is based only on their clock frequencies. Some applications might run more efficiently on AMD processors; other ones may perform better on Intel processors with the same clock frequency.

However, within one *processor family* (i.e., processors that are based on the same architecture but have different clock frequencies), such a comparison would be correct.

Thus, to increase the processor performance, it is expedient to raise its clock frequency. To be more precise, the improvement is made to the semiconductor core, the basis of this key computer component.

Each processor is intended to operate at the specified clock frequency. If the manufacturer declares that a processor is designed to run at 1,600 MHz, this is an objective reality, rather than simple declaration. Intel Pentium 4 processors of 1,600 MHz and 2 GHz are manufactured using the same technology, under the same conditions, and at the same technological line. However, various circumstances can cause deviations from specified parameters, which result in slightly different characteristics of the final products. To detect such deviations and their consequences, manufacturers perform technological control and testing of their products. Naturally, it is impossible to test each processor separately, especially taking into account the scale of production. The common practice is to perform selective testing of each party of the final product. During this testing, the manufacturer determines the general ability of the processors to run at a specific clock frequency. Then, the entire group of processors is marked according to that frequency. A specific processor purchased by a customer may not have undergone the procedure of selective testing; thus it may be capable of supporting a higher clock frequency than the declared one. Finally, each manufacturer provides some "reliability reserve" that accounts for static dispersion of parameters, because it is impossible to guarantee reproduction of manufacturing processes. As a result, most processors can run at increased clock frequencies (i.e., they can be successfully overclocked).

However, as processor manufacturing technologies become more advanced, the static parameter dispersion narrows. This enables manufacturers to supply more powerful processors and gradually decrease their "reliability reserve." As a result, low-end models are more promising to overclockers than high-end ones (Fig. 3.1).

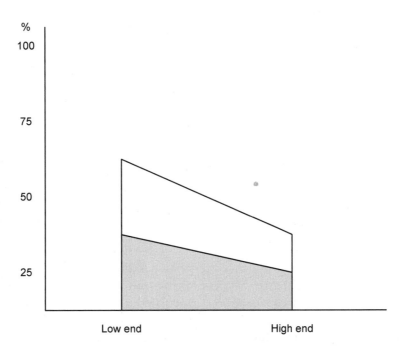

Fig. 3.1. Performance reserve for low-end and high-end processor
in various overclocking modes

Fig. 3.1 shows performance reserve for low-end and high-end processors in different overclocking modes. The dark area corresponds to moderate overclocking modes; the light area shows extreme modes, which sometimes can be implemented only under specific conditions.

Which effects and physical processes prevent unlimited growth of the internal frequencies of the semiconductor core?

Recall that contemporary processors installed in modern PCs comprise millions of elementary units made of transistors manufactured using *Complementary Metal-Oxide Semiconductor* (CMOS) technology. Furthermore, a semiconductor core, such as Northwood, created using 130-nanometer technology and serving as the basis for Intel Pentium 4 processors, comprises 55 million of transistors. Its successor, the Prescott core, manufactured according to the 90-nanometer technology, comprises more transistors. The size of each sophisticated unit is smaller than the size of a typical flu virus. These millions of transistors are connected to one another in specific ways, are concentrated in an extremely small area, and often operate at frequencies that already exceed 10 GHz. All these elements can produce negative effects on one another. This can be illustrated by an example of two adjacent conductors that connect elements of the processor core.

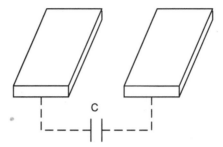

Fig. 3.2. Two adjacent conductors that connect elements
in the processor core

These conductors are characterized by *mutual capacitance*. This capacitance depends on the distance between them and on the area of the facing sides. The value of this capacitance is calculated according to a well-known formula $C = k \times S/d$, where C is the capacitance, S is the area, d is the distance, and k is permittivity coefficient, whose physical meaning will be considered later.

For a direct current, this configuration is a reliable dielectric; at high frequencies, mutual capacitance generates uncontrolled currents because the capacitor formed by the two conductors has a certain conductivity. Although conductors are small, the distance between them also is very small. The high values of the frequencies and the high number of conductors (there are millions of them) means their influence on the frequency properties of the internal core structures is not negligible. This is especially true because each capacitor, besides capacitance, is characterized by *resistance* and *inductance*. This means that the equivalent circuit of the configuration formed by two conductors represents a set of capacitors, resistors, and inductors. It has the properties of the integrating circuit with multiple resonance frequencies. Furthermore, there is mutual influence among several conductors. This statement is illustrated by Fig. 3.3, which presents the configuration that would be formed by three conductors.

Undisputedly, the frequency properties of such a configuration are considerably more complex than those of the diagram formed by two conductors. Both active (resistors) and reactive (capacitors and inductors) components of the impedance are distributed along the entire length of the conductors. This significantly complicates the behavior of such systems at high frequencies. The situation is worse because conductors do not operate in vacuum. On the contrary, they are surrounded by a medium with specific dielectric properties, which influences the values of mutual capacitance. Furthermore, materials used in chip manufacturing have permittivity that exceeds 1; therefore, the values of mutual capacity are higher than those produced by the cases just considered. An approximation that illustrates this situation is in Fig. 3.4.

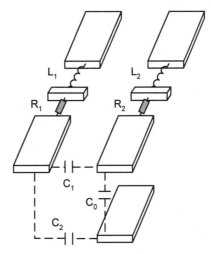

Fig. 3.3. Three neighboring conductors that connect core elements

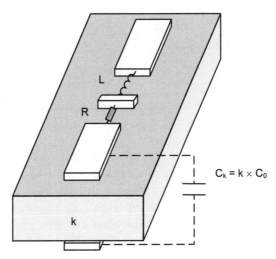

Fig. 3.4. Two conductors, with consideration for dielectric influence

Based on this illustration, it is clear why designers try to use materials with smaller values of permittivity (k) to insulate semiconductor chips.

The frequency characteristics in all these cases depend on a range of factors: the size of conductors, their mutual position, the chemical composition of conductors and of surrounding dielectrics, microscopic defects, etc. Any variation in these parameters changes the frequency characteristics. This explains why the "reliability reserve" is mandatory for sophisticated components operating at high frequencies.

Besides conductor topology, it is necessary to consider the influence of transistors, whose structure and physical nature are more complicated than those of individual conductors. Besides controlling currents, transistors themselves are powerful sources of electromagnetic radiation. Transistors also influence adjacent elements and are exposed to similar effects. The p-n-junctions present in their structure can perform detection of undesirable parasitic currents, their amplification, and their transmission. It is hard to imagine the intensity of the electromagnetic field within a processor chip; the elements are packed so densely that they are characterized by alternating fields of high intensity. These fields form a complicated structure that changes depending on the different operating frequencies of internal processor structures, forming maximums and minimums in different areas of the chip.

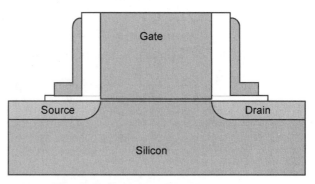

Fig. 3.5. Transistor structure

The general pattern is even more complicated, especially because at current transistor sizes, the influence of quantum effects is considerable and gradually increases. These effects, despite advances in transistor architecture, increase uncontrolled currents. Their total flow represents a combination of currents generated by insulation defects, those generated by leaks of a different nature via capacitors, and even the ones caused by the tunnel effect. This part of the uncontrolled current is large, and it tends to grow with an increase in clock frequency. This also requires manufacturers to provide reliability reserve in their products.

To compensate for negative effects and ensure stable CPU operation at higher frequencies, manufacturers have to increase core voltage. Compare the core voltages for low-end and high-end processors. For high-end models, the core supply voltages are always higher, no matter which architecture and manufacturing technology is used.

If you increase the clock frequency above the standard level and need to ensure reliable operation of the processor (as well as of the RAM modules, graphics processor of the video adapter, and video memory), you also need to increase the voltage. For moderate overclocking, this increase must not exceed the maximum values recommended by the manufacturer. These parameters are provided in technical documents known as *datasheets*. Usually, the limiting values established by processor manufacturers are approximately 10 percent above the standard value. Provided that normal operating conditions are ensured, which primarily relates to the temperature modes, such an increase doesn't result in a significant decrease of the processor's lifetime due to the rapid degradation of semiconductors.

Unfortunately, increasing the power-supply voltage and clock frequency also increases the temperature, which can be evaluated by the following formula:

$$P \approx C \times V^2 \times F$$

Here, P is the heat generated by the CPU, in watts; C is the correction factor that accounts for the mutual capacitance of the processor-core components, depending on its architecture; V is the power-supply voltage; and F is the clock frequency in gigahertz.

This formula can be expressed as follows:

$$P_k = P_0 \left(\frac{V_k}{V_0} \right)^2 \left(\frac{F_k}{F_0} \right)$$

The variables with the index of k designate overclocked parameters; the variables with the index of 0 represent standard values.

Table 3.1 presents an evaluation of the expected heat generation for an Intel Pentium 4 processor with a standard operating frequency of 2 GHz in different overclocking modes, with $P_0 = 52.4$ W and $V_0 = 1.50$ V.

Table 3.1. Evaluation of CPU Heat Generation (P_k) with Different F_k and V_k Values

F_k (GHz)	2.1	2.2	2.4	2.6
V_k (V)	1.50	1.50	1.55	1.60
P_k (W)	**55.0**	**57.6**	**67.1**	**77.5**

If a processor's clock frequency is decreased until it is below its standard value, the core voltage also can be decreased appropriately without disrupting overall system stability. According to the previous formula, this decreases the heat emitted by the processor. Such operations are usually performed automatically by combinations of specific hardware and software. Normally, they are intended to reduce power consumption and are typical for mobile computers. However, the same approach is also applicable to desktop computers.

Note that in recent years, the generated heat has increased even for standard operating modes. This happened despite PC designers' constant efforts to improve CPU internal structures and decrease the core voltage. Decreasing the core voltage became possible with the reduction of the transistor sizes, and, consequently, a decrease in the sizes of their *gates*. The gate controls the source-drain current. The thinner the gate, the lower the voltage required to maintain field intensity.

A reduction in the channel length is accompanied by a reduction of losses. The newest research aimed at improving transistor topology also helps improve parameters.

Thus, technological advances and improvement of processor architecture ensure an increase of CPU clock frequencies (Fig. 3.6).

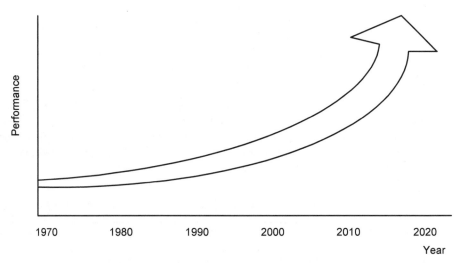

Fig. 3.6. Exponential growth of processor performance
(based on IDF data)

Unfortunately, this performance growth also has a dark side: increased heat emission. The area of the processor chip hardly changes; therefore, this growth in heat emission results from increased energy density.

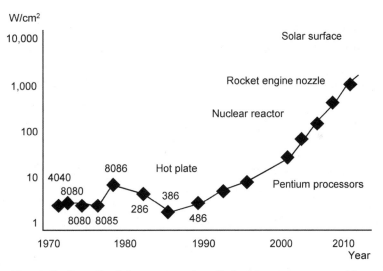

Fig. 3.7. Growth of the energy density inside a processor chip, compared to other densities (based on IDF data)

Under conditions of inadequate cooling, the high heat emission overheats the processor's internal structures, which negatively affects its reliability and speeds up the processes of semiconductor decay.

Semiconductors are sensitive to heating. The average energy of atom oscillations grows with the temperature. As a result, the number of broken links in the grid of the silicon crystal grows, and new pairs of electrons and holes appear. When the temperature limit is reached, semiconductor properties change. For example, conductivity of semiconductors and dielectrics grows as the temperature rises. As a result, the system begins to malfunction, and failures become persistent. To avoid these negative effects, it is necessary to use adequate cooling. Currently, no high-performance processor can operate without a high-quality cooler equipped with a massive heatsink and a powerful fan. It would be logical to suppose that by taking special steps to ensure CPU cooling, stable operation of chips designed for room temperature can be achieved. Note that such chips are usually overclocked to frequencies that considerably exceed the standard values. In particular, such measures (which are not actively promoted) were used at an Intel Developer Forum (IDF) session during a demonstration of standard processors in extreme overclocking modes.

Among the facilities that ensure extreme overclocking, a special place is held by the cooling facilities that reduce the CPU temperature below the ambient temperature. Specially designed freezers (or freezing chambers) are used for this purpose. This idea isn't new or revolutionary; most corporations specializing in high-end servers demonstrated temperature overclocking at least at an experimental level. Such manufacturers include Sun Microsystems, IBM, and Compaq. In 1991, Intel and NCR started "temperature overclocking under manufacturing conditions," a project known as Cheetah. The portfolio of patents registered within the range of this project later became the property of the six founders of KryoTech, who at that time were working as researchers for NCR. Later, these developments enabled KryoTech professionals to create a range of facilities that ensure efficient cooling of overclocked CPUs, at the expense of placing them, with motherboards, into freezing chambers.

Cryogenic methods of cooling overclocked components also can be considered variants of such solutions. Some details of such experiments that relate to extreme CPU overclocking will be presented later in this chapter. However, before proceeding to extreme overclocking, consider some aspects of traditional moderate overclocking modes.

Moderate Overclocking of Processors

(Based on materials and with the permission of Russian magazine *ComputerPress*.)

CPU overclocking is based on the performance growth of the processor's core and integrated L2 cache memory (and, consequently, on overall performance growth), caused by an increase in the operating clock frequency. Both the core and L2 cache operate at the *internal CPU clock frequency*.

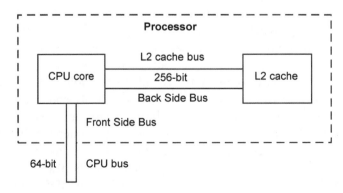

Fig. 3.8. Core, cache memory, and buses of an Intel processor

Besides the CPU clock frequency, other parameters must be considered, such as the *Front Side Bus* (FSB) *frequency* and the *memory-bus frequency*.

The FSB frequency is the main operating frequency of the entire computer system. All other frequencies, which define the operations of computer subsystems and the data exchange among them, are synchronized with it.

In contemporary computers based on the Intel Pentium 4 processor, the FSB frequency can take values of 100 MHz, 133 MHz, and 200 MHz. It is expected that the FSB frequency will increase with technological advances and improvement of the architecture of semiconductor elements. On this bus, the duration of one clock is determined by rectangular voltage pulses. The arrival time of each new pulse is defined by its front (leading edge).

The *processor bus*, also known as the *system bus*, connects the processor to the *North Bridge* of the chipset. This bus is used by the processor for communication with all the other devices.

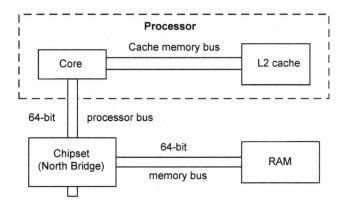

Fig. 3.9. CPU and RAM connection to the North Bridge

In computers based on the Intel Pentium 4 processor, data travel on the system bus at the frequencies of 400 MHz, 533 MHz, and 800 MHz. This means that in the Intel Pentium 4 processor, the data-transmission frequency is four times that of the FSB frequency, and the address-transmission frequency is twice that of the FSB frequency. If the FSB frequency is 100 MHz, then the data-transmission frequency is 400 MHz, and the address-transmission frequency is 200 MHz. If the FSB frequency is 133 MHz, then the data-transmission frequency is 533 MHz. At an FSB frequency of 200 MHz, data are transmitted at 800 MHz. This value usually is provided in CPU and motherboard specifications.

Besides the frequency, the processor bus is characterized by its *throughput* (i.e., by the maximum amount of data that can travel via this bus per second). The CPU bus has a width of 64 bits, which means that it can transmit 64 bits (8 bytes) per clock. Consequently, if it operates at 400 MHz, its throughput is 3.2 GB/sec (400 MHz × 8 bytes). At 533 MHz, its throughput will equal 4.2 GB/sec.

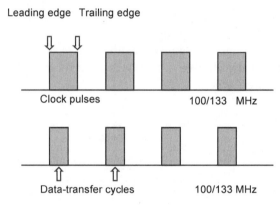

Fig. 3.10. Organization of data transfer
via the SDR SDRAM bus

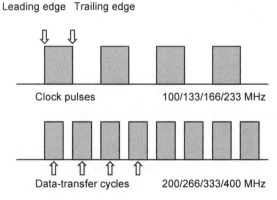

Fig. 3.11. Organization of data exchange
via the DDR SDRAM bus

The memory-bus frequency defines the speed of data exchange between the processor and the memory controller (located in the North Bridge). This frequency depends on the memory type and is synchronized with the FSB frequency. For the most common types of DDR memory, data transfer occurs twice per clock, both at the leading and trailing edges of the clock pulse. This means that the effective frequency of a memory operation is twice the clock frequency. The predecessor of DDR memory — SDR SDRAM — transmitted data at a frequency that coincided with the memory-bus frequency.

For DDR200, DDR266, DDR333, and DDR400, the effective frequency that defines the data-transmission speed is equal to 200 MHz, 266 MHz, 333 MHz, and 400 MHz, respectively. The clock frequency is 100 MHz, 133 MHz, 166 MHz, and 200 MHz, respectively. The memory-bus frequency is synchronized with the FSB frequency. For example, if the FSB frequency is 133 MHz, the memory frequency relates to the FSB frequency as shown in Table 3.2.

Table 3.2. Frequency Relationship between DDR Memory and FSB

DDR memory frequency (MHz)	FSB frequency (MHz)	Multiplier	Throughput (GB/sec)
200	133	1.5	1.6
266	133	2.0	2.1
333	133	2.5	2.6
400	133	3.0	3.2

Like the system-bus frequency and the memory-bus frequency, the CPU clock frequency is synchronized with the FSB frequency. The coefficient that relates the CPU clock speed and the FSB frequency is known as the *multiplier*. For example, if the FSB frequency is 133 MHz and the multiplier equals 18x, Intel Pentium 4 processor will operate at a frequency of 2.4 GHz. For an Intel Pentium 4 processor with a clock frequency of 2 GHz, the multiplier will equal 20x, provided that the FSB frequency is 100 MHz.

At first, it might seem that the easiest way to increase the internal (core) clock frequency of the processor is to increase the multiplier value. If you have an Intel Pentium 4 processor operating at 1.6 GHz with a standard multiplier of 16x (and an FSB frequency of 100 MHz), you can turn it into an Intel Pentium 4 with a frequency of 2.4 GHz by simply changing the multiplier to 24x. This method is simple and reliable, but, in all contemporary processors, including those of the AMD Athlon family, the possibility of changing the multiplier is disabled.

In AMD processors, it is still possible to sidestep this limitation using some tricks. (Information on this will be described in the appropriate sections of this book.) It is impossible to overcome this limitation in Intel Pentium 4 and Intel Pentium III.

Don't let this upset you. Recall that the CPU clock frequency is synchronized with the FSB frequency. Therefore, if you increase the FSB frequency, the CPU clock frequency will increase automatically. Motherboard manufacturers provide the capability of increasing the FSB frequency. For example, the nominal clock frequency of an Intel Pentium 4 processor is 2.4 GHz at an FSB frequency of 133 MHz (which means the multiplier is set to 18x). By increasing the FSB frequency to 180 MHz, the CPU frequency increases to 3.2 GHz (Table 3.3).

Table 3.3. Increasing the CPU and Memory Clock Frequencies with the FSB Frequency

FSB frequency (MHz)	CPU clock frequency (GHz), 18x multiplier	System bus frequency (MHz)	System bus throughput (GB/sec)	DDR266 memory frequency (MHz)	Memory throughput (GB/sec)
133	2.4	533	4.2	266	2.1
140	2.5	560	4.4	280	2.2
150	2.7	600	4.8	300	2.4
160	2.8	640	5.1	320	2.5
170	3.0	680	5.4	340	2.7
180	3.2	720	5.7	360	2.8

Overclocking a system by increasing the FSB frequency also increases the memory frequency, because RAM is synchronized with the processor clock frequency. This circumstance is important, although it often is overlooked by PC users. You can never know what will die first: the memory or the processor. Furthermore, the memory usually is the main hindrance to overclocking; it can prevent you from increasing the FSB frequency. If the processor is capable of operating at an FSB frequency of 180 MHz but the memory is unable to support FSB frequencies that exceed 150 MHz, you are limited to the FSB frequency of 150 MHz. For this reason, overclocking strongly depends on the quality of the memory modules.

There are two main ways of overcoming the limited capabilities of memory overclocking. First, by tuning the BIOS settings, it is possible to change the ratio between the FSB frequency and the memory frequency, making the frequency of the memory bus as small as possible. Because overclocking results in a proportional increase of the FSB and memory frequencies, it is possible to create conditions under which the processor is overclocked to higher frequencies than the memory. Suppose that the system is designed to run at an FSB frequency of 133 MHz and to use DDR266 memory modules. This means that 266 MHz is the nominal frequency for the memory. If you specify the coefficient that relates the FSB and memory frequencies as 1.5, then, at an FSB frequency equal to 133 MHz, the memory frequency will be 200 MHz. This will be below the nominal value. When you overclock the FSB frequency to 177 MHz, the processor also will be overclocked, and the memory will operate at its nominal frequency of 266 MHz. This method of artificially slowing the memory is used quite frequently. However, it has drawbacks: When the maximum FSB frequency is reached, the memory still may run at a frequency below the nominal value.

For example, suppose that you have an Intel Pentium 4 processor with a nominal frequency of 2.4 GHz (and a multiplier value of 18x). The nominal value of the FSB frequency is 133 MHz, and your computer is equipped with DDR266 memory modules. If the coefficient that relates the memory and FSB frequencies is set to 1.5, you might manage to overclock the FSB frequency to 160 MHz. In this case, the CPU clock frequency will be calculated as follows: 160 MHz × 18x = 2.88 GHz. (This is not a bad result.) However, the memory will operate at a frequency calculated as follows: 160 MHz × 1.5 = 240 MHz (i.e., below its nominal frequency). Which is better — to raise the CPU clock frequency and decrease the memory frequency, or to try to overclock both the CPU and RAM?

This example that synchronizes the CPU and memory operations is not an artificial one. Overall system performance depends on the CPU and memory frequencies. Thus, true overclocking means finding optimal values. The conditions that provide a maximum increase in overall system performance often have to be defined experimentally.

Another popular method uses faster memory than recommended in the motherboard specification. For example, DDR333 or even DDR400 memory modules can be used with motherboards supporting DDR266/200 memory. If you combine both approaches, you can achieve high FSB frequencies without being limited by the memory capabilities.

In addition to frequency, other important parameters influence memory performance. These are *memory timings*. In most cases, tuning these will achieve significant performance gain. These will be covered in more detail in the appropriate sections of this book. For the moment, however, it is necessary to make some important notes.

Before you start processor overclocking, it is necessary to improve the cooling system. You should correctly install the cooler and the heatsink. At first, it may seem that there are no difficulties here, but this impression is wrong. To achieve adequate cooling, a layer of thermal paste usually is placed between the surfaces of the processor and heatsink. The only exception is the so-called box coolers, included with the kits supplied by CPU manufacturers.

Fig. 3.12. Box kit comprising a CPU and cooler

Fig. 3.13. Box cooler

Such coolers have a special heat-insulation layer; therefore, they do not require thermal paste. In all other cases, thermal paste is a must. If there is not enough thermal paste (for example, the CPU surface isn't covered entirely), or if the paste has been dried up, you must remove the paste using a special dissolvent and apply a new layer. Never try to scratch off the paste with the knife; scratches on the surface of the heatsink or CPU will degrade heat dispersion. The new layer of thermal paste must be distributed evenly over the entire surface of the CPU cover. This layer mustn't be too thick; a heavy layer also would degrade heat dispersion. The optimal thickness of the layer is 0.5 mm.

You should consider purchasing a high-quality heatsink with a turbo-cooler. Box coolers usually are not intended for extreme modes. They do allow moderate overclocking, because box coolers have some power reserve.

Besides this, it is necessary to consider installing an extra cooler into the system unit. Although this will make the computer a little noisy, it will improve the efficiency of the cooling system considerably.

The right choice of motherboard also is of great importance. Its design, manufacturing quality, and used components must guarantee stable operation at high frequencies. Built-in tools, as well as BIOS, must support overclocked modes.

The ability to change the following is standard:

❑ FSB frequency
❑ Coefficient relating the memory and FSB frequencies
❑ Memory timings
❑ Processor and memory core supply voltage

Different manufacturers have different opinions about the overclocking problem. For example, on most Intel motherboards, this capability is locked. Other leading motherboard manufacturers, such as Abit, Asus, Gigabyte Technology, and MSI Computer, not only enable their users to change the previously listed standard settings, but they welcome the overclocking capability. Some manufacturers even include special overclocking utilities with their motherboards.

The advantage of special utilities used for system overclocking is that main settings are changed programmatically, rather than via traditional methods such as BIOS or special switches on the motherboard. Usually, this takes place when the operating system is up and running. As a result, it is not necessary to reboot the computer after each change is introduced — provided that the system operates reliably and remains stable. Otherwise, reboot is inevitable.

The functional abilities of such programs partially duplicate BIOS. Despite this, BIOS often provides a richer set of functionality, such as memory timing settings. However, special utilities significantly reduce the time required for system overclocking. Programs that support several motherboards can be purchased separately.

In concluding this section, it is necessary to mention that the final result of overclocking strongly depends on the quality of the components used. It also depends on the overclocker's skills and experience.

The examples of extreme overclocking confirm this statement.

Extreme Overclocking of Processors

For extreme overclocking of processors, characterized by extremely high values of clock frequencies, it is often necessary to increase the core supply voltage considerably. These processes are accompanied by exceedingly high heat emission. If the heat is never dispersed from the processor chip, the heat balance required for correct operation of the core will be disrupted. Furthermore, the uneven workloads on internal structures and units of the processor, as well as their different operating frequencies, make the heating and heat emission of different core areas uneven.

High temperatures of specific internal structures of the CPU chip limit the range of clock frequency growth. Besides this, high temperatures speed up semiconductor decay, which greatly reduces the processor durability. In addition, the processor becomes less stable, which influences overall system stability. Undesirable processes, even those that take place in recommended operating modes, significantly increase and speed up in extreme overclocking modes.

A powerful and efficient cooling system can help to withstand some decay in semiconductors. Such a cooling system can ensure acceptable conditions for the processor operation, even in the course of extreme overclocking.

Under conditions of extreme overclocking, the heat emission of the processor is so high that heat balance based on air-cooling support becomes inadequate. Liquid-cooling systems based on water are also unable to solve this problem. Water has the highest heat capacity of the natural substances that remain liquid in temperatures acceptable for semiconductors. Using water for cooling under normal conditions, including moderate overclocking, ensures efficient heat transmission from the hot chip to the heatsink equipped with a fan. Still, even a water-cooling solution cannot ensure the temperature required for extreme overclocking.

The inefficiency of traditional cooling methods in extreme overclocking modes is related to the overheating of the internal circuitry of the processor chip. Extra heat emitted from these areas likely will disrupt the operation of complex semiconductor circuits. Local overheating can even destroy these circuits. Under these conditions, semiconductors are unable to function. Traditional cooling facilities cannot always evacuate this heat efficiently, especially because of the limited thermal conductance of silicon (or any other material).

However, the value of *heat flux*, defined as the amount of heat passed per time unit, is proportional to the temperature gradient:

$$q \approx \left(\frac{dT}{dz} \right)$$

This means that the rate of heat transfer depends on the temperature difference between the heating zone and cooling zone. To ensure efficient cooling under conditions of extreme overclocking, it is best to use cryogenic temperatures at the surface of the cooled chip.

Normal ice can be used as cooling substance; *melting heat* — the energy produced by a transition from a solid state to a liquid state — is rather high. This circumstance ensures that relatively little ice will be needed during experiments. However, its melting temperature is only 0°C (32°F), which doesn't ensure high values of heat flux. Ice can be used in experiments in the field of extreme overclocking, but it is unlikely that high results would be achieved in such experiments.

The best temperature parameters are characteristic for so-called dry ice, or solid-state carbon oxide. Its temperature of phase transition is –70°C (–94°F). This, compared to normal ice, ensures far better values of heat flux. However, for carbon oxide, the temperature of phase transition into the gaseous state is much lower than the melting temperature of normal ice. This means more dry ice will be required for extreme overclocking experiments.

Liquid nitrogen is a more promising cooling substance because its boiling temperature is close to –196°C (–320°F). However, its phase-transition energy is very low. As a result, the heat absorbed during evaporation of this substance is also very low. To cool powerful processors characterized by high values of heat generation, large amounts of liquid nitrogen will be required. Despite these difficulties, it was liquid nitrogen that allowed research groups in many countries to achieve good results in extreme overclocking of standard processors.

Specific features and experimental results in the field of extreme overclocking of processors are provided in the following sections.

Extreme Overclocking of Intel Processors

(With the permission of **http://www.overclockers.ru**, a Russian-language Web site.)

Liquid nitrogen has become the chosen cooling agent for extremely overclocked processors because it has an exceedingly low evaporation temperature. The large difference between the temperatures of evaporating nitrogen and the CPU surface produces an intensive heat exchange that efficiently cools the overclocked CPU.

The use of liquid nitrogen required nonstandard facilities to play the role of processor cooler. To achieve this goal, researchers created a special container for nitrogen, installed on the top of the processor. This container was made from copper, the material with the best thermal conductance, after silver (which, unfortunately, is too expensive).

The cooling container could have been manufactured by soldering (from sheet copper), drilling (one piece of copper), or welding.

A stannic (tin) solder has never been recommended for such purposes, because standard solders of this type form unstable compounds at cryogenic temperatures. At temperatures below –40°C (–104°F), tin turns into mechanically unstable modification. Besides this, such a construction has lower thermal conductance than one manufactured from pure copper. This is because tin and its alloys have high thermal resistance. Another solution, which would require a container made from a solid piece of copper, was free from this drawback. Still, a large piece of expensive copper would be required, and most of this copper would be wasted. Furthermore, to manufacture this detail in such a way, special instruments would be required.

Therefore, the third method was chosen. Elements of the container were joined using *electron-beam welding*. During this technological process, the parts to be connected were heated to the required temperature by the beam of electrons sped up to a high speed. The bond obtained using this method was rather strong. In addition, the residual stresses that remained in the material after the welding operation were minimal, which ensured high strength under drastic temperature changes and no geometric distortions of the cooling container due to geometrical skew.

The dimensions of the cylindrical cooling container were chosen as follows:

❏ Height — 300 mm
❏ Diameter — 50 mm
❏ Thickness of walls — 2 mm
❏ Thickness of bottom — 3 mm

This construction was installed on the processor and fastened using metal rods with screws and nuts. The container was pressed against the board using an additional plate of metal. This means that on one side, the rods were screwed into the motherboard, which has special holes for fastening coolers, and on the other side, they were fastened to the metallic plate that pressed the cooling container against the processor.

The process of fastening this cooling system was as follows:

1. The copper cooling container was installed on an Intel Pentium 4 processor.
2. Metal rods with the appropriate screws were screwed into the holes in the motherboard and were fastened with nuts.
3. From above, the container was pressed against the board using a plate of aluminum, which had a hole in the center and several holes for fastening rods at its sides.

4. The rods were set into the holes, and the entire construction was fastened with nuts screwed from above.

5. A funnel made of stainless steel was installed into the central hole.

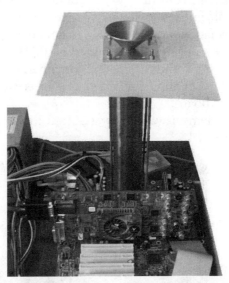

Fig. 3.14. Cooling system for extreme processor overclocking (assembled)

Fig. 3.15. Filling the cooling system with liquid nitrogen

After some time, a computer equipped with this cooling system stopped booting normally. The problem was related to condensation: A large amount of water accumulated near the processor slot. In the course of cooling, pieces of frozen condensate fell from the cooling container. On the motherboard, they melted and produced water. In other places on the motherboard, the water appeared because of the intense boiling of nitrogen, during which some drops fell on the motherboard. As a result, water appeared in cool regions of the motherboard.

Ice crystals falling from the copper cooling container caused another serious problem. This problem was solved using a normal household fan. A stream of air, directed from this fan toward the cooling container, diverted all crystals that otherwise would have fallen on the motherboard. However, because the fan blew a large amount of air around the cooling container, it increased the thickness of the frost that covered the cooling container. This layer was rather dense, and it didn't fall onto the motherboard.

As for the problem of water, it was solved by placing a sheet of foam rubber below the motherboard.

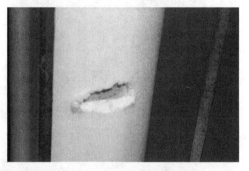

Fig. 3.16. Ice-crystal layer on the copper cooling container

Fig. 3.17. Motherboard covered with frost

Later, another method was found to help solve the problem of condensation. The basic idea of this method was as follows: The entire motherboard was covered evenly with liquid nitrogen. As a result, the entire motherboard was cooled below the freezing point of water, and ice caused significantly less harm to the motherboard.

These steps ensured stable operation of the system in the extreme overclocking mode of the processor. Of course, this could occur only if the cooling container contained liquid nitrogen and, consequently, if it ensured constant cooling of the processor.

Configuration of the Test System

Processors:

❐ Intel Celeron 1.8 GHz
❐ Intel Pentium 4 2.2 GHz
❐ Intel Pentium 4 2.4 GHz
❐ Intel Pentium 4 2.53 GHz

Motherboard:

❐ Epox 4BDA

RAM:

❐ Corsair XMS3000

Video adapter:

❐ VisionTek GeForce4 Ti4600

Software:

❐ Windows XP Professional/2000 Professional SP1
❐ Nvidia Detonator 29.42

Researchers had to abandon thermal paste. At the temperature of liquid nitrogen, it would freeze. As a result, the CPU surface would be covered with a layer of ice, which would decrease heat exchange considerably. The cooling container also would freeze to the processor's surface. Therefore, a long time would be required to replace the processor. Because of this, a cooling container often was installed on a heat-dissipating plate, the Integrated Heat Spreader (IHS) of Intel Celeron and Intel Pentium 4 processors, without thermal paste.

Fig. 3.18. Frozen thermal paste on the heat-dissipating plate
of the processor

Extreme Overclocking of Celeron Processors

Overclocking can be accomplished by increasing the FSB clock frequency while increasing the CPU core voltage (Vcore) to the maximum allowed by the motherboard. At a core voltage of 1.85 V, stable operation could be ensured at FSB frequencies to 140 MHz. This would result in a CPU frequency of 2,520 MHz (Fig. 3.19).

Several tests were performed for this mode. Test results obtained using SiSoftware Sandra are in Fig 3.20.

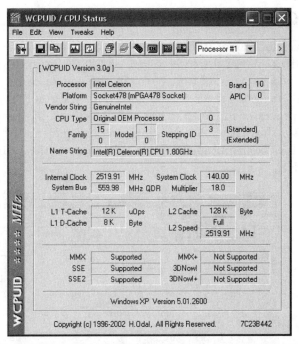

Fig. 3.19. Parameters of Intel Celeron 1.8 GHz overclocked to 2,519.91 MHz

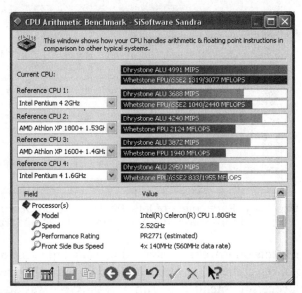

Fig. 3.20. Results of testing the overclocked CPU using SiSoftware Sandra

Extreme Overclocking of Pentium 4 Processors

Extreme overclocking of Intel Pentium 4 processors can be achieved by raising the FSB clock frequency at the core voltage of 1.85 V. As in the previous case, cooling was performed using liquid nitrogen. In the course of extreme overclocking, all CPU models exceeded the level of 3 GHz. The best result was achieved by the Intel Pentium 4 processor intended to run at 2.53 GHz. Being cooled by liquid nitrogen, this processor showed stable operation at a bus frequency of 185 MHz. Under conditions of the fixed multiplier value, this ensured the resulting clock frequency of 3,524 MHz.

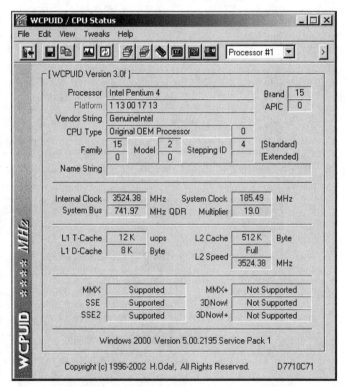

Fig. 3.21. Parameters of Intel Pentium 4 2.53 GHz overclocked to the maximum frequency of 3,524.38 MHz

In experiments on extreme overclocking using liquid nitrogen conducted by another group of researchers (see **http://holicho.lib.net**, a Japanese Web site), the Intel Pentium 4 processor intended to run at 3.06 GHz was successfully overclocked to 4.6 GHz. In these experiments, the FSB frequency equaled 200 MHz. Thus, one of the most powerful Intel processors implementing the NetBurst architecture, manufactured using 0.13-micrometer technology, was overclocked 1.5 times.

In extreme overclocking experiments, researchers used the Gigabyte 8INXP motherboard based on the Granite Bay (E7205) chipset. To achieve high results, the CPU core voltage was increased to 2.1 V. Because the motherboard doesn't support such voltage levels, the voltage was raised using its hardware modification.

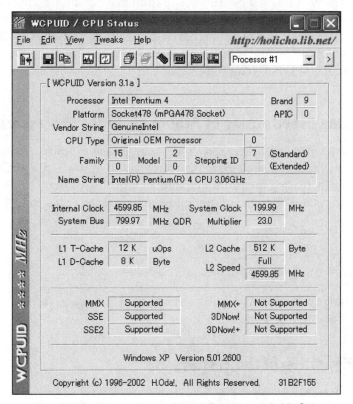

Fig. 3.22. Parameters of Intel Pentium 4 3.06 GHz
overclocked to 4,599.85 MHz

This example can be used to partially predict the performance of future processors with a clock frequency of 4.6 GHz and a bus frequency of 800 MHz. Such frequencies can be achieved only by the Prescott core, which has 1 MB of L2 cache memory manufactured using 0.09-micrometer technology.

Note that Intel processors are not exceptions. A similar procedure of extreme overclocking is applicable to AMD products. Materials from a range of sites (see *Chapter 19*) serve as evidence of this.

Extreme Overclocking of AMD Processors

Extreme overclocking of AMD processors in systems with liquid nitrogen cooling has its own specific features. AMD products have no heat-dissipating plate similar to IHS on Intel processors; therefore, with AMD products, there is a high risk of causing mechanical damage to the core. Besides this, the lack of the even, smooth, and large area formed by heat-dissipating plate creates additional difficulties when ensuring even contact of the cooling container and the processor. On the other hand, the lack of this plate can have a positive effect on the cooling quality, because there will be only one transition (core — cooling container) instead of two transitions (core — IHS — cooling container).

Extreme Overclocking of Athlon XP 1700+ Processors

Well-known overclocker YAO (see **http://www.piopioshardware.com**, a Chinese Web site) accomplished extreme overclocking of the AMD Athlon XP 1700+ processor by increasing the multiplier and EV6 processor bus.

The system operated at the following increased voltages:

❑ CPU core voltage (Vcore)

❑ North Bridge voltage (Vdd)

❑ RAM modules supply voltage (Vdimm)

The processor was cooled using liquid nitrogen; for the North Bridge chip, water cooling was used.

Configuration of the Test System

Processor:

❑ AMD Athlon XP 1700+ (Marking = AXDA1700DLT3C JIUHB0309UPMW, clock frequency = 1,467 MHz, FSB frequency = 266 MHz, L2 cache = 256 KB, Vcore = 1.5 V)

Motherboard:

❑ Epox EP-8RDA+, Rev.1.1, BIOS 3305

RAM:

❑ A-Data DDR400, 256 MB, 2.79 V (3-2-2-2.5 1CMD) × 2

Video adapter:

❑ Albatron MX420 (GeForce4 MX420)

Hard disk:

❑ Quantum (20 GB, 7,200 rpm).

Power supply unit:

❑ SevenTeam ST-300BLV

Driver:

❑ Nvidia nForce Driver 2.3, Nvidia Detonator 42.86

As a result, the processor was overclocked to the frequency of 3,107 MHz, at a multiplier raised to 13x and a system bus frequency increased to 239 MHz. The voltage at the North Bridge chip was increased to 1.92 V using the hardware modification of the motherboard. RAM voltage was raised to 2.79 V; the CPU core voltage reached 2.016 V.

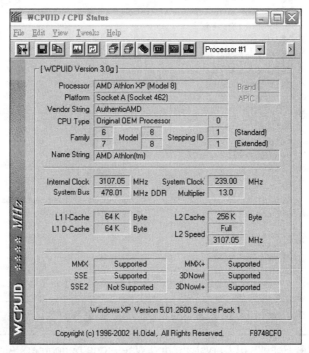

Fig. 3.23. Parameters of AMD Athlon XP 1700+ overclocked to 3,107.05 MHz

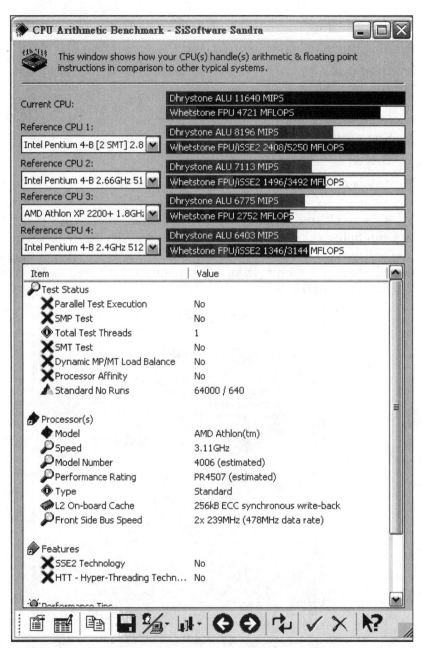

Fig. 3.24. Results of Dhrystone and Whetstone benchmark AMD Athlon XP 1700+ overclocked to 3,107.05 MHz

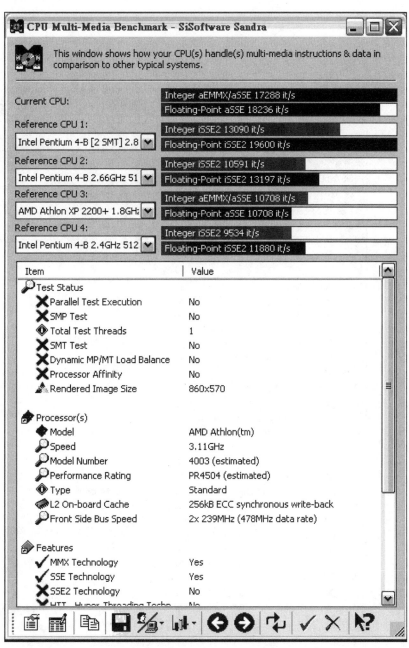

Fig. 3.25. Integer and floating-point results of testing AMD Athlon XP 1700+ overclocked to 3,107.05 MHz

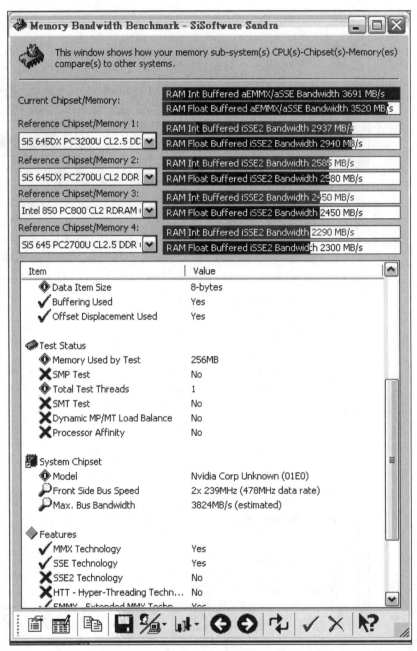

Fig. 3.26. RAM results of testing AMD Athlon XP 1700+
overclocked to 3,107.05 MHz

The performance of the AMD Athlon XP 1700+ processor overclocked to 3,107.05 MHz and cooled using liquid nitrogen can be evaluated according to the test results shown by SiSoftware Sandra.

Table 3.4. Testing Results Shown by SiSoftware Sandra

Tests	Results for Athlon XP 1700+ (3,107.05 MHz)	Results for Pentium 4 2.8 GHz
Dhrystone ALU (MIPS)	11,640	8,196
Whetstone FPU (MFLOPS)	4,721	2,408 5,250 (SSE2)
Integer aEMMX/aSSE (it/sec)	17,288	1,3090 (SSE2)
Floating-point (it/sec)	18,236	1,9600 (SSE2)
RAM integer buffered aEMMX/ aSSE bandwidth (MB/sec)	3,691	2,937 (SSE2)
RAM floating-point buffered aEMMX/aSSE bandwidth (MB/sec)	3,520	2,940 (SSE2)

As a result of extreme overclocking of the AMD Athlon XP 1700+ processor, its clock frequency (1,467 MHz) was increased 112% to 3,107 MHz. This corresponds to a rating of 4000+.

To conclude, it is necessary to emphasize that the results of extreme overclocking provided here were achieved only because of the art of overclockers and researchers, who used cryogenic cooling. These systems and methods are not suitable for home usage. Nevertheless, these data are interesting; they demonstrate the potential of modern computer technologies. The results provided in these experiments can be used to predict the potential of future products.

Chapter 4

Main Components and the Optimal Choice

The main computer hardware components are the processor, RAM, video adapter, motherboard, and hard disk. The entire system configuration depends on the components chosen. Functional capabilities of the computer and overall system performance in both nominal and overclocked modes depend on the properties of these components and the efficiency of their operation.

Depending on the configuration, the components supplied by different manufacturers might have different parameters and properties. Accounting for specific features allows you to choose the optimal configuration, based on financial limitations and planned tasks.

Processors

The processor is a central element of any computer system. Currently, the most popular and widely used processors are the ones manufactured by Intel (which holds more than 75% of the market) and AMD. Besides these market leaders, another large manufacturer of processors for PCs is Via Technologies.

Intel Pentium III/Celeron (Coppermine)

Intel Pentium III processors with the Coppermine core were based on experience accumulated by developing and running Pentium II, Pentium III, and Celeron (Mendocino).

The first representatives of the Pentium III processor line were released by the end of 1999. Pentium III processors based on the Coppermine core are manufactured using 0.18-micrometer technology. Similar to the earlier Pentium III processors based on the Katmai core, the successors support MMX and SSE. In contrast to their predecessors, they have an integrated L2 cache of 256 KB intended to operate at the core frequency. This makes them similar to the Celeron processors based on the Mendocino core. However, in Coppermine-based processors, L2 cache memory has become larger, the internal bus has been extended from 64 bits to 256 bits, the algorithm of operation has been enriched (256-bit Advanced Transfer Cache), and the core architecture has been improved. These factors allow the processor to achieve higher performance. Performance has improved not only in comparison to the overclocked Celeron (Mendocino) processors, but also in comparison to the Pentium III (Katmai) processors with 512 KB of cache memory, operating at the same frequencies.

In the Pentium III (Coppermine) processor line, some models are intended to operate at the bus frequencies of both 100 MHz and 133 MHz. The latter have the B character in their marking, distinguishing them from processors intended to operate at a 100 MHz bus frequency. Models that have the same frequencies as Pentium III (Katmai) processors are labeled with the E character.

As form factors, SECC2 (Slot 1) and FC-PGA (Flip Chip-Pin Grid Array) (Socket 370) were chosen. Gradually, processors designed using the Socket 370 standard have replaced their predecessors (Figs. 4.1–4.4).

Fig. 4.1. Pentium III processor with the SECC2 (Slot 1)
form factor, heatsink, and fan

Note that all Pentium III (Coppermine) processors have a fixed multiplier that relates internal and external frequencies; therefore, overclocking can occur only if the processor bus (external) frequency is increased.

Many of the first models of this processor line, intended for a 100 MHz bus frequency, easily allowed the Front Side Bus (FSB) frequency to be increased to 133 MHz or further.

Pentium III (Coppermine) processors have repeated the success of their predecessors. Their overclocking potential confirms that processors of this type have significant technological reserve. This reserve allows both external and internal frequencies to be increased considerably. This increase is accompanied by processor performance growth and, consequently, an increase in overall system performance.

Fig. 4.2. Slot 1 processor slot

Fig. 4.3. Pentium III processor with the FC-PGA (Socket 370) form factor

Fig. 4.4. Socket 370 processor slot

To provide a more precise evaluation of the temperature mode and appropriate selection of cooling devices, the data on the thermal power dissipated by Pentium III Katmai (512KB L2) and Coppermine (256KB L2) processors are provided in Tables 4.1–4.3.

Table 4.1. Pentium III Heat Dissipation (256KB L2, SECC2)

Processor model	Maximum thermal power (W)
533EB	14.0
550E	14.5
600E	15.8
600EB	15.8
650	17.0
667	17.5

continues

Table 4.1 Continued

Processor model	Maximum thermal power (W)
700	18.3
733	19.1
750	19.5
800	20.8
800EB	20.8
850	22.5
866	22.9
933	25.5
1000B	33.0

Table 4.2. Pentium III Heat Dissipation (256KB L2, PGA370)

Processor model	Maximum thermal power (W)
500E	13.2
533EB	14.0
550E	14.5
600E	15.8
600EB	15.8
650	17.0
667	17.5
700	18.3
733	19.1
750	19.5
800	20.8
800EB	20.8
850	22.5
866	22.9
933	24.5

Table 4.3. Heat Dissipation of Pentium III (SECC2) Based on the Katmai and Coppermine Cores

Processor model	L2 cache memory (KB)	Maximum thermal power (W)
450	512	25.3
500	512	28.0
533B	512	29.7
533EB	256	14.0
550	512	30.8
550E	256	14.5
600	512	34.5
600B	512	34.5
600E	256	15.8
600EB	256	15.8

Soon after the development and release of the first Pentium III processors based on the Coppermine core, similar low-end processors — Celeron (Coppermine) — were released. These processors appeared as a result of Intel's policy to separate market segments based on the performance and price of products, aimed at optimizing the price:performance ratio.

Celeron processors based on the Coppermine core, in contrast to their more powerful analogues, have less L2 cache memory: 128 KB (256-bit Advanced Transfer Cache). Like the previous core, these processors are intended to operate at a processor-bus frequency of 66 MHz; starting with the Celeron 800MHz processors, they operate at a bus frequency of 100 MHz. In all other aspects, the architecture of these processors resembles that of Pentium III (Coppermine) — including MMX and SSE support, which previously had been exclusive to Pentium III (Katmai) processors. As you may recall, Pentium III (Katmai) processors were oriented toward high-end computers.

Celeron (Coppermine) processors use the FC-PGA (Socket 370) standard.

The first processors of this line, including Celeron 533A (Coppermine), have a 1.5 V core supply voltage, a slightly lower voltage than the similar parameter for Pentium III (Coppermine) processors (1.6 V and 1.65 V). As a rule, this circumstance allows the core supply voltage for Celeron (Coppermine) to be raised to 1.6 V or 1.65 V without serious risks (only if efficient cooling is provided). This has a positive effect on system stability under conditions of extreme overclocking. For later, more powerful Celeron models, the core supply voltage was increased to the levels typical for standard processors based on the Coppermine architecture. This increase of the core supply voltage widens the overclocking capabilities for processors of this type. For example, Celeron 667 (Coppermine) allows overclocking to 1,000 MHz. Generally, Celeron (Coppermine) processors retain stable operation in overclocked modes even at standard core supply voltages, allowing the bus frequency to be exceeded by 30%. Some models allow both internal and external frequencies to be exceeded, providing the potential for 50% performance improvement.

Table 4.4 provides a more precise analysis of the temperature mode of the computer. The data show the thermal power dissipated by the first members of the Celeron processor family, based on the Coppermine core.

Table 4.4. Celeron Heat Dissipation (FC-PGA)

Processor model	Maximum thermal power (W)
533A	11.2
566	11.9
600	12.6
633	16.5
667	17.5
700	18.3

Intel Pentium III/Celeron (Tualatin)

Traditional processor architecture based on the Coppermine core and 0.18-micrometer technology reached its limit with the release of models characterized by a 1 GHz to 1.13 GHz clock frequency. For the latest processors based on the Coppermine core, this limit is 1.2 GHz to 1.3 GHz. This evaluation can be proved by analysis and approximation of the results obtained by overclocking various models of processors based on this core.

A greater increase in the CPU core frequency could be achieved only by improving the technological process. This occurred with the transition to the 0.13-micrometer scale. The new core, known as Tualatin, has become the basis for a new processor line.

The design of the Tualatin core, which used Coppermine as a prototype, makes it possible to increase the processor clock rate and solve problems with stable operation at an acceptable level of energy consumption and heat emission. The price of the new processors remains reasonable.

Using the Tualatin core, Intel released Pentium III processors with the following nominal frequencies: 1 GHz, 1.13 GHz, 1.20 GHz, or 1.33 GHz. The basic characteristics of these processors include the amount of L2 cache memory (256 KB) and the FSB frequency (133 MHz).

In addition to Pentium III processors, the traditional low-end line of Celeron processors was released (Fig. 4.5). This line comprises models with a clock frequency of 0.9 GHz, 1 GHz, 1.1 GHz, 1.2 GHz, 1.3 GHz, or 1.4 GHz. The amount of L2 cache memory is 256 KB (as in Pentium III); however, the FSB frequency is only 100 MHz.

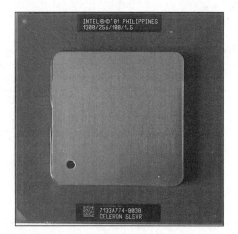 

Fig. 4.5. Celeron processor with the FC-PGA2 (Socket 370) form factor

The main feature of the new core based on 0.13-micrometer technology is a new approach to the core power supply.

Thinner transistor control gates, the basis of the processor core, made it possible to decrease the levels of the power supply voltage. The intensity of the field that controls the sink-gate current via transistors decreases with the decrease in distance between electrodes. This allowed Intel to lower the levels of the supply voltage to 1.475 V to 1.5 V. For comparison, this parameter in the Coppermine core is 1.6 V to 1.75 V.

However, this is not the sole feature that characterizes the power supply of the processors. When discussing products based on the Tualatin core, it is incorrect to only speak about core voltage.

This processor, in contrast to processors of previous generations, has no constant core voltage level.

The consumption currents of processors have reached a high value. For the latest models of Pentium III (Coppermine), this current reaches 20 amperes. Such a high level is a serious load — not only for processor cores (a surface area of 1 cm^2), but also for power supply units. High levels of electric power are danger-ous for processor chips because they inevitably are accompanied by significant heat emission. This often leads to local overheating of semiconductors. Besides violation of thermal modes required for proper operation of semiconductors, the chips are exposed to significant dynamic loads, which can destroy internal structures me-chanically due to uneven expansion of the chip.

To solve the problem of CPU temperature-mode optimization, Intel develop-ers replaced the constant core voltage level with a variable voltage level. The core voltage now depends on the consumption current, the value of which depends on the processor workload. The higher the current, the lower the processor's core voltage. This voltage decreases from the initial level, stated in the processor specifi-cation and set by the Voltage Identification (VID) contacts, to approximately 0.2 V at the maximum workload of the latest models.

As a result, it became necessary to introduce the changes into the Voltage Regulator Module (VRM) specifications. This module, integrated into the mother-board, converts standard voltage delivered by the power supply unit to the level required for correct operation of the processor core. For processors based on the Tualatin core, the VRM module of the motherboard must comply with the 8.5 specification (Fig. 4.6).

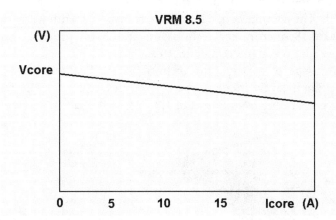

Fig. 4.6. Changing the core supply voltage, depending on the consumed current (Icore), in accordance with the 8.5 specification

The power supply of Pentium 4 and Celeron with Socket 478 slots is organized the same way.

The previously mentioned changes also relate to the FSB: The amplitude of transmitted pulses was decreased to 1.25 V. (Previously, this level was 1.5 V.)

Support for processors based on the Tualatin core is implemented in newer motherboards based on special chipset models. In models oriented toward desktop PCs, this is the modified version of the 810E2 chipset and the 815 (Step B) chipset family from Intel. The latter is represented by the following models: 815, 815P, 815G, 815E, 815EP, and 815EG.

Besides this, support for these processor models is implemented by system logic sets from Ali, SiS, and Via Technologies. These chipsets are based on well-known sets and usually have the T character in their marking. The list of such products includes Ali Aladdin Pro 5T from Ali; SiS630ET, SiS630ST, SiS633T, and SiS635T from SiS; and VIA Apollo PLET, VIA Apollo Pro133T, VIA Apollo Pro266T, VIA ProSavage PL133T, VIA ProSavage PN133T, and VIA ProSavageDDR PN266T chipsets designed and manufactured by Via Technologies.

Chipsets from Intel, Ali, SiS, and Via, in combination with VRM 8.5, implement support not only for processors based on the Tualatin core, but also for earlier processors based on the Coppermine core.

Intel Pentium 4/Celeron (Willamette, Northwood)

Intel Pentium 4 processors have principally new architecture (Fig. 4.7). They are based on the Intel NetBurst microarchitecture. The first models were released in 2000. They contained 42 million transistors and were created using a well-checked 0.18-micrometer technology, tested on previous-generation processors. The new core was named Willamette.

The usage of hyperpiping technology in the Pentium 4 architecture allowed Intel to significantly increase the operating frequency. The first processors of this line have operating frequencies of 1.3 GHz, 1.4 GHz, 1.5 GHz, and so on.

Fig. 4.7. Pentium III (Coppermine, Socket 370)
and Pentium 4 (Willamette, Socket 423) processors

To ensure nonstop operation of the long pipeline (20 steps) at a high frequency, significant modifications had to be introduced into internal core architecture. For example, the Advanced Dynamic Execution Engine technology improves branch prediction, and the Arithmetic Logic Unit (ALU) operates at the doubled core frequency.

High performance comes with efficient operation of the on-die L1 cache memory (8 KB) and L2 cache memory (256 KB in the Willamette core). As with Pentium III (Coppermine), L2 cache is connected via a 256-bit bus (Advanced Transfer Cache). It operates at the core frequency, ensuring high efficiency of cache operation.

The command set was extended to optimize the operation of internal core units. The additional command set, a further evolution of the MMX and SSE technologies, became known as SSE2 (Streaming SIMD Extensions 2, 144 new instructions).

Such innovations positioned Pentium 4 as a powerful processor oriented toward tasks with minimal branches, such as working with the Internet and processing multimedia information. The share of such tasks is growing steadily.

The high operating frequency required not only a radical redesign of the entire internal processor structure, but also the introduction of appropriate modifications into computer architecture. The processor bus at the 100 MHz frequency transfers data at the frequency of 400 MHz (quad-pumped, or 4X) when passing and processing the address portion at 200 MHz (2X). The next version of this standard implies increasing the bus frequency to 133 MHz, which ensures a data-transfer rate of 533 MHz, as a flow with a throughput of 4.3 GB/sec.

Pentium 4 (Willamette) processors are released in two forms of FC-PGA packaging, with provisions for Socket 423 and Socket 478 slots. The core voltage (Vcore) of processors complying with the Socket 423 standard is 1.7 V and 1.75 V; for processors with Socket 478, it is 1.75 V.

Tables 4.5 and 4.6 outline the main temperature parameters of Pentium 4 and Celeron processors based on the Willamette core. These processors are oriented toward systems with Socket 423 and Socket 478 processor slots, and with data-transfer rate through the system bus equal to 400 MHz. These tables provide clock frequencies, core voltage levels (Vcore), maximum thermal power, and maximum case temperature (Tcase).

Table 4.5. Temperature Parameters of Pentium 4 (Willamette, Socket 423, 400 MHz)

Processor (GHz)/Vcore (V)	Maximum thermal power (W)	Maximum Tcase (°C)
1.3/1.7	48.9	69
1.4/1.7	51.8	70

continues

Table 4.5 Continued

Processor (GHz)/Vcore (V)	Maximum thermal power (W)	Maximum Tcase (°C)
1.5/1.7	54.7	72
1.3/1.75	51.6	70
1.4/1.75	54.7	72
1.5/1.75	57.8	73
1.6/1.75	61.0	75
1.7/1.75	64.0	76
1.8/1.75	66.7	78
1.9/1.75	69.2	73
2.0/1.75	71.8	74

Table 4.6. Temperature Parameters of Pentium 4 (Willamette, Socket 478, 400 MHz)

Processor (GHz)	Maximum thermal power (W)	Maximum Tcase (°C)
1.4	55.3	72
1.5	57.9	73
1.6	60.8	75
1.7	63.5	76
1.8	66.1	77
1.9	72.8	75
2.0	75.3	76

Using the experience accumulated through developing, manufacturing, and operating Pentium 4 (Willamette), Intel has released a low-end processor line based on the same core. These processors received the traditional name: Intel Celeron. In contrast to the more powerful Pentium 4 processors, this line is characterized by a smaller L2 cache: 128 KB, instead of 256 KB. In other respects, the architecture remained practically unchanged.

Table 4.7 lists the temperature parameters of the first Celeron model based on the Willamette core.

Table 4.7. Temperature Parameters of Celeron (Willamette, Socket 478, 400 MHz)

Processor (GHz)	Maximum thermal power (W)	Maximum Tcase (°C)
1.7	63.5	76

The well-tested NetBurst microarchitecture was the basis for the next generation of Pentium 4 processors created with 0.13-micrometer technology. The Northwood core (Fig. 4.8), providing the Quad Pumped Bus (QPB) as the FSB, is used in this product line. The FSB frequencies are 100 MHz, 133 MHz, and 200 MHz. This ensures data-transfer rates of 400 MHz, 533 MHz, and 800 MHz. These processors have 512 KB of L2 cache memory.

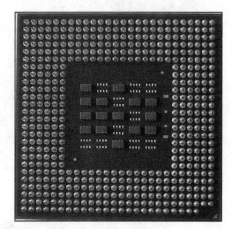

Fig. 4.8. Pentium 4 (Northwood, Socket 478) processor

Pentium 4 (Northwood) processors have FC-PGA2 packaging with provisions for the Socket 478 processor slot (Fig. 4.9).

Newer processor models intended for data-transfer rates of 533 MHz and 800 MHz have the C character in their markings and implement Intel's hyper-threading technology (Fig. 4.10). This technology allows the simultaneous execution of two tasks or two code sections of the same program on one physical processor. Thus, a single processor is interpreted by the OS as two logical devices operating in parallel. In two-processor systems, this technology allows work with four logical devices, and so on.

Fig. 4.9. Socket 478 processor slot

Fig. 4.10. Pentium 4 3 GHz is intended to operate at a 200 MHz bus
frequency, ensuring a data-transfer rate of 800 MHz

Tables 4.8–4.10 list the main temperature parameters of Pentium 4 (Northwood) processors, intended for operation at various bus frequencies and different core voltages set by VID. These processors can have the following VID values: 1.500 V, 1.525 V, and a `multiple`. The latter means that the exact VID setting can differ from the previous two values. It is set technologically, depending on the parameters of the processor chips being manufactured. For the models with a clock frequency to 2.8 GHz, the VID setting can take one of the following values: 1.475 V, 1.500 V, or 1.525 V. After overclocking, the VID setting can have one of the following values: 1.475 V, 1.500 V, 1.525 V, or 1.550 V.

Table 4.8. Temperature Parameters of Pentium 4 (Northwood, Socket 478, 400 MHz)

Processor (GHz)	Maximum thermal power (W)			Maximum Tcase (°C)		
	VID=1.500 V	VID=1.525 V	VID=multiple	VID=1.500 V	VID=1.525 V	VID=multiple
2A	52.4	54.3	54.3	68	69	69
2.2	55.1	57.1	57.1	69	70	70
2.4	57.8	59.8	59.8	70	71	71
2.5	59.3	61.0	61.0	71	72	72
2.6	–	62.6	62.6	–	72	72

Table 4.9. Temperature Parameters of Pentium 4 (Northwood, Socket 478, 533 MHz)

Processor (GHz)	Maximum thermal power (W)			Maximum Tcase (°C)		
	VID=1.500 V	VID=1.525 V	VID=multiple	VID=1.500 V	VID=1.525 V	VID=multiple
2.26	56.0	58.0	58.0	70	70	70
2.40B	57.8	59.8	59.8	70	71	71
2.53	59.3	61.5	61.5	71	72	72

continues

Table 4.9 Continued

Processor (GHz)	Maximum thermal power (W)			Maximum Tcase (°C)		
	VID=1.500 V	VID=1.525 V	VID=multiple	VID=1.500 V	VID=1.525 V	VID=multiple
2.66	–	66.1	66.1	–	74	74
2.80	–	68.4	68.4	–	75	75
3.06	–	–	81.8	–	–	69

Table 4.10. Temperature Parameters of Pentium 4 (Northwood, Socket 478, 800 MHz, multiple VID)

Processor (GHz)	Maximum thermal power (W)	Maximum Tcase (°C)
2.4C	66.2	74
2.6C	69.0	75
2.8C	69.7	75
3.0	81.9	70

With Pentium 4 processors based on the Northwood core, Intel released a Celeron processor line. As with models based on the Willamette core, these processors have 128 KB of L2 cache memory. Other parameters are similar to those of Pentium 4 (Northwood). The FSB clock frequency (100 MHz) and data-transfer rate (400 MHz) were inherited from the Celeron models based on the Willamette core (Table. 4.11).

Table 4.11. Temperature Parameters of Celeron (Northwood, Socket 478, 400 MHz, multiple VID)

Processor (GHz)	Maximum thermal power (W)	Maximum Tcase (°C)
2.0	52.8	68
2.1	55.2	69
2.2	57.1	70
2.3	58.3	70
2.4	59.8	71

For processors based on the NetBurst microarchitecture, Intel developed special chipsets: i850 and i850E for two Rambus memory channels, i845 line for the SDRAM (PC133) and DDR SDRAM, and i875 and i865 for dual-channel DDR SDRAM. Appropriate chipsets also have been released by Via Technologies and SiS.

The next core for high-performance Intel processors for desktop PCs was named Prescott. As all earlier members of the Pentium 4 family, this core is based on the NetBurst microarchitecture.

This core has several innovations, including increased L1 and L2 cache memory, an improved mechanism of branch prediction, more efficient hyperthreading technology, and 13 new instructions known as PNI (Prescott New Instructions).

The new chip has about 100 million transistors. It is manufactured using 0.09-micrometer technology with so-called strained silicon.

Future models with the Socket 478 are anticipated. They, in turn, are expected to be replaced by models intended for Socket 775 LGA.

The next core, the successor of Prescott, will be Tejas.

AMD Athlon/Duron (Thunderbird/Spitfire)

AMD Athlon and AMD Duron processors are supplied in a PGA case. Motherboards supporting these processors have a special slot known as Socket A (462 pins) (Fig. 4.11).

Athlon is based on the Thunderbird core; Duron uses the Spitfire core.

Athlon processors are oriented toward powerful computers. The architecture of these processors includes 128 KB of L1 cache and 256 KB of L2 cache memory.

Duron processors were developed for relatively inexpensive computers. Their architecture differs from Athlon only in the amount of the L2 cache memory: 64 KB (Figs. 4.12 and 4.13).

Both processor lines are intended to operate with the Alpha EV6 bus, designed by Digital Equipment Corp. (DEC) for its Alpha processors and licensed by AMD for its products. (The Alpha line is now a product of Hewlett-Packard.)

The Alpha EV6 bus, used as a processor bus (FSB), ensures data transmission on both fronts of the clock pulses (Double Data Rate). This increases the throughput, improving overall system performance. At 100 MHz, the Alpha EV6 FSB, usually named EV6, ensures data transfer at 200 MHz. In contract to EV6, the GTL+ and AGTL+ buses of Intel Celeron (Coppermine), Pentium II, and Pentium III processors have the same data rate and clock frequency.

Fig. 4.11. Socket A (462 pins) processor slot

Fig. 4.12. Athlon (Thunderbird, Socket A) processor

Fig. 4.13. Duron (Spitfire, Socket A) processor

Athlon and Duron processors require special motherboards with chipsets that support these processors. Such motherboards ensure stable operation of the processors, provided that sufficiently powerful power supply units are used. Usually, power supply units with a rating of no less than 235 W are recommended.

Athlon and Duron processors have significant technological reserve. Performance can be improved using overclocked modes that can be set, for example, by increasing the processor bus frequency.

Athlon and Duron, released in the PGA form factor, usually have fixed frequency multipliers. The form factor doesn't allow resistors to be changed, as in case with earlier specimens of Athlon. Therefore, frequency multipliers can be changed only by using specialized software and hardware.

The value of the frequency multiplier, relating internal and external processor frequencies, is set by the FID0–FID3 contacts. Supply voltage is set by VID0–VID4. Overclocking of such processors is easy: Most contemporary motherboards oriented toward these processors allow both the frequency multiplier and the core supply voltage of the processor to be changed. Some motherboards provide this functionality at the BIOS level (in BIOS Setup). Note that the processor core voltage can be increased no more than 10% above the nominal level. AMD's recommendations for specifying core supply voltages for Duron and Athlon are in Tables 4.12–4.14. This information changes with the release of new core implementations.

Table 4.12. Core Supply Voltages for Athlon/Duron (June 2000)

Processor	Frequency (MHz)	Minimum supply voltage (V)	Standard supply voltage (V)	Maximum supply voltage (V)
Athlon	650–850	1.60	1.70	1.80
	900–1,000	1.65	1.75	1.85
Duron	550–700	1.40	1.50	1.60

Table 4.13. Core Supply Voltages for Duron Model 7 (October 2001)

Minimum supply voltage (V)	Standard supply voltage (V)	Maximum supply voltage (V)
1.65/1.70	1.75	1.80/1.90

Table 4.14. Core Supply Voltages for Athlon/Duron Model 3 (November/June 2001)

Processor	Frequency (MHz)	Minimum supply voltage (V)	Standard supply voltage (V)	Maximum supply voltage (V)
Athlon	650–1,400	1.65	1.75	1.85
Duron	600–950	1.50	1.60	1.70

Information on the power of Duron and Athlon, needed for precise analysis of the temperature mode and evaluation of the required cooling devices, is in Tables 4.15–4.19.

Table 4.15. Power of Athlon (June 2000)

Processor frequency (MHz)	Normal power (W)	Maximum power (W)
650	32.4	36.1
700	34.4	38.3
750	36.3	40.4
800	38.3	42.6
850	40.2	44.8
900	44.6	49.7
950	46.7	52.0
1,000	48.7	54.3

Table 4.16. Power of Athlon (November 2001)

Processor frequency (MHz)	Normal power (W)	Maximum power (W)
900	45.8	51.0
950	47.6	53.1
1,000	49.5	55.1
1,100	54.1	60.3
1,133	55.7	62.1
1,200	58.9	65.7
1,266	60.1	66.9

continues

Table 4.16. Power of Athlon (November 2001)

Processor frequency (MHz)	Normal power (W)	Maximum power (W)
1,300	61.3	68.3
1,333	62.6	69.8
1,400	64.7	72.1

Table 4.17. Power of Duron (June 2000)

Processor frequency (MHz)	Normal power (W)	Maximum power (W)
550	18.9	21.1
600	20.4	22.7
650	21.8	24.3
700	22.9	25.5

Table 4.18. Power of Duron (June 2001)

Processor frequency (MHz)	Normal power (W)	Maximum power (W)
600	24.5	27.4
650	26.4	29.4
700	28.2	31.4
750	30.0	33.4
800	31.8	35.4
850	33.6	37.4
900	35.4	39.5
950	37.2	41.5

Table 4.19. Power of Duron Model 7 (November 2001)

Processor frequency (MHz)	Normal power (W)	Maximum power (W)
900	38.3	42.7
950	39.8	44.4
1,000	41.3	46.1
1,100	45.1	50.3

AMD Athlon XP/Duron (Palomino/Morgan)

AMD Athlon XP processors were the next step in the evolution of the AMD Athlon (Thunderbird) processor line.

The Palomino core became the foundation of the first processors of this line. This core is a new design of the Thunderbird core. As in its prototype, the 0.18-micrometer technological process is used, which employs aluminum compounds. Minor changes include the addition of SSE instruction support, data prefetching, and integration of the built-in thermal diode into the core. The core surface area is 129 mm^2.

To mark processors based on the Palomino core, AMD started using a processor rating, whose numeric value is different from the processor's operating frequency. This rating shows the approximate level of performance, in comparison to processors based on the Thunderbird core. The usage of this rating is supported by the QuantiSpeed architecture of AMD processors.

The Athlon XP (Palomino) line comprises processors with ratings from 1500+ to 2200+ (Fig. 4.14). These processors are intended for the 266 MHz bus (with a clock frequency of 133 MHz) implemented in models based on the Thunderbird core.

Fig. 4.14. Athlon XP (Palomino, Socket A) processor

Continuing its policy of targeting different market segments, AMD created the Morgan core, based on the Palomino architecture. The Morgan core is oriented toward processors for inexpensive computers.

The surface area of the Morgan core is 106 mm^2. Operating frequencies start from 1 GHz. This core is manufactured using 0.18-micrometer technology with aluminum compounds. The main difference from Palomino is that the Morgan core has reduced L2 cache: 64 KB. Processors based on this simplified core received the traditional name of AMD Duron.

Athlon XP (Palomino) and Duron (Morgan) are released in PGA cases and connect to motherboards using the Socket A slot.

AMD Athlon XP (Thoroughbred, Barton)

The Thoroughbred core (according to official AMD classification, it is Family 6, Model 8 in contrast to Palomino, which is Family 6, Model 6) was introduced as the next stage of Athlon XP architecture. This core shifted from the Palomino architecture to 0.13-micrometer technology. As a result of this technological advance, the surface area of the core has decreased to 80 mm^2. The heat emission also has been reduced (Table 4.20).

Table 4.20. Parameters of Athlon XP (Palomino, Thoroughbred)

Processor model	Clock frequency (MHz)	Surface area of the core (mm^2)	Core supply voltage (V)	Max. thermal power (W)
AMD Athlon XP (Palomino) 2000+	1,667	128	1.75	70.0
AMD Athlon XP (Palomino) 2100+	1,733	128	1.75	71.9
AMD Athlon XP (Thoroughbred) 2000+	1,667	80	1.60	60.3
AMD Athlon XP (Thoroughbred) 2100+	1,733	80	1.60	62.1

Athlon XP (Thoroughbred) processors use a 266 MHz bus; their ratings start from 1700+ (Fig. 4.15).

To further improve performance, AMD developers once again redesigned the core architecture. This new version is known as Thoroughbred-B among experts. The surface area of the modified core has increased slightly to approximately 84 mm^2. The core modifications make it possible to reduce heat emission and raise the maximum CPU operating frequency. Frequencies of the processor bus are 266 MHz and 333 MHz (with clock frequencies of 133 MHz and 166 MHz).

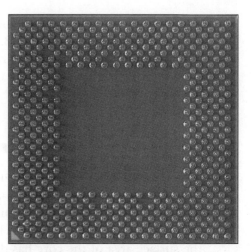

Fig. 4.15. Athlon XP (Thoroughbred, Socket A) processor

Fig. 4.16. Athlon XP (Barton, Socket A) processor

After Thoroughbred-B, AMD designed and released models based on the Barton core (Fig. 4.16). This core is manufactured using 0.13-micrometer technology with copper compounds. The amount of L2 cache memory (512 KB) is the distinguishing feature of this core. Processor bus frequencies are 333 MHz and 400 MHz (with clock frequencies of 166 MHz and 200 MHz).

Tables 4.21 and 4.22 provide the main characteristics of high-performance models of AMD Athlon XP processors. Examples that illustrate the marking of models based on Thoroughbred and Barton cores are shown in Figs. 4.17–4.19.

Table 4.21. Characteristics of the Barton and Thoroughbred-B Cores

Processor core	Barton	Thoroughbred-B
Fabrication technology (Fab 30) (micrometer)	0.13	0.13
Chip area (mm²)	101	84
Number of transistors (million)	54.3	37.6
Stepping	6-10-0	6-8-1
L1+L2 cache memory (KB)	128+512	128+256
Typical core voltage (V)	1.65	1.65
Maximum core temperature (°C)	85	85

Table 4.22. Characteristics of Newer Athlon XP Processor Models

Processor model	Core/bus frequency (MHz)	L2 cache (KB)	Core supply voltage (V)	Max. thermal power (W)
3200+	2,200/400	512	1.65	76.8
3000+	2,167/333	512	1.65	74.3
2800+	2,083/333	512	1.65	68.3
2500+	1,833/333	512	1.65	68.3
2700+	2,167/333	256	1.65	68.3
2600+	2,083/333	256	1.65	68.3
2600+	2,133/266	256	1.65	68.3
2400+	2,000/266	256	1.65	68.3

Fig. 4.17. Athlon XP 2700+ (Thoroughbred) marking: "3D" in the top-left group stands for 256 KB L2 and 133 MHz FSB

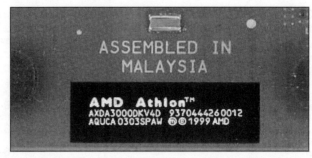

Fig. 4.18. Athlon XP 3000+ (Barton) marking: "4D" in the top-left group stands for 512 KB L2 and 133 MHz FSB

Fig. 4.19. Athlon XP 3200+ (Barton) marking: "4E" in the top-left group stands for 512 KB L2 and 200 MHz FSB

Table 4.23. Correspondence between Clock and Bus Frequency, Core Type, Cache-Memory Size, and Athlon XP Rating

Processor model	Core frequency (MHz)			
	Barton		Thoroughbred	
	400 MHz FSB	333 MHz FSB	333 MHz FSB	266 MHz FSB
3200+	2,200	–	–	–
3000+	–	2,167	–	–
2800+	–	2,083	2,250	–
2700+	–	–	2,167	–
2600+	–	–	2,083	2,133
2500+	–	1,833	–	–

continues

Table 4.23 Continued

Processor model	Core frequency (MHz)			
	Barton		Thoroughbred	
	400 MHz FSB	333 MHz FSB	333 MHz FSB	266 MHz FSB
2400+	–	–	–	2,000
2200+	–	–	–	1,800
2100+	–	–	–	1,733
2000+	–	–	–	1,667
1900+	–	–	–	1,600
1800+	–	–	–	1,533
1700+	–	–	–	1,467

The data in Table 4.23 indicate that the clock frequency of Athlon XP processors remains stable for some time. This is evidence that the architecture and technology of Athlon XP have reached their limit by clock frequency. The next stage of AMD processors will be AMD Athlon 64.

VIA C3

Among processors for desktop PCs manufactured by Via Technologies, the most common is VIA C3 (Fig. 4.20).

VIA C3 is the next step in evolution of the VIA Cyrix III line. VIA C3 processors are based on Samuel2, Ezra, Ezra-T, and Nehemiah cores manufactured with various technologies. The 0.13-micrometer process in newer VIA processors has increased the operating frequency, lowered the core voltage (1.35 V for the Ezra core, in comparison to 1.6 V for Samuel2), and reduced heat emission. VIA C3 processors have uniquely low energy consumption, which allows them to use coolers without cooling fans. Because of this, it is possible to create systems with low heat and noise emission, based on VIA C3. Such systems have become popular in multimedia complexes and compact computers such as Barebone.

VIA C3 processors often have significant technological reserve, providing for performance improvement through overclocking. As a rule, overclocking is achieved by increasing the processor bus frequency.

Fig. 4.20. VIA C3 (Ezra, Socket 370) processor

Random Access Memory

Computer performance depends not only on the internal CPU speed of data processing, but also on the rate of information exchange with other PC components.

Bandwidth

Data exchange is accomplished via special buses, the main characteristic of which is bandwidth. This key parameter determines the throughput, which depends on the clock frequency of the bus, the number of packets sent per clock, and the bus width. This dependence looks as follows:

$$Throughput = Clock\ frequency \times Number\ of\ packets \times Bus\ width$$

Maximum performance is achieved when the processor bus and the memory bus have matching bandwidths. Depending on the processor, this imposes stringent limitations on the memory subsystem architecture and the type of the modules used in the configuration.

SDRAM Modules

Synchronous Dynamic Random Access Memory (SDRAM) has long been the main type of memory used in computers. Operation of this memory is synchronized using an external signal. This is reflected by the name of this memory (Fig. 4.21).

Fig. 4.21. SDRAM module

Remember that the memory subsystem interacts with all other components via the appropriate chip of the chipset. Because of this, operation is synchronized with the chipset, rather than with the processor. This means that the processor bus and the main-memory bus can have the same clock frequencies and operate in synchronous mode, or different frequencies and operate in asynchronous mode. Note that even when operating in asynchronous mode, RAM, by its type and by its operating principles, remains synchronous memory: SDRAM.

SDRAM modules are designed to work at 66 MHz, 100 MHz, or 133 MHz. Accordingly, memory modules are marked PC66, PC100, or PC133. These modules, manufactured as Dual In-line Memory Modules (DIMM), have 168 pins and are intended for a supply voltage of 3.3 V. Memory modules are connected via a 64-bit memory bus.

Such modules ensure different performance levels of the RAM subsystem. To achieve maximum performance, it is necessary to choose the memory module variant appropriate for the processor bus clock frequency.

The values of the processor and memory bus throughput are listed in Table 4.24. They depend on the type of CPU and SDRAM modules.

Table 4.24. Parameters of Processors and SDRAM

Processor/ SDRAM module	Bus clock frequency (MHz)	Number of packets on the bus	Bus width (bytes)	Bus bandwidth (GB/sec)
Intel Celeron	66/100	1	8	0.5/0.8
Intel Pentium II/III	66/100/133	1	8	0.5/0.8/1.0

continues

Table 4.24 Continued

Processor/ SDRAM module	Bus clock frequency (MHz)	Number of packets on the bus	Bus width (bytes)	Bus bandwidth (GB/sec)
AMD Duron	100	2	8	1.6
AMD Athlon	100/133	2	8	1.6/2.1
Intel Pentium 4	100/133/200	4	8	3.2/4.2/6.4
AMD Athlon XP	100/133/166/200	2	8	1.6/2.1/2.7/3.2
PC66/100/133	66/100/133	1	8	0.5/0.8/1.0

As follows from Table 4.24, balance between the bandwidths of the FSB frequency and the memory-bus frequency is ensured only for Intel Celeron, Pentium II, and Pentium III. For all other processors, the FSB throughput in this mode exceeds the similar parameter of the memory bus. The same situation applies to asynchronous modes. Although configurations with SDRAM are common, this type of memory cannot reach the maximal performance level on powerful processors with high FSB frequencies. For these configurations, more advanced types of RAM are preferable.

Direct RDRAM Modules

Steady growth of processor performance and improvements in manufacturing technologies stimulate the development of new types of RAM. Direct Rambus DRAM (DRDRAM or Direct RDRAM), developed by Rambus and supported by Intel, became one such innovation (Fig. 4.22).

The release of Direct RDRAM required new packaging for memory modules. The Direct RDRAM chips are assembled into RIMM modules, similar in appearance to the standard DIMM.

RIMM modules can be used on motherboards with standard form factors such as ATX. However, RIMM modules can be used only in systems whose BIOS and chipset both support Direct RDRAM. For example, specialized chipsets from Intel, including i820, i850, and their modifications, provide this support.

The architecture of the Direct RDRAM subsystem gives provisions for up to four channels (buses). Each bus is 16 bits (18 bits, if Error Correction Code (ECC) support is provided). Data transmission takes place at high clock frequencies on both fronts of the clock pulse. This data rate is usually specified in the model marking. (It is twice the channel clock frequency).

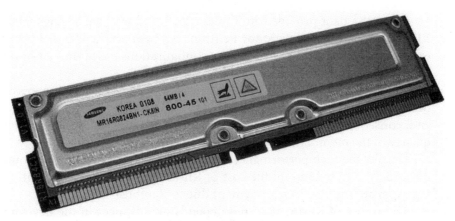

Fig. 4.22. RIMM module

For the systems based on Intel Pentium III processors and i820/820E chipsets, single-channel versions are used. In this case, the channel clock frequency can be up to 400 MHz, and the data-transmission rate can be up to 800 MHz. Three types of RIMM modules are used: PC600 for the clock frequency up to 300 MHz and the data rate up to 600 MHz, PC700 for the clock frequency up to 356 MHz and the data rate of 712 MHz, and PC800 for the clock frequency up to 400 MHz and the data rate of 800 MHz. When using PC800 modules, the bandwidth is 1.6 GB/sec.

For systems based on Intel Pentium 4 processors and 850/850E chipsets, dual-channel variants are used. In this case, the channel clock frequency is 400/533 MHz, and the data-transfer rate is 800/1,066 MHz. PC800 and PC1066 RIMM are used as memory modules. The bandwidth of a dual-channel variant using PC1066 modules is 4.2 GB/sec.

Table 4.25. Parameters of Processors and Direct RDRAM

Processor/Direct RDRAM module	Bus clock frequency (MHz)	Number of packets on the bus	Bus width (bytes)	Bus bandwidth (GB/sec)
Intel Pentium III	100/133	1	8	0.8/1.0
Intel Pentium 4	100/133	4	8	3.2/4.2
Single PC800/1066 channel	400/533	2	2	1.6/2.1
Two PC800/1066 channels	400/533	2	2	3.2/4.2

From the data provided in Table 4.25, it follows that a single-channel Direct RDRAM variant is sufficient for Pentium III, because the channel bandwidth even exceeds that of the processor bus. For configurations based on Pentium 4, the dual-channel variant is optimal.

When discussing specific features of RIMM modules, it is necessary to point out that they require intensive cooling. This relates to high power consumption and, consequently, intensive heat emission. These are caused by the high clock frequency of the memory chips.

Despite the high performance of the dual-channel variant, this configuration is not widely used because of the cost of RIMM modules: both the high manufacturing expenses and the license payment due to Rambus.

The future of RIMM modules depends on advances in the development of alternative types of memory, such as DDR SDRAM.

DDR SDRAM

Double Data Rate SDRAM (DDR SDRAM, or simply DDR) is an alternative to Direct RDRAM. This type of memory is the next step in the evolution of SDRAM. DDR SDRAM, like SDRAM, is synchronous memory. However, in contrast to SDRAM, DDR SDRAM data transmission takes place on both fronts of the clock pulse. SDRAM often is referred to as SDR SDRAM (Single Data Rate SDRAM).

Data transmission on both fronts of the clock pulse doubles the bandwidth.

DDR SDRAM modules are intended for clock frequencies of 100 MHz, 133 MHz, 166 MHz, and 200 MHz (Fig. 2.23). These modules are marked with their data rate: DDR200, DDR266, DDR333, and DDR400.

Fig. 4.23. DDR SDRAM module

Besides the data rate, the marking of DDR SDRAM modules includes bandwidth values. Thus, these memory modules are marked as PC1600, PC2100, PC2700, and PC3200 (Fig. 4.24).

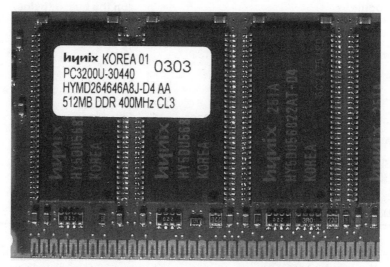

Fig. 4.24. Fragment of the PC3200 (DDR400) module

DDR SDRAM modules are manufactured in the DIMM form factor. They have 184 pins and are intended for a supply voltage of 2.5 V. These modules are connected using a 64-bit memory bus.

DDR SDRAM modules can be used in systems whose BIOS and chipset support this memory type. Such chipsets include i845 from Intel and Apollo KT400 from Via Technologies.

As with Direct RDRAM, dual-channel variants of DDR SDRAM are designed and implemented for high-performance systems. This doubles the memory subsystem throughput. Specialized chipsets that support a dual-channel memory subsystem include the i875 and i865 lines from Intel. Via Technologies and SIS have released similar chipset lines.

DDR200, DDR266, DDR333, and DDR400 modules ensure different performance qualities of the memory subsystem. To achieve maximum computer performance, depending on the processor bus frequency, it is necessary to choose the appropriate DDR SDRAM module.

The values of the bandwidths of the processor and memory buses, depending on the processor and DDR SDRAM module used in hardware configuration, are listed in Table 4.26.

Table 4.26. Parameters of Processors and DDR SDRAM

Processor/ DDR SDRAM module	Bus clock frequency (MHz)	Number of packets on the bus	Bus width (bytes)	Bus bandwidth (GB/sec)
Intel Celeron	66/100	1	8	0.5/0.8
Intel Pentium II/III	66/100/133	1	8	0.5/0.8/1.0
AMD Duron	100	2	8	1.6
AMD Athlon	100/133	2	8	1.6/2.1
Intel Pentium 4	100/133/200	4	8	3.2/4.2/6.4
AMD Athlon XP	100/133/166/200	2	8	1.6/2.1/2.7/3.2
Single-channel DDR 200/266/333/400	100/133/166/400	2	8	1.6/2.1/2.7/3.2
Dual-channel DDR 200/266/333/400	100/133/166/400	2	8	3.2/4.2/5.4/6.4

From the data provided in Table 4.26, it follows that for configurations based on Intel and AMD processors, it is possible to create well-balanced variants of the memory subsystem based on DDR SDRAM.

Motherboards

Contemporary motherboards support numerous processor bus frequencies within a wide frequency range. However, when comparing the parameters of motherboards, it is clear that different motherboards have not only different frequency values, but also different distributions within the frequency range. This occurs because contemporary motherboards use different frequency synthesizer chips.

Processor stability at high processor-bus frequencies is achieved by increasing of the processor supply voltage. When no built-in functions allow you to change the supply voltage, it is possible to use insulating varnish or another technique. This applies to almost any contemporary motherboard.

Currently, a processor-bus frequency above 250 MHz is not always a substantial advantage, although motherboards supporting even higher FSB values are announced regularly. No matter how advanced the motherboard might be, it is difficult to find other components (such as memory modules) capable of operating at such high frequencies. Besides this, not all high-frequency components of the motherboard would operate at such frequencies.

The memory-bus frequency, as well as the Accelerated Graphics Port (AGP) and Peripheral Component Interconnect (PCI) frequencies, are specified by the FSB frequency setting. Extremely high frequencies at these buses, depending on the motherboard architecture and chipset functionality, might cause hardware components to fail. This relates to RAM modules such as DIMM DDR SDRAM, video adapters (AGP or PCI), hard disks, and so on. However, many motherboards allow you to set fixed values of PCI/AGP frequencies (33/66 MHz) independent of the FSB frequency. These and other promising technologies are implemented in the architecture of the newest motherboard models, which appear on the market continually and in large quantities. Specialized chipsets, the basis of the motherboard architecture, ensure support of these new technologies.

Many chipsets and motherboard models are milestones in the history of computing.

Popular Chipsets

Intel Chipsets

Intel 440BX AGPset. The i440BX AGPset chipset is optimized for systems based on sixth-generation processors. Its architecture uses the Dual Independent Bus (DIB) with the Back Side Bus (BSB) interface, ensuring efficient operation of L2 cache memory (Fig. 4.25).

The i440BX AGPset supports FSB operation at 100 MHz. Dual-processor configurations are possible.

The support from FSB control functions built into the i440BX AGPset includes the following:

❑ Intel Celeron, Pentium II, and Pentium III (Slot 1 and Socket 370) processors
❑ Symmetric Multiprocessor (SMP) protocol for up to two processors
❑ Buffering, hardware facilities for dynamic command execution, the pipelined data-transfer method, and input/output Advanced Programmable Interrupt Controller (APIC) tools
❑ 60 MHz, 66 MHz, and 100 MHz FSB frequencies (64-bit host bus GTL+)

Built-in memory controller support includes the following:

❑ 64-/72-bit memory bus (64 +8 ECC)

❏ Extended Data Out (EDO) DRAM or SDRAM modules (60 MHz, 66 MHz, or 100 MHz) of 8 MB to 1 GB

❏ 3.3 V DIMM (Single/double density)
   • At 66 MHz: EDO DRAM (no worse than 60 nanoseconds) and SDRAM
   • At 100 MHz: SDRAM only (PC100)
   • Memory chips for 16- and 64-bit DRAM and up to four-sided DIMM (eight rows)

❏ Parity control and ECC (for SDRAM only)

❏ Unbuffered and registered SDRAM (x-1-1-1 at 66 MHz, and x-1-1-1 at 100 MHz)

❏ DIMM plug-and-play through the Serial Presence Detect (SPD) mechanism using Intel's SMBus (System Management Bus) interface

The chipset doesn't support the coexistence of EDO DRAM and SDRAM. The memory-bus frequency always equals the FSB frequency (synchronous mode).

Built-in interface controllers and control tools support the following:

❏ AGP Rev 1.0 (4/12/96) with 1X/2X modes (66/133 MHz, 3.3 V) and A6P sideband

❏ PCI Rev. 2.1 (3.3 V and 5 V, 33 MHz, 32 bits)

❏ Up to five PCI devices (in addition to the I/O bridge, PIIX4/PIIX4E)

❏ Two Integrated Drive Electronics (IDE) ports (four IDE devices), and two Universal Serial Bus (USB) ports

❏ System Management Bus (SMB), and bus mastering

❏ PC '98 specification of Advanced Configuration and Power Interface (ACPI) power management for mobile and desktop computers

❏ Wired for Management (WfM), Ultra DMA/33, and other devices

In systems based on i440BX, it is possible to use Ultra DMA/66 hard disks; however, they will operate in the Ultra DMA/33 mode.

The AGP and PCI bus frequencies are related to the processor-bus frequency. In the i440BX chipset, there are two coefficients relating AGP to FSB frequencies — 1:1 and 2:3. For the PCI bus, the value of this coefficient can be chosen from the following values — 1:2, 1:3, or 1:4. The last value is not supported by all motherboards; however, it is the one of the greatest interest to people who experiment with overclocking modes.

The i440BX AGPset chipset comprises two chips: 82443BX and 82371AB/EB. The 82443BX chip is known as the Host Bridge/Controller PCI AGP (PAC). The 82371AB/EB chip is the PCI-to-ISA/IDE Xcelerator (PIIX4/PIIX4E).

The problem caused by the lack of built-in Ultra DMA/66 and Ultra DMA/100 support in the i440BX chipset can be solved by installing an additional controller, implemented using specialized chips. For example, HPT366 or HPT370 from HighPoint Technologies can be used for this purpose.

In addition to the means of supporting Ultra DMA/66 and Ultra DMA/100 protocols, motherboard designers often add specialized chips for hardware monitoring, an essential architectural attribute of any contemporary system. This functionality is usually based on special chips such as Winbond W83782D.

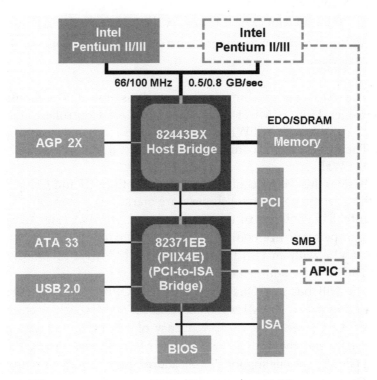

Fig. 4.25. Structure of a computer based on the i440BX AGPset chipset

Intel 815. Chipsets from the i815 line are based on Accelerated Hub Architecture (AHA). They are oriented toward high-performance computers with Pentium II/III processors (Slot 1 or Socket 370) and FSB frequencies of 66/100/133 MHz.

Built-in memory controller support includes the following:

❑ Up to 512 MB PC100/133 SDRAM
❑ Up to three DIMM modules
❑ 64-bit interface

Built-in tools support the following:

❑ AGP 1X/2X/4X (integrated graphics based on the i752 chip, with up to six PCI)
❑ Two (i815) or four (i815E) USB ports and two IDE ports (Ultra DMA/33/66 for 815, or Ultra DMA/33/66/100 for 815E)
❑ LAN controller (i815E)
❑ AC'97 audio with two (i815) or six (i815E) channels
❑ ACPI power management, hardware monitoring, and other functions or devices

The i815 chipset comprises three chips: the 82815 Graphics and Memory Controller Hub (GMCH), the 82801AA I/O Controller Hub (ICH), and the 82802 Firmware Hub (FWH).

The i815E chipset comprises three chips: 82815 GMCH, 82801BA ICH2, and 82802 FWH.

Besides this, variants of i815 support Pentium III and Celeron processors based on the Tualatin core. These chipsets are marked as B-step.

Intel 845. Chipsets of this line are based on AHA (Fig. 4.26) and are intended for high-performance computers based on Pentium 4 processors (Socket 478 and Socket 423) with an FSB frequency of 100/133 MHz (400/533 MHz for data and 200/266 MHz for addresses).

The FSB bus is a Quad Pumped Bus (QPB). At a 100 MHz clock frequency, it transmits data at 400 MHz and addresses at 200 MHz, which ensures a peak throughput of 3.2 GB/sec. At a clock frequency of 133 MHz, the data-transmission rate is 533 MHz, and the address rate is 266 MHz. In this mode, the peak throughput is 4.2 GB/sec. The bus supports 32-bit addressing, which ensures up to 4 GB RAM.

The built-in memory controller supports two types of memory: SDRAM (up to 3 GB with up to three DIMM modules, a 64-bit interface, PC100/133 SDRAM, etc.) or DDR SDRAM. The chipset version with DDR SDRAM is known as i845D.

The line of specialized i845 chipsets includes the following models: i845GL, i845GV, i845G, i845GE, i845E, and i845PE.

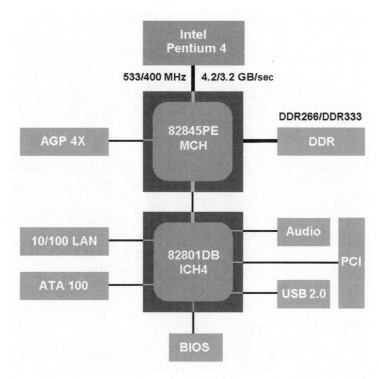

Fig. 4.26. Structure of a computer based on the i845PE chipset

The most popular chipset from this line is i845PE, based on i845 and i845E.

The i845PE chipset is oriented toward systems with Pentium 4 or Celeron (Socket 478) processors with a 100/133 MHz FSB (QPB).

The built-in memory controller (Intel 82845PE MCH) supports the following:

☐ DDR SDRAM and DDR266/333 modules
☐ Maximum memory of 2 GB
☐ 64 MB, 128 MB, 256 MB, and 512 MB SDRAM chips
☐ Unbuffered modules
☐ Unregistered 184 pin without ECC DDR

The maximum data-transmission rate is 2.1/2.7 GB/sec with DDR266/333.

The built-in graphics controller supports one AGP device for AGP 2X/4X modes.

The second component of the chipset, the Intel 82801DB ICH4 chip, manages peripheral devices. This chip is included in the base set of the i845PE chipset.

Built-in tools of the base set support the following:

☐ Two IDE channels with ATA 33/66/100/133 support (up to four IDE devices)
☐ Three USB 2.0 controllers (six ports) and six PCI devices (32 bit/33 MHz)
☐ AC'97 with support for six audio channels (20-bit AC-Link interface)
☐ Integrated 10/100 Base-TX Ethernet controller
☐ Low Pin Count (LPC), SMB, ACPI 2.0, and other functions and features

Because the i845PE chipset has considerable technological reserve, some motherboard manufacturers have released products that ensure support for a 200 MHz FSB (QPB).

Intel 850. Chipsets such as i850/i850E are based on AHA and are intended for high-performance computers with Pentium 4 (Socket 478 and Socket 423) processors operating at an FSB (QPB) clock frequency of 100/133 MHz (400/533 MHz for data and 200/266 MHz for addresses). The built-in memory controller supports two channels of up to 2 GB of Direct RDRAM, with up to four RIMM modules, PC800 RIMM, etc.

Built-in tools support the following:

☐ AGP 1X/2X/4X, with up to six PCI or four USB ports
☐ Two IDE ports with Ultra DMA/33/66/100 and a LAN controller
☐ AC'97 audio with six channels
☐ ACPI, hardware monitoring, and other features and functions

The i850 chipset comprises three chips: 82850 MCH, 82801BA ICH2, and 82802 FWH.

Intel 875. The i875P chipset, previously known as Canterwood, is oriented toward workstations and high-performance desktop computers (Fig. 4.27). It supports Pentium 4 processors with hyperthreading technology and manufactured using 0.13-micrometer technology. It is connected via the Socket 478 slot and has a FSB of the QPB type. The clock frequency can be 100 MHz, 133 MHz, or 200 MHz.

The built-in Intel 82875P (MCH) controller of the QPB-type FSB supports a bus operating frequencies of 100/133/200 MHz, which ensures a data-transmission rate of 400/533/800 MHz.

The memory controller provides support for the following features:

☐ Dual-channel and single-channel modes of DDR266/333/400 operation
☐ Up to 4 GB of memory

❑   128 MB, 256 MB, and 512 MB DDR SDRAM chips
❑   Memory modules with or without ECC

In configurations that ensure ECC support in dual-channel mode, a 144-bit bus is used; without ECC, the bus is 128 bits.

Various frequency modes for processor buses and memory are listed in Table 4.27.

Table 4.27. Frequency Modes for the Processor Bus and Memory

FSB frequency (MHz)	Memory frequency (MHz)	Coefficient	Bandwidth (GB/sec)
100	133	3:4	2.1
133	133	1:1	2.1
200	133	3:2	2.1
133	166	4:5	2.7
200	160	5:4	2.6
200	200	1:1	3.2

For synchronous operation of the DDR400 memory and 800 MHz bus, it is possible to implement the mode that ensures maximum performance of the memory subsystem: Intel Performance Acceleration Technology (PAT). In this mode, all delays related to synchronization are minimized.

The built-in graphics controller supports one 0.8/1.5 V AGP 3.0 device, operating in the AGP 8X mode.

Specific features of the MCH include implementation of a special interface (the CSA bus), which allows the implementation of Gigabit Ethernet. These features are ported from the ICH chip into MCH because of insufficient throughput of the local bus connecting MCH and ICH.

Control over peripheral devices is delegated to the second component of the chipset: ICH5, represented by Intel 82801EB chip. This chip is included in the base set of the i875P chipset.

Built-in control tools of this chip provide the following:

❑   Two IDE channels with ATA 33/66/100 support (up to four IDE devices)
❑   Two Serial ATA 150 ports, six USB 2.0 ports, and six PCI (32 bit/33 MHz)
❑   AC'97 with support for three audio channel codecs

❑ Integrated 10/100 Base-TX Ethernet controller
❑ LPC, SMB, ACPI 2.0, and other tools and features

Besides Intel 82801EB, it is possible to use an extended version of ICH5: ICH5R. This extended version is represented by the Intel 82801ER chip. It differs from its predecessor by the presence of RAID 0 functionality, implemented according to the Intel RAID 0 technology.

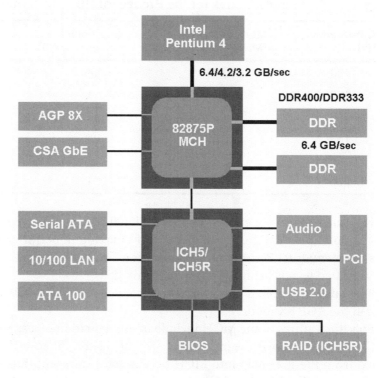

Fig. 4.27. Structure of a computer based on the i875P chipset

Intel 865. The i865 chipset line, previously known as Springdale Canterwood, is oriented toward high-performance desktop PCs. It supports Intel Pentium 4 processors with hyperthreading technology and it is manufactured using the 0.13-micrometer process. It is connected via Socket 478 and supports the Quad Pumped Bus (QBP) type of FSB. Its clock frequency can be 100 MHz, 133 MHz, or 200 MHz (with a 400 MHz, 533 MHz, or 800 MHz data-transfer rate).

The PAT technology isn't officially supported.

The chipset supports the following features:

❏ Dual-channel DDR266 memory (for any FSB frequency)
❏ DDR333 (for 533/800 MHz) and DDR400 (for 800 MHz only)
❏ AGP 8x and eight USB 2.0 ports
❏ Intel's Communication Streaming Architecture (CSA) bus (for Intel Gigabit Ethernet chips)
❏ Six PCI Busmaster devices
❏ AC'97 codec(s) (20 bit)
❏ Four IDE devices, with interface up to ATA 100, and two IDE devices with Serial ATA interface (with some limitations)

For the last two devices, it is possible to organize RAID 0, provided that the ICH5R South Bridge is used.

Via Technologies Chipsets

VIA Apollo Pro133A. The VIA Apollo Pro133A chipset supports Intel Celeron, Pentium II, and Pentium III (Slot 1 and Socket 370) processors. Among the most important characteristics of the Apollo Pro133A chipset is support for the following features:

❏ 66/100/133 MHz FSB, complying with the GTL+ standard
❏ Synchronous and asynchronous bus operating modes, allowing operating modes of RAM modules to be set above the FSB frequency (+33 MHz)
❏ Combined usage of SDRAM, Virtual Channel Memory (VCM) SDRAM, Enhanced SDRAM (ESDRAM), and EDO DRAM modules
❏ Maximum memory of 2 GB and eight memory banks

PC133 specifications recommend a limit of three DIMM or six banks at 133 MHz. (The maximum memory in this configuration is 1.5 GB.)

Synchronous and pseudosynchronous bus operation modes allow the operating frequency of memory modules to be set above (+33 MHz) or below (−33 MHz) the FSB frequency.

The chipset also supports the following:

❏ AGP 2.0 specifications, with the AGP 1X/2X/4X modes, and PC 2.1 specifications

❏ Ultra DMA/33/66 modes for Enhanced Integrated Drive Electronics (EIDE) and USB ports

❏ Keyboard and PS/2 mouse

❏ RTC/CMOS within the VT82C694X chip

The Apollo Pro133A chipset comprises two chips: VT82C694X North Bridge and VT82C596B Mobile South Bridge.

In Apollo Pro133A, the VT82C686A chip can be used as a South Bridge. The chipset comprising VT82C694X and VT82C686A chips allows the creation of high-performance multimedia systems. All interactions with the processor, memory, and graphics are the responsibility of the North Bridge (VT82C694X). The South Bridge (VT82C686A) controls peripheral devices. The South Bridge chip includes support for Ultra DMA/66, AC'97 (implementation of a cheap built-in modem and sound card), two USB, and so on.

For support of the processors based on the Tualatin core, Via Technologies has released the VIA Apollo Pro133T chipset.

VIA Apollo KT133. The VIA Apollo KT133 chipset is oriented toward systems using AMD Athlon and Duron with Socket A processor slots (Socket-462). It is intended to work with the EV6-type FSB. Chipset support includes the following:

❏ Asynchronous 64-bit memory bus with operating frequencies of 66/100/133 MHz

❏ Up to 1.5 GB of PC133 and PC100 SDRAM and VCM SDRAM

❏ Ultra DMA/33/66 and PCI 2.2

❏ Up to five PCI devices, four USB ports, and AGP 1X/2X/4X

❏ AC'97 audio, MC'97 modem, integrated I/O APIC, hardware monitoring, advanced mobile power management, and clock stop

The Apollo KT133 chipset comprises two chips: VT8363 North Bridge and VT82C686A South Bridge.

Via Technologies released an improved version of this chipset that became known as Apollo KT133A (North Bridge VT8363A). In contrast to its predecessor, this new chipset supports 200 MHz (100 MHz DDR) frequency, and is even capable of supporting 266 MHz (133 MHz DDR).

VIA Apollo Pro266. The VIA Apollo Pro266 chipset is oriented toward systems with Intel's Celeron, Pentium II, or Pentium III processors, or with Via Technologies' Cyrix III processors, with Socket 370 slot and FSB frequencies equal to 66/100/133 MHz. North Bridge and South Bridge are connected with the V-Link bus (266 MB/sec). The chipset supports DDR200/266 (PC1600/2100) SDRAM or PC66/100/133 SDRAM — up to 4 GB.

The North Bridge is represented by the VT8633 chip, and the South Bridge by the VT8233 chip.

To support processors based on the Tualatin core, Via Technologies has released the Apollo Pro266T chipset.

VIA Apollo KT266. The VIA Apollo KT266 chipset is oriented toward systems based on AMD Athlon and Duron (Socket A), with FSB frequencies of 100/133 MHz. The North Bridge and South Bridge are connected using the V-Link bus (266 MB/sec). The chipset supports DDR200/266 (PC1600/2100) SDRAM or PC66/100/133 SDRAM — up to 4 GB.

The North Bridge is represented by the VT8366 chip, and the South Bridge by the VT8233 chip.

Via Technologies has released an improved version of this chipset: Apollo KT266A with a VT8366A chip for the North Bridge. It uses a more powerful built-in memory controller.

VIA P4X266. The VIA Apollo P4X266 chipset is oriented toward systems using Pentium 4 (Socket 423 and Socket 478) with an FSB frequency of 100 MHz (400 MHz data bus and 200 MHz address bus). The North Bridge and South Bridge are connected using the V-Link bus (266 MB/sec). The chipset supports DDR200/266 (PC1600/2100) SDRAM or PC100/133 SDRAM — up to 4 GB.

North Bridge is represented by the P4X266 chip, and the South Bridge by the VT8233 chip.

Via Technologies has released an improved version of this chipset: P4X266A. This newer version includes support for Pentium 4 processors with an FSB frequency equal to 133 MHz (533 MHz data rate).

VIA Apollo KT400. The VIA Apollo KT400 chipset is oriented toward systems with AMD Athlon XP and Duron processors, with Socket A (Socket 462) and FSB frequencies of 100 MHz, 133 MHz, and 166 MHz. The FSB is of the EV6 type, and data transmission takes place on both fronts of the clock pulses (Fig. 4.28).

Traditionally, the chipset comprises two components — North Bridge and South Bridge — connected by a special local bus named 8X V-Link (Quad data pump per CLK, 533 MB/sec). The bus is bidirectional, with 266 MB/sec transmitted in any direction of data transfer.

The North Bridge, represented by the VT8377 chip, provides all functions specific for interfacing with the processor, AGP video adapter, main memory, and South Bridge.

The FSB controller built into VT8377 supports bus frequencies of 100/133/166 MHz.

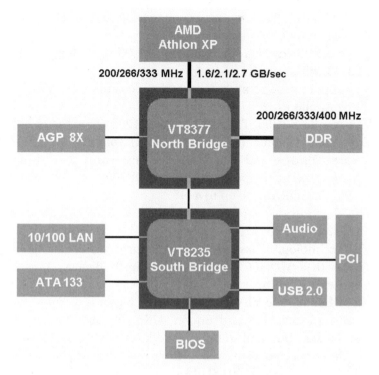

Fig. 4.28. Structure of a computer based on the Apollo KT400 chipset

The built-in memory controller ensures support for DDR SDRAM (Double Data Rate SDRAM) and DDR200/266/333, with maximum memory of 4 GB. The maximum data-transmission speed is 1.6/2.1/2.7 GB/sec at DDR200/266/333. Unofficially, this chipset also supports DDR400.

The built-in graphics controller supports one AGP device in 2X/4X/8X modes.

Control over peripheral devices is delegated to the South Bridge, represented by the VT8235 chip. This chip is included in the base set of the Apollo KT400 chipset.

The built-in tools of the base set support the following:

- ❏ Two IDE channels, with support for ATA 33/66/100/133 (up to four IDE devices)
- ❏ Three USB 2.0 controllers (six ports) and five PCI
- ❏ LPC Super I/O (Low Pin Count)

❑ AC'97 with support for six audio channels (Surround Sound AC-97 Audio)

❑ MC'97, VIA 10/100 Ethernet MAC (Media Access Control), Advanced Communications Riser (ACR), ACPI, advanced power management, and other devices and functions

Popular Motherboards

When evaluating the parameters of contemporary motherboards, it is expedient to consider high-performance motherboards that have the greatest popularity, are produced by well-known companies, and frequently are used in systems that operate in overclocked modes.

Abit BE6-II

Processors: Intel Pentium II/III, Celeron, Slot 1. *Chipset:* Intel 440BX AGPset. *FSB frequencies:* 66/75/83–200 MHz incremented at a step equal to 1 MHz. *Processor core supply voltage:* 1.3–2.3 V with a 0.05 V increment. *RAM:* Three DIMM, up to 768 MB SDRAM, ECC. *Video:* AGP 1X/2X. *ATA:* Two Ultra DMA/33 IDE ports, two Ultra DMA/66/33 (HPT366) ports. *I/O:* Two serial ports, one parallel port (ECP/EPP), two USB, PS/2, Infrared Data Association (IrDA), floppy. *Technologies:* ACPI; hardware monitoring; Wake-on-LAN header, Wake-on-Ring header, and waking on from events generated by the keyboard, mouse, network, and modem. *BIOS:* Award BIOS v.6, Plug-and-Play, Write-Protect Anti-Virus, SoftMenu III (or DIP switches for setting the CPU parameters). *Slots:* Five PCI, one ISA, one AGP. *Form factor:* ATX (305 × 200 mm).

Abit KT7

Processors: AMD Athlon/Duron, Socket A. *Chipset:* VIA Apollo KT133 (VT8363+VT82C686A). *FSB frequency:* 100 MHz (Alpha EV6). *Overclocking:* CPU core supply voltage of 1.1–1.85 V with an increment of 0.25 V. *FSB frequencies:* 100/101/103/105/107/110/112/115/117/120/122/124/127/133/136/140/145/150/155 MHz. *RAM:* Three DIMM, up to 1.5 GB PC100/PC133 SDRAM, memory-bus frequency of 100/133 MHz. *Video:* AGP 1X/2X/4X. *ATA:* Two IDE ports (up to four Ultra DMA/66/33 devices). *I/O:* Two PS/2 slots for connecting keyboard and mouse, one floppy port, one parallel port (EPP/ECP), two serial ports, two USB ports (with two additional), and so on. *BIOS:* Award Plug-and-Play. *Slots:* One AGP, six PCI, one ISA. *Form factor:* ATX (305 × 230 mm).

There is also an extended version of the Abit KT7 motherboard: Abit KT7-RAID. Architecture of this version employs the HPT370 (Ultra DMA/100, RAID) chip. RAID allows the operating speed to be increased and the reliability of data storage on hard disks to be improved. The presence of the HPT370 chip allows an increase to eight IDE devices.

The Abit KT7 motherboard allows the CPU frequency multipliers to be unlocked. However, this is possible only when L1 bridges on the surface of Athlon or Duron processors weren't cut during fabrication and testing by the manufacturer. If this isn't the case, you should use the technology for restoring these bridges.

After the release of the VIA Apollo KT133A chipset, Abit designed a new variant of its motherboard architecture, known as Abit KT7A. This board, in contrast to its prototype, has a wider range of FSB frequencies at which stable operation can be achieved. In addition to the possibilities of changing the frequency multiplier of the CPU, it provides optimal capabilities for overclocking.

Abit IT7-MAX2

Processor: Intel Pentium 4 and Celeron (Socket 478) with FSB QPB 400/533 MHz. *Chipset (for v.2.0):* Intel 845PE/ICH4, Ultra DMA 33/66/100 support, AGP slot with support for AGP 4X (only 1.5 V). *Memory:* Three 184-pin DIMM (unbuffered non-ECC DIMM), support for three DIMM DDR SDRAM 200/266 (maximum 2 GB). *Serial ATA:* Integrated two-channel Serial ATA interface, 1.5 Gbit/sec. *ATA133 RAID:* HighPoint Technologies HPT374 IDE RAID controller. *Media XP (add-on):* Support for Memory Stick, Secure Digital and Type I/II CompactFlash card readers, wireless devices and S/PDIF I/O for microphone/headphones/USB 2.0/ IEEE 1394. *Audio:* Six-channel AC'97 codec. *USB 2.0:* Ten USB 2.0 ports. *IEEE 1394:* Three IEEE 1394 ports. *Network controller:* Integrated RTL8100B 10/100M PCI Fast Ethernet. *BIOS:* SoftMenu technology for setting CPU parameters, Plug-and-Play support, ACPI interface support. *Internal I/O slots:* One AGP slot, four PCI slots, floppy drive for diskettes up to 2.88 MB, two Ultra DMA 33/66/100 slots, two Ultra DMA 33/66/100/133 (RAID) slots, two Serial ATA slots (1.5 Mbit/sec), six-channel FPIO audio splitter (for Media XP), two USB splitters, one IEEE 1394 splitter, two CD-IN sockets, one IrDA socket. *Sockets on the rear panel:* One PS/2 socket, one socket for PS/2 mouse, four USB connectors, two IEEE 1394 connectors, S/PDIF output, audio sockets (central speaker/subwoofer, speaker for stereo sound), audio sockets (front speakers, linear input, microphone input), two USB sockets, one RJ-45 LAN socket. *Form factor:* ATX. *Hardware monitoring:* Fan rotation speed, supply voltages, system temperature, Wake Up by LAN, Modem Ring, RTC Alarm, keyboard/mouse power-on, STR (Suspend to RAM).

DDR SDRAM modules can operate in either synchronous or asynchronous mode. To choose and set the required modes of operation for the processor, memory, and I/O devices, use the appropriate options from the BIOS Setup menu.

For overclocking fans, there are options that can be used to set the CPU overclocked modes. This can be done by increasing the FSB frequency and the memory-bus frequency, and by choosing the optimal values for DDR SDRAM parameters. A photo of this motherboard is in Fig. 4.29.

Fig. 4.29. Abit IT7-MAX2 Rev. 2.0 motherboard

Asus P3B-F

Processors: Intel Pentium II/III and Celeron, Slot 1. *Chipset:* Intel 440BX AGPset. *FSB frequency:* 66/100 MHz. *Overclocking:* 66/75/83/100/103/105/110/112/115/120/124/133/140/150 MHz. *Memory:* Four DIMM, 8 MB to 1,024 MB, PC100 SDRAM, ECC. *Video:* AGP 1X/2X. *ATA:* Two Ultra DMA/33, support for ATAPI IDE CD-ROM and LS-120. *I/O:* Two serial ports, one parallel port (ECP/EPP), two USB ports, IrDA, two PS/2, floppy (up to 2.88 MB). *Technologies:* Hardware monitoring, waking from keyboard. *BIOS:* 2 Mbit Flash Award BIOS v.6.0, ACPI, Plug-and-Play, Anti-boot Virus. *Slots (three variants):* Six PCI, zero ISA, and one AGP; six PCI, one ISA, and one AGP; or five PCI, zero ISA, and one AGP. *Form factor:* ATX (192 × 304 mm).

The Asus P3B-F motherboard has become one of the most popular high-performance motherboards.

Asus TUSL2-c

Processors: FC-PGA (PGA2) Intel Pentium III and Celeron, including Tualatin, Socket 370. *Chipset:* Intel 815EP (82815EP Step B, 82801BA, 82802AB). *FSB frequency:* 66/100/133 MHz. *Overclocking:* Capabilities are provided. *Memory:* Three DIMM, up to 512 MB PC100/PC133 SDRAM. *ATA:* Two Ultra DMA/33/66/100. *I/O:* Two serial ports, one parallel port (ECP/EPP), two built-in and two add-on USB ports, two PS/2, floppy. *Video:* AGP 4X. *Audio:* CMI8738 audio chip from C-Media. *Technologies:* Hardware monitoring and wake from modem, mouse, keyboard, and timer. *BIOS:* 4 Mbit Flash Award BIOS, ACPI, DMI, Green, Plug-and-Play, Trend Chip Away Virus, Symbios SCSI BIOS. *Slots:* Six PCI, one AGP, one CNR. *Form factor:* ATX (208 × 305 mm).

Asus P4PE

Processor: Intel Pentium 4 (HT support) and Celeron, Socket 478. *Chipset:* Intel 82845PE Memory Controller Hub (MCH), 82801DB Enhanced I/O Controller Hub (ICH4). *Overclocking:* Changing the FSB frequency from 100 MHz to 200 MHz with an increment of 1 MHz, and changing the core supply voltage for CPU, memory, and AGP. *Memory:* Three 184-pin DIMM DDR SDRAM 200/266/333 (maximum 2 GB). *Video:* AGP 4X. *Audio:* AC'97 codec, Analog Devices AD1980. *ATA:* Two Ultra DMA/33/66/100 and Promise PDC20376, supports Serial ATA (two channels). *I/O:* Two serial ports, one parallel port (ECP/EPP), two PS/2, floppy, six USB 2.0, two FireWire (VIA6307). *Network controller:* Broadcom BCM5702CKFB (Gigabit Ethernet). *BIOS:* 4 Mbit Award BIOS v. 6.0. *Slots:* Six PCI, one AGP. *Form factor:* ATX (305 × 230 mm).

Asus P4P800 Deluxe

Processors: Intel Pentium 4 (HT support) and Celeron, Socket 478. *Chipset:* 865PE Memory Controller Hub (MCH), 82801ER Enhanced I/O Controller Hub (ICH5R).

Overclocking: Changing the FSB frequency from 100 MHz to 400 MHz with an increment of 1 MHz, and changing the core supply voltage for the processor, memory, and AGP. *Memory:* Four DIMM DDR SDRAM, maximum memory of 4 GB, support for one or two memory channels. *Video:* AGP 4X. *Expansion slots:* AGP, five PCI. *I/O:* One FDD, two COM, one LPT, two PS/2, eight USB 2.0, two FireWire, IDE-controller integrated into the chipset (ATA100+SATA RAID), external IDE controller VIA VT6410 (ATA133 RAID). *Sound:* AC'97 Analog Devices AD1985 codec. *Built-in network controller:* 3COM Marvell 940-MV00 (Gigabit Ethernet). *BIOS:* 4 Mbit AMI BIOS v2.51. *Form factor:* ATX (305 × 245 mm).

A photo of this motherboard is in Fig. 4.30.

Fig. 4.30. Asus P4P800 Deluxe motherboard

Asus P4C800 Deluxe

Processors: Intel Pentium 4 (HT support) and Celeron, Socket 478. *Chipset:* Intel 875P/ICH5 (RG82875P + FW82801EB). *Memory:* Four DIMM DDR SDRAM, maximum physical memory of 4 GB, support for one or two memory channels. *Video:* AGP 4X. *Expansion slots:* AGP Pro, five PCI. *I/O:* One FDD, two COM, one LPT, two PS/2, eight USB 2.0, two FireWire, IDE controller integrated into the chipset (ATA100 + SATA), external IDE controller Promise PDC20378 (SATA/ATA133 RAID). *Sound:* AC'97 Analog Devices AD1985 codec. *Built-in network controller:* 3COM Marvell 940-MV00 (Gigabit Ethernet). *BIOS:* 4 Mbit AMI BIOS v2.51. *Form Factor:* ATX (305×245 mm).

A photo of this motherboard is shown in Fig. 4.31.

Fig. 4.31. Asus P4C800 Deluxe motherboard

Intel D845PEBT2

Processor: Intel Pentium 4 and Celeron processors (Socket 478) with FSB QPB operating at 400/533 MHz, support for hyperthreading technology. *Chipset:* Intel 82845PE (MCH)/82801DB (ICH4). *Memory:* Two slots (184-pin) for DIMM (unbuffered Non-ECC DIMM), DDR266/333, maximum memory of 2 GB. *Audio:* Integrated six-channel AC'97 codec (AC'97 Audio with SoundMAX Cadenza). *USB 2.0:* Up to six USB 2.0 ports with a data-transmission rate up to 480 Mbit/sec. *LAN:* Integrated 10/100 Mbit Ethernet network controller. *BIOS:* 4 MB Flash EEPROM, automatic configuration of IDE devices, Intel Rapid BIOS boot technology to speed up the POST routine. *Internal slots:* One AGP, six PCI, one floppy port (supports devices up to 2.88 MB), two Ultra DMA 100/66/33 connectors, two USB 2.0. *External slots:* One PS/2 keyboard, one xPS/2 mouse, four USB 2.0, RJ45-LAN network slot, one parallel port, one COM port, audio sockets (line-in, mic-in, line-out). *Hardware monitoring:* Voltage and temperature monitoring, automatic control over the fan rotation speed. *Form factor:* ATX.

Fig. 4.32. Intel D845PEBT2 motherboard

The Intel D845PEBT2 motherboard implements the Intel Rapid BIOS boot technology and Burn-In Mode technology for processor overclocking. Clock frequencies can be changed from the nominal as follows: –2%, –1%, +1%, +2%, +3%, and +4%. This mode is intended for professionals experimenting with system operating modes that differ in performance, heat emission, and stability. A photo of this motherboard is in Fig. 4.32.

Intel D875PBZ

Intel has designed the D875PBZ motherboard as a dual-channel solution for the main memory subsystem. The architecture of this motherboard, based on the Intel 875P (Canterwood) chipset, implements some promising new technologies. This motherboard is oriented toward high-performance computer systems and ensures support for Intel Pentium 4 processors with hyperthreading technology. It is intended to operate at FSB frequencies of 200 MHz and 133 MHz.

Processor: Intel Pentium 4 processors with hyperthreading technology (bus data rate of 533/800 MHz) in a 478-pin mPGA case. *Chipset:* Intel 82875P (MCH)/ 82801EB (ICH5R)/82802AC (FWH), two Serial ATA 150 ports with support for Intel RAID 0, Ultra ATA 66/100, five PCI slots, ACPI 1.0b, corresponding to PC2001 specifications. *RAM:* Four 184-pin slots for DIMM, DDR333/400, 2.5 V, ECC supported, maximum memory of 4 GB, support for one or two memory channels. *USB 2.0:* Six ports on the rear panel (one doubled and one quadrupled), two ports on the front panel (contact group for outputs on the front panel). *Video:* AGP 3.0 with support for the AGP 8X mode. *Audio:* Audio subsystem complying with the Flex 6 standard based on the AD1985 codec from Analog Devices (specific requirement from the customer). *LAN:* Integrated Gigabit Ethernet network controller (with the CSA interface). *BIOS:* 8 MB Flash EEPROM with Intel/AMI BIOS, automatic configuration of IDE devices, Intel Rapid BIOS boot technology to speed up the POST routine. *Internal slots:* One AGP, five PCI, one floppy port (supporting devices up to 2.88 MB), two Ultra DMA 33/66/100 connectors, two Serial ATA 150 connectors, two USB 2.0 connectors. *External connectors:* PS/2 keyboard and mouse, six USB 2.0 sockets, one RJ45-LAN network socket, one parallel port, one serial (COM) port, audio sockets (line-in, mic-in, line-out). *Hardware monitoring:* Temperature and voltage monitoring, automatic control over fan rotation speed (Intel Precision Cooling). *Form factor:* ATX 2.30 (237.5 × 240 mm).

Like Intel D875PBT2B, the Intel D875PBZ motherboard implements new technologies such as Intel Rapid BIOS boot and processor Burn-In Mode. Clock frequencies can be changed from the nominal as follows: –2%, –1%, +1%, +2%, +3%, and +4%. The overclocking mode is intended for professionals experimenting with modes of system operation that differ in performance, heat emission, and stability. A photo of this motherboard is shown in Fig. 4.33.

Fig. 4.33. Intel D875PBZ motherboard

Video Adapters

Video adapters based on video chips (also known as graphics processors) from Nvidia and ATI Technologies are currently the most popular. To achieve maximum performance and stable operation of their products, both Nvidia and ATI developed reference designs for video adapters based on their chips. These specifications, combined with recommendations from Nvidia and ATI, serve as the standard for companies manufacturing video adapters.

Data on the basic parameters, performance, and evolution of video adapters are provided in Table 4.28.

Table 4.28. Evolution of Nvidia and ATI Products

Graphics processor	Core frequency (MHz)	DDR SDRAM frequency (MHz)	Memory (MB)	Peak throughput (MB/sec)	Theoretical filling speed (million pixel per second)
Nvidia GeForce FX 5900 Ultra	400	850	256	27,200	3,600
Nvidia GeForce4 Ti4600	300	650	128	10,400	1,200
Nvidia GeForce4 Ti4400	275	550	128	8,800	1,100
Nvidia GeForce4 Ti4200	250	500	128	8,200	1,000
Nvidia GeForce3 Ti500	240	500	64	8,000	960
Nvidia GeForce3	200	460	64	7,360	800
Nvidia GeForce3 Ti200	175	400	64	6,400	700
Nvidia GeForce2 Ultra	250	460	64	7,360	1,000
Nvidia GeForce2 Ti	250	400	64	6,400	1,000
Nvidia GeForce2 Pro	200	400	64	6,400	800
ATI Radeon 9700	276	540	128	17,200	2,200
ATI Radeon 8500	275	550	64	8,800	1,100
ATI Radeon 7500	290	460	64	7,360	580

Hard Disks

A hard disk is a device for storing large amounts of data. Each disk comprises four basic elements that contribute to the disk parameters: media (platters), read/write heads, positioning device that positions the head to the needed track, and controller that ensures data transfer.

Hard disk performance depends on various parameters. The most important are write density, data-access time, amount of cache memory, and interface.

Increasing the write density increases the disk capacity and data-transmission speed, provided that the disk rotation speed remains the same. Hard disk capacity tends to double each year.

The data-access time includes the interval needed to position the head to the required track and the latency (the wait for the needed sector to appear under the head). The latency depends on the rotation speed.

For now, hard disks with a rotation speed of 7,200 rpm, 2 MB cache memory, and a capacity of 120 GB to 180 GB are the optimal choice for desktop PCs.

The most common models have a parallel ATA interface (i.e., IDE, EIDE, or ATAPI) with a data-transmission speed of 100 MB/sec. However, these are being replaced by the Serial ATA interface, which ensures a transmission rate of 150 MB/sec.

Hard disks have low overclocking potential. Acceleration of more than 20% may result in data loss, even under conditions of adequate cooling. This risk and the possibility of disk failure indicate that it is not wise to overclock hard disks.

Power Supply Units

(Based on materials and with the permission of **http://www.fcenter.ru**, a Russian-language Web site.)

As a rule, when purchasing a new computer, buyers pay serious attention to the CPU clock frequency, amount of memory, hard disk size, and so on. If some attention is paid to the system unit case, it mainly relates to its appearance. The importance of purchasing a power supply unit with the case is often overlooked.

Specific Features of Power Supply Units

Not only stable operation, but also the existence of entire computer system depends on the power supply unit. Minor problems with power supply units are hard to diagnose. Persistent failures or unstable operation of the power supply unit might look like memory failures, chipset malfunctions, or OS internal errors. The PC user who experiences such problems may replace the memory, upgrade the BIOS, or reinstall device drivers, but never see a positive result. Major problems frequently cause a complete failure of the system unit. To avoid such problems, it is necessary to strictly observe the following rule: Purchase only high-quality power supply units.

Pay attention to the power declared by the manufacturer of the unit. Most power supply units with a declared power of 300 W can't handle this load. The exceptions are world-class brands, such as Fong Kai, Enermax, PowerMaster, PowerMan, HEC, and Delta Electronics products. Even these products may differ significantly from model to model; various models of power supply units from the same manufacturer can have different parameters and designs.

It is possible to obtain a lot of information by opening the case of the power supply unit. Under the hood, there is an internal device with a range of units and components. The input filter, which suppresses electric noise, is one of the most important parts of the power supply unit. Electric interference may be incoming and outgoing (i.e., from the power supply unit to the mains).

A full-featured power supply unit usually has two capacitors and is capable of protecting the computer from pulse noise and short-time blackouts. Nevertheless, the power supply unit and computer powered by it are the sources of a wide range of noise. A correctly designed filter should prevent this noise from propagating in the system and disturbing the operation of other electronic appliances, such as TV sets or other computers.

However, manufacturers of supply units often economize on throttles, and sometimes even on capacitors. Two fragments of power supply units are in Fig. 4.34. The left photo shows a high-quality filter; the right photo shows a poor-quality board, with jumpers instead of throttles.

Fig. 4.34. Fragment of a power supply unit with (*left*) and without (*right*) a filter

Besides the filter, many so-called no-name manufacturers economize on the capacitors and heatsinks. They also may install diodes and transistors that lack the power required for correct and smooth operation. The usage of low-powered elements intended for low currents and voltages is the most common cause of failures for power supply units. Transistors cannot withstand the load and fail.

Unfortunately, it is difficult to check the quality of the electronic components in power supply units. Therefore, it is only possible to draw conclusions from indirect indications.

The degree of voltage deviation from nominal values is the main parameter for the quality of a power supply unit. These deviations are always determined at the nominal workload.

Intel requirements for power supply units are outlined in the ATX specification. The maximum deviations of voltage for the ATX 2.01 and ATX 2.03 specifications are in Table 4.29.

Table 4.29. ATX Specification Requirements

Voltage (V)	ATX 2.01	ATX 2.03
+5	5% = 0.25 V	5% = 0.25 V
−5	5% = 0.25 V	10% = 0.5 V
+12	5% = 0.6 V	5% = 0.6 V
−12	5% = 0.6 V	10% = 1.2 V
+3.3	4% = 0.132 V	4% = 0.132 V
+5 Vsb (standby voltage)	5% = 0.25 V	5% = 0.25 V

As follows from these data, the ATX 2.03 specification requirements are less stringent. However, even these are not always met by a power supply unit.

Good power supply units must have large and efficient heatsinks and fans whose rotation speed can be controlled. As a rule, the more electronic components in the power supply unit, the better the quality — and the higher the price.

The following sections provide some examples of power supply units.

Examples of Power Supply Units

Enermax EG365AX-VE

Enermax Technology is one of the world's leading manufacturers of high-quality power supply units, such as the EG365AX-VE (Fig. 4.35).

This power supply unit is equipped with two fans. One of them is of the standard size (80 × 80 mm) and is placed at the rear panel. Another fan (90 × 90 mm) is on the top cover.

Fig. 4.35. Enermax EG365AX-VE power supply unit

The rotation speed of the first fan can be adjusted manually using the regulator (variable resistor) located on the rear panel. The rotation speed can be changed from 1,500 rpm to 3,500 rpm.

The second fan is controlled automatically by the thermal sensor built into the power supply unit. Besides this, a special socket for connecting to the motherboard allows the use of a built-in hardware-monitoring functionality that controls the fan rotation speed.

This power supply unit is compact and well-assembled (Fig. 4.36).

Fig. 4.36. Internal structure of the Enermax EG365AX-VE power supply unit

This unit is based on the UCC3817N, UC3842BN, and TPS3510P chips.

Most power supply units use two 200 V capacitors at the input. This Enermax unit uses a single capacitor at the input (220 µF, 400 V). At each output, a pair of capacitors (2,200 µF and 3,300 µF) and a throttle have been installed.

The power supply unit is equipped with nine sockets for supplying power to peripheral devices. One of them is intended for motherboards in which processor stabilizers are supplied not only from the ATX12V socket, but also from peripheral power connector. Note that no more than two connectors are on the same cable, and the main power supply buses — 5 V, 3.3 V, and 12 V — in ATX and AUX connectors are made of thick 16AWG wire.

Tests of this unit confirmed its high workload and voltage stability.

The results of testing the EG365AX-VE are in Table 4.30.

Table 4.30. Enermax EG365AX-VE Test Results

	12 V	5 V	3.3 V
Minimum (V)	11.93	5.03	3.31
Maximum (V)	12.91	5.16	3.43
Minimum/maximum (%)	7.6	2.5	3.5

KM Korea GP-300ATX

The power supply unit in Fig. 4.37 was removed from a Sereno case.

The network filter is present. However, important components such as a heatsink, transformer, and group stabilization throttle are very small. The 12 V channel lacks the traditional diode assembly. Instead, two discrete diodes are installed. The 5V channel — S16C40C from MOSPEC diodes are installed (40 V, 16 A current), 3.3 V channel is equipped with the SBL1040CT assembly (40 V, 10 A current). The unit based on such components can't ensure the claimed parameters.

The voltage stabilizer is based on the KA7500B chip from Fairchild Semiconductor and is an analogue to the well-known TL494 controller.

At the input, there are two capacitors (330 µF). At the output, there are two capacitors (1,000 µF) for 5 V and 3.3 V and one capacitor (1,000 µF) for 12 V. The throttle is only at the 12 V output; on the other outputs, only jumpers are installed.

The output diodes failed during testing because they could not withstand the currents specified on the power supply label. This power supply unit was unable to provide even 250 W, to speak nothing about 300 W.

Fig. 4.37. Internal structure of the KM Korea GP-300ATX power supply unit

Delta Electronics DPS-300TB rev. 01

This power supply unit (Fig. 4.38) is manufactured by one of the best-known power supply manufacturers — Delta Electronics.

The assemblage is very accurate. The components of the high-voltage circuits are insulated by a special thermo-contractable tube. All power transistors and diode assemblies are fastened by nuts and bolts onto heatsinks, on which the thermal compound is applied.

This power supply unit is equipped with a thermal regulator that controls the fan rotation speed. Immediately after power-on, the fan rotates slowly; it increases to full rotation speed only under serious workloads.

The fan in this power supply unit has low power and is intended only for cooling the power supply itself. Because of this, it is expedient to use a separate vacuum fan in the computer case. The optimal construction of this power supply unit makes it silent.

All required units, including the filters, are soldered accurately. There is a full-fledged network filter, and there are throttles on all power outputs: 5 V, 12 V, and 3.3 V. Capacitance of the input capacitors is 470 μF. At the 12 V output, there is one Chemi-Con KZE capacitor (1,200 μF); at the 5 V output, there are two

Rubycon ZL capacitors (2,200 μF); and at the 3.3 V output, there are two Taicon PW capacitors (2,200 μF).

Fig. 4.38. Internal structure of the Delta Electronics DPS-300TB power supply unit

Testing confirmed the parameters (Table 4.31). At the 5 V bus, oscillations were practically unnoticeable even at the maximum workload. At the 12 V bus, the pulsation amplitude was about 15 millivolts, which is a good result.

Table 4.31. Delta Electronics DPS-300TB Test Results

	12 V	5 V	3.3 V
Minimum (V)	11.81	4.94	3.31
Maximum (V)	12.92	5.15	3.39
Minimum/maximum (%)	8.6	4.1	2.4

IPower LC-B250ATX

The power supply unit supplied with the E-Star model 8870 "Extra" case is shown in Fig. 4.39.

Fig. 4.39. Internal structure of the IPower LC-B250ATX power supply unit

There is no network filter here — only jumpers, instead of throttles. Half of the filtering capacitors at the output are missing. Two capacitors usually are installed on each bus before and after the throttles. In this unit, one of the capacitors has disappeared, along with the throttle. The capacitance of the capacitors of the high-voltage rectifier is 330 μF; the output capacitors are 1,000 μF for each bus.

This is not all. This power supply unit lacks even insulating plastic lining between the case and the high-voltage part of the circuit. Because of this, the assembling quality is unsatisfactory.

Five output connectors are connected by short 20AWG wires. There is no thermal regulator.

Testing showed unstable output voltages — for example, 15% for 12 V and 7% for 5 V.

These examples should illustrate the importance of carefully choosing a high-quality power supply unit.

Chapter 5

BIOS as Additional Performance Reserve

The efficiency of computer-hardware operation strongly depends on the Basic Input/ Output System (BIOS). BIOS code is stored in nonvolatile RAM and is an integral part of the architecture of any contemporary PC. Newer versions of this code can eliminate bugs related to controlling the existing hardware, as well as extend the range of components. Additionally, improved BIOS code often enhances PC functionality and improves its performance.

The contemporary PC comprises a large number of highly integrated semiconductor chips. They are distributed among various components that form the foundation of the entire system. Components and their elements are known as *computer hardware*, controlled by system and application software.

In multilayer software organization, a part of the system programs, the BIOS, is stored in Read-Only Memory (ROM).

The BIOS is an integral part of any contemporary PC. It implements the simplest and most universal functions required to control standard peripheral devices (input/output organization), relieving the operating system from accounting for the specific features and details of individual peripheral devices. The BIOS "hides" architectural features of specific PC models and ensures software independence on peripheral devices. The BIOS contains standard device drivers, test programs, and a *bootstrap loader*. The bootstrap loader is system-independent; it can work with any OS designed to run on the IBM PC architecture, which serves as the basis for contemporary PCs.

BIOS functions fall into the following categories:

❏ Power-On Self-Test (POST) routine — Initializes and tests computer hardware
❏ BIOS Setup — Configures and fine-tunes the entire computer system
❏ Bootstrap loader — Loads the operating system
❏ BIOS Hardware Interrupts — Performs maintenance and controls interrupts
❏ ROM BIOS Services — Processes software calls to system devices

On contemporary PCs, BIOS code resides in flash memory — on a Flash ROM chip. This allows PC users to modify or update BIOS versions using built-in computer hardware and software.

The motherboard BIOS is responsible for correct operation of the entire computer system. Overall system stability and performance strongly depend on the quality and efficiency of BIOS code. This is especially true for overclocked modes. Motherboard manufacturers, in cooperation with BIOS developers, make significant efforts to improve BIOS code. As a result, improved BIOS versions constantly appear, both for new products and for existing models of motherboards.

Improved versions of BIOS software code are intended for the newest components. They take into account the advanced architecture of these components, as well as improvements related to installation and operation. New BIOS versions often compensate for the drawbacks of earlier models.

Because flash-memory chips store BIOS code, PC users can periodically update the system BIOS. Some computers equipped with older motherboards might experience problems when working with contemporary components under control of contemporary operating systems such as the Windows 9*x*/ME or Windows 2000/XP.

In this situation, it is expedient to update the BIOS version. Most motherboard manufacturers, including Abit, Asus, and Chaintech, strongly recommend that PC users update older BIOS versions. This deserves consideration, particularly if you are using the newest models of processors. A BIOS update may be helpful if you are using Intel Pentium III with a motherboard whose specification states the product can be used with Intel Pentium II, but provides no information about Intel Pentium III support. In many cases, the BIOS must be updated when using Intel Pentium III with the Coppermine core. The same recommendation applies to Intel Pentium 4 processors when migrating to models that support hyperthreading technology.

Some motherboards have hidden potential. A BIOS upgrade can help reveal these hidden capabilities and make them available. For example, it is possible to widen the range of supported system-bus frequencies and core voltages for many motherboards. In most cases, this allows the newest processor models to be used with older motherboards.

The Asus P3B-FB motherboard, which was once widely known and popular, serves as a good example. Versions manufactured before the release of Intel Pentium III with the Coppermine core can work with processors of this type after a BIOS upgrade.

Another example that demonstrates the implementation of hidden capabilities of motherboard architectures is the use of hyperthreading technology after a BIOS upgrade. The manufacturer itself recommends this approach: Intel provided all the necessary information on the Intel Pentium 4 processors and its Hyper-Threading technology to motherboard manufacturers, which enabled them to develop code files. As a rule, motherboard manufacturers provide information required for a BIOS upgrade to their distributors; they also place it on their Web sites so that it is available to the PC user community. Most manufacturers even offer several BIOS versions on their Web sites. Usually, these sites also provide special utilities for upgrading the BIOS, as well as documentation explaining the functionality that will become available after a BIOS upgrade.

Upgrading BIOS

Special utilities are required for performing a BIOS upgrade. This procedure is very important and potentially dangerous; therefore, it must be performed carefully and according to instructions. As a rule, all required instructions, BIOS upgrading utilities, and documentation explaining possible failures and useful recommendations are available at the Web sites offering files with new BIOS versions.

A BIOS upgrade completely replaces the entire BIOS code and data. If any failure occurs during this process, the computer system might become unusable. If this happens, it is necessary to call a service center for support. Usually, the repair operations require special equipment or, at least, a second (usable) computer with the same type of motherboard.

Note that the recommendations given here are only a generalized scenario of a BIOS upgrade. Before proceeding with an actual BIOS upgrade, it is necessary to carefully study the technical documentation or contact a trained specialist. Remember that any specific case might have particular nuances that can greatly influence the final result.

As a rule, you should perform the following steps to accomplish a motherboard BIOS upgrade:

1. Precisely identify the model of your motherboard. Different motherboard versions require different utilities and different files containing BIOS upgrade codes. Each motherboard is usually labeled with the manufacturer name, product name, and version number.

2. Download the file containing the newest BIOS version from the manufacturer's Web site.

3. Unpack the downloaded file containing the BIOS upgrade. Quite often, the downloaded file is a self-extracting archive with the .exe filename extension. To unpack the BIOS upgrade, it is usually sufficient to run this file. The archive will be automatically unpacked into the required file format, such as into a file with the .bin extension.

4. Disable the BIOS protection function in BIOS Setup. Some motherboards have the **Flash BIOS Protection** parameter in the **See & CHIPSET SETUP** menu of BIOS Setup. You must set the **Disabled** option for this function before proceeding with the BIOS upgrade.

5. Start the system without loading any Terminate and Stay Resident (TSR) programs. Some utilities for upgrading the BIOS operate correctly only when there are no memory-resident programs. This is why you are advised to boot the system from the boot diskette that contains only the system and the command.com file, or to skip the processing of the autoexec.bat and config.sys files when booting DOS/Windows.

6. Start the BIOS updating program (the flash utility) to update flash memory containing BIOS code.

7. The flash utility often is supplied with the motherboard. The file containing the BIOS update must reside in the same directory as the flash utility. It would be wise to memorize the name of the file containing the new BIOS version.

Generally, BIOS updating utilities are interactive programs. They usually request the following information from the PC user:

❏ Fully-qualified name (with extension) of the file containing the new BIOS version
❏ Fully-qualified filename where you will save the current BIOS version (oldbios.bin)
❏ Confirmation of the update process (Y/N)

After accomplishing the update process, you must restart your computer.

These steps can be accomplished not only in a DOS environment, but also under other operating systems. Recently, BIOS updating utilities appeared that operate under Windows-like systems. Furthermore, some motherboard manufacturers supply special tools that allow the BIOS to be updated via the Internet, directly from a manufacturer's Web site.

Time will show if this approach is justified. However, it is our duty to warn potential users of such tools: You might render your computer unusable if you choose this updating method. A situation even may occur in which the operating system fails during the update process.

BIOS and Computer Performance

Computer performance and functionality don't depend solely on the CPU. On the contrary, they depend on all components of the computer system. The motherboard, whose architecture includes the chipset and the BIOS, plays the central-coordination role. Although the chipset plays the most important role in determining the motherboard parameters, it is not a component that can be replaced. BIOS code, written into the BIOS chip and influencing the operation of most computer subsystems, can be replaced using a special program.

Development and use of new BIOS code can correct existing inconsistencies between BIOS code and motherboard architecture, as well as account for features of new computer components. Besides this, updating BIOS code allows you to benefit from the new features of system and application software, decrease the probability of hardware conflicts, enhance available functionality, and improve overall system performance. For these reasons, it is highly advisable to pay attention to information about the release of new BIOS versions from the moment you purchased a new motherboard.

The functionality enhancements and performance gain that result from updating BIOS code can be illustrated through an example with the following hardware configuration: the Abit BE6-II motherboard and the Intel Pentium 550E processor. Note that the motherboard used in this configuration is considered as one of the most advanced motherboards, providing the broadest range of functional capabilities. Nevertheless, after updating BIOS code, new settings will be available via the BIOS Setup. The test results that follow are evidence of the performance growth achieved with a BIOS update.

Testing the Abit BE6-II Motherboard

The following system configuration was used for testing:

❑ Motherboard — Abit BE6-II
❑ Processor — Intel Pentium III 550E (Coppermine core, L2 cache of 256 KB, operating at the full core frequency, Slot 1, in box)
❑ Hard disk — IBM DPTA-372050 (20 GB, 2 MB cache memory, 7,200 rpm, Ultra DMA/66)
❑ RAM — 128 MB, PC100, and M-Tech
❑ Video adapter — Asus AGP-V3800 TV (TNT2 video chipset, 32 MB SGRAM)
❑ CD-ROM drive — Asus CD-S400/A (40x)
❑ Operating system — Windows 98 with Ultra DMA/66 hard-disk controller drivers installed

The following initial BIOS version was used:

❑ 12/30/99 (beh_po)

The following new BIOS versions were tested:

❑ 2/1/00 (beh_qj)
❑ 5/8/00 (beh_rv)

BIOS Update and Testing

The stages of updating BIOS code are outlined in Figs. 5.1 and 5.2.

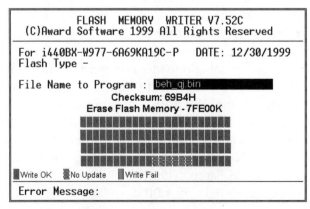

Fig. 5.1. Entering the name of the file containing the updated BIOS code

```
          FLASH  MEMORY  WRITER V7.52C
   (C)Award Software 1999 All Rights Reserved

 For i440BX-W977-6A69KA19C-P   DATE: 12/30/1999
 Flash Type -

 File Name to Program : beh_qj.bin




 Error Message:
```

Fig. 5.2. Writing the updated BIOS code into flash ROM

We used WinBench 99 v1.1 tests: CPUmark 99 and FPU WinMark. Test results are in Table 5.1 and in Figs. 5.3 and 5.4.

Table 5.1. BIOS Test Results Using CPUmark 99 and FPU WinMark

BIOS version	CPUmark 99	FPU WinMark
BIOS initial code 12/30/99	46.1	2,950
BIOS 2/1/00	50.7	2,970
BIOS 5/8/00	51.1	2,973

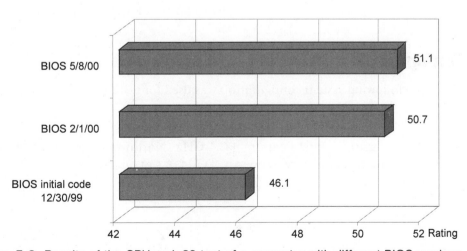

Fig. 5.3. Results of the CPUmark 99 test of a computer with different BIOS versions

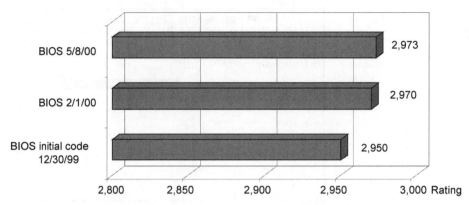

Fig. 5.4. Results of the FPU WinMark test of a computer with different BIOS versions

As a result of updating BIOS code (beh_po) 12/30/99 with newer versions, the following functional capabilities became available:

☐ BIOS (beh_qj) 2/1/00:

- Elimination of problems with some AGP video adapters at the system-bus frequency of 133 MHz
- Support for Intel Pentium III processors up to 800 MHz
- Improved SDRAM compatibility

☐ BIOS (beh_rv) 5/8/00:

- Improved parameters at the system-bus frequency of 133 MHz

Testing the Abit IT7-MAX2 v2.0 Motherboard

The following system configuration was used for testing:

☐ Motherboard — Abit IT7-MAX2 v2.0

☐ Processor — Intel Pentium 4 2.4 GHz (Northwood core, L2 cache of 512 KB, operating at full core frequency, FC-PGA slot, in box)

☐ Hard disk — IC35L120AVV207-0 (180GXP, 120 GB, 2 MB cache, 7,200 rpm, Ultra DMA/100)

☐ RAM — 512 MB, DDR266, Kingston

☐ Video adapter — GeForce4 Ti4200, 128 MB

❑ CD-ROM — Asus CD-S400/A (40x)

❑ Operating system — Windows XP, Service Pack 1

The following initial BIOS version was used:

❑ 12/16/02 (it7pdf)

The following new BIOS version was used:

❑ 3/27/03 (it7pd6)

As a result of updating BIOS code, the following improvements and functional capabilities were added:

❑ The problem with detection of a low-speed cooler was eliminated. This problem sometimes caused the system to power down automatically without passing the POST routine.

❑ The settings for the SP_LED indicator were corrected. After the BIOS code was updated, this indicator corresponded to the following specifications:
  - S0 — Always on
  - S1 — Blinks at high frequency
  - S3 — Blinks at low frequency
  - S4 — Always off
  - S5 — Always off

❑ The problems with the processor multiplier were eliminated.

❑ The processor microcode was updated: 0F24/18, 0F27/33, 0F29/0E.

❑ HPT374 BIOS revision 1.23 was used.

The 3DMark2001 SE Pro program was used for testing.

Table 5.2. BIOS Test Results Using 3DMark2001 SE Pro

BIOS version	3DMark2001
BIOS initial code 12/16/02	10,046
BIOS 3/27/03	10,120

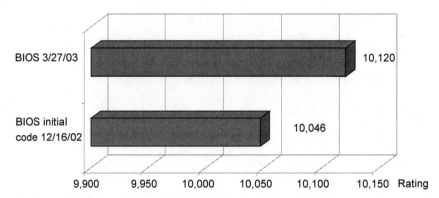

Fig. 5.5. Results of the 3DMark2001 SE Pro test of a computer
with different BIOS versions

Chapter 6

Computer Hardware Monitoring

The complex hardware and advanced functionality of modern computers require the operation of the main computer subsystems to be monitored and controlled. This can be achieved using built-in tools known as hardware-monitoring tools. These tools have become a de facto standard of the architecture implemented in most contemporary motherboards. They are supported both by BIOS Setup and by special-purpose software, including such popular programs as Motherboard Monitor (MBM).

Designers and manufacturers of contemporary hardware, under the extremely competitive conditions of the market, always try to implement the highest potential performance of hardware components. Aiming for this goal, they provide various functions for implementing overclocked modes.

This trend for computer-hardware optimization, along with the overclocked modes that can provide maximum performance, often requires strict control over the main operating parameters. This ensures the selection of an efficient operating mode, as well as a level of protection. Therefore, motherboard manufacturers often provide built-in hardware-monitoring tools, ensuring support for diagnostics and control over the most important operating parameters of the main computer subsystems and components.

In general, the list of such parameters includes the following:

❐ Temperature of the CPU, motherboard, air within the case, etc.
❐ Core voltage of the CPU, motherboard components, etc.
❐ Rotation speed of the coolers installed on the processor, power supply unit, etc.

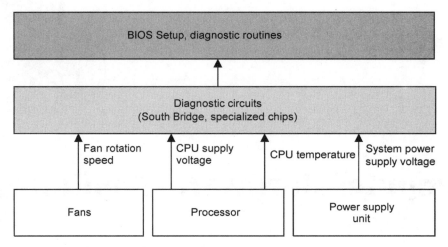

Fig. 6.1. Diagram of computer hardware monitoring

Hardware-Monitoring Facilities

Hardware-monitoring tools and facilities gradually are becoming mandatory attributes of the architecture of any contemporary computer system. Such tools usually are built into contemporary chipsets.

Unfortunately, unlike Via chipsets and others, the most popular Intel chipsets are not equipped with built-in hardware-monitoring tools.

However, despite the lack of such tools in the Intel chipset architecture, some motherboards implement these capabilities. They use advanced special-purpose chips such as LM78 and LM79 from National Semiconductor or W83781D and W83782D from Winbond Electronics. A diagram that shows the use of the Winbond W83782D chip is in Fig. 6.2.

Note that some motherboard manufacturers that release products based on advanced chipsets with hardware-monitoring facilities are not satisfied with the standard functional capabilities provided by such chipsets. Because of this, they often use the special-purpose chips previously mentioned, or their analogues. For example, Asus, one of the leading motherboard manufacturers, often uses its own monitoring chips. The PC Health Monitoring function implemented on the basis of the Application-Specific Integrated Circuit (ASIC) AS99127F chip serves as a good example of this approach (Fig. 6.2). Asus and other manufacturers use the same approach when implementing networking functions and several additional controllers, such as IEEE1394.

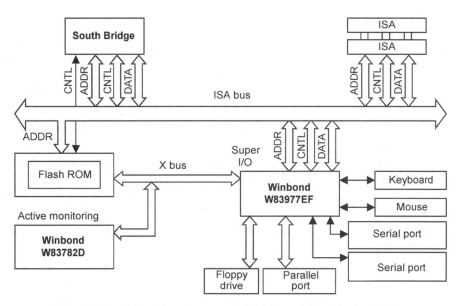

Fig. 6.2. Including hardware-monitoring and input/output chips
in the computer architecture

Fig. 6.3. Hardware-monitoring chip on the Asus motherboard

The use of specialized hardware-monitoring chips is justified because they often provide better parameters than the built-in hardware-monitoring facilities of the chipset components. These parameters include the number of monitored parameters and measurement accuracy. The latter is crucial in overclocked modes, especially when approaching maximum voltages. In these modes, even one-hundredth of a volt becomes important. Inadequate measurement precision can distort the result, cause incorrect actions, and, consequently, increase the probability of failure.

Fig. 6.4 shows the structure of a hardware-monitoring chip from Winbond: the W83782D Winbond H/W Monitoring IC. Fig. 6.5 shows the LM78/LM79 chip from National Semiconductor. These illustrations also show possible connections of probes and sensors, as well as variants of supplying voltages of different values and polarity to the chip inputs. These chips often are used for hardware monitoring in the architecture of contemporary motherboards.

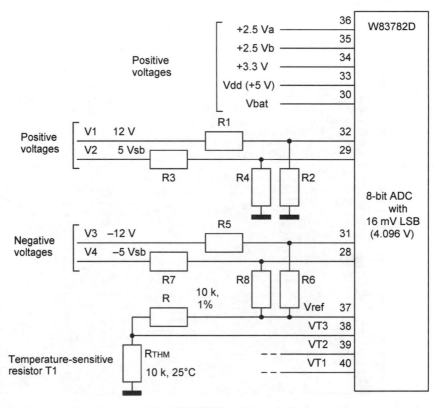

Fig. 6.4. Internal structure of the W83782D chip and diagram of probe connections

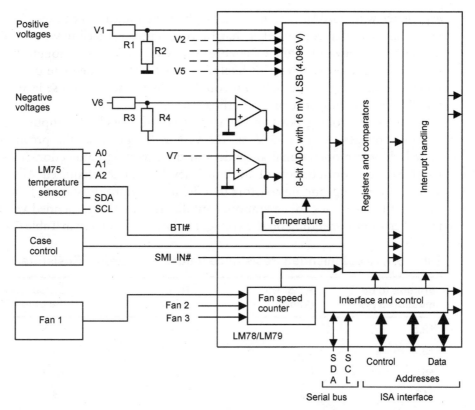

Fig. 6.5. Internal structure of the LM78/LM79 chip and diagram of probe connections

The 8-bit Analog-to-Digital Converter (ADC) serves as the basis for the internal structure of these and similar devices. It ensures the input and conversion of 256 input-signal values with positive polarities. The operating range of the ADC is 0 V to 4.096 V, with an increment of 16 millivolts (mV): 4.096/256 = 0.016. To widen the range of input voltages, external or internal resistor dividers must be used. The nominal values of their elements depend on the voltage levels being controlled. This allows the processing of voltages within a range of 5 V to 12 V.

To ensure correct operation of the measurement methods, it is necessary to coordinate their input resistance with the output resistances of the probes. This gives the best signal-to-noise ratio. Coordination can be achieved using sequential resistors or special electronic circuits such as repeaters (with a common collector (CC), common source (CS), etc.).

The nominal resistance of the coordinating resistors influences the voltage measurement results. This probably causes the problems some motherboards experience with hardware monitoring, such as the indication of excessive values of the voltages under control. The hardware-monitoring facilities installed on the motherboard may indicate a CPU core supply of 1.7 V, even though the installed value didn't exceed 1.65 V. This likely is caused by an inadequate design of additional coordinating cascades, but, it could be due to the high noise level, related to unsatisfactory wiring of such motherboards.

Besides controlling positive voltages, it is also possible to input and control negative voltages, such as −5 V or −12 V. For this purpose, the previously mentioned chips use operational amplifiers in the inverting connection (as shown in Fig. 6.5). The coordination of the input levels with the required ADC range is achieved using appropriate resistors that define the input resistance of cascades and values of the feedback for operational amplifiers. The recommended values of external resistors, depending on the voltages to be measured, are in Table 6.1.

Table 6.1. Recommended Resistance Values for External Resistors

Voltage to be measured (V)	R1 or R3 (kilohm)	R2 or R4 (kilohm)	Output voltage of the chip (V)
+2.5	0	−	+2.5
+3.3	0	−	+3.3
+5	6.8	10	+2.98
+12	30	10	+3
−12	240	60	+3
−5	100	60	+3

The previously mentioned chips also provide the possibility of measuring the temperatures of the elements being controlled. Generally, *thermal resistors* are used as sensors. The resistance of thermal resistors depends on the temperature. Usually, these sensors are connected as shown in Fig. 6.4. The internal resistance of the thermal resistor changes with the temperature being measured. The electric current and voltage of this element (which is connected to the supply voltage via the 10-kilohm resistor) change accordingly. The change of the voltage on this thermal resistor is registered by the ADC in the hardware-monitoring chip, similar to the method used to control supply voltages.

Instead of a thermal resistor, a transistor in diode connection can be used for temperature measurement, as shown in Fig. 6.6, *a*. The operating principle of such sensor is based on the dependence between the threshold opening voltage of the p-n-silicon junction and the temperature. As a result of this effect, the threshold voltage changes almost linearly with the temperature, with a negative gradient of 2.3 mV/sec ($dV \sim 1/T$). In Fig. 6.6, *a*, the voltage on the 2N3904 transistor, connected via the resistor to the reference voltage of 3.6 V, will decrease with the temperature growth. To test this effect experimentally, you can mount a circuit comprising a silicon diode, a resistor, and a standard battery (4.5 V). The voltage on the diode will decrease if you heat it with a soldering iron (for no longer than 3 seconds).

With a method similar to the one that uses a transistor to control the temperature mode of the CPU, thermal diodes sometimes can be integrated with the Pentium III processor chips. The use of thermal diodes, instead of traditional thermal resistors, can be explained quite easily. Most contemporary chips, including processors, are created on the basis of p-n-junctions that perform the functions of transistors, diodes, and even resistors and capacitors. The recommended minimum value of the current for a built-in thermal diode is –5 micro-ampere (μA); the maximum value is –300 μA.

The diagram for the connection of the thermal diode built into the Pentium III processor to the W83782D chip is in Fig. 6.6, *b*. The reference voltage is 3.6 V.

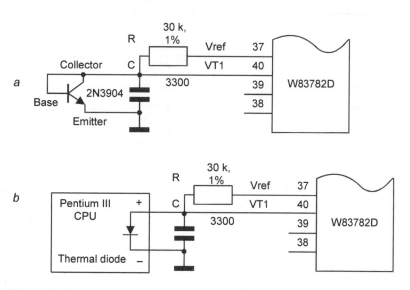

Fig. 6.6. Methods for connecting the W83782D chip with different semiconductor thermal sensors: the 2N3904 transistor (*a*) and the thermal diode built into the Pentium III chip (*b*)

When evaluating the readings taken from such sensors, it is necessary to account for the maximum values of the CPU core temperature (the maximum T-junction, shown as T1) and of error (T2). This error is caused by the spatial temperature gradient within the processor chip and the finite speed of the heat propagation. It is also necessary to take into account the effects of the constantly changing spatial temperature distribution, caused by the CPU workload fluctuations. Because of this, the developers advise increasing the T2 value by another error related to temperature measurements. The value of this error is approximately 1°C (33°F).

Thus, when using a thermal diode as a temperature sensor for the Pentium III FC-PGA and SC242 (Slot 1) processors, it is best to take the value of T1-T2-1 as the maximum allowed temperature.

For the Pentium 4 processor, the thermal diode is connected in a similar way.

When using a traditional thermal resistor as a temperature sensor, it is expedient to consider the maximum temperature value of Pentium III/4 processors equal to the maximum case temperature. This usually equals 75°C (167°F). (See Tables 6.2 and 6.3.)

Table 6.2. Temperature Parameters of the Pentium III FC-PGA Processors

Processor	T1 (°C)	T2 (°C)
500E	85	1.9
533EB	85	2.0
550E	85	2.1
600E	82	2.3
600EB	82	2.3
650	82	2.5
667	82	2.5
700	80	2.7
733	80	2.8
750	80	2.8
800	80	3.0
800EB	80	3.0
850	80	3.3
866	80	3.3
933	75	3.6

Table 6.3. Outputs of the Thermal Sensors of the Pentium III/4 Processors

Thermal diode output	SC242 (Slot 1) PIII (contacts)	FC-PGA PIII (contacts)	423 PGA P4 (contacts)
Anode	B14	AL31	H38
Cathode	B15	AL29	E39

AMD Athlon and AMD Duron processors, as well as early Intel products, have no built-in thermal sensors. Therefore, control of the thermal mode of such processors is implemented using external sensors, usually installed near the Slot A or Slot 1 processors, or within the Socket A (Socket 462) or Socket 370 slots for the processors of the PGA or FC-PGA form factors (Figs. 6.7 and 6.8). To ensure normal operation of thermal sensors and to obtain correct temperature values, motherboard manufacturers provide thermal contact between the sensors and processor cases. To prevent mechanical deformation or even damage to the thermal sensor connection, it is wise to control the quality of the thermal contact.

When considering specific characteristics of temperature measurements using LM78/LM79 chips, note that the LM75 chip is recommended for use as a sensor. Despite the single input contact for connecting the external thermal sensor, it is possible to connect up to eight LM75 devices. In this case, the available ISA, I^2C SDA, SCL, A0, A1, and A2 interface lines are used.

Note that the previously mentioned chips and similar ones used in hardware monitoring do not need calibration. In general, they do not provide such functions to end users. Correct, precise operation is achieved using sensors and connection methods recommended by manufacturers. As a rule, chip architecture is programmable.

Fig. 6.7. External temperature sensor for Slot 1 processors

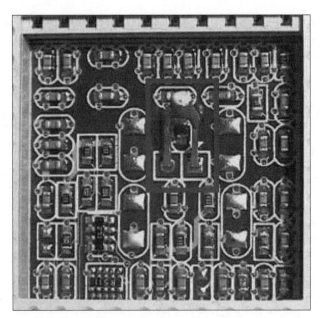

Fig. 6.8. External temperature sensor installed within the Socket A slot

The main parameters of the previously described chips — as well as those of other chips, such as W83781D, W83783S, and W83L784R from Winbond, that are oriented toward relatively inexpensive systems and mobile computers — are outlined in Tables 6.4–6.6. For comparison, the main parameters of the hardware-monitoring tools integrated into the VT82C686A chip are also presented. Until recently, this chip was often used in Via chipsets.

Table 6.4. Main Parameters of Winbond Chips

Parameters	W83781D	W83782D	W83783S	W83L784R
Temperature control (input lines)	3	3	3	2 and 1-on-chip
Voltage control (input lines)	5(+), 2(−)	9	6	4
Fan control (input lines)	3	3	3	2
Case integrity control, open/closed (input lines)	1	1	1	—

continues

Table 6.4 Continued

Parameters	W83781D	W83782D	W83783S	W83L784R
Typical values of monitored voltage (V)	VcoreA, VcoreB, +3.3, +5, +12, −12, −5	Vcore, +3.3, +5, +12, −12, −5, +5 Vsb, Vbat, 1 reserved	Vcore, +3.3, +5, +12, −12, −5	Vcore, +3.3, +5, Battery
Voltage precision (%) (max.) +/−	1	1	1	1
Temp. precision (°C) (max.) +/−	3	3	3	3
Built-in ADC (bits)	8	8	8	8
Interface	ISA, I²C	ISA, I²C	ISA, I²C	ISA, I²C
Supply voltage (V)	5	5	5	5
Current (mA)	1	5	5	2
Case form-factor	48p LQFP	48p LQFP	24p SOP	20p SSOP

Table 6.5. Main Parameters of National Semiconductor Chips

Parameters	LM78 and LM79
Temperature control (input lines)	1 and sensor-on-chip
Voltage control (input lines)	5(+), 2(−)
Fan control (input lines)	3
Typical values of monitored voltage (V)	2.5Va, 2.5Vb, +3.3, +5, +12, −5, −12
Voltage precision (%) (max.)	1
Temperature precision (°C) (max.)	3
Fan rpm precision (%) (max.)	10
Built-in ADC (bits)	8
Interface	ISA, I²C
Supply voltage (V)	5
Current (mA)	1
Case form-factor	VGZ44A (PQFP)

Table 6.6. Main Hardware-Monitoring Parameters in VT82C686A

Parameters	VT82C686A
Temperature control (input lines)	2 and 1-on-chip
Voltage control (input lines)	4(+) and 1-on-chip
Fan control (input lines)	2

Most motherboard manufacturers continue to release motherboards that include hardware-monitoring facilities based on specialized chips, even though more advanced chipsets that implement improved architecture are designed and released constantly by manufacturers such as Intel, Via Technologies, Ali, and SiS. These chipsets are more sophisticated and offer a significantly wider range of functional capabilities than their predecessors. As a rule, these chipsets provide various monitoring tools, including hardware-monitoring.

Software-Monitoring Tools

Hardware-monitoring tools based on specialized chips or built into chipset components, and complemented with appropriate sensors, usually only provide measurement capabilities. To perform the control, output the measured results, and analyze them, you'll need special-purpose software. Relatively simple programs that provide this kind of service are built into the BIOS Setup program of most motherboards. Functionality, the number of measured parameters, and measurement precision usually depend on the chips used for this purpose, as well as on the BIOS code version. Fig. 6.9 shows the **PC Health Status** menu, included in the BIOS Setup program of most popular motherboards.

Although BIOS built-in functions often provide a wide range of capabilities, there are also specialized software applications that ensure control, analysis, and screen output of the diagnostic parameters. Such programs often use the built-in tools of popular operating systems (such as Windows). As a rule, motherboard manufacturers provide such software tools along with their products. The Winbond Hardware Doctor is a typical example of such a program. The screenshot in Fig. 6.10 illustrates its operation.

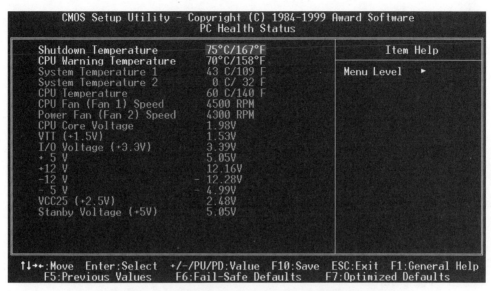

Fig. 6.9. Hardware monitoring in BIOS Setup

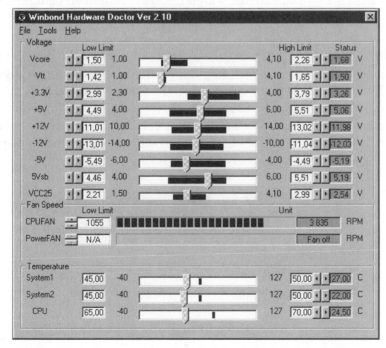

Fig. 6.10. Typical screenshot of the Winbond Hardware Doctor application

The Winbond Hardware Doctor provides the capability of monitoring system parameters. The main parameters are as follows:

☐ Voltage (supply voltage):
  - Vcore — CPU core voltage
  - Vtt — Additional CPU supply voltage
  - +3.3 V — Chipset, frequency generator, and PCI bus
  - +5 V — Chips of the motherboard, PCI bus, and ISA
  - +12 V — ISA bus
  - −5 V — ISA bus
  - 5 Vsb — Supply voltage in hibernation mode
☐ Fan speed (speed of fan rotation):
  - CPU fan
  - Power-supply fan
☐ Temperature:
  - System1 — Temperature within the system (motherboard or case)
  - System2 — Temperature within the system (motherboard or case)
  - CPU temperature

The Winbond Hardware Doctor allows you to install the boundaries that serve as limiting values allowable for computer hardware — maximum (**High Limit**) and minimum (**Low Limit**) for each parameter being monitored (Fig. 6.11). For temperature control, only the maximum allowed values are important (Fig. 6.12). For fan speed, only the lower limits play a role (Fig. 6.13). If the value of the parameter being monitored goes beyond the valid range, the system displays a warning message accompanied by a sound (Fig. 6.14).

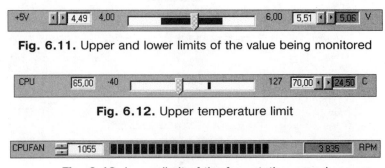

Fig. 6.11. Upper and lower limits of the value being monitored

Fig. 6.12. Upper temperature limit

Fig. 6.13. Lower limit of the fan rotation speed

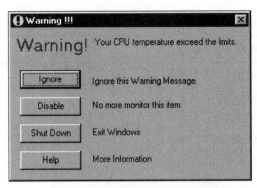

Fig. 6.14. Warning message

Note that the example application has one significant drawback: It is bound to a specific motherboard (or motherboard series) equipped with specific hardware-monitoring tools. Other programs provide more universal system-monitoring tools. The popular Motherboard Monitor (MBM) software is a good example of such a utility.

There are currently two significantly different versions of this tool: 4.*xx* and 5.*xx*. The first releases of version 5.*xx* contained several bugs that made the system unstable with some motherboards. Because of this, most PC users prefer version 4.*xx*. Fortunately, the most recent releases of the MBM software are free of these bugs. Table 6.7 lists the most popular chips supported by the MBM program. Note that this list grows with each new release of this popular program.

Table 6.7. Monitoring Chips Supported by MBM 4 and MBM 5

Supported monitoring chips	MBM 4	MBM 5
Analog Devices ADM1025	X	X
Analog Devices ADM9240	X	X
Asus AS99127F	X	X
Fairchild Semiconductor FMS2701	X	X
Genesys Logic GL518SM	X	X
Genesys Logic GL520SM	X	X
National Semiconductor LM78	X	X
National Semiconductor LM78j	X	X
National Semiconductor LM79	X	X

continues

Table 6.7 Continued

Supported monitoring chips	MBM 4	MBM 5
National Semiconductor LM80	X	X
National Semiconductor LM87		X
SIS SiS5595	X	X
Texas Instruments THMC50	X	X
Via Technologies VIA686A	X	X
Via Technologies VIA686B		X
Winbond Electronics W83627HF	X	X
Winbond Electronics W83697HF	X	X
Winbond Electronics W83781D	X	X
Winbond Electronics W83782D	X	X
Winbond Electronics W83783S	X	X

Figs. 6.15–6.18 show examples illustrating the operation of the MBM program.

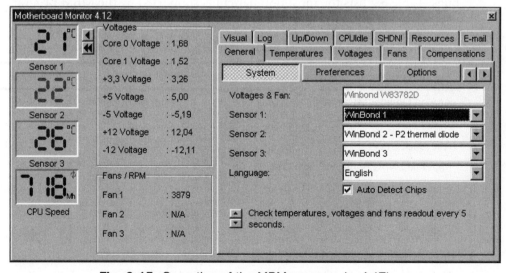

Fig. 6.15. Operation of the MBM program (v. 4.17)

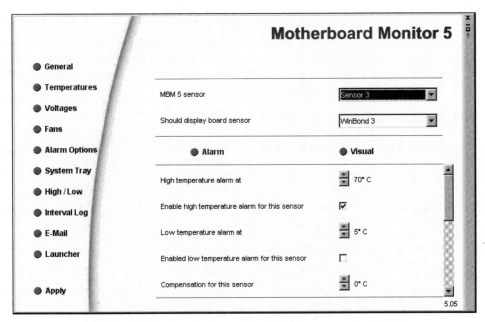

Fig. 6.16. Customization of the MBM program (v. 5.05)

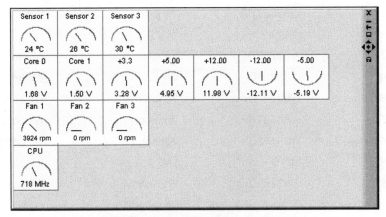

Fig. 6.17. Operation of the MBM program (v. 5.05)

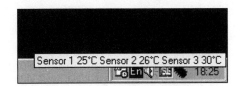

Fig. 6.18. MBM (v. 5.05)

Tables 6.8–6.19 briefly outline the parameters of the motherboards from several leading manufacturers. These motherboards, according to the data provided by the MBM developer, are supported by MBM v. 5.3. These tables list the chips integrated into the motherboard architecture to ensure the capabilities of monitoring the most important parameters.

Table 6.8. Abit Motherboards

Motherboard	Monitoring chip	Temperature sensor within the case	CPU temperature sensor
AT7	W83627HF	Winbond 1	Winbond 2
AT7 MAX2	W83627HF	Winbond 2	LM90 or Winbond 1
BD7 II	W83627HF	Winbond 1	Winbond 2
BD7 RAID	W83627HF	Winbond 1	Winbond 2
BE6	W83783S	Winbond 2	Winbond 1
BE6-2	W83782D	Winbond 1 or 3	Winbond 2 (P2 diode)
BE7 RAID	W83627HF	Winbond 1	Winbond 2
BF6	W83782D	Winbond 3	Winbond 2 (P2 diode)
BG7	W83627HF	Winbond 1	Winbond 2
BH6	LM79	LM79	–
BL7	W83782D	Winbond 1	Winbond 2 (P2 diode)
BM6	W83782D	Winbond 3	Winbond 2
BP6	W83782D	Winbond 3	Winbond 2 or 1
BW7	W83697HF	Winbond 1	Winbond 2 (P2 diode)
BX133 RAID	W83782D	Winbond 3	Winbond 2 (P2 diode)
BX6	LM79	LM79	–
BX6-2	W83782D	Winbond 1	Winbond 2 (P2 diode)
IT7	W83627HF	Winbond 1	Winbond 2 (P2 diode)
KA7-100	VIA686A	VIA686A 2	VIA686A 3
KG7	VIA686B	VIA686B 2	VIA686B 3
KG7 RAID	VIA686B	VIA686B 2	VIA686B 3
KR7A RAID	W83697HF	Winbond 1	Winbond 2
KT7	VIA686A	VIA686A 2	VIA686A 3

continues

Table 6.8 Continued

Motherboard	Monitoring chip	Temperature sensor within the case	CPU temperature sensor
KT7 RAID	VIA686A	VIA686A 2	VIA686A 3
KT7A	VIA686B	VIA686B 2	VIA686B 3
KT7A RAID	VIA686B	VIA686B 2	VIA686B 3
KX7	W83697HF	Winbond 1	Winbond 2
KX7 RAID	W83697HF	Winbond 1	Winbond 2
NF7-S	W83627HF	Winbond 1	Winbond 2
NV7 133R	W83627HF	Winbond 1	Winbond 2
SA6R	W83627HF	Winbond 1	Winbond 2 (P2 diode)
SA7	SiS950/ITE8705F	SiS950/ITE8705F 2	SiS950/ITE8705F 1
SE6	W83627HF	Winbond 1	Winbond 2 (P2 diode)
SH6	W83627HF	Winbond 1	Winbond 2 (P2 diode)
SR7-8X	W83627HF	Winbond 1	Winbond 2 (P2 diode)
ST6-RAID	W83627HF	Winbond 1	Winbond 2 (P2 diode)
TH7 II RAID	W83782D or W83627HF	Winbond 3 or 1	Winbond 2 (P2 diode)
VA6	VIA686A	VIA686A 3	VIA686A 2
VH6	VIA686A	VIA686A 3	VIA686A 2
VP6	VIA686B	VIA686B 1	VIA686B 2 or 3
VT6X4	VIA686A	VIA686A 3	VIA686A 2
ZM6	W83782D	Winbond 3	Winbond 2

Table 6.9. Acer Motherboards

Motherboard	Monitoring chip	Temperature sensor within the case	CPU temperature sensor
V66M	W83781D	Winbond 1	Winbond 2
Veriton 3200PC	ADM1024	ADM1024 1	ADM1024 2

Table 6.10. A-Trend Motherboards

Motherboard	Monitoring chip	Temperature sensor within the case	CPU temperature sensor
ATC 6220	W83781D	Winbond 1	Winbond 2

Table 6.11. AOpen Motherboards

Motherboard	Monitoring chip	Temperature sensor within the case	CPU temperature sensor
AK 73	VIA686B	VIA686B 1	VIA686B 2
AK 77Pro	W83697HF	Winbond 1	Winbond 2
AX 34	VIA686A	VIA686A 1	VIA868A 2
AX 6BC	GL518SM	–	GL518SM
AX 6L	GL518SM	–	GL518SM
AX 6S	W83627HF	Winbond 1	Winbond 2 (P2 diode)
MX 64	VIA686A	VIA686A 1	VIA686A 2

Table 6.12. Asus Motherboards

Motherboard	Monitoring chip	Temperature sensor within the case	CPU temperature sensor
A7A266	AS99127F	Asus 1	Asus 2
A7M266	AS99127F	Asus 1	Asus 2
A7M266 D	AS99127F	Asus 1	Asus 2
A7N266	AS99127F	Asus 1	Asus 2
A7N266 C	AS99127F	Asus 1	Asus 2
A7N266 VM	AS99127F	Asus 1	Asus 2
A7N8X	ASB100	Asus 1	Asus 2 and W83L785TS-S
A7N8X	ASB100	Asus 2	Asus 1 and W83L785TS-S
A7S333	SiS950/ITE8705F	SiS950/ITE8705F 1	SiS950/ITE8705F 2
A7V	AS99127F	Asus 1	Asus 2
A7V Pro	AS99127F	Asus 1	Asus 2

continues

Table 6.12 Continued

Motherboard	Monitoring chip	Temperature sensor within the case	CPU temperature sensor
A7V133	AS99127F	Asus 1	Asus 2
A7V266	AS99127F	Asus 1	Asus 2
A7V266 E	AS99127F	Asus 1	Asus 2
A7V333	ASB100	Asus 1	Asus 2 or 4
A7V8X	ASB100	Asus 1	Asus 2 socket or 4
CUBX	AS99127F	Asus 1	Asus 2
CUBX E	AS99127F	Asus 1	Asus 2
CUBX L	AS99127F	Asus 1	Asus 2
CUR DLS	AS99127F	Asus 1	Asus 2
CUSL2	AS99127F	Asus 1	Asus 2 CUSL2
CUSL2 C	AS99127F	Asus 1	Asus 2 CUSL2
CUSL2 LS	AS99127F	Asus 1	Asus 2 CUSL2
CUSL2 M	AS99127F	Asus 1	Asus 2 CUSL2
CUV266	AS99127F	Asus 1	Asus 2
CUV4X	AS99127F	Asus 1	Asus 2
CUV4X C	AS99127F	Asus 1	Asus 2
CUV4X D	AS99127F	Asus 1	Asus 2
CUV4X DLS	AS99127F	Asus 1	Asus 2
CUV4X E	AS99127F	Asus 1	Asus 2
CUV4X M	AS99127F	Asus 1	Asus 2
CUV4X V	AS99127F	Asus 1	Asus 2
K7M	W83782D	Winbond 1	Winbond 2
K7V	W83782D	Winbond 1	Winbond 2
K7V T	W83782D	Winbond 1	Winbond 2
KN87X	LM78	LM78	—
MEW AV rev 1.6	W83781D	Winbond 1	Winbond 2
P2B	W83781D	Winbond 1	Winbond 2

continues

Table 6.12 Continued

Motherboard	Monitoring chip	Temperature sensor within the case	CPU temperature sensor
P2B D	W83781D	Winbond 1	Winbond 2
P2B DS	W83781D	Winbond 1	Winbond 2
P2B F	W83781D	Winbond 1	Winbond 2
P2B L	W83781D	Winbond 1	Winbond 2
P2B LS	W83781D	Winbond 1	Winbond 2
P2B S	W83781D	Winbond 1	Winbond 2
P2L97	LM78	LM78	–
P2L97 DS	LM78	LM78	–
P2L97 S	LM78	LM78	–
P3B F	AS99127F	Asus 1	Asus 2
P3C 2000	AS99127F	Asus 1	Asus 2
P3C D	AS99127F	Asus 1	Asus 2 or 3
P3C E	AS99127F	Asus 1	Asus 2
P3C L	AS99127F	Asus 1	Asus 2
P3C LS	AS99127F	Asus 1	Asus 2
P3C S	AS99127F	Asus 1	Asus 2
P3V 133	W83781D	Winbond 1	Winbond 2
P3V 4X	AS99127F	Asus 1	Asus 2
P4B	AS99127F	Asus 1	Asus 2
P4B533	ASB100	Asus 1	Asus 2
P4B533 E	ASB100	Asus 1	Asus 2
P4B533 V	ASB100	Asus 1	Asus 2
P4B533 VM	Mozart2	Mozart2-2	Mozart2-1
P4G8X	ASB100	Asus 1	Asus 2
P4G8X Deluxe	ASB100	Asus 1	Asus 2
P4PE	ASB100	Asus 1	Asus 2
P4S333	ASB100	Asus 1	Mozart2-1

continues

Table 6.12 Continued

Motherboard	Monitoring chip	Temperature sensor within the case	CPU temperature sensor
P4S533	ASB100	Asus 1	Asus 2
P4S533 VM	Mozart2	Mozart2-2	Mozart2-1
P4S8X	ASB100	Asus 2	Asus 1
P4T	AS99127F	Asus 1	Asus 2
P4T 533C	AS99127F	Asus 1	Asus 2
P4T E	AS99127F	Asus 1	Asus 2
P4T F	AS99127F	Asus 1	Asus 2
P5A	W83781D	Winbond 1	Winbond 2
P5A B	W83781D	Winbond 1	Winbond 2
Terminator P4	Mozart2	Mozart2-2	Mozart2-1
TUA266	AS99127F	Asus 1	Asus 2
TUSI M	SiS950/ITE8705F	SiS950/ITE8705F 1	SiS950/ITE8705F 2
TUSL2 C	AS99127F	Asus 1	Asus 2
TX97	LM78	LM78	LM75 2
TX97 E	LM78	LM78	LM75 2
TX97 LE	LM78	LM78	LM75 2
TX97 X	LM78	LM78	LM75 2
TX97 XE	LM78	LM78	LM75 2
TX97 XV	LM78	LM78	LM75 2

Table 6.13. Chaintech Motherboards

Motherboard	Monitoring chip	Temperature sensor within the case	CPU temperature sensor
6ATA2	VIA686A	VIA686A 3	VIA686A 2
6BTM	W83781D	Winbond 1	Winbond 2
6LTMPII	LM78	LM78	–
7AJA	VIA686A	VIA686A 3	VIA686A 2

continues

Table 6.13 Continued

Motherboard	Monitoring chip	Temperature sensor within the case	CPU temperature sensor
7AJA 2E	VIA686B	VIA686B 3 or 1	VIA686B 2 or 3
7KDD	ITE8712F	ITE8712F 3	ITE8712F 1 and 2
7NJS	ITE712	LM90	LM90
7VJ D/2	SiS950/ITE705	SiS950/ITE705 2	SiS950/ITE705 1
7VJ L	SiS950/ITE705	SiS950/ITE705 2	SiS950/ITE705 1
9E JL1	ITE8712F	ITE8712F 1	ITE8712F 2

Table 6.14. Elitegroup Motherboards

Motherboard	Monitoring chip	Temperature sensor within the case	CPU temperature sensor
6BXA+	W83781D	Winbond 1	Winbond 2
D6VAA	VIA686B	VIA686B 3	VIA686B 2
K7AMA	GL520SM	GL520SM 2	GL520SM 1
K7S5A	SiS950/ITE705	SiS950/ITE705 2	SiS950/ITE705 3
K7S5A pro	SiS950/ITE705	SiS950/ITE705 2	SiS950/ITE705 3
K7S6A	SiS950/ITE705	SiS950/ITE705 1	SiS950/ITE705 2
K7SEM	SiS950/ITE705	SiS950/ITE705 2	SiS950/ITE705 3
K7VMA	VIA686B	VIA686B 3	VIA686B 2
K7VTA	SiS950/ITE705	SiS950/ITE705 2	SiS950/ITE705 3
K7VTA	SiS950/ITE705	SiS950/ITE705 1	SiS950/ITE705 2
K7VZA	VIA686B	VIA686B 3	VIA686B 2
L7VTA	SiS950/ITE705	SiS950/ITE705 1	SiS950/ITE705 2
P4I BMS	ITE8712F	ITE8712F 1	ITE8712F 2
P4I TA	W83781D	Winbond 3 or 2 2N3904	Winbond 2 or 3
P4S5A	SiS950/ITE705	SiS950/ITE705 2	SiS950/ITE705 3 or 1
P4S5MG GL	SiS950/ITE705	SiS950/ITE705 1	SiS950/ITE705 2
P4VXASD+	SiS950/ITE705	SiS950/ITE705 2	SiS950/ITE705 1
P6BAPA+	GL520SM	GL520SM 1	GL520SM 2

Table 6.15. Epox Motherboards

Motherboard	Monitoring chip	Temperature sensor within the case	CPU temperature sensor
3VWB+	VIA686B	VIA686B 3	VIA686B 2
4G4A+	W83627HF	Winbond 3	Winbond 2
EP3 SPA3L	W83627HF	Winbond 3	Winbond 2
EP4 BDA	W83627HF	Winbond 1	Winbond 2
EP4 BEAR	W83627HF	Winbond 3	Winbond 2
EP5 1MVP3EMAT	LM78	LM78	–
EP5 8MVP3CMAT	LM78	LM78	–
EP5 8MVP3CMAT	W83781D	Winbond 1	Winbond 2
EP6 1BXAM	LM78	LM78	LM75 5
EP6 1BXBS	LM78	LM78	ADM1021 7 + ADM1021 8
EP7 KXA	VIA686A	VIA686A 3	VIA686A 2
EP8 K3A	W83697HF	Winbond 1	Winbond 2
EP8 K3A+	W83782D	Winbond 1	Winbond 2
EP8 K3A+	W83697HF	Winbond 1	Winbond 2
EP8 K3AE	W83697HF	Winbond 1	Winbond 2
EP8 K5A2	W83697HF	Winbond 1	Winbond 2
EP8 K7A	VIA686B	VIA686B 1 or 3	VIA686B 2
EP8 K9A	W83697HF	Winbond 1	Winbond 2
EP8 KH+	W83697HF	Winbond 1	Winbond 2
EP8 KHA	W83697HF	Winbond 1	Winbond 2
EP8 KTA	VIA686A	VIA686A 3	VIA686A 2
EP8 KTA3	VIA686B	VIA686B 3	VIA686B 2
EP8 RDA+	W83697HF	Winbond 3	Winbond 2
EPZ XA	LM78	LM78	LM75 5
KP6BS	LM78	LM78	ADM1021 7
KP6BS	LM78	LM78	LM75 5

continues

Table 6.15 Continued

Motherboard	Monitoring chip	Temperature sensor within the case	CPU temperature sensor
MVP 3EM	W83781D	Winbond 1	Winbond 2
MVP 3G5	W83781D	Winbond 1	Winbond 2
MVP 3GM	W83781D	Winbond 1	Winbond 2
MVP 4A	VIA686A	VIA686A 3	VIA686A 2

Table 6.16. FIC Motherboards

Motherboard	Monitoring chip	Temperature sensor within the case	CPU temperature sensor
AN11	W83627HF	Winbond 1	Winbond 2
AZ11	VIA686A	VIA686A 2	VIA686A 3
AZ11 EA	VIA686A	VIA686A 2	VIA686A 3
FB11	W83782D	Winbond 3	Winbond 2
KA31	VIA686A	VIA686A 1	VIA686A 2
PAG2130	VIA686A	VIA686A 2	VIA686A 3
SD11	VIA686A	VIA686A 2	VIA686A 3
VA503A	VIA686A	VIA686A 2	VIA686A 3
VB601	W83781D	Winbond 1	Winbond 2

Table 6.17. Gigabyte Technology Motherboards

Motherboard	Monitoring chip	Temperature sensor within the case	CPU temperature sensor
GA586 BA	W83781D	Winbond 1	Winbond 2
GA586 SG	SiS5595	SiS5595	–
GA686 BX	W83781D	Winbond 1	Winbond 2
GA686 BXB	W83781D	Winbond 1	Winbond 2 or 3
GA686 LX4	W83781D	Winbond 1	Winbond 2
GA6BX 7	W83781D	Winbond 1	Winbond 2
GA6BX D	W83781D	Winbond 1	Winbond 2 or 3

continues

Table 6.17 Continued

Motherboard	Monitoring chip	Temperature sensor within the case	CPU temperature sensor
GA6BX E	W83782D	Winbond 1	Winbond 2
GA6BX E	W83782D	Winbond 1	Winbond 3
GA6O MM7E	ITE8712F	ITE8712F 1	ITE8712F 3
GA6O XM7E	ITE8712F	ITE8712F 1	ITE8712F 3
GA6V M7A+	VIA686A	VIA686A 1	VIA686A 2
GA6V TXDR	VIA686B	VIA686B 1	LM75 1 or 2
GA6V X74X	VIA686A	VIA686A 3	VIA686A 2
GA6V X7B4X	VIA686B	VIA686B 3	VIA686B 2
GA6V XC74XP	VIA686B	VIA686B 3	VIA686B 2
GA6V XDC7	VIA686B	VIA686B 1	VIA686B 2 + VIA686B 3
GA7 DPXDW	W83627HF	Winbond 3	Winbond 1 or 2
GA7 DPXDW C	W83627HF	Winbond 3	Winbond 1 or 2
GA7 DX	VIA686B	VIA686B 3	VIA686B 2
GA7 DXR	VIA686B	VIA686B 3	VIA686B 2
GA7 IX	W83782D	Winbond 1	Winbond 2
GA7 IXE	W83782D	Winbond 1	Winbond 2
GA7 IXE4	W83782D	Winbond 1	Winbond 3
GA7 VAC	SiS950/ITE8705F	SiS950/ITE8705F 1	LM90
GA7 VAX	SiS950/ITE8705F	SiS950/ITE8705F 1	LM90
GA7 VAXP	SiS950/ITE8705F	SiS950/ITE8705F 1	LM90
GA7 VRX	SiS950/ITE8705F	SiS950/ITE8705F 1	SiS950/ITE8705F 2
GA7 VRX	SiS950/ITE8705F	SiS950/ITE8705F 1	LM90
GA7 VRX	SiS950/ITE8705F	SiS950/ITE8705F 1	LM90
GA7 VRXP rev 1.0	SiS950/ITE8705F	SiS950/ITE8705F 1	SiS950/ITE8705F 2
GA7 VRXP rev 2.0	SiS950/ITE8705F	SiS950/ITE8705F 1	LM83 7
GA7 VTX	SiS950/ITE8705F	SiS950/ITE8705F 1	SiS950/ITE8705F 2
GA7 ZM	VIA686A	VIA686A 3	VIA686A 2

continues

Table 6.17 Continued

Motherboard	Monitoring chip	Temperature sensor within the case	CPU temperature sensor
GA7 ZMM	VIA686B	VIA686B 3	VIA686B 2
GA7 ZX	VIA686A	VIA686A 3	VIA686A 2
GA7 ZXR	VIA686B	VIA686B 3	VIA686B 2
GA8 IDX	ITE8712F	ITE8712F 1	ITE8712F 3
GA8 IDX3	ITE8712F	ITE8712F 1	ITE8712F 3
GA8 IEXP	ITE8712F	ITE8712F 1	ITE8712F 3
GA8 IHXP	W83627HF	Winbond 1	Winbond 3
GA8 INXP	ITE8712F	ITE8712F 1	ITE8712F 3
GA8 IRXP	SiS950/ITE8705F	SiS950/ITE8705F 1	SiS950/ITE8705F 2
GA8 PE667	ITE8712F	ITE8712F 1	ITE8712F 3
GA8 PE667 Ultra 2	ITE8712F	ITE8712F 1	ITE8712F 3
GA8 PE667U	ITE8712F	ITE8712F 1	ITE8712F 3
GA8 SG667	SiS950/ITE8705F	SiS950/ITE8705F 1	SiS950/ITE8705F 2
GA8 SINXP1394	SiS950/ITE8705F	SiS950/ITE8705F 1	SiS950/ITE8705F 3
GA8 SR533	SiS950/ITE8705F	SiS950/ITE8705F 1	SiS950/ITE8705F 2
GA8 SRX	SiS950/ITE8705F	SiS950/ITE8705F 1	SiS950/ITE8705F 3
GA8 TX	W83627HF	Winbond 1	–
GABX 2000	W83782D	Winbond 1	Winbond 2
GABX 2000+	W83782D	Winbond 1	Winbond 2
ZXH	VIA686B	VIA686B 3	VIA686B 2

Table 6.18. Intel Motherboards

Motherboard	Monitoring chip	Temperature sensor within the case	CPU temperature sensor
D815 EEAL	ADM1025	ADM1025 1	ADM1025 2
D845 BG	ADM1025	ADM1025 1	ADM1025 2
D850 GB	ADM1025	ADM1025 1	ADM1025 2

continues

Table 6.18 Continued

Motherboard	Monitoring chip	Temperature sensor within the case	CPU temperature sensor
D850 MD	ADM1025	ADM1025 1	ADM1025 2
D850 MV	ADM1025	ADM1025 1	ADM1025 2
OR840	ADM1025	ADM1025 1	ADM1025 2
PD440 FX	LM78	LM78	–
RP440 FX	LM78	LM78	–
SE440 BX	ADM9240	ADM9240	–
SE440 BX2	ADM9240	ADM9240	–
VC820	ADM1025	ADM1025 1	ADM1025 2
VX440 FX	LM78	LM78	–

Table 6.19. MSI Computer Motherboards

Motherboard	Monitoring chip	Temperature sensor within the case	CPU temperature sensor
645 Ultra C (MS-6547)	W83627HF	Winbond 1	Winbond 2
648 MAX (MS-6585)	W83697HF	Winbond 1	Winbond 2
654 Ultra (MS-6547)	W83627HF	Winbond 1	Winbond 2
694 T Pro (MS-6309)	VIA686A	VIA686A 2	VIA686A 3
6SBA	W83781D	Winbond 1	Winbond 2
745 Ultra (MS-6561)	W83627HF	Winbond 1	Winbond 2
815 E Pro (MS-6337)	W83627HF	Winbond 1	Winbond 2
815 EM Pro (MS-6315)	W83627HF	Winbond 1	Winbond 2
815 EMT Pro (MS-6315)	W83627HF	Winbond 1	Winbond 2
815 EP Pro (MS-6337)	W83627HF	Winbond 1	Winbond 2
815 EP Pro-R (MS-6337)	W83627HF	Winbond 1	Winbond 2
815 ET Pro (MS-6337)	W83627HF	Winbond 1	Winbond 2
850 Pro 5 (MS-6545)	W83627HF	Winbond 1	Winbond 2

continues

Table 6.19 Continued

Motherboard	Monitoring chip	Temperature sensor within the case	CPU temperature sensor
K7D Master L	W83627HF	Winbond 1	Winbond 2 or 3 2N3904
K7N 415 (MS-6373)	W83627HF	Winbond 1	Winbond 2
K7N 420 (MS-6373)	W83627HF	Winbond 1	Winbond 2
K7T 266 Pro (MS-6380)	W83697HF	Winbond 1	Winbond 2
K7T 266 Pro 2 RU (MS-6380)	W83627HF	Winbond 1	Winbond 2
K7T 266 Pro TD (MS-6380)	W83627HF	Winbond 1	Winbond 2 or 3
K7T 266 Pro2 (MS-6380)	W83627HF	Winbond 1	Winbond 2
K7T 266 Pro2 A (MS-6380)	W83627HF	Winbond 1	Winbond 2
K7T Pro (MS-6330)	VIA686B	VIA686B 3	VIA686B 2
K7T Pro Turbo (MS-6330)	VIA686A	VIA686A 3	VIA686A 2
K7T Pro Turbo 2 (MS-6330)	VIA686B	VIA686B 3	VIA686B 2
K7T Pro Turbo R (MS-6330)	VIA686B	VIA686B 3	VIA686B 2
KM 133A Pro (MS-6340)	VIA686B	VIA686B 2	VIA686B 3
KM 133A Pro 5 (MS-6340)	VIA686B	VIA686B 2	VIA686B 3
KT2 Combo L (MS-6764)	W83697HF	Winbond 1	Winbond 2
KT3 Ultra 2 (MS-6380e)	W83697HF	Winbond 1	Winbond 2
KT3 Ultra ARU (MS-6380e)	W83697HF	Winbond 1	Winbond 2
KT4 Ultra (MS-6590)	W83697HF	Winbond 1	Winbond 2
MS-5158	LM78	LM78	–
MS-6119	W83782D	Winbond 1	Winbond 2
MS-6163	W83781D	Winbond 1	Winbond 2
MS-6199	W83781D	Winbond 1	Winbond 2
MS-6231	VIA686A	VIA686A 2	VIA686A 3
MS-6309 LE5	VIA686A	VIA686A 2	VIA686A 3
MS-6337 LE5	W83627HF	Winbond 1	Winbond 2
MS-6340	VIA686B	VIA686B 2	VIA686B 3

continues

Table 6.19 Continued

Motherboard	Monitoring chip	Temperature sensor within the case	CPU temperature sensor
MS-6341	VIA686A	VIA686A 2	VIA686A 3
MS-6528 LE	W83627HF	Winbond 1	Winbond 2
MS-6528 LE	W83627HF	Winbond 1	Winbond 2
MS-694DPro 66VIA	VIA686A	VIA686A 1	VIA686A 2 or 3
MS-694Pro	VIA686A	VIA686A 3	VIA686A 2
MS-845E MAX2 (MS-6389)	W83627HF	Winbond 1	Winbond 2
MS-845E MAX2 BLR (MS-6389)	W83627HF	Winbond 1	Winbond 2
MS-845E MAX2 L (MS-6389)	W83627HF	Winbond 1	Winbond 2
MS-845E MAX2 LR (MS-6389)	W83627HF	Winbond 1	Winbond 2
MS-845PE MAX2 R (MS-6704)	W83627HF	Winbond 1	Winbond 2
MS-K7 Pro	W83781D	Winbond 1	Winbond 2
MS-P6 DBU	W83781D	Winbond 1	Winbond 2
OL5158	LM78	LM78	–

Most motherboards based on Via chipsets have built-in hardware-monitoring tools. Specialized software tools for hardware-monitoring are usually supplied with these motherboards. Shepherd is a good example of such a program (Figs. 6.19 and 6.20).

It is recommended that you start monitoring programs during system startup and never close them during computer operation. Such programs can issue a warning sound or even power down the computer if the temperature rises above the predefined limit. This feature is especially important for overclocked systems.

Note that such programs often run in background mode. Most of these applications do not consume many system resources. For example, on a computer equipped with a Pentium III 700 processor, the CPU workload is less than 1%, which means it corresponds approximately to the measurement error. This makes workload analysis unnecessary.

When evaluating the capabilities of hardware monitoring for subsystems and components, it is necessary to emphasize that contemporary hardware monitoring isn't limited to reading and analyzing the values of motherboard and CPU parameters. Today's high-performance video adapters are equipped with monitoring

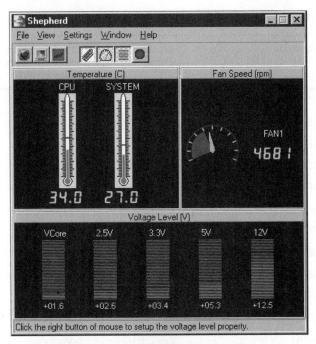

Fig. 6.19. Operation of the Shepherd program

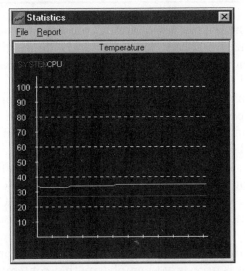

Fig. 6.20. Temperature graph built using Shepherd

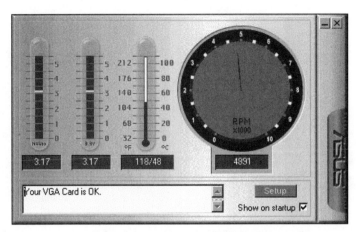

Fig. 6.21. SmartDoctor at work

facilities that control the temperature of the video chipset, supply voltage, etc. The SmartDoctor program supplied with a range of Asus video adapters (Fig. 6.21) is a good example of such a software tool.

Note that in contemporary computers, hardware-monitoring functions control several parameters: two or three temperature values, three to nine voltage values, the rotation speed of two or three fans, and so on. Complemented by appropriate software and supported by add-on circuitry on the motherboard, they ensure protection of the computer from hardware instability or a malfunction, issuing a series of warning signals (and possibly powering down an overheated system). These functions provide the possibility of automatic overclocking as well. The range of such smart motherboards includes products from MSI Computer, Gigabyte Technology, and Soltek Computer.

Leading hardware manufacturers continue their efforts to improve hardware-monitoring facilities. Undoubtedly, new technologies that make use of their advanced functionality will further stimulate the growth of computer performance and extend their standard functional capabilities.

Chapter 7

Stages of PC Overclocking and Testing

Depending on the capabilities of the motherboard, specifying the parameters settings that define CPU overclocked modes can be done either by using BIOS Setup or by setting the motherboard jumpers. Evaluation of the overall system performance and stability can be done using specialized tools, which usually include test programs.

There are two ways of changing the system parameters. The first one is to use the appropriate settings in BIOS Setup. Most current motherboards that provide built-in overclocking capabilities, such as **SoftMenu** from Abit, allow the bus frequency and various voltages to be measured directly in BIOS Setup. All such capabilities are described in the documentation supplied with the motherboard. However, many motherboards only allow parameters to be measured using jumpers and switches located on the motherboard itself.

It is first necessary to figure out which method of overclocking is provided by the motherboard. Then, you'll have to carefully read the documentation on your motherboard, especially the sections that describe overclocking capabilities and methods.

Step-by-Step Use of BIOS Setup

1. Determine the main CPU characteristics, usually labeled on the processor. The main parameters include the CPU frequency, the processor-bus frequency, and the supply voltage. It would be helpful to write down these data.

2. Consider providing intense, or at least adequate, processor cooling.

3. Power down the computer and enter the BIOS Setup program. (This usually is done by pressing the <Del> key at system startup.)

4. Enter the main menu that allows you to manage the processor parameters, such as **SoftMenu** or **CPU Frequency/Voltage Settings**.

5. Decide how to overclock the processor, which settings must be changed, and how to make the necessary adjustments.

6. Following the manual's instructions, change the CPU bus frequency and/or the multiplier value that sets the ratio between clock frequencies of the CPU and its bus.

7. Save the settings and exit the BIOS Setup program.

8. If the computer operates normally, which will be shown by successful completion of the Power-On Self-Test (POST) routine and loading of the BIOS Setup (CMOS Setup), proceed to Step 17.

9. If the computer didn't start successfully, reset the settings. First try to power down the computer several times (usually two or three times), then power it up (after no less than 5 seconds). If the computer started successfully, proceed to Step 15.

10. If the computer didn't start, reset the complementary metal-oxide semiconductor (CMOS) settings by disconnecting the jumper on the motherboard.

11. Remove the case from the system unit and consult the documentation provided for the motherboard.

12. When working with the opened case of the system unit, avoid static electricity, which can damage sensitive semiconductor elements. It is recommended that you touch the case with your hand before proceeding. It would be even better to hold the case with one hand during your work. Besides this, always try to avoid dropping any objects, especially metallic ones, on the device boards. If an object does fall, remove it immediately. Everything must be done carefully and accurately.

13. Locate the jumper responsible for resetting the BIOS settings on the motherboard. It usually is close to the CMOS battery, which is responsible for storing parameters set in BIOS Setup. Remove the jumper for two or three seconds, then return it to its initial position.

14. Power on the computer.

15. Enter the BIOS Setup program. Try to increase the supply voltage of the CPU and/or the memory. All these operations must be performed according to the instructions provided in the documentation.

16. After you accomplish these operations, the computer still may not start successfully. If this occurs, forget about overclocking to this specific frequency and try to set other values for the system-bus multiplier instead. If the computer won't start with the values that you have set, you'll need to reset the CMOS settings. Some motherboards do this automatically.

17. If the operating system has booted correctly, start testing the overclocked computer. The most popular and recommended tests include Winstone, WinBench, SYSmark, and 3DMark. The more tests passed successfully, the better. Modern computer games also are good tests. If you have successfully tested the game, then the CPU overclocking procedure was completed successfully. If this occurs, you can proceed with the optimization and fine-tuning of all other subsystems. (These topics will be covered in the appropriate sections of this book.) Note that some motherboards don't provide independent management of the memory, Peripheral Component Interconnect (PCI), and Accelerated Graphics Port (AGP) buses on the Front Side Bus (FSB) frequency. For such motherboards, CPU overclocking is done in parallel with that of other subsystems.

18. If system operation is unstable, either reduce the frequency or increase the voltage as appropriate. (See Steps 15 and 16.)

19. Do not try to raise the voltage until necessary. Raising the supply voltage increases heat generation. If the cooling facilities remain unchanged, this will increase the CPU temperature. Overheating has a negative effect on the stability of operation and decreases the time before failure. This is why efficient cooling should never be neglected.

20. When increasing supply voltage levels for each element, always remember: failure may occur if the parameter values exceed the maximal values.

Step-by-Step Use of Jumpers

1. Identify all important CPU characteristics, labeled on the CPU case, marked on the box, or specified in the documentation. These data include processor clock frequency, CPU bus frequency, and supply voltage. It is recommended that you memorize or write down this information.

2. Power down the computer, remove the case from the system unit, and consult the documentation supplied with the motherboard.

3. When working with the opened case of the system unit, avoid static electricity, which can damage sensitive semiconductor elements. It is recommended that

you touch the case with your hand before proceeding. It would be even better to hold the case with one hand during your work. Besides this, avoid dropping any objects, especially metallic ones, on the device boards. If an object does fall, remove it immediately; be very careful when performing this operation.

4. Locate the motherboard jumpers responsible for setting the values of the multiplier, the CPU bus frequency, and the CPU core voltage.

5. Consult the documentation to check the jumper settings, then figure out the required settings for the multiplier, the CPU bus frequency, and the CPU supply voltage. Memorize or write down these data.

6. Consider efficient CPU cooling. This is very important!

7. Carefully consider and plan processor overclocking, including the most important parameters and the procedure of setting these values.

8. Following the instructions provided in the documentation, change the CPU bus frequency and/or multiplier.

9. Check all settings carefully.

10. Power on the computer.

11. If your computer operates normally, the POST routine was completed successfully, and the BIOS Setup (CMOS Setup) was loaded, proceed to Step 15.

12. If the computer doesn't start, power it down, restart the computer, then try to slightly increase the supply voltage of the CPU and/or the memory. Before proceeding with these operations, it is necessary to consult the documentation.

13. If the computer still does not start successfully (the BIOS is not loaded), then abandon your attempts to overclock the processor to this frequency and set new values for the multiplier and bus frequency.

14. Enter the BIOS Setup program and change the required values, if necessary.

15. If the operating system started successfully, start testing. The list of recommended tests includes such popular programs as Winstone, WinBench, SYSmark, and 3DMark. In general, the more tests you run, the better. Contemporary games also can be good tests. If the tests were successful, the overclocking procedure has been accomplished. Proceed with the optimization of other subsystems. (This topic will be covered in more detail later in this book.) Note that if your motherboard doesn't provide the capability of managing PCI and AGP frequencies independent of the FSB frequency, processor overclocking must be accomplished in parallel with other subsystems.

16. If tests were accomplished correctly, you successfully overclocked your computer.

17. If there were failures during the tests, repeat Steps 12–16.

18. A general recommendation is as follows: Do not increase the voltage if there is no need to do so. A voltage increase is accompanied by greater heat generation. If cooling facilities are not improved, this increases CPU overheating, which has a negative effect on overall system stability and decreases the time before failure. Because of this, efficient cooling should never be neglected.

19. Increasing the supply voltages of specific elements increases the risk of overheating and failure.

20. The newest operating systems, such as Windows 2000/XP/Server 2003, may become unstable after overclocking. Windows 9x/ME might operate smoothly. This disparity is the result of the high requirements imposed by Windows 2000/XP/Server 2003 on computer hardware. Running these powerful operating systems on overclocked hardware is a test in itself. If this test is passed successfully (i.e., the system retains its stability), then it's OK. If the system couldn't withstand this test, overclocking is unstable and unreliable. Therefore, to ensure smooth operation, it is necessary to set other parameters.

Testing

Testing and optimizing computer hardware and software frequently requires an analysis of multiple parameters. It is often necessary to evaluate the efficiency of specific settings and chosen procedures of testing both hardware and software configurations. Because numerous parameters and settings influence overall system efficiency and stability, it is difficult to evaluate the influence of these parameters; they can be interrelated and dependent. However, their influence sometimes is mutually exclusive.

Erroneous solutions at the stages of optimization, fine-tuning, and especially upgrading computer hardware often prevent the user from fully implementing functionality and achieving maximum performance. Such errors frequently result in additional and unjustified expenses. In such cases, it is necessary to develop objective criteria that simplify the process of analyzing the influence of specific parameters.

To evaluate the influence of established parameter values, specialized software tools can be used. Tests usually can be run to analyze the performance of various computer subsystems using different combinations of the chosen parameters, and to select optimal values. Software tests solve the problem of backtracking and introduce some objectivity, the value of which depends on the software used during testing and the number of tests conducted.

For testing purposes, programs oriented toward the analysis of a specific computer subsystem can be used. An evaluation of hard disk performance often is done using the HDDSpeed program; processors frequently are evaluated using Million Instructions Per Second (MIPS). There are special tests intended for RAM and cache memory. For example, by changing memory timings in BIOS Setup, such programs can be used to evaluate the effect of these subsystems on overall system performance. Such programs often help reveal the capabilities of memory modules and optimize their operation, achieving maximum performance.

Contemporary computer games frequently are used as tests because they impose stringent requirements on computer subsystems. The list of such games includes versions of the popular Quake and Unreal. These games have long been de facto testing standards, used to evaluate both overall system performance and the performance of specific subsystems. It has become a tradition to provide the results of game tests when evaluating the performance of processors and video adapters in various output modes.

Although these programs are widely spread, the tools that allow complex analysis of computer systems have become the most popular.

When running operating systems such as Windows 9x/2000/XP/Server 2003, you can choose tests such as CheckIt, WinCheckIt, WinBench, Winstone, 3DMark, SiSoftware Sandra, and SYSmark. These programs perform complex analyses of specific devices included in computer subsystems and of their operation in coordination with other devices when performing different tasks. Besides this, some tests lay a significant workload on the system, which can be used to evaluate stability. Popular sets of tools and specialized utilities intended for heating and testing processors, such as burnP6, burnK7, CPUburn, etc., serve the same purpose.

Figs. 7.1–7.4 show WinBench 99 and CheckIt tests. Most companies that manufacture hardware components for testing their products use these utilities. This list includes such leading manufacturers as Intel, AMD, Via Technologies, Asus, and Abit. To confirm this statement, just visit these companies' Web sites.

Unfortunately, testing can't be universal. Each test usually gives preference to one or more specific tasks, such as office tasks or 3D graphics tasks.

The SYSmark 2002 test (Fig. 7.5) is a good example. It includes two parts: **Internet Content Creation** and **Office Productivity**. Each part of this test starts a set of popular applications and measures the time required to execute each operation. The first part of this test is oriented toward the system intended for creating Internet content. It includes testing the use of the following software products:

❑ Macromedia Dreamweaver 4
❑ Adobe Photoshop 6.0.1

- ❏ Adobe Premiere 6.0
- ❏ Microsoft Windows Media Encoder 7.1
- ❏ Macromedia Flash 5

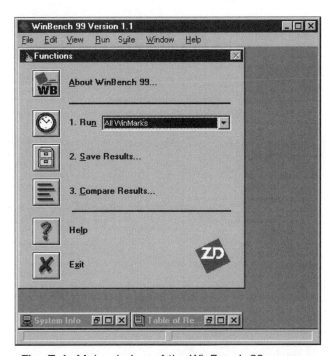

Fig. 7.1. Main window of the WinBench 99 program

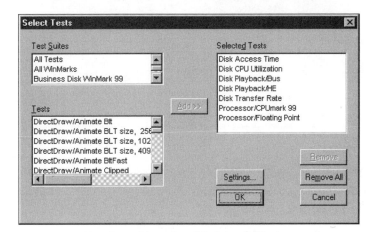

Fig. 7.2. Choosing WinBench 99 tests

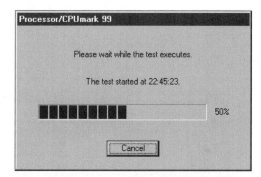

Fig. 7.3. Example of a WinBench 99 test

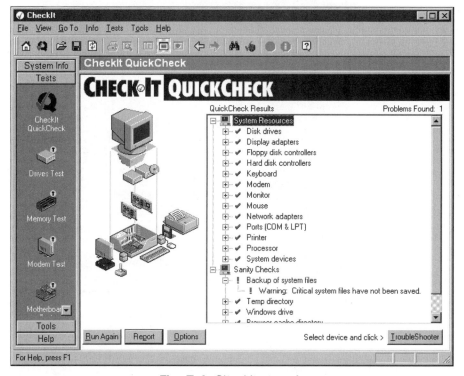

Fig. 7.4. CheckIt at work

Office Productivity comprises tests based on standard office tasks, such as creating documents, presentations, mail messages, etc. The following applications are used in the course of testing:

❑ Microsoft Word 2002

❏ Microsoft Excel 2002
❏ Microsoft PowerPoint 20002
❏ Microsoft Access 2002
❏ Microsoft Outlook 2002
❏ Dragon NaturallySpeaking 5
❏ Netscape Communicator 6.0
❏ WinZip 8.0
❏ McAfee VirusScan 5.13

The advantage of this test over artificial tests (such as WinBench or CPUmark) is the test data replicate the performance of the system when it executes these applications. New releases of these tests are already available. The main difference of the new releases from the version discussed here is that they use newer versions of the related applications.

Fig. 7.5. SYSmark 2002 test

3DMark is one of the most popular tests of the 3D graphics subsystem. Many versions of this test have been released, including 3DMark 98, 3DMark 99, and 3DMark2001. Currently, the most popular version of this product is 3DMark2001 Second Edition (Figs. 7.6 and 7.7), which has been used actively even after the release of 3DMark03 for DirectX 9.0.

Fig. 7.6. 3DMark2001 SE

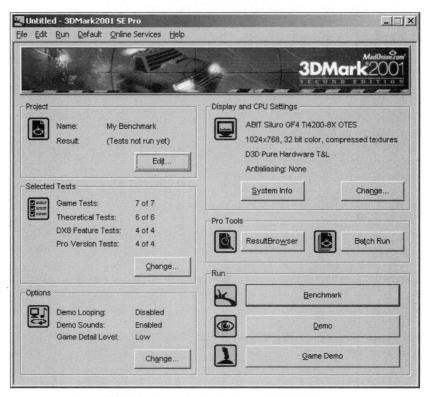

Fig. 7.7. Window of the 3DMark2001 SE test

This test plays numerous video clips, checking the performance of the video subsystem as well as that of the CPU and RAM. Having completed testing, the program produces a report that includes parameters such as the Frames Per Second (FPS) and total execution time for each clip.

For the input/output subsystem, the popular WinBench 99 test is recommended. However, most manufacturers and overclockers use data produced by the Iometer test (Fig. 7.8).

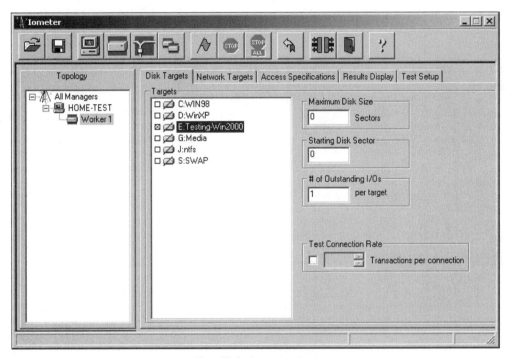

Fig. 7.8. Iometer test

SiSoftware Sandra is a good set of integrated tests and system analyzers. Unfortunately, early versions of this product often contained errors and inconsistencies. However, the latest version, SiSoftware Sandra 2003, has been improved and extended considerably. This newest release includes tests for almost all components and subsystems of the contemporary computer. Functional capabilities of this program are represented by appropriate icons, used to call various components of the program (Fig. 7.9). Having completed testing, this program provides an intuitive and illustrative graphical report that shows how the tested system relates to other popular configurations. Figs. 7.10–7.12 show the results of the CPU arithmetic, RAM throughput, and network bandwidth tests.

Encoding video data in the MPEG3 format (also known as MP3 or MPEG 1 Layer 3) is a good test. Unfortunately, there currently are no standard tests of this kind. Nevertheless, you can choose any audio file and encode it in MPEG3 using any available program. This procedure, when accomplished on computers with different architecture, will allow you to evaluate the performance of the processor. This method can be used during system overclocking. Consider audio compression using the Audiograbber program and the LAME codec (Fig. 7.13).

Fig. 7.9. Choosing a test in SiSoftware Sandra 2003

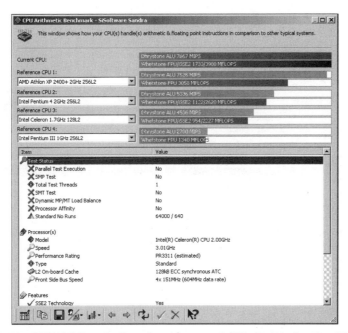

Fig. 7.10. CPU Arithmetic Benchmark test of SiSoftware Sandra 2003

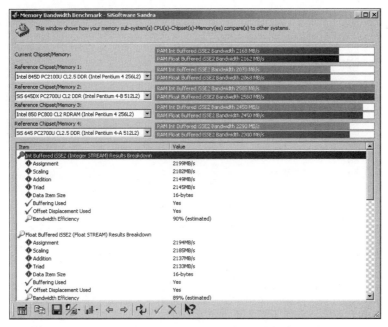

Fig. 7.11. Memory Bandwidth Benchmark test of SiSoftware Sandra 2003

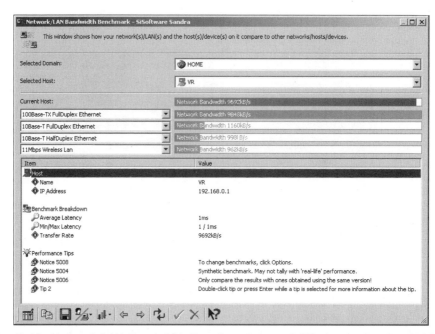

Fig. 7.12. Network/LAN Bandwidth Benchmark test of SiSoftware Sandra 2003

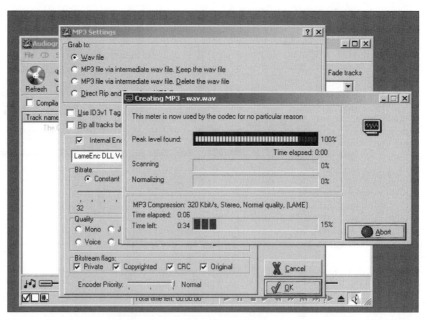

Fig. 7.13. Audio compression using the Audiograbber program and the LAME codec

Utilities and analyzers included in the SiSoftware Sandra toolkit will allow you to learn more about your computer.

CPUmark 99 (Fig. 7.14) is a popular synthetic test of the CPU subsystem.

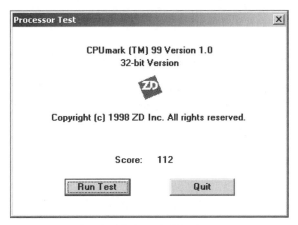

Fig. 7.14. CPUmark 99 test

When considering the functional capabilities of specialized programs, never forget standard tools. For example, the built-in monitoring tools of the Windows 9*x* operating system might be helpful.

Using this program, you can determine the workload of the CPU, RAM, hard disk, the size of a swap file, and so on, without exiting any system or application programs. As a result, it is easy to detect both software and hardware that tend to monopolize resources of computer subsystems. After determining the requirements of application software in resources such as RAM and virtual memory, it is easy to choose optimal strategies for upgrading and fine-tuning the computer. This may allow you to improve overall performance while minimizing financial expenses. Depending on the results of testing and monitoring, you could choose and install RAM modules for optimal information exchange.

Additionally, it is possible to specify the size and status of the swap file that virtual memory uses to operate. To increase the speed of working with this file, place it at the beginning of the hard disk (or, at least, in its first quarter); this can be achieved easily by installing the system on a new and sufficiently large disk. As a rule, this results in significant improvement of system performance. With the value of virtual memory dedicated by the system for system and application software, it is possible to choose the optimal amount of RAM to be installed on the computer.

To start the System Monitor utility, click the **Start** button and choose **/Programs/Accessories/System tools/System monitor**.

Illustrations in Figs. 7.15–7.17 demonstrate the settings and operation of the System Monitor utility. In Fig. 7.15, the four initial peaks on the **Kernel: Processor Usage (%)** graph correspond to the startup of the System Monitor and Microsoft Word 7, loading a file in Word 7, and the startup of Microsoft Excel. In Fig. 7.17, Microsoft Word 97 is loaded and a file is opened in this program.

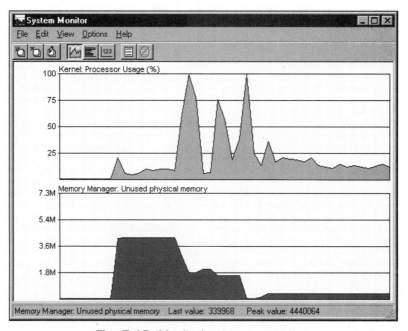

Fig. 7.15. Monitoring two parameters

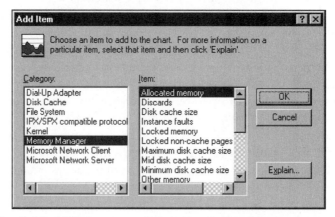

Fig. 7.16. Adding a parameter in the System Monitor program

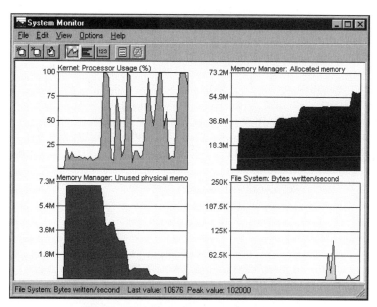

Fig. 7.17. Monitoring four parameters

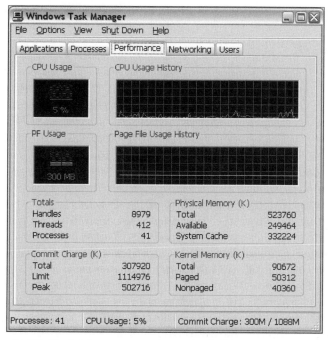

Fig. 7.18. Task Manager monitors the CPU and RAM workload

To get acquainted with the functional capabilities of the System Monitor and learn the specific features of its operation, you should read its technical documentation and use the help system built into Windows 9*x*.

Note that in Windows NT-based systems such as Windows 2000/XP/Server 2003, another monitoring tool — Windows Task Manager — allows you to monitor the system workload and the amount of occupied and available RAM (Fig. 7.18). Besides this, Task Manager displays a list of running processes and the amount of resources consumed by these processes. For example, the avp32.exe process takes about 85% of resources and 12 MB of RAM (Fig 7.19).

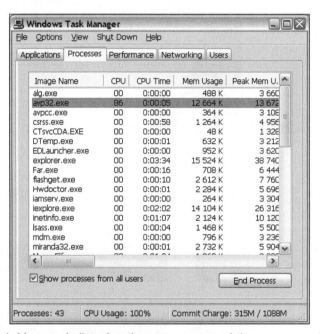

Fig. 7.19. Task Manager's list of active processes and the resources they consume

The most important capability of the Task Manager is it can be used to "kill" a process that has stopped responding or is consuming too many resources. It is also possible to stop all undesirable processes. You should not stop all processes one by one, because some of them are required for the system to run.

When evaluating the functionality of the Task Manager program, pay special attention to the possibility of changing the priority of the user process. The higher the process priority, the more processor time available to that process. This allows you to manage and control the tasks running in the system and to optimize the operation of computer hardware, optimized and fine-tuned beforehand using the previously described programs.

Chapter 8

Approaches
to Processor Overclocking

Processor overclocking usually is achieved by increasing the FSB frequency or by changing the multiplier. However, the best computer performance can be achieved by using a complex approach that accounts for component parameters and characteristics specific to the chosen modes.

Processors have significant technological reserve ensured by manufacturers. This reserve allows the CPU performance to be improved by overclocking, which can be achieved by raising the FSB frequency or other methods.

Increasing the FSB Frequency

When you consider using overclocked modes, remember that practically all processors have a fixed value for the multiplier — the coefficient that relates the core frequency to the external frequency. This is especially true for Intel products, the majority of the processor market. The list of Intel processors includes Pentium II, Pentium III (Katmai, Coppermine, and Tualatin), Pentium 4 (Willamette and Northwood), and Celeron. There is no indication that this situation will change in the near future. This means that increasing the FSB frequency remains the main method of overclocking.

The early IBM XT computers equipped with an Intel 8088 processor, intended to operate at 4.7 MHz, could be overclocked to 12 MHz. Numerous processors of Intel's 386 family and their clones were intended to run at 33 MHz; however, they usually were used at 40 MHz. These capabilities often were provided and ensured by manufacturers. Although such facts were rarely promoted, most computers of that time had a **Normal/Turbo** button on the front panel for switching the system to the overclocked mode.

Hardware implementation of the Turbo mode ensured considerable performance growth while retaining the required level of stability. Although these modes didn't correspond to specifications of the computer components, such architecture was standard: Manufacturers of such systems offered warranties for their products.

Since the times of 386 computers, CPU architecture has become more complicated. Clock frequencies have multiplied more than 100 times. The operating speed of these computer components has grown even more significantly. However, establishing forced operating modes by increasing the CPU clock frequency remains the most popular method of implementing potential capabilities of contemporary processors and obtaining maximal performance.

Increasing the CPU clock frequency, as well as overclocking other components and subsystems, is achieved by raising the FSB clock frequency. Depending on the type of motherboard, the required value of the FSB clock frequency is chosen by setting Dual In-line Package (DIP) switches or parameters in BIOS Setup.

Fig. 8.1. Setting the FSB frequency using DIP switches

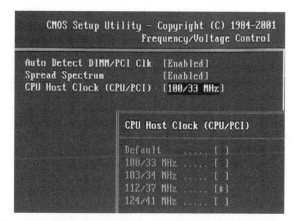

Fig. 8.2. Setting the FSB frequency using BIOS Setup

The range of FSB frequencies — and, consequently, the theoretical growth of computer performance — is determined by the motherboard. This depends on the elements used in the motherboard's construction, its design, the quality of its manufacturing, the BIOS software code, the functional capabilities, and so on.

The performance of Celeron (Northwood) overclocked via increased FSB frequency is shown in Table 8.1 and in Figs. 8.3 and 8.4.

Table 8.1. Overclocking Celeron (Northwood)

CPU frequency (MHz) = FSB frequency × multiplier	SYSmark 2002 rating (Internet content creation)	3DMark2001 rating
2,000 = 100 × 20	246	8,893
3,000 = 150 × 20	279	9,656

Like the Intel processors, AMD products such as Duron, Athlon (Thunderbird), and Athlon XP (Palomino, Thoroughbred, and Barton), usually have fixed multipliers, although in some cases, the multiplier can be unlocked and changed.

As a consequence of the Socket A form factor, for which Athlon is designed and which doesn't allow operations with resistors, frequency multipliers can be changed using special hardware and software of the motherboard.

Features and secrets of implementing the potential functional capabilities of these hardware and software tools, which allow the correction of frequency multipliers of AMD's Socket A processors, will be analyzed in the next section of this chapter. Here, consider a traditional method based on increasing the FSB frequency, also used on Intel processors.

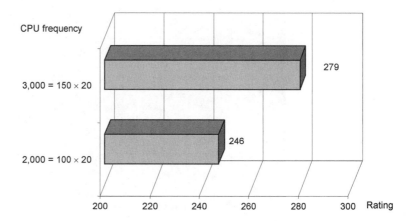

Fig. 8.3. Overclocking Celeron (Northwood) (tested using SYSmark 2002)

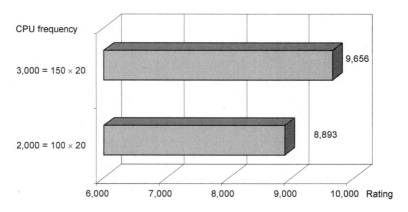

Fig. 8.4. Overclocking Celeron (Northwood) (tested using 3DMark2001)

This method, when used on Duron and Athlon, is achieved at the expense of increasing the external frequency (i.e., the FSB EV6 bus frequency).

The performance of Duron and Athlon achieved by increasing the FSB EV6 bus frequency is shown in Tables 8.2 and 8.3 and in Figs. 8.5 and 8.6.

Table 8.2. Overclocking Duron by Increasing the Bus Frequency

CPU frequency (MHz) = FSB frequency × multiplier	CPUmark 99 rating	FPU WinMark rating
600 = 100 × 6	51.4	3,260
690 = 115 × 6	59.4	3,760

Table 8.3. Overclocking Athlon (Thunderbird) by Increasing the Bus Frequency

CPU frequency = FSB frequency × multiplier	CPUmark 99 rating	FPU WinMark rating
700 = 100 × 7	64.7	3,810
784 = 112 × 7	72.5	4,270

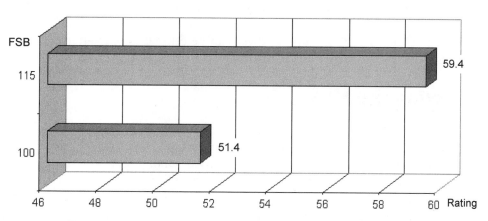

Fig. 8.5. Overclocking Duron by increasing the bus frequency (tested using CPUmark 99)

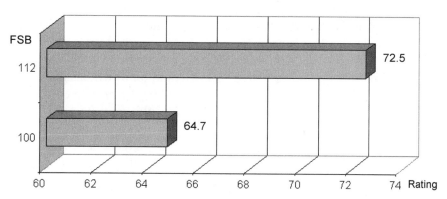

Fig. 8.6. Overclocking Athlon (Thunderbird) by increasing the bus frequency (tested using CPUmark 99)

Detailed information on the overclocking of Duron, Athlon, and Athlon XP will be given in *Chapter 18*.

Despite the insignificant performance growth of systems based on the VIA Apollo KT133 chipset from Via Technologies, obtained by processor overclocking at the expense of increasing clock frequencies of the FSB EV6 bus, this method has become popular. After the release of more advanced chipsets (such as Apollo KT133A, KT266A, KT333, and KT400) intended for operation at a wider range of FSB EV6 clock frequencies (including 133 MHz and 166 MHz), this overclocking method became even more popular. Complemented by the capability of changing the values of the frequency multipliers for Duron, Athlon, and Athlon XP (provided by motherboards, rather than the processors), this method allowed impressive results. The true value of these can be estimated only after considering overclocking methods that involve changing the multiplier.

Changing the Multiplier

As previously explained, the frequency multiplier in Duron, Athlon (Thunderbird), and Athlon XP (Palomino, Thoroughbred, and Barton) is fixed. Nevertheless, many motherboards ensure the capability of changing it. The multiplier value can be corrected using specific contacts: FID0–FID3, where FID stands for Format Identification. This relates only to the first releases of these processors. AMD has limited this capability for most of its products. For such processors, the signal lines, responsible for changing the multiplier, are usually broken. However, overclocking fans are fortunate that AMD performs this procedure using special bridges on the surface of the processor. Usually, these are the L1 bridges. Their locations on the processor are shown in Fig. 8.7.

By closing the disconnected bridges, the possibility of changing the frequency multiplier can be restored.

For Duron and Athlon, this procedure can be accomplished using a soft, sharpened pencil containing a large core of graphite, which has good conductivity. Using such a pencil, you can fill the gaps created by the broken contacts of the L1 bridges on the processor. Try to form small "hills;" this ensures good contact of the graphite with the metal and sufficient conductivity of the new connection. When performing this procedure, avoid closing the contacts between adjacent bridges. The results of this procedure are demonstrated in Figs. 8.8 and 8.9, where you can see fragments of the Duron processor.

The advantages of this method are the simplicity of its implementation and the possibility of quickly restoring the original appearance of the processor using a cloth and alcohol.

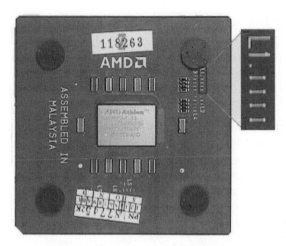

Fig. 8.7. Locations of L1 bridges

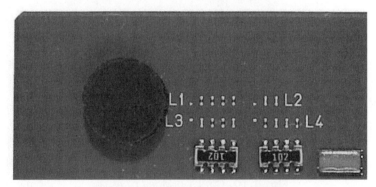

Fig. 8.8. Cut L1 bridges of Duron

Fig. 8.9. Restored L1 bridges of Duron

A special silver pencil, intended for correcting printed circuits, achieves a better result. To restore a broken bridge, you also can use a small piece of soldering paste, shaped like a thin wire and used like the graphite pencil.

In addition to these methods, broken contacts can be restored using quick soldering with a low-temperature soldering paste or special glues based on fine, dispersible silver. The main drawback of these methods is the irreversibility of the operations and, consequently, the loss of warranty for the processor.

Note that for AMD processors based on Palomino and Thoroughbred cores, it is impossible to connect broken bridges using a graphite or silver pencil. Fine soldering paste also can't be used here. For processors of this type, it is only possible to use soldering or conductive glue. The conductivity of connections created by graphite, silver, or soldering paste is not sufficient for these processors. Furthermore, in the course of manufacturing, the bridges are cut to form small pits.

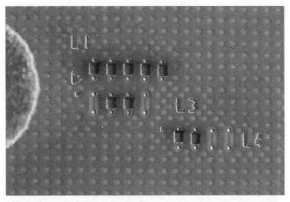

Fig. 8.10. Cut L1 bridges of Athlon XP (Palomino)

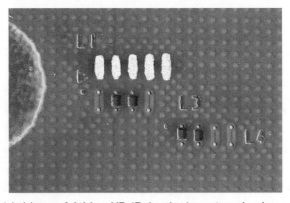

Fig. 8.11. L1 bridges of Athlon XP (Palomino), restored using a special glue

Before using conductive glue, you must eliminate the pits in the bridge gaps. This can be done using epoxy resin or any suitable varnish that has good insulating capabilities. The latter is especially important, because the bottom of such a pit is usually conductive and is connected to the common power supply line.

For Athlon XP processors based on the Thoroughbred core, the capability of changing the multiplier using motherboard functionality usually can be restored by closing the last L3 bridge (**http://www.amdnow.ru**) (Fig. 8.12). All remaining bridges can be left unchanged.

Fig. 8.12. Athlon XP (Thoroughbred) (the marked fragment contains the L3 bridges)

Fig. 8.13. L3 bridge responsible for the multiplier of Athlon XP (Thoroughbred)

After the broken bridges are restored on AMD processors, it becomes possible to change the frequency multiplier using motherboard functionality. If the bridges responsible for the processor frequency multiplier are not cut during the manufacturing process, the restoration procedure isn't required (Fig. 8.14).

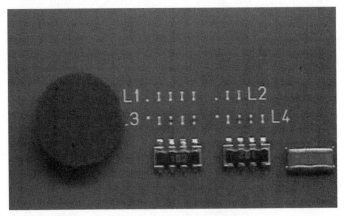

Fig. 8.14. L1 bridges that do not require restoration

Performance of Duron and Athlon (Thunderbird) overclocked by changing the frequency multiplier is shown in Tables 8.4 and 8.5 and in Figs. 8.15 and 8.16.

Table 8.4. Overclocking Duron by Changing the Multiplier

CPU frequency (MHz) = FSB frequency × multiplier	CPUmark 99 rating	FPU WinMark rating
600 = 100 × 6	51.4	3,260
900 = 100 × 9	68.3	4,900

Table 8.5. Overclocking Athlon (Thunderbird) by Changing the Multiplier

CPU frequency (MHz) = FSB frequency × multiplier	CPUmark 99 rating	FPU WinMark rating
700 = 100 × 7	64.7	3,810
800 = 100 × 8	71.8	4,350

Details of the results of overclocking Duron and Athlon will be considered later in this chapter.

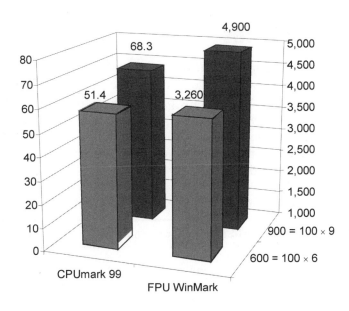

Fig. 8.15. Overclocking Duron by changing the multiplier

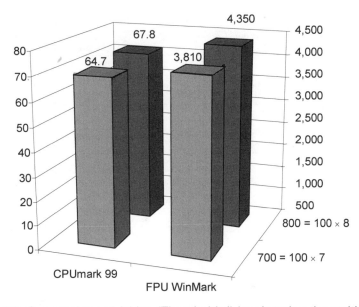

Fig. 8.16. Overclocking of Athlon (Thunderbird) by changing the multiplier

Using Both Methods

To achieve high performance, it is recommended that you combine both methods: increasing the processor bus frequency and changing the multiplier value. To set and evaluate different values of the processor bus frequency and its frequency multiplier, you must choose the optimal combination of these values, corresponding to the maximum performance.

For example, the results of overclocking Duron using both methods are presented in Table 8.6 and Fig. 8.17.

Table 8.6. Overclocking Duron by Combining Methods

CPU frequency (MHz) = FSB frequency × multiplier	CPUmark 99 rating
600 = 100 × 6	51.4
690 = 115 × 6	59.4
900 = 100 × 9	68.3
896 = 112 × 8	71.2

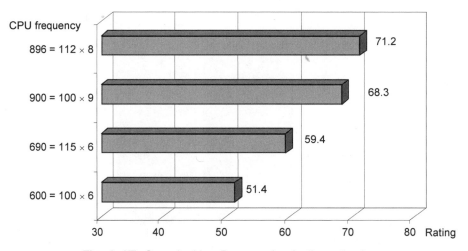

Fig. 8.17. Overclocking Duron using both methods

In the example provided in Table 8.6 and Fig. 8.17, maximum performance is achieved using a bus frequency of 112 MHz and multiplier of 8x (112 MHz × 8 = = 896 MHz), even though the maximum operating frequency of the processor corresponds to an FSB frequency of 100 MHz and a multiplier of 9x (100 MHz × 9 = 900 MHz). The difference in performance, according to the CPUmark 99 test, is approximately 5%.

Higher performance usually corresponds to combinations with high FSB frequencies, on which the frequencies of other buses are dependent. By increasing the FSB frequency, you increase the throughput of this bus and other buses of the computer system, as well as the performance of the processor and other subsystems. These include the video adapter, the hard disk, PCI devices, and RAM modules.

However, the increase of the clock frequencies and subsystem performance is limited not only by the capabilities of the components and technologies that they implement, but also by the chipset architecture and motherboard design. Furthermore, when approaching the limit, the computer system becomes unstable.

As a result of these limitations, it is often impossible to fully implement the potential of the CPU when overclocking it exclusively by increasing the FSB frequency. Because of this, it is recommended that you use the combined approach, increasing the FSB frequency and changing the processor multiplier.

Thus, simultaneous usage of both overclocking methods allows you to increase overall system performance and ensure the required level of stability.

To conclude this section, it is expedient to mention once again that changing the processor multiplier is only possible in combination with specialized motherboards that support this function. Examples of processor overclocking will be considered and analyzed in the next few sections.

Hardware Correction of Parameters

Most motherboards allow the correction of the voltage supplied to the CPU core (Vcore). When this capability is lacking, you can do it manually.

Usually, the processor automatically sets the required value of the supply voltage using the binary code set at specific contacts. These contacts typically are labeled as VID0, VID1, and so on (VID stands for Voltage Identification).

If it is necessary to change the value of the supply voltage and motherboard doesn't support this functional capability, the only recourse is to change the coding at these contacts.

In Slot 1 processors, which recently were quite popular, it is possible to change the supply voltage by closing the required contact (such as by gluing it). As a result, the value of 1 will be established on that contact.

Table 8.7. Voltage Identification for Pentium II

Voltage (V)	VID0	VID1	VID2	VID3	VID4
1.80	1*	0	1	0	0
1.85	0**	0	1	0	0
1.90	1	1	0	0	0
1.95	0	1	0	0	0
2.00	1	0	0	0	0
2.05	0	0	0	0	0
2.10	0	1	1	1	1
2.20	1	0	1	1	1
2.30	0	0	1	1	1
2.40	1	1	0	1	1
2.50	0	1	0	1	1
2.60	1	0	0	1	1
2.70	0	0	0	1	1
2.80	1	1	1	0	1
2.90	0	1	1	0	1
3.00	1	0	1	0	1
3.10	0	0	1	0	1
3.20	1	1	0	0	1
3.30	0	1	0	0	1
3.40	1	0	0	0	1
3.50	0	0	0	0	1

* 1 means the contact is free
** 0 means the contact is connected to the supply voltage

Motherboards automatically detect the required voltage levels by analyzing the code set by the VID0–VID4 contacts. As a result, the required supply voltage is set.

Note that using this method, it is only possible to change the value of 0 to 1; the reverse action is impossible. Therefore, this method is not applicable to the processors that have a supply voltage of 2.8 V. Such processors include Pentium II 233 MHz, 266 MHz, and 300 MHz.

However, this method can be used to correct the supply voltage of 2 V processors. Such processors include Pentium II 333 MHz, 350 MHz, 400 MHz, and 450 MHz and Celeron 266, 300, 300A, and 333.

Table 8.8. VID0–VID4 Locations on the CPU Board

Input	VID0	VID1	VID2	VID3	VID4
Contact	B120	A120	A119	B119	A121

The A1–A121 contacts are on the same side as the cooler or heatsink; the B1–B121 contacts reside on the opposite side. They are easy to find: Usually, it is sufficient to count from the contact whose number is labeled on the processor board.

Table 8.9 specifies which contacts can be glued (they are marked with an X) to obtain the required voltage.

Table 8.9. CPU Supply Voltage Correction

Voltage (V)	B119	B120	A119	A120	A121
2.0					
2.2	X		X		X
2.4	X			X	X
2.6	X				X
2.8			X	X	X
3.0			X		X
3.2				X	X
3.4					X

The required contacts can be glued with varnish or adhesive tape. If desired, you can also cut the contact. This task has can be accomplished in numerous ways. However, you must proceed carefully: By cutting the wrong contact, you can accidentally increase the voltage to such a level that the core would be destroyed immediately after you power on the computer.

When increasing the CPU supply voltage, remember that the power consumed by the processor will grow accordingly. Consequently, it will be necessary to provide additional cooling for the processor.

Like Pentium II, Pentium III for Socket 1 automatically specifies the required power supply voltage via the binary code set on the five output contacts. These contacts again are named VID0, VID1, VID2, VID3, and VID4 (VID stands for Voltage Identification).

Table 8.10. Voltage Identification for Pentium III

Voltage (V)	VID0	VID1	VID2	VID3	VID4
1.30	1*	1	1	1	0
1.35	0**	1	1	1	0
1.40	1	0	1	1	0
1.45	0	0	1	1	0
1.50	1	1	0	1	0
1.55	0	1	0	1	0
1.60	1	0	0	1	0
1.65	0	0	0	1	0
1.70	1	1	1	0	0
1.75	0	1	1	0	0
1.80	1	0	1	0	0
1.85	0	0	1	0	0
1.90	1	1	0	0	0
1.95	0	1	0	0	0
2.00	1	0	0	0	0
2.05	0	0	0	0	0
2.10	0	1	1	1	1
2.20	1	0	1	1	1
2.30	0	0	1	1	1
2.40	1	1	0	1	1
2.50	0	1	0	1	1
2.60	1	0	0	1	1
2.70	0	0	0	1	1
2.80	1	1	1	0	1

continues

Table 8.10 Continued

Voltage	VID0	VID1	VID2	VID3	VID4
2.90	0	1	1	0	1
3.00	1	0	1	0	1
3.10	0	0	1	0	1
3.20	1	1	0	0	1
3.30	0	1	0	0	1
3.40	1	0	0	0	1
3.50	0	0	0	0	1

* 1 means the contact is free

** 0 means the contact is connected to the supply voltage

As with Pentium II, motherboards automatically detect the required voltage levels by analyzing the code at the VID0–VID4 output contacts.

Method and features of voltage correction coincide to those previously described. By insulating a contact, it is possible to change the value of the code specified. Insulating a contact sets its value to 1. The location table of the VID0–VID 4 remains unchanged, because it is determined by the Slot 1 standard.

Fig. 8.18. Celeron installed in Socket 370

Migration from the Slot 1 standard to the Socket 370 standard has caused significant changes in PC architecture. Different versions of Pentium III and Celeron have appeared, based on different cores and technologies and created for different form factors. The most popular version was Celeron based on the Tualatin core and using the 0.13-micrometer technology.

However, these architectural changes didn't eliminate the necessity of manually correcting the required parameters.

Like previous models created for Slot 1, processors corresponding to the Socket 370 standard allow you to change the core supply voltage. For these elements, motherboards also detect the required voltage levels automatically by analyzing the code specified by the appropriate contact. As a result of this analysis, the motherboard establishes the required level of core voltage.

To correct the core voltage, it is necessary to change the state of the contacts that determine the level of supply voltage. This can be done by insulating the respective contacts. Insulating a contact ensures its transition to the 1 state. Besides this, connecting the contact to the ground ensures its transition to the 0 state. Choosing the states of VID0, VID1, VID2, and so on, specifies the binary code according to which the required level of supply voltage is established.

To correct the voltage, take the following steps:

1. Visit **http://www.intel.com** and download the document that contains description of your processor.
2. This document usually contains a table that summarizes the states (codes) of the VID contact group, along with their corresponding voltage levels supplied to the CPU core. State 1 means the contact is free, and state 0 means it has the supply voltage (Vss, also referred to as ground) potential.
3. To find the required pins, consult the map of contacts, usually at the end of the document. Contacts responsible for the core voltage are usually located in the top-right corner of the chart.
4. Using the information collected in Step 3 and the "key" (processor skew), identify the physical contacts on the processor.
5. To set a chosen contact from the VID group to state 1, insulate the contact. You can use insulation from a thin wire (such as Teflon insulation from an electric wire). You also can use special insulating varnish, even cut the pin from the processor, or drill a hole for this contact in the Socket 370 slot. The latter approach is not recommended; if you choose it, you'll be unable to return to the previous variants or keep the warranty.

6. To set a chosen contact from the VID group to state 0, connect this contact, using a thin wire, to the nearest Vss contact.

7. After a careful check, install the processor into the Socket 370 slot, install the cooler, and power on your computer.

8. When manipulating the processor, remember to avoid static electricity. When performing the operations, periodically discharge the static charge. An even better approach would be to use a special antistatic bracelet. Instead of the bracelet, you could wrap your wrist in wire without insulation and ground it via the 1 megohm (Mohm) resistor.

This can be illustrated using Celeron (Tualatin). The correspondence of core voltage levels and VID contact states are in Table 8.11.

Table 8.11. Voltage Identification for Celeron (Tualatin)

VID25mV	VID3	VID2	VID1	VID0	Voltage (V)
0**	1	1	1	1	1.300
1*	1	1	1	1	1.325
0	1	1	1	0	1.350
1	1	1	1	0	1.375
0	1	1	0	1	1.400
1	1	1	0	1	1.425
0	1	1	0	0	1.450
1	1	1	0	0	1.475
0	1	0	1	1	1.500
1	1	0	1	1	1.525
0	1	0	1	0	1.550
1	1	0	1	0	1.575
0	1	0	0	1	1.600
1	1	0	0	1	1.625
0	1	0	0	0	1.650
1	1	0	0	0	1.675
0	0	1	1	1	1.700

continues

Table 8.11 Continued

VID25mV	VID3	VID2	VID1	VID0	Voltage (V)
1	0	1	1	1	1.725
0	0	1	1	0	1.750
1	0	1	1	0	1.775
0	0	1	0	1	1.800
1	0	1	0	1	1.825

* 1 means the contact is free

** 0 means the contact is connected to the supply voltage

Fig. 8.19 shows a fragment of the contact map of this Celeron processor, manufactured using 0.13-micrometer technology. The fragment shows the labels only for those contacts related to the manual correction of the processor parameters.

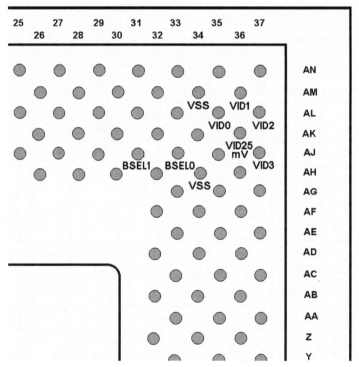

Fig. 8.19. Fragment of the contact map of Celeron (Tualatin)

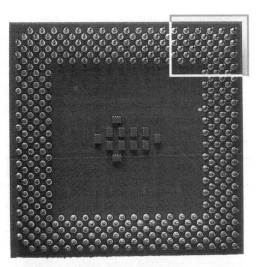

Fig. 8.20. Celeron (Tualatin) (view of the contacts side)

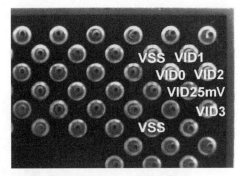

Fig. 8.21. Fragment of Celeron (Tualatin), with the VID and Vss contacts marked

Besides voltage correction, which is performed by changing the state of the contacts responsible for selection of the core supply voltage, you can choose another clock frequency of the processor bus. Celeron processors corresponding to the Socket 370 standard have inherited many features from Intel's Pentium III products: the case, the core architecture, and even the size and operating principles of L2 cache. However, Celeron processors always have a lower FSB frequency than their predecessors. Starting with Celeron (Coppermine), processors of this class were intended to run at the bus frequency of 100 MHz. Despite a more advanced technological process, new core, and the capability of operating at high frequencies, the newer models remained at the same bus frequency. Most Celeron (Tualatin) users increase the bus frequency (and, consequently, the core frequency) using the built-in functionality of a motherboard. When a motherboard doesn't support such functions, it is still possible to accomplish these operations by manipulating the appropriate contacts of the processor.

The processor has two contacts responsible for choosing bus frequency. Their possible states and the corresponding values of the FSB frequency are outlined in Table 8.12.

Table 8.12. Selecting the Bus Frequency

BSEL1	BSEL0	Bus frequency (MHz)	Processor
0**	1	100	Celeron
1*	1	133	Pentium III

* 1 means the contact is free

** 0 means the contact is connected to the supply voltage

As follows from Table 8.12, to choose an FSB frequency of 133 MHz for a Celeron processor, it is sufficient to insulate the BSEL1 contact. The CPU clock frequency will grow accordingly.

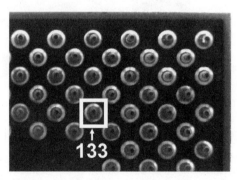

Fig. 8.22. Fragment of Celeron, with the contact marked
that allows you to set the FSB frequency to 133 MHz

The advantage of this method is the possibility of changing the FSB frequency even when the motherboard architecture doesn't provide the tools for supporting overclocked modes. The key drawback of this approach is its installation of intermediate values. Besides this, not all Celeron (Tualatin) processors can operate at this frequency. However, experience has shown that a high percentage of models intended to run at a clock speed of 900 MHz, 1 GHz, 1.10 GHz, or 1.2 GHz show stable operation at an FSB frequency set to 133 MHz. As a rule, the first three of these models don't even require you to raise the CPU core voltage. When you can't ensure stable operation of the computer at the FSB frequency of 133 MHz, the only recourse is to increase the core supply voltage. If the motherboard doesn't support the required functionalities, you can try the previously described method for choosing the supply voltage.

Figs. 8.23 and 8.24 give examples of increasing the FSB frequency and CPU core voltage for Celeron (Tualatin). The nominal mode is outlined in Table 8.13.

Table 8.13. Nominal Mode of Celeron (Tualatin)

VID25mV	VID3	VID2	VID1	VID0	CPU core voltage (V)	FSB frequency (MHz)
0**	1*	0	1	1	1.5	100

* 1 means the contact is free

** 0 means the contact is connected to the supply voltage

Fig. 8.23. Implementation of the FSB frequency of 133 MHz and core voltage of 1.7 V

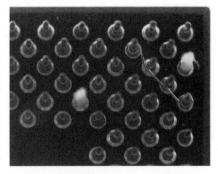

Fig. 8.24. Implementation of the FSB frequency of 133 MHz and core voltage of 1.75 V

When considering the management of supply voltage, it is necessary to emphasize some features of AMD processors.

For Athlon XP, the core supply voltage is determined by the configuration of the L11 group of bridges.

Fig. 8.25. L1 and L11 bridges of Athlon XP (Palomino)

Fig. 8.26. L3 and L11 bridges of Athlon XP (Palomino)

Possible configurations of the bridges from the L11 group, and their Vcore values, are provided in Table 8.14.

Table 8.14. Configuration of L11 Bridges and Their Core Voltages

1	2	3	4	5	Vcore voltage (V)
1*	0*	0	0	0	1.475
1	0	0	0	1	1.500
1	0	0	1	0	1.525
1	0	0	1	1	1.550
1	0	1	0	0	1.575
1	0	1	0	1	1.600
1	0	1	1	0	1.625
1	0	1	1	1	1.650
1	1	0	0	0	1.675
1	1	0	0	1	1.700
1	1	0	1	0	1.725
1	1	0	1	1	1.750

continues

Table 8.14 Continued

1	2	3	4	5	Vcore voltage (V)
1	1	1	0	0	1.775
1	1	1	0	1	1.800
1	1	1	1	0	1.825
1	1	1	1	1	1.850

* 1 means the contact is free
** 0 means the contact is connected to the supply voltage

Influence of Temperature on Pentium 4 Performance

(Translated from **http://www.fcenter.ru/forprint.shtml?processors/5798#** and **http://www.fcenter.ru/forprint.shtml?processors/5814#** with the permission of **http://www.fcenter.ru**, a Russian-language Web site.)

Contemporary processors with high energy-consumption (including both AMD and Intel processors) can have a cooling problem because they produce considerable thermal power. It is highly desirable that this heat be not only evacuated from the processor core, but also from the system unit case, so that the temperature of the air flowing around the heatsink be as low as possible.

With the release of each new Pentium 4 model, experts renew their requirements for PC manufacturers, especially those related to the temperature modes of the processor. Among these requirements are the maximum temperature of the CPU core, the maximum temperature of the air inside the system unit cover, and the recommended thermal resistance of the installed cooler. Provided that these requirements are observed, Intel guarantees stable operation of its processors. AMD also specifies similar requirements for PCs equipped with Athlon XP. The main issue is whether or not the PC manufacturer observes these requirements, and if yes, to what extent.

With well-known brands such as Hewlett-Packard or Dell Computer, the manufacturer has carefully tested the temperature characteristics of each component chosen for assembling the computer, including the case and cooler. However, if you purchased your computer from a less well-known vendor or even assembled it yourself, the situation is quite different. Are you sure that all requirements of Intel or AMD for temperature modes have been met? Even the calculations of the component manufacturers might be useless, if you implement modes that differ from the nominal or recommended ones. Overclocking increases the power consumption and heat generation of respective components. The CPU core temperature grows accordingly. This often results in instable operation of the component and the entire computer system.

Instable operation of an overclocked computer is an ordinary occurrence. If an overclocked processor operates slower than expected, the situation is different. Such situations are typical on Pentium 4. At first, they may seem surprising. Such behavior is caused by overheating of the processor chip — to be precise, by the operation of the Thermal Control Circuit. This system controls the processor performance, depending on its temperature. The following experiments confirm this.

Thermal Monitor and Thermal Control Circuit

Intel developers have implemented new technology known as the Thermal Control Circuit in Pentium 4. This technology is aimed at ensuring stable operation and at protecting processors from damage caused by overheating. The architecture of all Pentium 4 processors includes two built-in temperature sensors, which actually are specialized thermal diodes. One of these sensors, integrated into the chip, informs the system BIOS and the hardware-monitoring subsystem of the CPU core temperature. Another sensor located in the "hottest" zone of the core — near the Arithmetic Logic Unit (ALU) — is an integral part of the Thermal Monitor layout.

It is necessary to mention that Athlon XP contains a similar sensor. However, the difference between Athlon XP and Pentium 4 is significant. The thermal diode of Athlon XP informs the motherboard of the temperature of the CPU core. Special logical circuits of the motherboard process the received data and power down the system if the CPU temperature reaches the temperature threshold. Thus, the hardware control circuits prevent the processor from being damaged by overheating. If this happens when the OS is running and data is being processed, all unsaved data probably will be lost.

Temperature monitoring in Pentium 4 is based on different principles. As a result, the computer retains overall stability even when the temperature threshold is reached. The system is powered down only in emergencies. This means that the processor protects itself from overheating and is capable of continuing stable operation of the system and application programs.

To meet this requirement, the Pentium 4 core contains a special integrated circuit that compares the current and threshold temperatures. This circuit, known as the Thermal Monitor, complements Thermal Control Circuit logical boards that control the heat generation of the CPU.

The operating principle of the Thermal Monitor is based on the comparison of two currents: one flowing through the thermal diode, and one taken from a separate source as a predefined reference value. The resistance of the thermal diode depends on its temperature. Consequently, the current flowing through the thermal diode will change with the CPU core temperature. By comparing the reference value of the current passing through the thermal diode, it is possible to determine whether or not the temperature threshold has been reached. The Thermal Monitor is designed to complete a simple task: If the temperature in the hottest location of the CPU exceeds the threshold, the Thermal Monitor generates the PROCHOT# signal. As a result, the Thermal Control Circuit is activated to reduce the generated heat and prevent the temperature from rising.

Erroneous opinions related to the operation of the Thermal Control Circuit are common. One of the most frequent fallacies states that Pentium 4 reduces its clock frequency when overheated. Suppose that the processor operated at 2.2 GHz when cooled adequately. If it became overheated, the Thermal Control Circuit would reduce its clock frequency to 1.8 GHz or even lower. To understand this, you must know how the operating frequency is generated in the CPU.

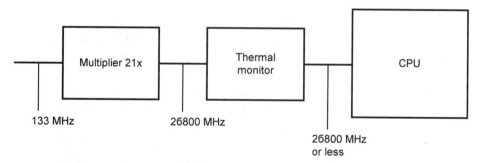

Fig. 8.27. Generation of the operating frequency in Pentium 4

Suppose that the motherboard supplies a frequency of 133 MHz via the FSB to the processor. In the processor, this frequency is multiplied by the multiplier value. (Pentium 4 2.8 GHz has a multiplier of 21x). The resulting frequency (2.8 GHz, in this case) of the generated signal used by internal components is the value marked on the CPU. This value is read by programs such as WCPUID. It is this high-frequency signal that determines the CPU clock speed and operation of the ALU. This signal is controlled by the Thermal Control Circuit.

Thus, under normal temperatures, clock pulses supplied to the arithmetic units of Intel Pentium 4 2.8 GHz have a frequency of 2.8 GHz. However, when the processor temperature reaches the threshold, the Thermal Monitor issues the

PROCHOT# signal. As a result, the Thermal Control Circuit is activated. The Thermal Control Circuit, in turn, modulates the signal supplied to the processor, and determines how many pulses must be discarded to decrease the heat generated by the CPU. Modification of the clock signal is illustrated in Fig. 8.28.

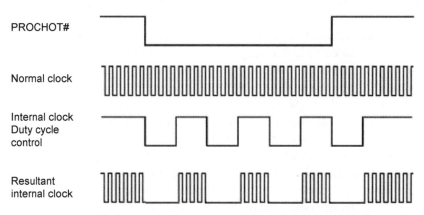

Fig. 8.28. Modification of the clock signal supplied to Pentium 4 by the thermal control system

A portion of the clock pulses generated by the CPU's multiplying unit is discarded by the thermal control system. As a result, the operating intensity of the calculation units of the processor, which idle during idle clocks, is decreased. Consequently, the processor performance and heat generation decrease, even though both the motherboard and the internal clock pulse generator specify a value of 2.8 GHz.

According to the data provided by Intel, the resulting frequency can be lower than the nominal by between 30% and 50%, depending on the processor model.

As the core temperature decreases, the Thermal Control Circuit logical unit gradually returns the processor to the normal mode of operation, reducing the number of discarded clock cycles and increasing the intensity of operation for internal CPU circuitry. When the CPU core temperature drops approximately 1°C (33.8°F) below the threshold (the so-called value of temperature hysteresis), the Thermal Monitor will stop issuing the PROCHOT# signal. After that, the idle cycles enforced by the Thermal Control Circuit will disappear, and the internal CPU circuits will run at the specified clock frequency (in this example, 2.8 GHz).

By default, the Thermal Control Circuit is disabled for all processors of the Pentium 4 family. To initialize it, you must include an appropriate functionality in the motherboard BIOS. The Thermal Control Circuit is enabled when the computer is powered on, or later at the operating system boot (via special drivers or system software).

What benefits are provided by the Thermal Control Circuit technology? To answer this question, it is sufficient to imagine a situation in which a Pentium 4 processor is inadequately cooled. Such a situation can arise if the computer is equipped with an inferior cooler, if there is no thermal paste between the CPU surface and heatsink, or if the case of the system unit is stuffed with electronic components and has no extra coolers. As a result, the processor overheats, and its performance will be much lower than the performance of a CPU that operates in an optimal temperature mode.

Another common situation is related to an overclocked processor. Such a processor generates more heat than a CPU that runs at the nominal frequency. An overclocked processor may demonstrate performance even lower than that of a processor running at the nominal frequency. This is possible because, under conditions of inadequate cooling, a core that operates at a high intensity can reach the temperature threshold, which would cause the Thermal Monitor to activate. After the Thermal Monitor was activated, the Thermal Control Circuit would force the processor to discard clock cycles. Consequently, at the computer boot time (at the stage of the POST routine) and later, when the programs such as WCPUID start, the user would be shown the clock frequency to which the processor was overclocked. However, the real performance of that processor might be much lower.

When considering the Thermal Control Circuit technology, it is necessary to mention that its implementation allows you to prevent processor overheating, but it won't preserve system stability (for example, if the cooler fails). To prevent processor damage in such emergencies, another temperature sensor has been integrated with the core. This sensor tracks another temperature value — the one that prompts the THERMTRIP# signal, which initiates system shutdown. This value is lower than the level at which CPU semiconductor circuits are destroyed. Even if the fan of the processor cooler fails, the computer will be powered down before it reaches the fatal core temperature. The temperature measurement interval is no more than several dozen nanoseconds; therefore, the Thermal Control Circuit will save the overheated processor even if you physically remove the CPU cooler. The temperature that prompts the THERMTRIP# signal is about 135°C (275°F), according to the manufacturer.

Testing the Temperature Control Facilities

The primary goals of this test were to determine the threshold that activates thermal protection and to reveal the dependence between the Pentium 4 processor and its core temperature.

Configuration of the Test System

- ❐ Processor — Intel Pentium 4 3.06 GHz
- ❐ Cooler — GlacialTech Igloo 4310 Pro
- ❐ Motherboard — Asus P4PE
- ❐ Hard disk — IBM DTLA 15 GB, 7,200 rpm
- ❐ RAM — 256 MB PC2100
- ❐ Video adapter — GeForce4 MX440-8X
- ❐ Sound card — SoundBlaster Live! Value
- ❐ Disk drive — IBM DTLA 15 GB, 7,200 rpm
- ❐ CD-ROM drive — CD-ROM 24X
- ❐ Case — InWin J-536 (system unit fan disabled)
- ❐ Operating system — Windows XP Professional

To investigate the influence of Thermal Monitor and Thermal Control Circuit operation on the processor performance, it was necessary to ensure a smooth increase in its temperature. Reaching the temperature threshold was determined by the change of performance, which had to be controlled constantly.

Unfortunately, the fan speed control using Zalman FanMate was insufficient.

Fig. 8.29. Zalman FanMate regulator

First, it was impossible to smooth the increase in CPU temperature. Furthermore, the lower the fan speed, the lower the cooler efficiency. At low rotation speed, the dependence of the cooling efficiency on the rotation speed was nonlinear. Because of this, another method was chosen.

The processor temperature at a constant workload, if the same cooler is used, will depend almost linearly on the temperature of the air within the system unit case, which, in turn, depends on the ambient temperature. By smoothly increasing the ambient temperature, it is possible to smoothly increase the processor temperature.

Measuring the room temperature with a precision of 1°C is difficult; however, this precision was desirable for testing purposes. This was achieved using the MIR-253 thermally isolated chamber from Sanyo. This device has a case with the dimensions of 162×50×70 cm. The ATX system unit can be placed within it. A special outlet in the case of the thermal camera allows the connection of the monitor, keyboard, mouse, and power cable. The computer case is placed into the thermally isolated medium, the temperature of which doesn't depend on the ambient temperature and can be set manually.

Fig. 8.30. MIR-253 thermally isolated chamber from Sanyo

MIR-253 includes a heating element and cooling system similar to the ones used in refrigerators. The incubator consumes 220 W and is capable of supporting an internal temperature ranging from −10°C (+14°F) to +50°C (+122°F), with a precision of 0.1°C (32.18°F). However, such measurement precision could not be achieved, because a computer is a constant and powerful source of heat. Consequently, the temperature within the incubator constantly changes by 0.5°C (32.9°F) to 1°C (33.8°F).

This precision was sufficient for performing the planned measurements.

Using MIR-253, it became possible to measure the ambient temperature for the computer with a precision of 1°C. This ensured adequate measurements of the CPU temperature.

A decision was made to trace the CPU performance and its dependence on the temperature using a real application, rather than synthetic test. For this purpose, the Unreal Tournament 2003 game and Fraps program were used. The latter displays in real-time the number of frames per second achieved in a Direct3D application. In contrast to the built-in tools of performance measurements implemented in various games, such as Unreal Tournament or Quake III Arena, Fraps displays the result in a large font, which is important when starting the application in a window with low resolution. Generally, Fraps also consumes system resources and influences the displayed results. However, this isn't important, because it is the change of the performance parameters that is of interest in this case. The settings of the Unreal Tournament were changed to decrease the workload on the video adapter as much as possible, making performance more dependent on the processor. The game was started at a screen resolution of 320 × 240 with a 16-bit color depth, in the Instant Action mode, at the DM-Asbestos level. After the game started, a spot was chosen with a constant number of frames per second. At this point, the main personage was stopped. From this moment, the tester touched neither the keyboard nor the mouse. During the investigation, the rendering speed was registered for the same scene depending on the processor temperature. Because the game was started in a window, rather than in full-screen mode, it was possible to constantly monitor the processor temperature using the Asus PC Probe program supplied with the motherboard, without stopping the testing process. All that remained after starting Unreal Tournament was to gradually increase the temperature within the thermally isolated chamber.

Influence of Hyper-Threading on the CPU Temperature

Hyper-Threading technology, first implemented in Intel Pentium 4 3.06 GHz, is one of the newest achievements of Intel. This technology allows two tasks or two code fragments of the same program to be executed simultaneously on one physical processor. Thus, one processor is interpreted by the operating system as two logical devices, which operate in parallel. This functional capability can be enabled or disabled in BIOS Setup.

In the course of analyzing the temperature influence on the CPU performance, there arose the problem of detecting the dependence of the thermal power on the usage of hyperthreading technology.

In experiments conducted at 20°C (68°F), the following testing programs were used: CPUburn, SiSoftware Sandra 2003, and Unreal Tournament 2003. The first program from this list loads the processor with intense calculations. As a result, the processor heats. Other programs are used as tests.

The CPU temperatures achieved as a result of running these programs, as well as the temperature of the CPU in the idle mode, are shown in Fig. 8.31. Temperature measurements were conducted using Asus PC Probe.

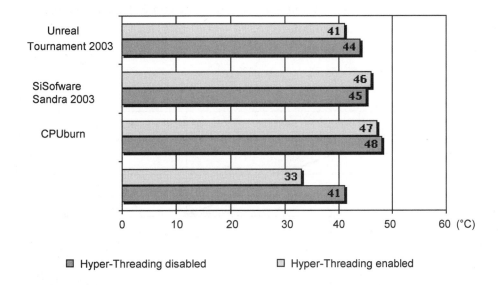

Fig. 8.31. Influence of hyperthreading technology on the CPU temperature

As is obvious from the illustration, the CPU temperature in the idle mode decreased when hyperthreading technology was enabled. For Unreal Tournament, the CPU temperature without hyperthreading was much higher. This is why the decision was made to disable hyperthreading technology when investigating the operation of the Thermal Monitor and the Thermal Control Circuit. This had to simplify the CPU heating.

Test Results

Investigation of Thermal Monitor and Thermal Control Circuit operation was started at the following parameter values:

❏ Temperature within the thermally isolated chamber — 28°C (82.4°F)
❏ CPU temperature — 69°C (156.2°F)
❏ Unreal Tournament 2003 — 115 frames per second

In the course of testing, the temperature of the ambient air was increased smoothly, and changes of the following parameters were registered:

❏ Temperature of the ambient air (Line 1)
❏ Temperature of the ambient air within the computer case (Line 2)
❏ CPU temperature (Line 3)
❏ Speed of the game test (Line 4)

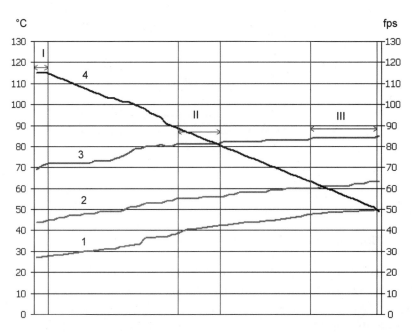

Fig. 8.32. Influence of the Thermal Monitor and the Thermal Control Circuit on the CPU performance (1 = temperature of the ambient air, 2 = temperature of the air within the computer case, 3 = CPU temperature, and 4 = speed in the game test)

This test showed that the speed of the game test didn't change until the CPU temperature approached the threshold of 72°C (161.6°F) (Section I). From this moment, the speed in Unreal Tournament started to decrease rapidly. Before conducting measurements, it seemed possible that the Thermal Control Circuit would decrease the CPU speed with each additional 1°C increase of its temperature. However, in Fig. 8.32, there are regions in which the CPU temperature doesn't change, even though the speed continues to decrease (Sections II and III). This is evidence that the implementation of protective elements allows Pentium 4 to resist the increase of its core temperature and even to support the temperature at a constant level for some time.

As a result, the ambient temperature in the course of testing has risen from 27°C (80.6°F) to 50°C (122°F). The temperature within the computer case rose from 44°C (111.2°F) to 63°C (145.4°F), and the CPU temperature changed from 69°C (156.2°F) to 85°C (185°F).

It became possible to experimentally determine the threshold at which the Thermal Monitor starts to issue the PROCHOT# signal and the Thermal Control Circuit starts to slow the operation of the internal processor circuitry. For the Pentium 4 3.06 GHz processor being investigated, this was 72°C (161.6°F).

Increasing the CPU temperature 13°C (55.4°F) from this threshold resulted in a more than twofold performance drop. The frames per second in Unreal Tournament decreased from 115 to 49.

Unfortunately, a further increase of the temperature was impossible because of the limited temperature range of MIR-253: the maximum temperature that can be supported by this device is 50°C (122°F). Because of this, the CPU cooler fan had to be switched. As a result, the CPU temperature increased to 94°C (201.2°F) in less than a minute, and the computer was powered down. During this time, the speed measured by Unreal Tournament hardly changed. Therefore, it appears that decreasing performance 2.3 times is the maximum, at least for the used model of Pentium 4 3.06 GHz.

To perform an additional check of this hypothesis, an experiment was conducted using CPU RightMark 2 RC3. This test displays the CPU performance in real-time mode and allows its changes in the course of the test to be traced. Taking into account the relatively short time during which this test created a graph, the testing method was changed. To increase the temperature, the cooler fan was switched off. In such a case, the CPU temperature rises at a rapid rate. This allows data that serve as evidence of the performance decrease to be registered. Still, the CPU temperature increase is not sufficient to cause a system hangup.

The results of the conducted experiment are shown in Fig. 8.33. These results can be used to determine the limit at which the CPU speed can be controlled. In this case, the performance decreased 2.7 times.

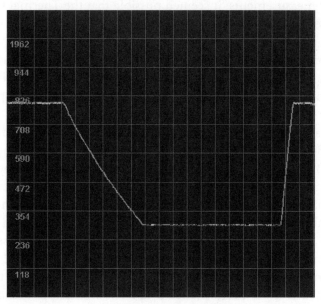

Fig. 8.33. Results of the CPU RightMark 2 RC3 test (Intel Pentium 4 3.06 GHz)

Based on the results of investigations of Thermal Monitor and Thermal Control Circuit operation, several conclusions can be drawn.

The protective tools implemented in Pentium 4 cannot retain CPU stability when the CPU cooler fan is switched off. However, they are capable of significantly widening the operating temperature range. At the same time, Pentium 4 prevents core overheating at the expense of an almost threefold performance drop.

As the testing results have shown, a 3°C increase in the CPU core temperature (from 72°C to 75°C) degraded performance 10% (for Pentium 4 3.06 GHz).

If cooling is inadequate, the operation of Pentium 4 can slow. Because of this, overclocked processors can be even slower than the ones running at nominal clock frequencies: The Thermal Control Circuit will always determine the ratio between performance and temperature independently of the reason that overheating occurred. Replacing the cooler with more powerful one or installing an additional fan into the computer case can solve the problem. However, to choose optimal cooling facilities, it is necessary to know both the thermal power of the CPU and the temperature threshold that activates the protection system.

This investigation relates only to Pentium 4 3.06 GHz. The parameters Thermal Monitor and Thermal Control Circuit of earlier Pentium 4 models are also interesting.

Investigating Earlier Pentium 4 Models

As previously mentioned, there are two thermal sensors in Pentium 4. The first sensor is an integral part of the Thermal Monitor circuit. It is installed at the hottest point of the core and is used by the Thermal Monitor to compare the CPU temperature to the threshold value at which the PROCHOT# signal is issued. This sensor is unavailable to hardware-monitoring programs, and it is impossible to read the values that it registers. The second sensor is also installed in the processor core; however, it is impossible to tell where it resides. The values measured by this sensor are available to the motherboard BIOS and hardware-monitoring programs. These sensors are installed separately. There is some distance between them, and it is possible to guess that the CPU temperature measured by them will be different. However, for the practical purposes, assume that in Pentium 4, they show the same temperature (i.e., the temperature displayed by the hardware-monitoring program corresponds to the temperature of the Thermal Monitor sensor).

Configuration of the Test System

- ❏ Processors — Intel Pentium 4 with clock frequencies of 1.6 GHz, 1.8 GHz, and 2.0 GHz
- ❏ Cooler — Standard cooler supplied with Pentium processors
- ❏ Motherboard — Asus P4PE
- ❏ Hard disk — IBM DTLA 15 GB, 7,200 rpm
- ❏ RAM — 256 MB PC2100
- ❏ Video adapter — GeForce4 MX440-8X
- ❏ Sound card — SoundBlaster Live! Value
- ❏ CD-ROM drive — CD-ROM 24X
- ❏ Case — InWin J-536
- ❏ Operating system — Windows XP Professional

The method of testing was similar to the one previously described and comprised two stages. In the first stage, the Unreal Tournament 2003 game and Fraps program were used for testing. In the second stage, during which the CPU performance was measured under conditions of quick heating, the CPU RightMark 2 RC3 test was used (the CPU overclocking module).

Fig. 8.34. Standard cooler supplied with Pentium processors

Intel Pentium 4 1.6 GHz

This processor is based on the Willamette core with 256 KB L2 cache memory operating at a frequency of 100 MHz, which ensures data transmission at a frequency of 400 MHz. The model under consideration was Stepping 2, Revision D0.

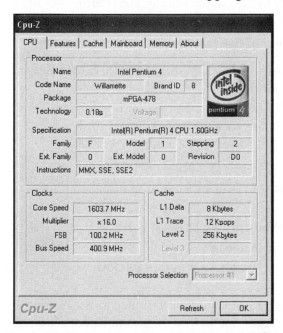

Fig. 8.35. Parameters of Intel Pentium 4 1.6 GHz

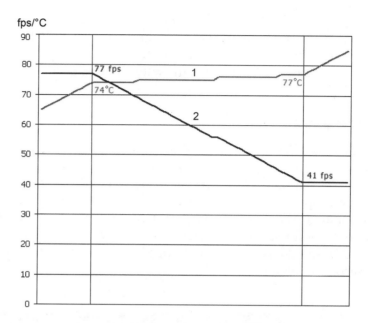

Fig. 8.36. Influence of the Thermal Monitor and the Thermal Control Circuit on the performance of Pentium 4 1.6 GHz (1 = CPU temperature, and 2 = speed shown by the Unreal Tournament test)

The temperature threshold that activated the Thermal Monitor and the Thermal Control Circuit was 74°C (165.2°F). Starting from this temperature, the performance of the CPU decreased. As can be seen from the results in Fig. 8.36, the temperature in this test grew to 77°C (170.6°F), and the performance dropped from 77 frames per second to 41 frames per second, or about 1.8 times.

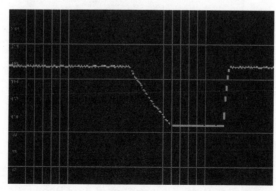

Fig. 8.37. Results of the CPU RightMark 2 RC3 test (Intel Pentium 4 1.6 GHz)

During the CPU RightMark 2 RC3 test, the CPU performance smoothly decreased 1.9 times as a result of the core heating. After the CPU cooler was powered up, the performance returned to its initial value.

The temperature threshold of the system power-down was 110°C (230°F).

Intel Pentium 4 1.8 GHz

This processor has the Northwood core with 512 KB of L2 cache memory operating at a clock frequency of 100 MHz, which ensures data transmission at 400 MHz and a core voltage of 1.5 V. The model under consideration was Stepping 4, Revision B0.

The temperature threshold that activated the Thermal Monitor and the Thermal Control Circuit was 68°C (154.4°F). At this temperature, the CPU performance started to decrease. In the course of this test, the temperature grew to 72°C (161.6°F), and the performance dropped from 87 frames per second to 38 frames per second, or about 2.28 times.

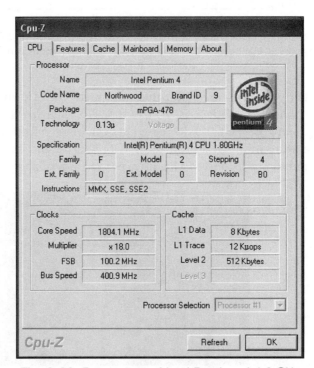

Fig. 8.38. Parameters of Intel Pentium 4 1.8 GHz

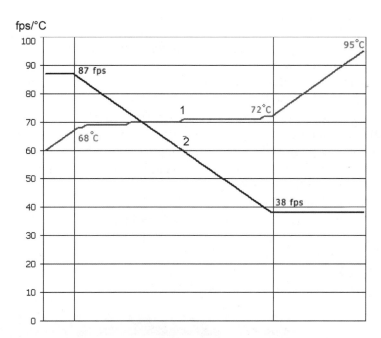

Fig. 8.39. Influence of the Thermal Monitor and the Thermal Control Circuit on the performance of Pentium 4 1.8 GHz (1 = CPU temperature, and 2 = speed shown in the Unreal Tournament test)

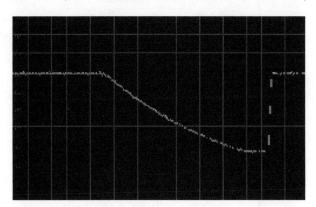

Fig. 8.40. Results of the CPU RightMark 2 RC3 test (Intel Pentium 4 1.8 GHz)

In the course of the CPU RightMark 2 RC3 test, the CPU performance smoothly decreased 2.7 times. After the cooler fan was turned on again, the CPU temperature decreased and performance returned to initial value.

The temperature threshold of the complete system power-down was 95°C (203°F).

Pentium 4 2.0 GHz

This processor is based on the Northwood core with 512 KB L2 cache operating at a 100 MHz clock frequency, which ensures data transmission at a frequency of 400 MHz. The core supply voltage is 1.5 V. The model being investigated was Stepping 7, Revision C1.

The temperature threshold that activated the Thermal Monitor and the Thermal Control Circuit was 73°C (163.4°F). Starting from this temperature, the processor performance decreased. During testing, the temperature grew to 77°C (170.6°F), and the performance decreased from 92 frames per second to 41 frames per second, or about 2.2 times.

In the course of testing using CPU RightMark 2 RC3, processor performance smoothly decreased 2.62 times due to heating. After the CPU cooler was powered up again, the performance returned to its initial value.

The temperature threshold at which the system powered down was 98°C (208.4°F).

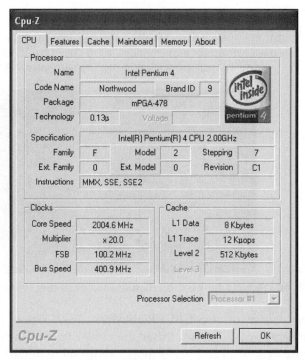

Fig. 8.41. Results of the CPU RightMark 2 RC3 test (Intel Pentium 4 2.0 GHz)

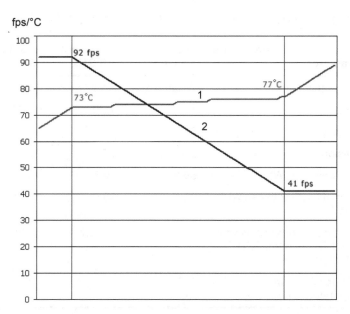

Fig. 8.42. Influence of the Thermal Monitor and the Thermal Control Circuit on the performance of Pentium 4 2.0 GHz (1 = CPU temperature, and 2 = speed shown in the Unreal Tournament test)

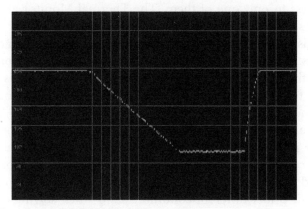

Fig. 8.43. Results of the CPU RightMark 2 RC3 test (Intel Pentium 4 2.0 GHz)

Summary Data

The main parameters of the Pentium 4 models used in these tests and of their built-in Thermal Monitor and Thermal Control Circuit temperature protection tools are provided in Table 8.15.

Table 8.15. Parameters and Test Results of the Processors

Parameter	Processor	Pentium 4 1.6 GHz	Pentium 4 1.8 GHz	Pentium 4 2.0 GHz	Pentium 4 3.06 GHz
Core architecture		Willamette	Northwood	Northwood	Northwood
Voltage (V)		1.75	1.50	1.50	1.60
Stepping		2	4	7	7
Revision		D0	B0	C1	C1
Heat emission (W)		60.8	49.6	54.3	81.8
Thermal Monitor threshold value (°C)		74	68	73	72
Performance drop shown by Unreal Tournament/CPU RightMark (times)		1.8/1.9	2.3/2.7	2.2/2.6	2.3/2.7
CPU power-down temperature (°C)		110	95	98	94

To conclude, it is necessary to mention once again that the CPU core has two built-in thermal sensors. The built-in motherboard hardware-monitoring tools have access to only one of them. The Thermal Monitor and the Thermal Control Circuit use information from the second sensor to control the processor performance. This sensor is located in the core area, for which high heat emission and temperatures are characteristic. These values strongly depend on the calculation intensity and the workload of the units located in this area. It is necessary to point out that the temperatures of the sensors can be different from each other and can change independently of the tasks being solved.

In the experiments described here, the threshold of temperature protection was based on readings of the hardware-monitoring sensor. The readings of this sensor may not coincide with the readings of the thermal protection sensor. Therefore, the threshold values for the temperature protection activation depend on the tasks being solved. Under different conditions, and when solving other tasks, these values can be different from the ones presented in Table 8.15.

Chapter 9

Software Tools for Cooling

Additional protection from overheating for the CPU can be ensured by specialized software aimed at controlling the processor workload and, consequently, heat generation.

Operation of contemporary high-performance components of PC hardware is characterized by intense heat generation. As a result, the operation of most hardware components is impossible without special tools that support optimal temperature modes. Such hardware components are numerous; they include contemporary high-performance processors whose thermal power exceeds 80 W. For future models, the level of thermal power is expected to exceed 100 W.

Ensuring optimal temperature modes is given mainly to traditional cooling devices, such as massive heatsinks and high-performance fans. Special software tools also can help prevent the CPU from overheating. Some of these tools can control the computational workload on the CPU, reducing heat generation.

Software coolers are a good example of such programs.

Working Principles of Software Coolers

Most software coolers issue special halt commands when the CPU is idle. An idle processor consumes less power, and thus, generates less heat. Similar functions are included in newer operating systems, such as Windows NT/2000/XP/Server 2003 and Linux. These operating systems perform the so-called halt cycle in low-priority tasks. During this cycle, the processor core temporarily stops; other subsystems continue to operate.

When the CPU is cooled by the traditional heatsink and fan, the temperature of its case drops. Because of this, software tools supporting these functions became known as software coolers.

As a rule, software coolers are most efficient under nonuniform processor workloads. Such a situation is created when the CPU executes tasks that require relatively long cycles of data transfer, which do not require the processor's participation. When the processor is loaded to the limit of its capabilities, software cooling based on the previously described principles becomes less efficient. In this case, traditional hardware solutions play the key role.

Still, some software coolers can dynamically increase their priority depending on the CPU temperature, improving their efficiency in Windows NT/2000/XP/Server 2003. In this case, idle clock cycles will increase, the temperature will decrease, and all other programs will slow.

Many tools that ensure the software cooling of processors were created for Windows 9x. This family of operating systems still retains its leading position in some areas. Table 9.1 gives data on the prevalent operating systems used by visitors to our Web site, accumulated during a fixed period.

Table 9.1. Evaluation of Prevalence among Windows Operating Systems

Operating system	Percentage of users (%)
Windows 98	39.1
Windows XP	33.5
Windows 2000	22.4
Windows NT	2.1
Windows 95	1.0
Windows ME	0.5

Examples of Software Coolers

For operating systems of the Windows 9x family, special software tools and drivers perform the functions of software cooling by temporarily halting the CPU. The list of such software is long; it includes such popular programs as CpuIdle, Rain, and Waterfall Pro. Using programs of this type, it is possible to achieve good results when overclocking processors, even if only standard cooling facilities are available. If additional cooling hardware is employed, the results will be even better.

Screenshots illustrating the operation of CpuIdle 5.6 are in Figs. 9.1 and 9.2.

Fig. 9.1. CpuIdle window

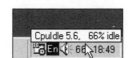

Fig. 9.2. CpuIdle at work

CpuIdle 5.6 supports the following types of processors:

❑ AMD — K5, K6, K6-2, K6-III, and Athlon (K7)

❑ Intel — Pentium, Pentium Pro, Pentium with MMX technology, Pentium II, Pentium III, and Celeron

❑ Via Technologies/Cyrix — Cx486S/S2/D/D2/DX/DX2/DX4, Cx5x86 (M1SC), Cx6x86 (M1), and Cx6x86MX (M2)

❑ IBM — BL486DX/DX2 (Blue Lightning), 5x86, and 6x86

❑ Texas Instruments — TI486DX2 and TI486DX4

❑ Other x86-compatible processors supported by the Windows family of operating systems (even if CpuIdle is unable to determine the processor type, it will run correctly and perform its functions adequately)

To evaluate the efficiency of CpuIdle as a tool intended for optimization of the CPU temperature mode, we performed a series of tests.

Testing CpuIdle

To test the processor in the overclocked mode, we performed a series of temperature measurements, both with CpuIdle and without this software cooler.

Configuration of the Test System

❏ Motherboard — Abit BE6-II (440BX chipset, Slot 1, May 2000 BIOS)
❏ Processor — Intel Pentium III 550E (Coppermine) (256 KB L2 cache operating at full core frequency, Slot 1, in box)
❏ Hard disk — IBM DPTA-372050 (20 GB, 2 MB cache, 7,200 rpm, Ultra DMA/66)
❏ RAM — 128 MB, PC133
❏ Video adapter — Asus AGP-V3800 TV (TNT2 video chipset, 32 MB SGRAM)
❏ CD-ROM drive — Asus CD-S400/A (40x)
❏ Operating system — Windows 98 with Ultra DMA/66 drivers installed

The system was overclocked to a 130 MHz processor-bus frequency with a 5.5x multiplier, making the CPU frequency 715 MHz ($130 \times 5.5 = 715$).

Test Results

The Motherboard Monitor 4.12 diagnostic program was selected for testing the CPU temperature. The processor temperature (Sensor 1) without software cooling was 37°C (99°F), which was 14°C (26°F) higher than the ambient temperature (Sensor 2) of 23°C (73°F) (Fig. 9.3). After CpuIdle was loaded, the processor temperature dropped to 25°C (77°F), which is only 2°C (4°F) above the ambient temperature (Fig. 9.4). Thus, CpuIdle performed software cooling of the processor and managed to decrease its temperature 12°C (22°F), sufficient even for extreme overclocking. The temperature decrease achieved programmatically depends on the processor workload: The lower the workload, the more efficient the software cooling.

It is necessary to point out that CpuIdle is not limited to providing software cooling of the processor. Sometimes it even optimizes its operation. Contemporary processors provide a set of extended functions that can help improve performance.

If these functions are not enabled, CpuIdle can activate them. To achieve this, set the **Optimize CPU features** checkbox (Fig. 9.5).

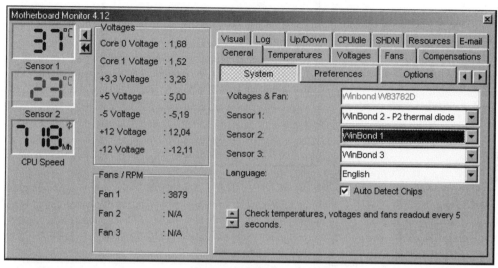

Fig. 9.3. CPU temperature in an overclocked system without software cooling

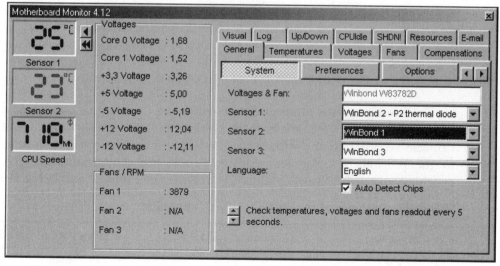

Fig. 9.4. CPU temperature in an overclocked system with software cooling

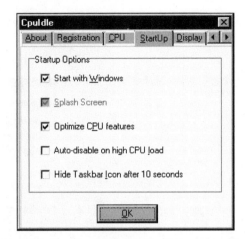

Fig. 9.5. Customizing the CpuIdle parameters

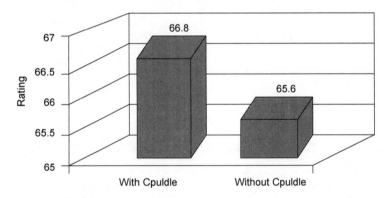

Fig. 9.6. Comparison of the CPUmark 99 test results

To investigate the optimization capabilities of CpuIdle, we conducted a series of tests using FPU WinMark from WinBench 99 v1.1 — both with the initialized CpuIdle 5.6 program and without it. Configuration of the test system was similar to the previous test for temperature monitoring. The results of testing the optimization capabilities of CpuIdle are presented in Table 9.2 and in Fig. 9.6.

Table 9.2. Analysis of the Optimization Capabilities of CpuIdle

Test program	Rating with CpuIdle	Rating without CpuIdle
CPUmark 99	66.8	65.6
FPU WinMark	3,850	3,850

Although the performance growth shown by CPUmark 99 when testing the optimization capabilities of CpuIdle is insignificant (less than 2%), it still exists. Because of this, it is possible to conclude that CpuIdle optimizes the operation of the CPU, as claimed in its description.

CpuIdle analyzes the processor workload and allows the user to evaluate these results (as shown in Fig. 9.2). It is possible to customize the output mode of the analysis results by choosing a digital or graphic CPU workload indicator on the taskbar, the refresh interval, and so on (Fig. 9.7).

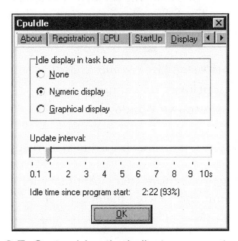

Fig. 9.7. Customizing the indicator parameters

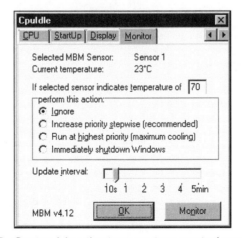

Fig. 9.8. Customizing the temperature control parameters

Cpuldle is also capable of controlling the CPU temperature. If this temperature exceeds the value specified by the PC user, Cpuldle can raise the temperature priority to cool the processor or even initiate the shutdown process. To use this functionality, it is necessary to have a system that supports CPU monitoring parameters (including the temperature). It also is necessary to install the Motherboard Monitor program. Fig. 9.8 illustrates the customization of Cpuldle capabilities for controlling the CPU temperature.

These settings allow the PC user to specify the threshold temperature. After reaching this value, Cpuldle will perform the appropriate action and activate the required functions. The following options are available:

❏ **Ignore**
❏ **Increase priority stepwise** (*recommended*)
❏ **Run at highest priority** (*maximum cooling*)
❏ **Immediately shutdown Windows**

Select the last option in this list if the system supports automatic power-down of the computer.

When solving problems related to optimal cooling of computer hardware components, we recommend viewing materials that can be downloaded from the Internet. (A list of Web addresses is provided in *Chapter 19.*)

Chapter 10

Choosing Cooling Devices and Parameters

To guarantee the reliability and stability of computer elements and subsystems in normal — and especially overclocked — modes, you must cool them properly. This can be achieved with heatsinks and fans.

(Based on materials from and with the permission of **http://www.fcenter.ru**, a Russian-language Web site.)

Cooling can be achieved in the following ways:

- ❏ Choosing and using an appropriate case
- ❏ Acquiring an effective heatsink
- ❏ Acquiring an effective cooling fan

For the architecture of modern computers, the best case is a standard ATX. Considering the intensive heat flux from elements used in overclocked modes, it makes sense to direct your attention toward mini ATX cases or even the larger midi ATXs, which guarantee better temperature conditions for all components of the system.

It's advisable to add a fan or fans to the case you select. This will lower the air temperature inside the case and improve the efficiency of all local cooling devices.

Beginning with 486DX2/66 processors, heatsinks have become an integral part of all processors. With the growth of CPU processing power, heat flux increases; thus, the heatsink size also has to be increased. Starting with Pentium processors, cooling fans have been mounted onto heatsinks. These devices are known simply as coolers.

In contemporary computers, most components must be cooled, including processors, video adapters, the chipset, and even the hard disk.

To improve the heat contact between the body of the element being cooled and the attached heatsink, it makes sense to buy and use special thermal grease, or *thermal tape*. These thermal compounds eliminate tiny air gaps that form between the body of the element and the heatsink attached to it. This improves heat transfer to the heatsink, providing more efficient cooling.

Heatsinks and Fans

Heatsinks allow you to guarantee the best temperature conditions for electronic components. Heatsinks intensify the heat exchange between cooled elements, such as the CPU or video chipset, and their environment. This occurs because the heatsink area is significantly larger than the area of the cooled element. The greater the heatsink surface area, the more intense the heat dissipation from the cooled element. Numerous technologies are used for heatsink manufacturing, and these affect the quality. Note that most high-quality heatsinks are not only effective, but expensive as well. Usually, these high-priced heatsinks are the best choices for a cooling system.

A heatsink must have good *thermal conductance* and *thermal resistance*. Thermal conductance determines the speed of heat propagation. For a heatsink, thermal conductance must be as high as possible, because the area of the cooled object is often several times smaller than the area of the heatsink base. If thermal conductance is low, the heat from the cooled object won't be distributed evenly over the volume of the heatsink, including all its fins. On the other hand, if the heatsink is manufactured from a material with high thermal conductance, the temperature will be the same throughout it. As a result, the heat will be dispersed with equal efficiency from the entire heatsink area. This means one part of the heatsink will never be very hot while another part remains cold (and, consequently, doesn't radiate heat into the ambient air).

As illustrated in Table 10.1, two materials are the most suitable for heatsink manufacturing: aluminum and copper. Aluminum is a good choice because of its low cost and high thermal conductance; copper also has high thermal conductance. Silver is too expensive to be used for heatsink manufacturing. Disregarding its relatively high price, this metal is best for manufacturing only heatsink bases because of its high thermal conductance.

Table 10.1. Thermal Properties of Materials

Material	Thermal conductance (W/m × K)	Specific heat (J/kg × K)	Density (g/cm³)
Aluminum	238.0	880	2.7
Copper	398.0	385	8.9
Gold	322.0	130	19.3
Lead	35.1	130	11.3
Nickel	90.1	460	8.9
Silver	418.7	235	10.5

Heatsinks are usually made from aluminum — an inexpensive material with high thermal conductance (Fig. 10.1). Copper is better, but much more expensive. Copper also weighs much more, which would increase the weight of the heatsink and complicate mounting.

Fig. 10.1. Heatsink for a processor

Dark objects radiate heat better than light ones. This is why the preferred heatsink color is black. Note that the black color is achieved through special technology, such as chemical treatment or applying special coating by means of sputtering. You couldn't just paint the heatsink black; paint is a heat insulator, rather than a conductor.

The most important characteristics of a heatsink are its *thermal conductance factor* and *thermal resistance factor*. Thermal resistance is a variable — the opposite of thermal conductance — that largely depends on the material from which the heatsink is made. Thermal resistance is measured in °C/W. Keep in mind that the value of this parameter is affected not only by the material of the heatsink, but also by its size, its form, the technology used, the quality of manufacturing, etc. Thermal resistance is the increase in the heatsink temperature relative to the temperature of its immediate surroundings when a cooled element, such as a processor, with a 1 W power capacity is dissipating heat. For example, with a thermal resistance of 2°C/W and dissipation from a processor that uses 15 W, the temperature will increase 30°C. The value of this parameter is usually between 0.5°C/W and 2°C/W. The design of the heatsink plays a key role, one more important than even its size. This is why bigger is not necessarily better.

The best cooling devices have a construction that consists of a heatsink and a fan. The fan is usually set over the heatsink, which is attached to the object to be cooled. The fan moves hot air from the heatsink while supplying it with cool air. (Fig. 10.2).

Fig. 10.2. Fan for a CPU cooler

There are several types of fans; the most common ones on CPU heatsinks are *sleeve-bearing fans* and *ball-bearing fans*. Fans with ball bearings are preferable, because sleeve bearings (also known as slide or plain bearings) generally are less reliable and make more noise. On average, fans that use ball bearings work twice as long as the ones that use sleeve bearings. Note that most popular fans labeled "ball bearing" actually have one ball bearing and one sleeve bearing. Most overclockers highly recommend buying purely ball-bearing fans, also known as *double ball-bearing coolers*. By using a double ball-bearing cooler, the service life of the fan is at least 1.5 times longer than the life estimated for a cooler that uses both types of bearings.

The life of a fan is usually two to three years. At least once a year, you should clean the dust that collects on the fan. The dust accumulates with time and may degrade the parameters of the cooling equipment significantly or even stop the fan completely. If the cooler fails, the cooled component (processor, video chip, etc.) also will fail soon because of overheating. To avoid processor overheating caused by a fan failure, modern hardware and software components including the processor, motherboard, BIOS, and system software provide a system of preventive defense against overheating. Such a system includes sensors that control both the temperature and the voltage. When buying hardware components, make sure that this function is present.

There are three basic performance parameters of the fan: *cubic feet per minute*, *linear feet per minute*, and *revolutions per minute*.

❏ The volumetric flow rate is measured in cubic feet per minute (cfm). It shows how many cubic feet of air the fan blows per minute. For most modern CPU fans, this parameter is between 10 cfm and 12 cfm.

❏ The linear flow rate of the air is measured in linear feet per minute (lfpm). Typical values are between 500 lfpm and 600 lfpm. Multiplying the lfpm value by the cross-section area of the airflow from the fan returns the cfm value.

❏ The fan speed is measured in revolutions per minute (rpm). Typical values for this parameter are between 4,000 rpm and 6,000 rpm.

The larger the value of each parameter, the higher the performance of the fan, and the better its performance as a cooling system element.

The dimensions of fans for modern processors are usually 50 × 50 × 10 mm.

The noise level, measured in decibels (dB), also characterizes the quality of the fan. A high noise level may irritate and annoy you. High-quality fans have a noise level of between 20 dB and 25 dB. (The lower the noise level, the better.) Sometimes, a high noise level is caused by the construction of the fan. Therefore, another sign of a high-quality fan is the absence of strong vibrations. If you feel the fan vibrating while you hold it in your hand, then the fan is not of a high quality, and you should look for a better one.

Usually, a cooling device consists of two parts: a heatsink and a fan, which work together as an efficient high-performance cooler. When selecting the best cooler, pay attention to the brand-name products of well-known manufacturers. In general, these products are highly reliable and have stable parameters. Examples of such coolers include the products from companies such as Intel, Titan, Thermaltake, Iwill, Asus, Sanyo, and AVC.

Fig. 10.3. Intel cooler recommended for Celeron 2 GHz

The Intel cooler shown in Fig. 10.3 is supplied with Intel Celeron 2 GHz processors in the box version. This cooler is optimal for these processors and can be used with them in both nominal and moderate overclocked modes (10%–20%). However, if you are using extreme overclocked modes, characterized by high frequencies and voltage levels, you should use either Intel coolers supplied with more powerful models or implement more intense cooling. Such cooler models include TTC-D2T, TTC-D3T, and TTC-D3TB from Titan, and Chrome Orb and Super Orb from Thermaltake.

Without covering the constructive details of popular coolers, we should point out that their parameters are similar. This is especially true for the products from Titan and Thermaltake. Tests have shown that the temperature modes of the processors supported by coolers from these vendors differ within a range of 3–5 degrees Celsius. Within between 50°C (122°F) and 60°C (140°F), this difference is insignificant. Other factors, such as cable layout (which influences air circulation within the system unit) and supplementary fan positions, frequently have a greater effect on the temperature modes of the processor.

Keep in mind that the processor is not the only component that requires intensive cooling. Intensive cooling often is required by the integrated circuits that form chipsets, by video adapters, and by certain types of memory chips. It is also strongly recommended that you cool high-performance, large-capacity hard drives; their operation is accompanied by considerable heat release, especially in overclocked modes.

Cooling Processors

For Intel and AMD processors, three main platforms have become the most common: Socket 370, Socket 478, and Socket 462 (Socket A). The number in the standard name specifies the number of contacts for each processor. These standards are not compatible; for example, Intel Pentium III complying with the Socket 370 standard can't be installed on a motherboard with any other socket. For each type of the processor, there are also specific standards for coolers.

Intel Pentium III, Intel Celeron (Coppermine and Tualatin) and VIA C3C are compatible with Socket 370 systems. AMD Duron and AMD Athlon based on the Thunderbird, Palomino, Thoroughbred, and Barton cores are oriented toward Socket A. Socket 370 and Socket A have the same dimensions. However, standards recommended by AMD to motherboard manufacturers are different from similar specifications created by Intel.

The Socket A slot has three special ledges at the front and rear sides for fastening the cooler. Initially, it was assumed that Athlon processors would be equipped with powerful coolers that would require a rigid fastening because a ledge might break under the cooler. Besides this, AMD recommended that motherboard manufacturers leave free zones to the right and left of the socket. These zones must not contain any elements that might create an obstacle for installing a rectangular cooler whose length exceeds 55 mm (the width of the CPU socket). Thus, a cooler with dimensions of 60×80 mm and a height limited only by the case size can be installed on AMD processors.

Most motherboards for Athlon and Duron have four holes around the socket. This provides another method of installing the cooler — fastened to the motherboard, rather than to the socket. On one hand, this method is more reliable. On the other hand, to replace the cooler or processor, it will be necessary to remove the motherboard.

Athlon processors generate intense heat even if they are not overclocked. Because of this, developers of coolers for contemporary processors actively use copper in their heatsinks. Some manufacturers, attempting to increase the cooler efficiency, coat the copper heatsink with nickel, silver, or another material with high thermal conductance. Fans installed on such coolers usually have dimensions of $60 \times 60 \times 25$ mm, although recently, larger models with lengths of 70 mm or 80 mm are becoming popular. Such coolers have a lower rotation speed and produce dramatically lower noise levels.

Coolers for Socket 370 processors are fastened using two socket clips. Usually, coolers have cross-section dimensions from 50×50 mm to 60×60 mm. As a rule, Intel Pentium III processors emit less heat than AMD Athlon processors; therefore, they are easier to cool. In most cases, coolers with heatsinks made entirely from aluminum can be used with Pentium III. Heatsinks with copper bases are rare, because aluminum or bimetallic heatsinks are far cheaper than ones made entirely from copper.

In computers based on Pentium 4 and Celeron, complying with the Socket 478 standard, the cooler is fastened to a special lever on the motherboard (Figs. 10.4–10.6). Power consumption of the Intel Pentium 4 2.8 GHz processor is about 64 W; for Intel Pentium 4 3.0 GHz, this parameter is about 80 W.

Fig. 10.4. Socket 478 slot and levers for fastening a cooler

Fig. 10.5. Cooler for a Pentium 4 3 GHz processor installed
on the levers on the motherboard

Fig. 10.6. Cooler for Pentium 4 3 GHz (underside view)

Coolers for Socket 478 Processors

Because CPU coolers ensure stability and reliability of operation for the entire
computer system, and often provide additional possibilities for overclocking, it is
necessary to choose the right cooler. The next few sections provide brief descrip-
tions of the most popular cooler models and the results of testing them.

GlacialTech Igloo 4200 and Igloo 4200 Pro

GlacialTech was founded relatively recently. Nevertheless, GlacialTech coolers for Pentium 4 or Celeron processors, complying with the Socket 478 standard, have become common. User reviews published on the Internet and in numerous print magazines indicate that GlacialTech manufactures high-quality coolers. Coolers such as Igloo 4200 and Igloo 4200 Pro are supplied in box versions. (These boxes are rather small and made of white cardboard.)

Fig. 10.7. Igloo 4200 cooler from GlacialTech

Igloo 4200 and Igloo 4200 Pro coolers have almost identical designs and differ only in the rotation speeds of their fans. Both coolers have 83 × 70 × 35 mm aluminum heatsinks manufactured with pressing technology. Each heatsink has 29 fins, 15 of which are 27 mm high and 14 of which have a height of 24 mm. Fins on the heatsink are alternated by the height; there is one low fin between every two high fins. GlacialTech engineers say that this helps distribute the air from the fan more efficiently (Fig. 10.7).

In Igloo coolers, the silver thermal compound is already applied to the base of the heatsink and covers a square area the size of a Pentium 4 processor complying with the Socket 478 standard. The procedures for installing or removing the cooler are straightforward.

The fan in an Igloo 4200 or Igloo 4200 Pro cooler is not placed in the center of the heatsink. Its developers argue that the fan center, which covers a so-called dead space, must not coincide with the position of the processor core. The reason is obvious: In the dead space below the fan center, there is practically no airflow. If the fan is offset from the CPU core, its propeller blades will be located directly above the core, and air will be directed to the part of heatsink located above the hottest spot on the CPU.

The fan used in Igloo 4200 is unusual; its dimensions are $60 \times 60 \times 20$ mm. Usually, fans with a surface area of 60×60 mm have a height of 10 mm or 25 mm. The fan is connected to the motherboard via a three-pin Molex connector. For fastening, rotor ball bearings are used.

In Igloo 4200, the nominal (stated by the manufacturer) rotation speed is 3,000 rpm, the performance is 13.3 cfm, and the noise level is 25 dB. Igloo 4200 Pro is faster (4,800 rpm), has higher performance (22.8 cfm), and is equipped with a noisier fan (35 dB). GlacialTech recommends both coolers for use with Pentium 4 processors running at the frequencies up to 2.4 GHz.

GlacialTech Igloo 4300

This model of the cooler (Fig. 10.8) is supplied as a retail box version, in a colorful box. Installation instructions and technical parameters of the product are included.

Igloo 4300 has the same heatsink as Igloo 4200, also prepared with the silver-based thermal compound. The fins of this heatsink also have different heights. The only difference of the 4300 model from the two previous ones is the fan: In Igloo 4300, the fan has dimensions of $70 \times 70 \times 15$ mm. Like the 4200 and 4200 Pro models, the 4300 model uses ball bearings to suspend the rotor. The nominal rotation speed is 5,000 rpm, and the fan has a performance of 30 cfm. The noise level of this model is 37 dB. Igloo 4300 is recommended for Pentium 4 processors running at 2.4 GHz or higher.

Fig. 10.8. Igloo 4300 cooler from GlacialTech

GlacialTech Diamond 4000

The Diamond 4000 cooler is similar to Igloo 4200. This cooler also is supplied in a small white cardboard box. In contrast to Igloo 4200, the technical parameters of the cooler are labeled on the box, along with some diagrams of its fan operation.

Diamond 4000 uses a fan with automatic temperature control (Fig. 10.9). This means that the rotation speed of the fan, its performance, and its noise level are not constant: They depend on the temperature of the ambient air at the point where the thermal sensor built into the fan is installed.

In the Diamond 4000 cooler, the thermal sensor is installed in the lower part of the fan. This sensor is constantly hit by air moving from the fan. The higher the temperature of this air, the faster the rotation speed. This approach to thermal control is not always correct: The air temperature below the fan is usually different from the CPU core temperature, which is the main parameter. Consequently, the fan rotation speed is often either insufficient or excessive. Besides this, the fan rotation speed strongly depends on the temperature of the ambient air within the computer case, the way its ventilation is organized, the dimensions of the system unit case, the amount of room within it, and the number of components installed on the computer.

The fan used in Diamond 4000 has dimensions of 60 × 60 × 20 mm. GlacialTech says that at an ambient air temperature below 25°C, its rotation speed will be approximately 2,700 rpm. This parameter will grow with the temperature and, at 40°C, it will reach 4,800 rpm. The noise level will change from 23 dB to 35 dB, and performance will increase from 12.4 cfm to 22.8 cfm.

Fig. 10.9. Diamond 4000 cooler from GlacialTech

The manufacturer recommends using Diamond 4000 with Pentium 4 processors running at the frequencies up to 3.06 GHz.

Titan TTC-W2T

Titan is one of the best-known manufacturers in the cooling device market. It produces coolers ranging from simple and cheap models to sophisticated and expensive ones.

The standard supply of the TTC-W2T cooler includes a syringe with silver thermal compound. Currently, Titan supplies this thermal compound with most of its products.

The aluminum heatsink, with dimensions of 70 × 70 × 40 mm, has fins of different heights, from 20 mm to 35 mm. The 2 outermost large fins have 11 small fins that are 6 mm high (Fig. 10.10).

Fig. 10.10. TTC-W2T cooler from Titan

The surface of the heatsink base is polished so that it shines like a mirror. This base is 12 mm wider than the heatsink. This left space to install two steel clamps for fastening the cooler to the motherboard.

The standard supply of TTC-W2T includes a fan with dimensions of 60 × 60 × 10 mm. The rotation speed is 4,500 rpm, nominal performance is 19 cfm, and the noise level is 31 dB. The fan is connected to the motherboard via a three-pin Molex connector. Slide bearings are used to suspend the rotor.

Titan TTC-W5TB

This cooler, also named "Silver Glacier," is one of the expensive models (Fig. 10.11). Titan positions it as a model for experienced users.

The cooler has an entirely aluminum heatsink with dimensions of $83 \times 67 \times 37$ mm. The fins are very thin, nearly flat, and have a smooth surface without scratches or imperfections. The heatsink base, like the rest of the surface, is smooth and mirror-like.

TTC-W5TB is equipped with a shiny fan whose dimensions are $70 \times 70 \times 25$ mm. The fan is suspended on one ball bearing and one slide bearing. Like the GlacialTech Diamond 4000, this cooler has automatic temperature control over the fan rotation speed. In contrast to GlacialTech cooler, the temperature sensor of TTC-W5TB is installed on the heatsink base. This allows a precise reaction to the CPU temperature. Depending on the temperature of the heatsink base, the rotation speed can change from 1,900 rpm at 35°C (with performance of 19.34 cfm and a noise level of 22 dB) to 3,320 rpm at 80°C (with performance of 33.8 cfm and a noise level of 28 dB). Titan recommends using TTC-W5TB with Pentium 4 processors running at the frequencies up to 2.66 GHz.

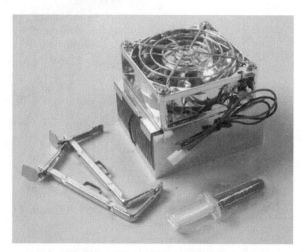

Fig. 10.11. TTC-W5TB cooler from Titan

Thermaltake Volcano 478 for Pentium 4

Thermaltake was one of the first companies to supply coolers for Socket 478 processors. One such model is the Volcano 478 cooler (Fig. 10.12). This model is positioned as a cheap cooler for Pentium 4.

This model employs an aluminum heatsink with dimensions of 70 × 70 × 45 mm and a base with the length of 85 mm. The heatsink is manufactured using the pressing technology. Its fins are relatively thick. The thickness of the base is 10 mm.

Volcano 478 employs Berguist 225U material as the heat-exchange interface. This material is a polymeric heat-conductive padding. When heated, this padding softens and fills all the gaps between the CPU core and the heatsink base. However, this heat-exchange interface is cheap, and experience has shown that no thermal padding can replace a high-quality thermal compound that includes silver particles. Because of this, to obtain better results, it is recommended that you replace this thermal padding with thermal paste.

This cooler is equipped with a 70 × 70 × 15 mm fan hanging from ball bearings. Its nominal power is 2.5 W, its rotation speed is 4,800 rpm, its performance is 30 cfm, and its noise level is 37 dB.

A noise level of 37 dB is rather high for a cooler intended for Pentium 4, especially because Thermaltake recommends using this model with processors running at the frequencies up to 2.0 GHz. Volcano 478 is a rather old model. Nevertheless, it is common and still available in computer stores.

Fig. 10.12. Volcano 478 cooler from Thermaltake

Thermaltake Dragon 478

Initially, Dragon 478 was an expensive and prestigious high-end model. Because of this, it is offered in a beautiful plastic box. Besides the cooler, the box contains an adapter for connecting the three-pin Molex connector of the fan to the four-pin

PC-Plug, a packet of thermal compound, and sticker with the Thermaltake logo intended for the CPU case. The first supplies of Dragon 478 also included a three-position rotation speed controller. Today this component is often missing.

The cooler has an oval heatsink with the fins positioned at an angle to the airflow, as in the Golden Orb series (Fig. 10.13).

The heatsink of Dragon 478 has dimensions of $80 \times 67 \times 35$ mm and comprises a copper base and aluminum fins. The fins of the cooler branch off radially from the base. The upper part of the base has a needle-shaped form that represents a small copper heatsink. The only drawback of this form is its location: under the fan center and, therefore, not hit by direct airflow.

The fan of the Dragon 478 cooler has dimensions of $70 \times 70 \times 25$ mm. Its power is 8.4 W, its rotation speed is 6,000 rpm., its performance is 49.4 cfm, and its noise level is 43 dB. Because of its high power, it is dangerous to install this cooler on some motherboards; the poser elements might fail at such a high workload. Because of this, Thermaltake engineers have equipped the fan with two Molex connectors. One of them (the one with two wires) supplies power to the electric motor of the fan; the second one (with one wire) is connected to the CPU-Fan slot on the motherboard and passes to the motherboard information on the fan rotation speed. Thus, the fan can be connected to the computer's power supply unit via the PC-Plug-Molex adapter, supplied with the cooler, and it will continue to inform the motherboard of the fan rotation speed.

Because of the powerful fan, Thermaltake recommends Dragon 478 for use with Pentium 4 processors running at frequencies up to 3.06 GHz.

Fig. 10.13. Dragon 478 cooler from Thermaltake

Testing

The main characteristics of the previously described coolers are summarized in Table 10.2.

Table 10.2. Parameters of Coolers for Socket 478 Processors

Cooler	Heatsink dimensions (mm)	Fan dimensions (mm)	Rotation speed (rpm)	Airflow (cfm)	Noise level (dB)	Price ($)
Igloo 4200	83 × 70 × 35	60 × 60 × 20	3,000	13.3	25	8.50
Igloo 4200 Pro	83 × 70 × 35	60 × 60 × 20	4,800	22.8	35	10.00
Igloo 4300	83 × 70 × 35	70 × 70 × 15	4,800	30.0	37	13.00
Diamond 4000	83 × 70 × 35	60 × 60 × 20	2,700–4,800	12.4–28.0	23–35	17.00
TTC-W2T	70 × 70 × 40	60 × 60 × 10	4,500	19.0	31	8.50
TTC-W5TB	83 × 67 × 37	70 × 70 × 25	1,900–3,320	19.3–33.8	22–28	10.00
Volcano 478	70 × 70 × 45	70 × 70 × 15	4,800	30.0	37	8.50
Dragon 478	80 × 67 × 35	70 × 70 × 25	6,000	49.4	43	18.50

The Abit IT7-MAX2 motherboard, based on the Intel 845E chipset, and the Intel Pentium 4 2.8 GHz processor, based on the Northwood core, were used in the course of testing. The processor operated at a nominal voltage of 1.5 V. The temperature and fan rotation speed were taken using Winbond Hardware Doctor 2.70. The air temperature was 23°C (73°F).

The coolers were tested in two stages.

In the first stage, the Windows XP operating system was booted, and the Winbond Hardware Doctor was started. The computer remained idle for 30 minutes, after which temperature readings were taken.

In the second stage, the Burn-in module of the SiSoftware Sandra 2002 test was started under Windows XP. This module constantly started the CPU Multimedia Benchmark test. After 60 cycles of the test, the CPU temperature was registered. At this stage, the maximum workload temperature was taken.

For comparison, the standard Intel cooler was used, which is supplied with all retail versions of Intel processors. In Fig. 10.14, its parameters are labeled Intel Stock Cooler. For the fans with temperature control over fan rotation speed, the maximum rotation speed achieved during the test also was registered.

When testing different coolers, temperature measurements within the case were performed. This task was accomplished using the built-in thermal sensor on the motherboard. This temperature is also shown in Fig. 10.14.

The lowest temperatures were achieved by the GlacialTech coolers, and absolute winner in this category is Igloo 4300. The worst maximum workload temperatures occurred with Titan coolers. When using these models, the CPU temperature reached 67.5°C (153.5°F).

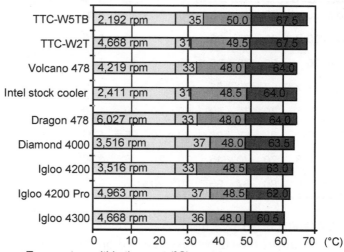

Fig. 10.14. Results of testing coolers for Socket 478 processors

Besides the performance, some other cooler properties were evaluated, including noise level and the convenience of installation and removal. Each parameter was rated subjectively on a scale of 0 to 5 (where 5 is ideal). The final ratings of the tested devices are summarized in Table 10.3.

Table 10.3. Ratings of the Tested Coolers

Cooler	Appearance	Convenience of installation	Convenience of removal	Supply	Noise level	Total rating
TTC-W5TB	5	3	4	4	5	**4.2**
Igloo 4200	4	4	5	2	5	**4.0**

continues

Table 10.3 Continued

Cooler	Appearance	Convenience of installation	Convenience of removal	Supply	Noise level	Total rating
Diamond 4000	4	4	5	2	5	**4.0**
Igloo 4200 Pro	4	4	5	2	4	**3.8**
Igloo 4300	4	4	5	2	3	**3.6**
Dragon 478	5	3	1	5	0	**2.8**
TTC-W2T	3	2	2	3	3	**2.6**
Volcano 478	2	3	3	1	4	**2.6**

Coolers for Socket A Processors

As previously described, computers oriented toward AMD Socket A processors have become popular.

Fanner Speeze 5R266B1H3 (EagleStream)

Fanner, whose main fields of activity are developing, manufacturing, and selling computer coolers, has two departments. Spire is related to expensive and high-quality products; Speeze is dedicated to cheaper models.

The differences between Spire and Speeze models often are minimal. Frequently, the same cooler model has two modifications: with a fan on ball bearings, or with a fan on slide bearings. The first modification is supplied under the Spire trademark; the second one is available under the Speeze trademark.

The 5R266B1H3 cooler supplied by Speeze is also known as EagleStream.

This cooler is supplied in large plastic pack, which also contains an installation manual in nine languages. On the back of the box are photographs illustrating the installation process. The box says this cooler corresponds to the ISO 9002 standards. However, this cooler is not in the lists of coolers that AMD recommends for Athlon XP or Duron.

The cooler comprises an aluminum heatsink with dimensions of $60 \times 70 \times 45$ mm. Its 27 fins are relatively thin, approximately 1 mm (Fig. 10.15). The base of the heatsink has a width of 10 mm.

On the top of the heatsink a plastic frame is installed to which the fan ($60 \times 60 \times 10$ mm) is mounted. The fan has 11 propeller blades. This fan has a nominal power of 3.36 W. Despite this high wattage, the fan rotation speed is quite low and does not exceed 4,800 rpm. The performance of the fan is 22.1 cfm, and the noise level is 30 dB. This fan has two ball bearings for suspending the rotor. It uses a standard connection to the motherboard — via a three-pin Molex connector. From above, the propeller is protected by a grid. The presence of a protective grid on the fan is one of the ISO 9002 standard requirements.

The EagleStream cooler has a steel fastening clamp that hitches all six ledges of the processor socket. The cooler is recommended for Athlon processors operating at speeds up to 1,400 MHz and for Athlon XP processors up to 2800+.

Fig. 10.15. Speeze 5R266B1H3 (EagleStream) cooler from Fanner

EverCool ND18-715CA

This cooler is supplied in a plain cardboard box, which also contains a pack with thermal compound.

The ND18-715CA cooler has an aluminum heatsink. The heatsink base has the same dimensions as the processor slot. The heatsink widens from bottom to top, increasing its surface area and providing the capability of installing a small fan on its top (Fig. 10.16).

The heatsink has fins of different height. The fins are rather thin — less than 1 mm. From the inner side, the heatsink base has a bulging shape, and its thickness reaches 12 mm. When considering trapezoidal heatsinks, it makes sense to use terms such as "maximum size" and to measure dimensions at the upper part of the heatsink, where values are the largest. For the cooler under consideration, the maximum heatsink dimensions are 70 × 80 × 43 mm.

A 48 × 50 mm copper plate is mounted onto the heatsink base. This plate, in contrast to the copper cylinder of the EagleStream cooler, almost completely covers the surface of the aluminum heatsink base. Consequently, it distributes and dissipates the heat emitted by the processor core better than a cylinder. Interestingly, the surface of this copper plate is not polished like those of most other EverCool coolers.

A fan with dimensions of 70 × 70 × 15 mm is installed on top of the ND18-715CA heatsink. The nominal power of this fan is 2.16 W; the nominal rotation speed is 3,500 rpm. The fan performance is 27.96 cfm; the noise level is 28 dB. According to the cooler marking ("S" stands for slide bearings) the cooler uses slide bearings for the rotor.

Newer EverCool models for Athlon XP and Duron processors use a steel clamp to fasten the cooler, which is clutched at all six clips on the socket. This design securely fastens the cooler. The ND18-715CA cooler is recommended by the manufacturer for all Pentium III and Celeron processors complying with the Socket 370 standard, as well as for all Duron and Athlon XP processors up to 2800+.

Fig. 10.16. ND18-715CA cooler from EverCool

Neng Tyi KN02

The KN02 model is intended exclusively for cooling AMD processors complying with the Socket A standard (Fig. 10.17). This cooler is supplied in a white cardboard box without any labels or markings.

The box doesn't contain an installation manual. Besides the cooler, the box contains a small syringe with thermal compound. The thermal compound has a gold tinge. This is a special thermal paste, which is 5% silver and 10% copper.

Fig. 10.17. KN02 cooler from Neng Tyi

The heatsink in this cooler has dimensions of 62.5 × 80 × 35 mm. The heatsink has 26 flat fins mounted onto the base. The manufacturer says the fins are made from material that is 99.95% aluminum; this means that they do not contain replenishers or admixtures. In contrast to many heatsinks of similar design, the fin height is inconsistent. At the edges of the heatsink, the fins have the same height; as they near the center, the fin height decreases, then increases again at the center, below the fan motor (Fig. 10.18). As a result, there is free space below the fan propeller. This extra space makes it possible to preserve the high speed of airflow at the fan outlet and to decrease the noise level.

Fig. 10.18. KN02 heatsink from Neng Tyi

The heatsink base is made of copper and coated with nickel. Generally, nickel has lower thermal conductance than copper. Therefore, at first, it doesn't make any sense to cover copper with nickel. Nevertheless, this coating is thin, and it prevents surface corrosion of the copper base.

On top of the heatsink of the KN02 cooler, a Y.S. Tech fan is installed. The fan's dimensions are $60 \times 60 \times 25$ mm, its nominal power is 2.16 W, its rotation speed is 4,200 rpm, its performance is 26.1 cfm, and its noise level is 35 dB. Ball bearings are used to suspend the rotor. Fans manufactured by Y.S. Tech are considered to be among the best. Because of this, they are used in expensive coolers. Y.S. Tech claims a high value of the Mean Time Before Failure (MTBF) parameter — about 75,000 hours. For fans with two ball bearings, this value usually is 50,000 hours.

The KN02 cooler is installed on top of the processor socket and fastened with a steel clamp against all six special-purpose clips. The clamp has a small clip that allows you to install or remove the cooler without using a screwdriver. If manual installation is inconvenient, the clamp has special catches for installing the cooler using a screwdriver.

The KN02 cooler is recommended by the manufacturer for the entire line of Duron processors and for Athlon XP up to 2800+.

ElanVital FSCUG9C-6FC

ElanVital is the member of the Asus Group. It specializes in manufacturing computer cases, power units, and coolers. ElanVital coolers are often labeled and sold under the Asus trademark.

The ElanVital FSCUG9C-6FC cooler is supplied in a small cardboard box, which doesn't contain anything in addition to the cooler — not even an installation manual. The box only has a graph of the dependence between the cooler noise level and CPU temperature painted on it. The FSCUG9C-6FC model has a fan with automatic regulation of its rotation speed, depending on the temperature measured by the built-in thermal sensor (Fig. 10.19).

Fig. 10.19. FSCUG9C-6FC cooler from ElanVital

The design of FSCUG9C-6FC is rather original. The heatsink in particular is distinguished by its unusual design. It comprises a copper base to which fins are glued, which are formed by two folded aluminum plates. The fins are attached to the base using a heat-conducting glue. The usage of glue is a drawback; if contact between the fins and the heatsink base is poor, the heat won't be transmitted effectively to the fins, and cooler efficiency will decrease. Besides this, when using thermal glue, the quality of heat contact between the fins and the heatsink base will be different for different production lots. Therefore, coolers of the same model but from different production lots will have different efficiencies.

The heatsink base in this model is not flat, in contrast to Socket A coolers from other manufacturers. The FSCUG9C-6FC base has a protruding area in the center. The cooler has contact only with the processor core and doesn't adjoin damper pads at the surface of Athlon, Athlon XP, or Duron. As a result, when installing this cooler, there is a danger of damaging the processor core. Such a cooler hardly will be recommended by AMD. Surprisingly, ElanVital, which has considerable experience designing and manufacturing coolers, has recommended this model for AMD processors.

The FSCUG9C-6FC model uses a thermal plastic lining as a thermal interface. It is expedient to replace this thermal lining with a layer of thermal compound.

On this cooler, a fan with dimensions of $60 \times 60 \times 10$ mm and a nominal power of 3 W is installed. Although the cooler can control the fan rotation speed, the fan has no full-featured temperature regulator. It is connected by a normal three-pin Molex connector to a small control unit mounted on the side wall of the heatsink. The frequency changes within relatively narrow range, from 3,200 rpm to 4,800 rpm. Accordingly, the noise level changes from 29 dB to 36.5 dB.

Fastening of the FSCUG9C-6FC cooler is inherited from earlier models intended for Socket 370 processors. The steel clamp of the fastening clutches only two clips of the processor slot.

ElanVital recommends the FSCUG9C-6FC model for cooling Pentium III, Celeron, Athlon, and Duron processors with the frequencies up to 1,500 MHz.

Testing

The main characteristics of the previously described Socket A coolers are summarized in Table 10.4.

Table 10.4. Parameters of Coolers for Socket A Processors

Cooler	Heatsink dimensions (mm)	Fan dimensions (mm)	Rotation speed (rpm)	Airflow (cfm)	Noise level (dB)
Speeze 5R266B1H3	$60 \times 70 \times 45$	$60 \times 60 \times 15$	4,800	22.10	30.0
EverCool ND18-715CA	$70 \times 80 \times 43$	$70 \times 70 \times 15$	3,500	27.96	28.0
Neng Tyi KN02	$62.5 \times 80 \times 35$	$60 \times 60 \times 25$	4,200	26.10	35.0
ElanVital FSCUG9C-6FC	$66.6 \times 58 \times 40$	$60 \times 60 \times 10$	3,200–4,800	14.20–21.20	29.0–36.5

The configuration of the system used for testing these coolers is as follows:

❏ Processor — AMD Athlon XP 2200+ (Thoroughbred)
❏ Motherboard — Epox 8K9A (VIA KT400)
❏ Hard disk — IBM DTLA 15 GB, 7,200 rpm

❏ Video adapter — Albatron GeForce4 MX440-8x, 32 MB
❏ Sound card — SoundBlaster Live! Value
❏ CD-ROM drive –– CD-ROM 24X
❏ Case — InWin-J535
❏ Operating system — Windows XP Professional

The values of the temperature and the fan rotation speed were obtained using Motherboard Monitor 5.20.

The temperature of the ambient air during testing was 21°C (70°F).

The standard thermal interface was removed from all tested coolers, and the Thermaltake thermal paste was used instead of it.

After booting the operating system, the computer remained idle for 10 minutes. During this time, the temperature within the case became stable. After that, the Burn-In Wizard of the SiSoftware Sandra 2003 ran for 10 minutes. This module ensured 100% workload for the processor. After accomplishing the test, the temperature was monitored for 10 minutes while the system cooled, returning to the stable temperature mode within the system unit case.

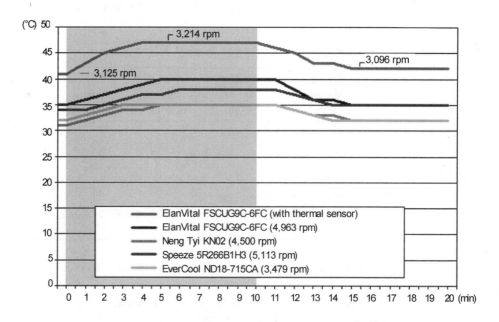

Fig. 10.20. Results of testing coolers for Socket A processors

The ElanVital FSCUG9C-6FC cooler was tested in two modes: with temperature control (standard mode) and without temperature control.

As can be seen from Fig. 10.20, the worst results were shown by the ElanVital cooler. However, it is still possible to improve its efficiency by disabling the thermal control over the fan rotation speed. The best results were shown by Neng Tyi KN02, although this cooler, during the final 10 minutes of the test, was unable to decrease the CPU temperature to the value that it had before Burn-In was started.

Cooling Motherboards

Usually, only one component of a motherboard may become overheated — the North Bridge of the chipset. This element of the chipset is responsible for the operation of the processor, AGP, and memory buses, as well as for connection with the South Bridge. Besides this, the North Bridge performs several other important functions. As a result, it emits large amounts of heat and needs to be cooled.

Motherboards are sold ready to use, with appropriate coolers already installed on the North Bridge chips (Figs. 10.21 and 10.22). As a rule, cooling devices consist only of heatsinks. Sometimes, however, fully functional air coolers equipped with both heatsinks and fans are used. On most motherboards, coolers are glued tightly to the chips. Consequently, it is difficult to dismount and replace them if they fail. However, if you do remove the standard chipset cooler from the motherboard, you can easily find another cooler for the system chipset.

Fig. 10.21. Heatsink installed on an Intel 875 chipset

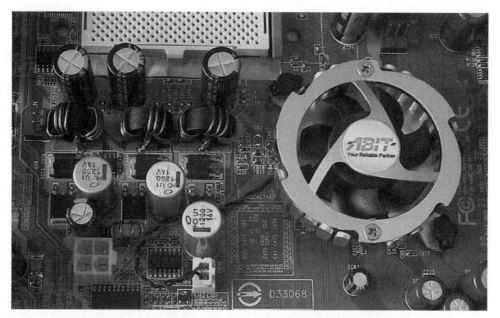

Fig. 10.22. Cooler, with a fan, installed on the North Bridge

Several manufacturers, such as Thermaltake and Titan, provide production-run coolers for chipsets. These cooling devices can be used both with motherboards and with video adapters. As a rule, these cooling devices include fans. They are powered from 12 V sources via three-pin Molex connectors. Thermaltake's devices, known as Blue Orb or Crystal Orb, also can be used to cool any chipset. Usually, the standard supply of these coolers includes a double-sided sticker that can be used to install the cooler on any surface.

Note that in most cases, the standard cooler installed by the motherboard manufacturer is sufficient. The only exceptions are those on cheap motherboards.

Cooling Video Adapters

Numerous video adapters are currently on the market — from expensive adapters for modern video games to relatively cheap ones for office workstations, which can handle only the simplest tasks.

The facilities used to cool video adapters change with the adapter's price.

In practice, an efficient cooler for a video adapter can cost about $10. Most manufacturers won't install such a cooler on a simple, low-end device, because it will increase the adapter cost rather considerably. Therefore, cheap video adapters often are equipped with the simplest cooling devices, usually standard heatsinks. Sometimes, however, even budget products are equipped with cheap coolers comprising a heatsink and low-power fan (Fig. 10.23).

When the power of a standard cooling device is insufficient, it is possible to replace it. However, replacement of a standard cooler installed on a video adapter is expedient only if you plan to overclock the adapter.

Fig. 10.23. Cooler installed on a video adapter

Fig. 10.24. Video adapter equipped with the OTES cooling system

Manufacturers often provide a significant reserve in the cooling system installed on the video adapter; they regularly install large heatsinks and powerful fans. Sometimes, even the adapters that are already overclocked might be encountered. The Abit Siluro OTES adapter is a good example (Fig. 10.24).

Cooling Hard Disks

Not all hard disks require cooling. This includes drives with a spindle rotation speed of 5,400 rpm. Disk drives intended for the home or office rarely require cooling.

Nevertheless, there are many high-performance disk drives available. These drives include models with a rotation speed ranging from 7,200 rpm to 15,000 rpm. They often include a large amount of cache memory and high-performance chips in the built-in controller. The operation of these electronic components, combined with the operation of mechanical elements, causes intensive heat emission. As a result, high-performance hard disks frequently require appropriate cooling, especially if they are installed in compact computer cases.

The replacement life of the hard disk depends on its operating temperature. When the drive temperature rises above the limit specified by the hardware manufacturer, it is advisable to use specialized cooling devices. For example, the temperature limit for the IBM hard disks is 55°C (131°F).

Some computer cases, such as the Thermaltake Xaser, can ensure a constant flow of cool air around the hard disk. For sufficient air cooling, 80 mm fans are installed in the hard disk compartments of these cases that constantly blow cool air around the disks. Some cases have special compartments where additional fans can be installed when necessary. When air-cooling is not sufficient, it is possible to install an additional cooler for hard disks. Such devices are not hard to find.

There are several types of hard disk coolers. The first type includes coolers for the electronic components of a hard disk. These devices usually comprise only one fan. The fan is fastened below the disk and cools its controller. Such coolers rarely require additional room within the case. Because they direct the airflow toward the lower part of the hard disk drive, they can decrease the temperature not only of the chips, but also of the mechanical components of the disk. Unfortunately, the design of some cases doesn't provide the possibility of using such coolers.

The second type of cooling device of the second type is a heatsink fastened to the drive. They are used mainly to cool the hard drive case. Because the surface of the hard disk case is rarely flat, it can be difficult to fasten the heatsink to the disk. The general efficiency of such devices is far from perfect, because they usually adjoin only part of the disk case surface. Because of this, heatsinks for hard disk are used rarely as standalone coolers.

The third type includes devices that ensure ventilation for the entire hard disk. This device blows cool air around the entire disk case. Such coolers are stationary containers for hard disks. Disk is fastened within the container using screws, just as the disk is fastened within the case. The entire unit is placed into an available compartment of the 5-inch drive within the system unit case. Fans are installed on the front panels of such devices. These fans blow cool air from the room into the system unit. Depending on the modification, such coolers can have from one to three fans on the front side. Both the efficiency and the noise level depend on these fans. An example of such a cooler is shown in Fig. 10.25.

Fig. 10.25. HardCano 3 cooler for hard disks

Finally, the fourth type of device is a combined cooler. They can provide all combinations of the previously listed cooling facilities. They typically comprise heatsinks for cooling the disk case and fans for air-cooling. Such coolers take one 5-inch compartment in the case, and the hard disk is fastened within the device in a manner similar to that for the third type of coolers. The top surface of the disk being cooled adjoins the heatsink; cool air is supplied from the front and/or from below. Such coolers are the most efficient and, therefore, the most expensive.

Ventilation within the Case

The main task of ventilation in the computer case is decreasing the interior temperature. This is achieved by installing additional fans that ensure an additional flow of cool air into the computer case or that push hot air from it. Because the PC case is not hermetically sealed, the temperature within the case always will decrease as hot air flows out of the case and cool air flows in. For efficient ventilation of the computer case, the correct number and location of the fans must be chosen, and the direction of the airflows created by those fans must be calculated.

The most common additional system unit fans have dimensions of $80 \times 80 \times 25$ mm, although 90 mm or 60 mm fans can be encountered. As a rule, they lack brand names — for example, System Fan ATX 80mm. It is better to purchase retail versions, which will give the fan characteristics and will supply small ironware elements for fastening the cooler to the case, as well as a PC-Plug adapter (if the fan has Molex connector).

Recently, fans with automatic control of the rotation speed have become popular. In these fans, the rotation speed is based on the temperature of the ambient air. When the workload is low (as in the Sleep mode), the temperature of the air within the case is also low, and the fan rotates at the minimal speed. As the workload increases, the temperature within the case also rises, which increases the fan rotation speed. An example of such fan is the Thermaltake Smart Case Fan (Fig. 10.26). It has dimensions of $80 \times 80 \times 25$ mm, and the rotation speed, depending on the temperature, varies from 3,000 rpm to 5,000 rpm. The minimum rotation speed is achieved at 27°C (81°F); the maximum speed is reached at 47°C (117°F).

Fig. 10.26. System cooler from Thermaltake

Chapter 11

Problems with Using Thermoelectric Elements

Some tools and facilities ensure optimal temperature modes for semiconductor components whose operation is characterized by intensive heat emission (processors, video chips, etc.). These tools and facilities can employ special elements, such as Peltier modules. Sufficiently powerful modules support a temperature of protected components below the ambient temperature. However, the procedures for choosing and running such tools have specific features and often require the user to perform calculations.

The operation of high-performance electronic components, the architectural basis of a modern computer, releases a significant amount of heat, especially in overclocked modes. Efficient operation of such components requires adequate cooling that ensures the required temperature conditions. It is a common practice to use special cooling devices or coolers to ensure optimum temperature conditions. Generally, these coolers are based on traditional heatsinks and fans.

The reliability and performance of such cooling devices are improved constantly as technology advances, designs improve, and control facilities are implemented, including various sensors. This ensures the possibility of integrating such facilities with computer systems and providing diagnostic and control facilities for monitoring temperature conditions. This improves the reliability and prolongs the trouble-free operation of hardware components.

The parameters of traditional coolers also are improved continually. Other cooling devices, such as semiconductor Peltier coolers, recently appeared on the market. These new cooling devices quickly became popular.

Peltier coolers contain special semiconductor thermoelectric modules. Their operating principles are based on the Peltier effect, discovered in 1834. These cooling devices are impressive and have been successfully used in various branches of science and technology.

In the 1960s and 1970s, multiple attempts were made to implement small household refrigerators based on the Peltier effect. Unfortunately, an insufficient level of technology and relatively high prices did not allow such a device to be created, except in a few experimental instances.

Fortunately, the Peltier effect and thermoelectric modules were never reduced to an interesting but neglected topic of scientific research. As technology improved, it became possible to diminish most of the negative effects. As a result of these efforts, efficient and reliable semiconductor coolers appeared.

Currently, modules based on the Peltier effect are used to cool various electronic components of modern computers, such as processors.

The unique properties of Peltier modules can be used to cool computer components as required without encountering technical problems or making considerable financial investments. Peltier coolers are promising because they save space and are reliable, convenient, and very efficient.

The most promising semiconductor coolers are those used for overclocked systems, especially for ones operating in extremely overclocked modes. Extreme overclocking ensures a large gain in performance, but the temperature conditions of elements in such modes often are near the limits of modern hardware endurance.

Note that high-performance processors are not the only components whose operation is accompanied by significant heat release. Modern video adapters and sometimes memory modules also require a sufficient cooling, even in normal operating modes.

Peltier Modules

Peltier coolers are thermoelectric refrigerators based on the Peltier effect — a phenomenon named after French watchmaker and amateur physicist Jean C. A. Peltier (1785–1845).

Peltier made his discovery almost 170 years ago, in 1834. The idea behind this phenomenon was revealed several years later, in 1838, by German physicist Heinrich F. E. Lenz (1804–1865). While experimenting with an electric current flowing through the junction of two dissimilar conductors, Lenz placed a drop of water into a small cavity at the junction of two bars made of bismuth (Bi) and antimony (Sb). When the electric current flowed in one direction, the drop of water froze.

When the current flowed in the opposite direction, the frozen water melted. This experiment showed that when an electric current flows through the junction of two dissimilar conductors, that junction will either absorb or release heat, depending on the direction of the current flow. This phenomenon was named the Peltier effect.

This effect is the reverse of a discovery made in 1821 by German physicist Thomas J. Seebeck (1770–1831). This phenomenon takes place in a closed electric circuit consisting of dissimilar metals or semiconductors. If there is a temperature difference at the two junction points of dissimilar metals or semiconductors, voltage is induced in the circuit.

According to the well-known Joule's law, a conductor carrying a current generates heat proportional to the product of the resistance (R) of the conductor and the square of the current (I). Thus, Joule heat that evolves during a period of time (t) is calculated using the following formula:

$$Q_J = R \times I^2 \times t \qquad \text{(Formula 11.1)}$$

In contrast to Joule heat, Peltier heat is proportional to the current, and the direction of heat transfer is reversed if the current is reversed. Experiments have shown that Peltier heat can be expressed by the following formula:

$$Q_P = P \times q \qquad \text{(Formula 11.2)}$$

Here, q is the electric charge ($q = I \times t$), and P is the so-called Peltier factor, the value of which depends both on the properties of the dissimilar materials carrying the current and on their temperatures.

Peltier heat is positive if it is released; otherwise, it is negative.

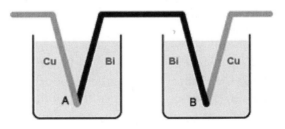

Fig. 11.1. Arrangement for measuring Peltier heat (Cu — copper, Bi — bismuth)

In the experiment conducted as shown in Fig. 11.1, the same Joule heat will be released in each calorimeter if both wires have the same resistance (Cu + Bi). This heat can be calculated using the following formula:

$$Q = R \times I^2 \times t \qquad \text{(Formula 11.3)}$$

Peltier heat, on the other hand, will be positive in one calorimeter and negative in the other. This experiment measured Peltier heat and derived the Peltier factor values for different pairs of conductors.

Note that the Peltier factor strongly depends on the temperature. Several Peltier factor values for different combinations of metals and alloys at different absolute temperatures (Kelvin scale, or °K) are provided in Table 11.1.

Table 11.1. Peltier Factors for Pairs of Conductors

Fe – constantan		Cu – Ni		Pb – constantan	
T(°K)	P(mV)	T(°K)	P(mV)	T(°K)	P(mV)
273	13.0	292	8.0	293	8.7
299	15.0	328	9.0	383	11.8
403	19.0	478	10.3	508	16.0
513	26.0	563	8.6	578	18.7
593	34.0	613	8.0	633	20.6
833	52.0	718	10.0	713	23.4

The Peltier factor, an important technical characteristic of materials, can be calculated using the Thomson coefficient, rather than having to be measured, as follows:

$$P = \alpha T \qquad \text{(Formula 11.4)}$$

Here, P is the Peltier factor, α is the Thomson coefficient, and T is the absolute temperature.

This discovery had a huge effect on subsequent developments in physics and, later, in engineering.

The idea of the effect is this: When an electric current flows through the junction of two dissimilar materials, besides Joule heat (which always is produced), additional heat known as Peltier heat is either produced or absorbed, depending the direction of the current or of the temperature gradient. The degree to which this effect is manifested largely depends on the chosen conductors and the electric modes used.

A classic theory explains the Peltier effect. Electrons, moved by the current from one conductor to another, speed up or slow because of the internal potential difference at the junction point. In the first scenario, the kinetic energy of the electrons increases and is subsequently released as heat. In the second situation, the kinetic energy of the electrons decreases, and this energy loss is compensated by heat absorption. The second material, as a result, will cool.

The Peltier effect, like other thermoelectric phenomena, most strongly manifests itself in semiconductor circuits, composed of n- and p-type semiconductors.

Consider the thermoelectric processes that take place at the contact of such semiconductors. Suppose that the electric field direction causes electrons in the n-semiconductor and holes in p-semiconductor to move toward one another. After passing through the boundary, an electron enters the p-semiconductor zone and takes the place of a hole. This recombination releases heat (Fig. 11.2).

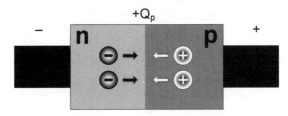

Fig. 11.2. Release of Peltier heat at the contact
of n- and p-type semiconductors

If the direction of the electric field is reversed, the electrons and holes will move in opposite directions. Holes moving from the boundary will increase in number because new pairs will be generated when electrons pass from the p-semiconductor to the n-semiconductor. The generation of such pairs consumes energy, and this energy loss is compensated by heat oscillations of the atomic lattice. Electrons and holes, generated as a result of appearing pairs, will be driven in opposite directions by the electric fields. Therefore, new pairs will continue to appear as long as there is a current through the contact. This will result in heat absorption (Fig. 11.3).

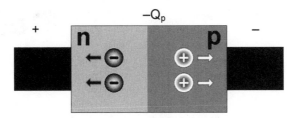

Fig. 11.3. Absorption of Peltier heat at the contact
of n- and p-type semiconductors

Thus, depending on the direction of the electric current through the contact of different types of semiconductors (p-n- and n-p-junctions), heat will be released or absorbed as electrons (n) and holes (p) interact and as new pairs of charges are recombined or generated. The usage of p- and n-semiconductors in thermoelectric refrigerators is illustrated in Fig. 11.4.

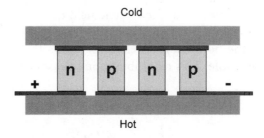

Fig. 11.4. Using p- and n-semiconductors in thermoelectric refrigerators

Joining large numbers of n- and p-semiconductor junctions creates cooling elements — Peltier modules of significant capacity. The structure of a semiconductor Peltier module is shown in Fig. 11.5.

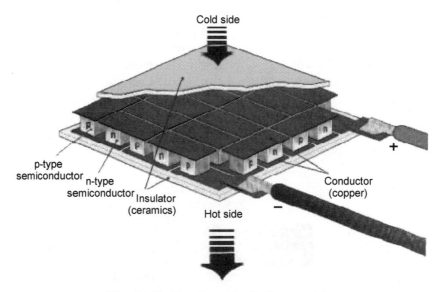

Fig. 11.5. Structure of a Peltier module

The Peltier module is a thermoelectric refrigerator that consists of coupled p- and n-type semiconductors, which constitute p-n- and n-p-junctions. Each junction has heat contact with one of two heatsinks. If an electric current of a certain polarity passes through the junction, the temperature between the heatsinks in the Peltier module will drop: One heatsink will work as a refrigerator, and the other will generate and remove the heat. When the cold side of the Peltier module is joined to the surface of the object being protected, this module acts as a heat pump. This heat pump moves the heat from this object to the hot side of the module, which is cooled by air or water. Like any heat pump, it can be described by thermodynamic formulas. Therefore, Peltier modules can be called not only thermoelectric, but also thermodynamic modules.

Fig. 11.6 shows an external view of a typical Peltier module.

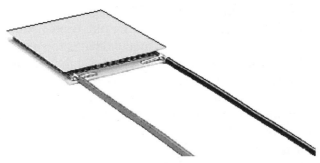

Fig. 11.6. External view of a typical Peltier module

In a typical module, temperature can differ tens of degrees. If the hot side is cooled adequately, the other side will reach negative Celsius temperatures. To increase the temperature difference, it is possible to cascade properly cooled Peltier modules. This method provides a simple, reliable, and inexpensive way of obtaining a temperature difference that will cool electronic components efficiently.

Fig. 11.7 shows an example of cascaded Peltier modules.

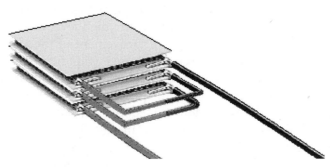

Fig. 11.7. Cascaded Peltier modules

A cooling component based on Peltier modules is often called an active Peltier cooler, or simply a Peltier cooler.

Peltier modules make coolers more efficient than standard coolers based on the traditional heatsink-and-fan combination. In the process of designing and running coolers that use Peltier modules, you must keep in mind certain traits. These features are the results of the modules' construction, the principles of their operation, the architecture of the hardware of a modern computer, and the functional capabilities of the system and application software.

A key role is played by the power of the Peltier module, which generally depends on its size. A weak module will not be able to guarantee the necessary level of cooling, which may lead to overheating and failure of a cooled electronic element, such as a processor. However, using a Peltier module that is too powerful may lower the temperature of the cooling heatsink to such a level that the moisture in the air condenses — a dangerous situation for electronic circuits. Water constantly formed by condensation may cause the electronic circuits of the computer to short-circuit. This is the time to recall that the distance between lead wires in modern circuit boards is often only a fraction of a millimeter.

Nevertheless, powerful Peltier modules in high-performance coolers and additional cooling systems allowed KryoTech and AMD, in a combined research project, to overclock AMD processors created with traditional technology beyond 1 GHz. They almost doubled the operating frequency. However, the given performance level was reached under conditions that ensured the stability and reliability of the processors working in overclocked modes. The result of such experimental overclocking was a performance record among 80x86 processors.

KryoTech is famous for more than its experiments related to extreme processor overclocking. Its facilities for cryogenic freezing of computer components also have become widely known. They have been equipped with appropriate electronic components and employed as platforms for many high-performance servers and workstations. Meanwhile, AMD confirmed the high level of its products and received experimental materials for further improvement of the architecture of its processors. Similar research has been conducted with Intel Celeron, Pentium II, and Pentium III processors and has increased performance significantly.

Note that Peltier modules, in the process of operating, give off a relatively large amount of heat. For this reason, you should not only have a powerful fan for your cooler, but also a means of lowering the temperature of the inside of the computer's case to avoid overheating the rest of the components. To do this, you should use additional fans in the construction of the case.

An external view of an active cooler that uses semiconductor Peltier modules is presented in Fig. 11.8.

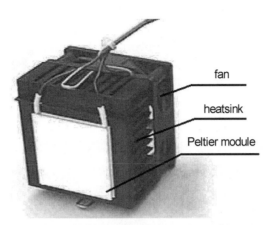

Fig. 11.8. External view of a cooler with a Peltier module

Examples of Peltier modules manufactured in lots are Osterm products (**http://www.osterm.ru**). They are distinguished by their maximum consumed current (Imax, in amperes), their maximum voltage (Umax, in volts), cooling power (Qcmax, in watts), the maximum temperature drop (dTmax, in kelvins) between the hot and cold sides measured in a vacuum without a workload, and their dimensions.

Table 11.2 lists the working parameters for some Peltier modules manufactured in lots.

Table 11.2. Peltier Modules from Osterm

Serial number	Imax (A)	Umax (V)	Qcmax (W)	dTmax (°K)	L × W × H (mm)
K1-127-1/0.8	6.0	15.4	50.0	71	30 × 30 × 3.1
K1-241-1/0.8	6.0	29.2	95.0	71	40 × 40 × 3.1
K1-127-1/1.3	3.9	15.4	33.4	73	30 × 30 × 3.6
K1-241-1/1.3	3.9	29.2	63.4	73	40 × 40 × 3.6
K1-127-1/1.5	3.0	15.4	27.0	73	30 × 30 × 3.8
K1-241-1/1.5	3.0	29.2	51.2	73	40 × 40 × 3.8
K1-71-1.4/1.1	8.5	8.6	41.9	71	30 × 30 × 3.8
K1-127-1.4/1.1	8.5	15.4	75.0	71	40 × 40 × 3.8
K1-71-1.4/1.5	6.0	8.6	30.0	73	30 × 30 × 3.9
K1-127-1.4/1.5	6.0	15.4	53.0	73	40 × 40 × 3.9
K1-127-2/1.5	13.0	15.5	120.0	73	55 × 55 × 4.6

Keep in mind that cooling systems based on Peltier modules are used not only in electronic systems, but also in computers. Similar modules are used to cool various high-precision devices. This primarily applies to experiment-based research in physics, chemistry, and biology.

Examples of several Peltier modules released by Osterm are shown in Figs. 11.9–11.13.

Fig. 11.9. Semiconductors of p- and n-types in a Peltier module

Fig. 11.10. Tiny Peltier module

Fig. 11.11. Shaped Peltier module

Fig. 11.12. Peltier module with one ceramic platter removed

Fig. 11.13. Cascaded Peltier module

Information on modules in Peltier coolers, including their features and the results of their usage, can be found on the Internet at Web addresses including:

❑ http://www.tomshardware.com
❑ http://rudteam.narod.ru/english/index.html
❑ http://www.kryotech.com
❑ http://www.melcor.com
❑ http://www.supercool.se
❑ http://www.computernerd.com

Features of Operation

Peltier modules, when used to cool electronic elements, have relatively high reliability. In contrast to refrigerators created using traditional technology, they do not have moving parts. To increase the efficiency of their operation, these modules can be cascaded. Cascading allows protected electronic components to cool below 0°C (32°F), even with significant power dissipation.

Besides the obvious advantages, Peltier modules have some specific properties that must be considered when using them in cooling equipment. Some of these properties have been mentioned, but to correctly use a Peltier module, you need to take a more detailed look at these characteristics. The following operating features are among the most important:

❑ Peltier modules release a large amount of heat in the course of operation. They require in the cooler heatsinks and fans capable of efficiently deflecting surplus heat from the cooling modules. Thermoelectric modules are noted for their relatively low efficiency coefficient; when they act as heat pumps, they are powerful sources of heat. Using these modules in cooling devices, intended to protect the electronic components of the computer, dramatically increases the temperature within the system unit. This sometimes requires additional cooling devices within the computer case. If you don't use additional cooling, the high temperatures complicate operating conditions — even for the modules. Note that using Peltier modules creates a relatively heavy extra load for the power supply to handle. Including the values of currents required by Peltier modules, the power supply unit installed on the computer must be 250 W. Therefore, it makes sense to choose an ATX motherboard and case with a powerful power supply unit. Doing so will simplify the task of organizing optimum temperature conditions and electric modes for the components of the computer.

❐ If a Peltier module fails, the cooled element is isolated from the heatsink of the cooler. This leads to a speedy breakdown of the stable temperature conditions of the element, quickly followed by a breakdown of the element itself from overheating. Because of this, it is wise to choose high-quality modules from well-known brands. Such modules are characterized by high reliability. Their mean time between failures (MTBF) often exceeds 1 million hours.

❐ The low temperatures produced by the operation of Peltier coolers can be too powerful and cause moisture from the air to condense. This is dangerous for electric components; water can short-circuit elements. To avoid such a danger, choose a Peltier cooler with the optimal power for your needs. Condensation depends on a few parameters; the most important are the temperature of the surrounding area (the air inside the case), the temperature of the object being cooled, and the humidity of the air. The warmer and the more humid the air inside the case, the greater the likelihood of condensation, and, thus, the greater chance that electronic elements of the computer will break down. Table 11.3 illustrates how the temperature at which moisture will condense depends on the amount of moisture in the air and the air temperature. Using this table, you can easily figure out whether or not there is a danger of condensation. For example, if the temperature inside the case is 25°C (77°F), and the humidity is 65%, then condensation of moisture on the cooled object will occur when its surface temperature drops below 18°C (64°F).

Table 11.3. Temperatures at Which Moisture Will Condense

Temperature (°C)	Humidity (%)													
	30	35	40	45	50	55	60	65	70	75	80	85	90	95
30	10.5	12.9	14.9	16.8	18.4	20.0	21.4	22.7	23.9	25.1	26.2	27.2	28.2	29.1
29	9.7	12.0	14.0	15.9	17.5	19.0	20.4	21.7	23.0	24.1	25.2	26.2	27.2	28.1
28	8.8	11.1	13.1	15.0	16.6	18.1	19.5	20.8	22.0	23.2	24.2	25.2	26.2	27.1
27	8.0	10.2	12.2	14.1	15.7	17.2	18.6	19.9	21.1	22.2	23.3	24.3	25.2	26.1
26	7.1	9.4	11.4	13.2	14.8	16.3	17.6	18.9	20.1	21.2	22.3	23.3	24.2	25.1
25	6.2	8.5	10.5	12.2	13.9	15.3	16.7	18.0	19.1	20.3	21.3	22.3	23.2	24.1
24	5.4	7.6	9.6	11.3	12.9	14.4	15.8	17.0	18.2	19.3	20.3	21.3	22.3	23.1

continues

Table 11.3 Continued

Temperature (°C)	Humidity (%)													
	30	35	40	45	50	55	60	65	70	75	80	85	90	95
23	4.5	6.7	8.7	10.4	12.0	13.5	14.8	16.1	17.2	18.3	19.4	20.3	21.3	22.2
22	3.6	5.9	7.8	9.5	11.1	12.5	13.9	15.1	16.3	17.4	18.4	19.4	20.3	21.2
21	2.8	5.0	6.9	8.6	10.2	11.6	12.9	14.2	15.3	16.4	17.4	18.4	19.3	20.2
20	1.9	4.1	6.0	7.7	9.3	10.7	12.0	13.2	14.4	15.4	16.4	17.4	18.3	19.2
19	1.0	3.2	5.1	6.8	8.3	9.8	11.1	12.3	13.4	14.5	15.5	16.4	17.3	18.2
18	0.2	2.3	4.2	5.9	7.4	8.8	10.1	11.3	12.5	13.5	14.5	15.4	16.3	17.2
17	−0.6	1.4	3.3	5.0	6.5	7.9	9.2	10.4	11.5	12.5	13.5	14.5	15.3	16.2
16	−1.4	0.5	2.4	4.1	5.6	7.0	8.2	9.4	10.5	11.6	12.6	13.5	14.4	15.2
15	−2.2	−0.3	1.5	3.2	4.7	6.1	7.3	8.5	9.6	10.6	11.6	12.5	13.4	14.2
14	−2.9	−1.0	0.6	2.3	3.7	5.1	6.4	7.5	8.6	9.6	10.6	11.5	12.4	13.2
13	−3.7	−1.9	−0.1	1.3	2.8	4.2	5.5	6.6	7.7	8.7	9.6	10.5	11.4	12.2
12	−4.5	−2.6	−1.0	0.4	1.9	3.2	4.5	5.7	6.7	7.7	8.7	9.6	10.4	11.2
11	−5.2	−3.4	−1.8	−0.4	1.0	2.3	3.5	4.7	5.8	6.7	7.7	8.6	9.4	10.2
10	−6.0	−4.2	−2.6	−1.2	0.1	1.4	2.6	3.7	4.8	5.8	6.7	7.6	8.4	9.2

Besides the features already mentioned, you must consider situations that use thermoelectric Peltier modules to cool high-performance CPUs in powerful computers.

The efficiency of Peltier module usage depends on the model and its operating modes. Choosing a nonoptimal model and setting incorrect operating modes can lead to dangerous situations, because such choices do not ensure the required operating conditions for the cooled components. They can even result in the failure of the components to be protected. The optimal choice of a Peltier module is not a trivial task.

Fig. 11.14 illustrates one of the calculation methods used to select a Peltier modules. (This graph is published with the permission of Osterm.) The graph shows the thermoelectric characteristics of a Peltier modules manufactured in lots. The measurements are as follows:

❏ Th (Th) — Temperature of the hot side of the Peltier module (in kelvins)
❏ Imax (I) — Maximum allowed current (in amperes)

❏ dTmax (*dT*) — Maximum temperature difference between the hot and cold sides of the Peltier module, measured in a vacuum without a workload (in kelvins)

❏ Umax (*U*) — Maximum allowed voltage (in volts)

❏ Qcmax (*Qc*) — Maximum cooling power (in watts)

❏ RdTm — Module resistance to the alternate current (in ohms)

The values of these parameters of the Peltier module depend on the temperature of its hot side. They are different from the values specified in documentation, where all characteristics are provided for a temperature of 300°K (27°C).

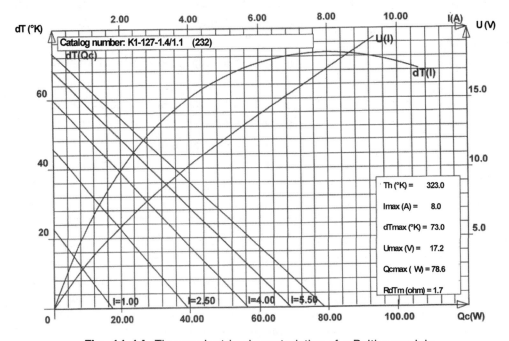

Fig. 11.14. Thermoelectric characteristics of a Peltier module

Performing calculations based on this graph implies the following:

1. Using the *U(I)* graph, for the selected *U* voltage, determine the *I* current that flows through the Peltier module. The value of the *I* current must fit within the range of the ascending part of the *dT(I)* curve.

2. For the value of the I current, choose characteristic using the curves that determine the dependence of dT on Qc (in the lower left part of the graph).

3. With the known values of Th and dT, determine the temperature of the cold side of the Peltier module (Tc), calculated according to the following formula:

$$dT = Th - Tc \qquad \text{(Formula 11.5)}$$

Here, Tc is the temperature of the cold side of the module, Th is the temperature of the hot side of the module, and dT is the temperature difference.

From the graphs of the functions illustrating the dependence of dT on Qc, it is obvious that as the thermal power (Qc) of the cooled element increases, the temperature drop between the hot (Th) and cold (Tc) sides of the Peltier module decreases. (See Formula 11.5.) At the same time, the higher the current flowing through the module (defined by the U voltage), the greater the dT difference, provided that the Qc thermal power is fixed.

The following example illustrates the calculation required to choose a Peltier module. It is based on the following initial conditions: The supplied voltage is 12 V; the thermal powers of the element to be cooled are 20 W, 40 W, and 60 W; and the temperature of the hot side of the Peltier module (equal to the temperature of the base of the heatsink installed on the Peltier module) is 50°C. The calculation produces the following:

1. For a voltage of 12 V, the current is 5 A.

2. For a current of 5 A and a thermal power of the cooled element equal to 20 W, the temperature difference (dT) is approximately 45°K (45°C). At 40 W, it is 25°K (25°C), and at 60 W, it is 4°K (4°C).

3. Given the values of temperature difference (dT) and of the temperature of the hot side of the Peltier module, which is 323°K (50°C) in this example, it is possible to calculate the Tc temperature for each Qc value. When the thermal power of the cooled element is 20 W, the temperature of the cold side of the Peltier module is 278°K (5°C). At 40 W, it is 298°K (25°C), and at 60 W, it is 319°K (46°C).

If a more powerful Peltier module is used, it is possible to achieve a greater temperature difference between the hot and cold sides. For example, a module with a Qc of 131 W, an I of 8.5 A, and a U of 28.8 V will ensures a temperature difference of 308°K (35°C) to 313°K (40°C) for objects with a thermal power equal to 60 W.

When choosing an appropriate module based on cooling power, keep in mind the module's thermal power. For example, when the module under consideration operates in the chosen modes ($U = 12$ and $I = 5$), this power is 60 W. There also is the thermal power of the element being cooled. The heat flux generated by these sources is a heavy burden for a cooling system.

Correctly chosen and appropriately run Peltier modules are efficient cooling devices that ensure a temperature for the case of the cooled element below the ambient temperature.

Cooling devices normally composed of a heatsink and a fan must not only dissipate rather powerful heat flux, they also must ensure a low temperature on the hot side of the Peltier module. The module ensures the temperature difference between its hot and cold sides; therefore, the lower the temperature supported on its hot side, the lower the temperature of its cold side. (See Formula 11.5.)

If traditional cooling devices can't ensure the required parameters, one possible solution is a water cooling system. Again, the temperature of the cold side of the Peltier module, and, consequently, that of the adjoining surface of the cooled element, depends both on the temperature difference and on the value of the temperature on the hot side of the Peltier module.

When choosing a Peltier module of appropriate cooling power, it is necessary to ensure that the entire surfaces of its cold and hot sides are used. Otherwise, the parts of the module that do not have contact with the surface of the protected object (such as a processor chip) will only waste power and emit heat, decreasing overall cooling efficiency (Fig. 11.15).

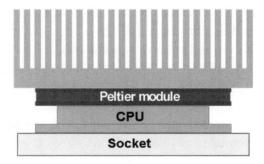

Fig. 11.15. Incorrect usage of a large Peltier module

If the surface of the cold side of the module exceeds the area of contact with the cooled object, it is necessary to use thermal padding of sufficient dimensions and thickness. This padding must be manufactured from material with good heat conductivity, such as copper (Fig. 11.16).

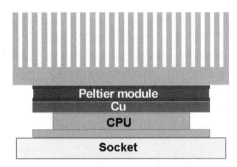

Fig. 11.16. Correct usage of a large Peltier module
with heat-conductive padding (Cu)

Unfortunately, problems with using Peltier modules are not limited to the previously mentioned aspects. The architecture of contemporary processors and certain system software permit modification of the energy consumed, depending on the workload of the processor. This allows you to optimize the amount of energy used. This is also the result of energy-saving standards supported by functions built into the hardware and software of modern computers. Under normal conditions, optimizing the operation and energy consumption of the processor positively affects the thermal conditions of the processor, as well as the general thermal balance. However, note that modes with periodic fluctuations in the amount of power consumed might not harmonize with cooling equipment that uses Peltier modules. This is because existing Peltier coolers are intended for constant operation. If the processor is changed to a mode in which the amount of power consumed, and, therefore, the heat flux has been lowered, the temperature of the processor chip and core also will be lowered considerably. In certain cases, if the processor core is too cool, the processor may experience a temporary cessation of operation, which will cause the computer system to hang up persistently. Corresponding documentation from Intel says the minimum temperature that guarantees proper functioning of Pentium II and Pentium III processors is 5°C (41°F).

As previously mentioned, low temperatures may result in water condensation. Water condenses on the cold parts of the cooling system, such as the cold side of the Peltier module and the cooled surface of the object being protected (such as the CPU). Furthermore, when heat-conductive padding is used, it also will also collect water. This effect can be neutralized by isolating the cold areas of the cooling system. One way to achieve this is to apply special foam rubber (Fig. 11.17).

Certain problems may arise from the work of a series of built-in functions, such as those that control the fans in the cooler. In part, the mode that controls energy consumption of the processor provides for changes in the rotation speed of the cooling fan, using hardware built into the motherboard. Under normal conditions, this greatly improves the heating rate of the processor. However, if you are using one of the simpler Peltier coolers, lowering the rotation speed of the fan may worsen the heating rate, with fatal consequences for the processor, which will be overheated by the operating Peltier module. Remember that the Peltier module, besides performing the functions of a heat pump, is a powerful source of heat.

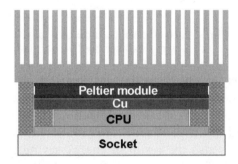

Fig. 11.17. Isolating cold areas of the cooling system by using foam rubber (Cu is the heat-conductive padding)

As in the case of central processors, Peltier coolers may be a good alternative to the traditional means of cooling video chipsets used in modern, high-performance video adapters. The work of such video chipsets is accompanied by significant heat flux and rarely is subject to sharp changes in its functional modes.

To avoid problems with modes that change power consumption, which can lead to condensation, overcooling, and possibly overheating of protected elements, you should not use such modes or built-in functions. However, as an alternative, you can use a cooling system that provides intelligent control of Peltier coolers. This will control not only the work of the fan, but also will change the work modes of the thermoelectric modules used in active coolers. In the simplest situation, this might be a miniature thermal relay based on a bimetallic plate, fastened on the Peltier module and controlling the operation of the fan cooling that module.

Information recently appeared on experiments that built miniature Peltier modules directly into the processor chips to cool their most critical structures. This solution favors better cooling that results from decreased heat resistance and allows considerable increases in the operating frequency and performance of the processor.

Many research laboratories conduct investigations to improve systems that ensure optimal temperature modes of electronic components. Cooling systems based on Peltier modules are considered rather promising.

Examples of Peltier Coolers

Recently, some simple, reliable, and relatively inexpensive ($5–$20) Peltier modules have appeared on computer market. (As a rule, the cooling fan is not supplied with the kit.) These modules show the prospects of cooling devices, and even now are used regularly to cool PC components.

A wide range of Peltier coolers is available, from miniature products with relatively low cooling power, which can operate with simple coolers that use small heatsinks, to powerful Peltier modules, which require a water cooling system for proper operation.

Numerous cooling devices are supplied by Supercool (**http://www.supercool.se**) (Fig. 11.18).

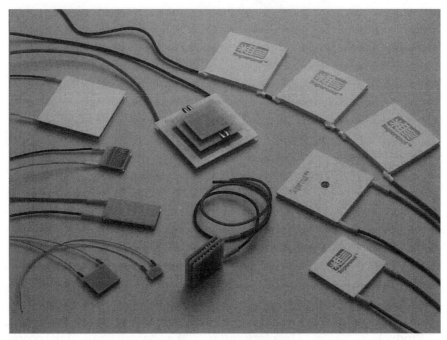

Fig. 11.18. Thermoelectric modules from Supercool

For efficient operation of powerful thermoelectric modules, a water cooling system is required. Supercool supplies these components as well, including those shown in Figs. 11.19 and 11.20.

Some manufacturers supply processor coolers based on Peltier modules. Examples of such products are listed in Table 11.4.

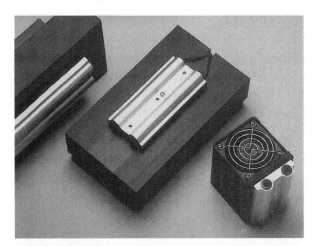

Fig. 11.19. Components of a water cooling system

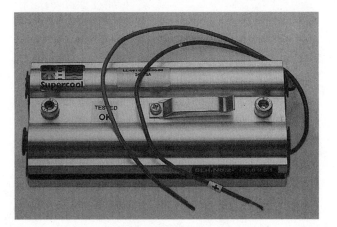

Fig. 11.20. Element of a two-circuit water cooling system

Table 11.4. Industrial Coolers Based on Peltier Modules

Product	Manufacturer/ vendor	Fan description	Intel processor
PAX56B	ComputerNerd	Ball bearing	Pentium/MMX, to 200 MHz and 25 W
PA6EXB	ComputerNerd	Dual ball bearing, tachometer	Pentium MMX, to 40 W

continues

Table 11.4 Continued

Product	Manufacturer/ vendor	Fan description	Intel processor
DT-P54A	DesTech Solutions	Dual ball bearing	Pentium
AC-P2	AOC Cooler	Ball bearing	Pentium II
PAP2X3B	ComputerNerd	Triple ball bearing	Pentium II
STEP-UP-53X2	Step Thermo-dynamics	Dual ball bearing	Pentium II, Celeron
PAP2CX3B-10 BCool PC-Peltier	ComputerNerd	Triple ball bearing, tachometer	Pentium II, Celeron
PAP2CX3B-25 BCool-ER PC-Peltier	ComputerNerd	Triple ball bearing, tachometer	Pentium II, Celeron
PAP2CX3B-10S BCool-EST PC-Peltier	ComputerNerd	Triple ball bearing, tachometer	Pentium II, Celeron

The PAX56B cooler was developed to cool Intel Pentium and Pentium with MMX technology, Cyrix, and AMD processors that work at a frequency of 200 MHz. The 30×30 mm thermoelectric modules allow the cooler to support a processor temperature of less than 63°C (145°F), at a power dissipation of 25 W and an internal temperature of 25°C (77°F). Most processors dissipate less heat; therefore, this cooler supports a much lower processor temperature than many alternative cooling systems, consisting of just heatsinks and fans. The power supply of the Peltier module included in the PAX56B cooler is from a source of 5 W; it can support a maximum current of 1.5 A. This cooler's fan requires 12 V and a maximum current of 0.1 A. The parameters of the fan are as follows: ball bearing, 47.5 mm, 65,000 hours, and 26 dB. The dimensions of the entire cooler are $25 \times 25 \times 28.7$ mm.

The PA6EXB cooler is intended to cool more powerful Pentium processors with MMX technology, which dissipate a power of 40 W. This cooler is compatible with all processors from Intel, Cyrix, and AMD that use Socket 5 or Socket 7. The thermoelectric Peltier modules included in PA6EXB are 40×40 mm. The maximum current is 8.0 A (but usually 3.0 A) at a voltage of 5 V when connected through the standard power socket of the computer. The dimensions of the entire cooler are $60 \times 60 \times 52.5$ mm. To install the cooler correctly and ensure optimal heat exchange between the heatsink and its surroundings, make sure that there is space of at least 10 mm above it and 2.5 mm to the sides. PA6EXB guarantees a processor temperature of 62.7°C (144.9°F) at a dissipation power of 40 W and an internal temperature of 45°C (133°F). Taking into consideration the way the thermoelectric module inside PA6EXB works, you must avoid using programs that place the processor in hibernation mode for long periods of time; this will prevent condensation and possibly short-circuiting.

The DT-P54A cooler (also known as the PA5B from ComputerNerd) was developed for Pentium processors. However, some companies that sell the cooler also recommend it to users of Cyrix/IBM or AMD processors. The cooler heatsink is relatively small, 29 × 29 mm. A thermal sensor built into the cooler will inform you when there is danger of overheating. It also monitors the Peltier module. An external controlling device also is included. This device tracks the voltage, the operation of the Peltier element and the fan, and the temperature of the processor. The device will give a warning signal if the Peltier element or the fan breaks, if the fan rotates at less than 70% of its normal speed (4,500 rpm), or if the temperature of the processor has climbs higher than 63°C (145°F). When the processor temperature surpasses 38°C (100°F), the Peltier element automatically turns on. If the temperature is below this, the Peltier element is kept off. This last function eliminates problems connected with moisture condensation. Unfortunately, the Peltier element is so securely attached to the heatsink that you won't be able to remove it without destroying the construction. This means that you don't have the ability to install it on another, more powerful heatsink. The fan parameters are as follows: The voltage is 12 V, the rotating speed is 4,500 rpm, the air supply speed is 6 cfm, the power consumed is 1 W, and the noise level is 30 dB. This cooler performs fairly well and is useful for overclocking. In certain cases, however, overclocking the processor simply requires a bigger heatsink and a good fan.

The AC-P2 cooler was developed for Pentium II processors. Included are a 60 mm fan, a heatsink, and a 40 mm Peltier element. It does not work well with Pentium II processors of 400 MHz and higher, because the SRAM chips are not cooled.

The PAP2X3B cooler (Fig. 11.21) is similar to the AC-P2. It comes with two 60 mm fans. The problem of cooling the SRAM is not dealt with. Keep in mind that the cooler is not recommended for use with cooling programs such as CpuIdle, or with the Windows NT or Linux operating systems, because moisture condensation on the processor is more likely to occur.

The STEP-UP-53X2 cooler has two fans that blow through the heatsink.

Fig. 11.21. External view of the PAP2X3B cooler

The BCool series from ComputerNerd (PAP2CX3B-10 BCool PC-Peltier, PAP2CX3B-25 BCool-ER PC-Peltier, and PAP2CX3B-10S BCool-EST PC-Peltier) were developed for Pentium II and Celeron processors. All have similar characteristics, which are presented in Table 11.5.

Table 11.5. Coolers of the BCool Series

Parameter	PAP2CX3B-10 BCool PC-Peltier	PAP2CX3B-25 BCool-ER PC-Peltier	PAP2CX3B-10S BCool-EST PC-Peltier
Recommended processors	Pentium II, Celeron	Pentium II, Celeron	Pentium II, Celeron
Number of fans	3	3	3
Type of central fan	Ball bearing, tachometer (12 V, 120 mA)	Ball bearing, tachometer (12 V, 120 mA)	Ball bearing, tachometer (12 V, 120 mA)
Dimensions of central fan (mm)	60 × 60 × 10	60 × 60 × 10	60 × 60 × 10
Type of external fan	Ball bearing	Ball bearing, tachometer	Ball bearing, thermistor

continues

Table 11.5 Continued

Parameter	PAP2CX3B-10 BCool PC-Peltier	PAP2CX3B-25 BCool-ER PC-Peltier	PAP2CX3B-10S BCool-EST PC-Peltier
Dimensions of external fan (mm)	60 × 60 × 10	60 × 60 × 25	60 × 60 × 25
Voltage (V), current (mA)	12, 90	12, 130	12, 80–225
Total area covered by fans (cm^2)	84.9	84.9	84.9
Power (W), total current for fans (mA)	300, 3.6	380, 4.56	280–570, 3.36–6.84
Heatsink pins at center	63 long, 72 short	63 long, 72 short	63 long, 72 short
Heatsink pins on each side	45 long, 18 short	45 long, 18 short	45 long, 18 short
Total number of heatsink pins	153 long, 108 short	153 long, 108 short	153 long, 108 short
Heatsink size at center, with thermoelectric module (mm)	57 × 59 × 27	57 × 59 × 27	57 × 59 × 27
Heatsink size on each edge (mm)	41 × 59 × 32	41 × 59 × 32	41 × 59 × 32
Total heatsink size, with thermoelectric module (mm)	145 × 59 × 38	145 × 59 × 38	145 × 59 × 38
Total cooler size (mm)	145 × 60 × 50	145 × 60 × 65	145 × 60 × 65
Cooler weight (g)	357	416	422
Warranty (years)	5	5	5
Estimated price (2000)	$74.95	$79.95	$84.95

Note that BCool coolers include devices that have similar characteristics but do not include Peltier elements. Such coolers are cheaper, but they cool computer components less effectively.

Chapter 12

Overclocking and Fine-Tuning RAM

The memory subsystem is one of the most important computer subsystems in terms of performance. Memory chips are mounted on special boards, called memory modules *(Fig. 12.1), installed in special slots on the motherboard. The operating speed of the RAM subsystem — and, consequently, overall system performance — depends on the RAM settings specified in BIOS Setup.*

Usually, the required parameters that determine the operation of RAM modules are set automatically. This typically is accomplished via a special parameter known as **DRAM Timing**. In the BIOS Setup of most contemporary motherboards, it can have two settings: By SPD (Serial Presence Detect) or Manual.

Fig. 12.1. RAM module

The By SPD value ensures settings recommended by the RAM manufacturer, hard-encoded into the modules. Note that manufacturers usually try to ensure stable operation of their products in all possible computer configurations. In doing so, they tend to raise the latency value too far. This decreases the speed of the memory subsystem and, consequently, degrades overall system performance.

It is possible to improve the performance of the memory subsystem by switching to Manual and setting optimal parameters for the specific memory module.

The rest of this chapter focuses on an investigation of the performance dependence on various settings of the RAM parameters that influence the operating speed of the memory subsystem. (This information is published with the permission of **http://www.3dnews.ru**, a Russian-language Web site. The English version of this site can be found at **http://www.digital-daily.com**.)

Performance of a System with DDR266

The following system configuration was used for testing:

- ❑ Processor — AMD Athlon XP 1600+
- ❑ Motherboard — Abit KX7-333 (AMD Athlon/Duron, Socket A, VIA KT333 chipset, DDR333/266 memory support, Ultra DMA/33/66/100) (Fig. 12.2)
- ❑ Hard disk — IBM DTLA 307030, 30 GB
- ❑ RAM — Samsung, 256 MB, PC2100, DDR SDRAM
- ❑ Video adapter — MX440 Nvidia GeForce4, 64 MB (Nvidia Detonator v28.32)
- ❑ Sound card — Creative Live 5.1
- ❑ Power supply unit — PowerMan, 250 W
- ❑ Operating system — Windows 2000 SP1

The SiSoftware Sandra 2002 test was used to demonstrate the potential for optimal tuning of the memory subsystem. Besides this, a game test was performed using Quake III. To make the results more illustrative, one parameter was changed at a time. For each set of parameters, performance results are provided.

Fig. 12.2. KX7-333 motherboard from Abit

Default Settings

The default settings (with FSB and memory frequencies of 133 MHz) are as follows (Fig. 12.3):

- ☐ **Bank Interleave** — Disable
- ☐ **DRAM Command Rate** — 2T
- ☐ **DRAM CAS Latency** — 2.5T
- ☐ **Precharge to Active (Trp)** — 3T
- ☐ **Active to Precharge (Tras)** — 6T
- ☐ **Active to CMD (Trcd)** — 3T

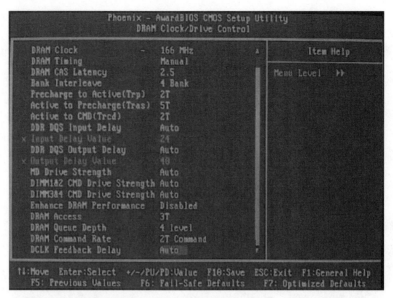

Fig. 12.3. DRAM Clock/Drive Control menu in BIOS Setup

Table 12.1. Performance Evaluation of the Default Parameters

Test	Rating
SiSoftware Sandra (integer)	1,907
SiSoftware Sandra (floating point)	1,776
Quake III (fastest)	218.1 frames per second

Bank Interleave

The **Bank Interleave** parameter manages access to the open memory banks. Possible values are as follows: disable, 2 Bank (sometimes 2-Way), and 4 Bank (sometimes 4-Way). The best performance is achieved when the 4 Bank value is chosen.

Table 12.2. Performance Evaluation (Bank Interleave = 2 Bank)

Test	Rating
SiSoftware Sandra (integer)	1,911
SiSoftware Sandra (floating point)	1,791
Quake III (fastest)	222.9 frames per second

Table 12.3. Performance Evaluation (Bank Interleave = 4 Bank)

Test	Rating
SiSoftware Sandra (integer)	1,925
SiSoftware Sandra (floating point)	1,806
Quake III (fastest)	227.3 frames per second

DRAM Command Rate

Using the **DRAM Command Rate** parameter, it is possible to specify manually the delays for data transfers between the chipset and the memory. The command (or CMD) rate has the greatest influence on the performance of the memory subsystem. Possible values are 1T and 2T. The greatest performance is achieved when the minimum value is set — 1T.

For the performance evaluation, the 1T setting was chosen. (The **Bank Interleave** option was set to 4 Bank.)

Table 12.4. Performance Evaluation (DRAM Command Rate = 1T)

Test	Rating
SiSoftware Sandra (integer)	1,965
SiSoftware Sandra (floating point)	1,864
Quake III (fastest)	235.0 frames per second

Column Address Strobe (CAS) Latency

The **CAS Latency** parameter sets the delay (in clocks) specific for operations with RAM. The smaller this value, the faster RAM modules react to requests (i.e., the faster the memory subsystem). For performance, this is probably the most important parameter. Possible values are 2T and 2.5T.

For the performance evaluation, the value of 2T was chosen. (The previously selected settings were retained: **Bank Interleave** was 4 Bank, and **DRAM Command Rate** was 1T.)

Table 12.5. Performance Evaluation (CAS Latency = 2T)

Test	Rating
SiSoftware Sandra (integer)	2,024
SiSoftware Sandra (floating point)	1,901
Quake III (fastest)	239.7 frames per second

As a rule, the process of fine-tuning the memory subsystem has been accomplished at this stage. However, if you have high-quality memory modules, it is possible to achieve better performance by changing the following parameters: **Precharge to Active (Trp)**, **Active to Precharge (Tras)**, and **Active to CMD (Trcd)**.

Trp, Tras, and Trcd

The default values of the **Trp**, **Tras**, and **Trcd** parameters are as follows: 3T, 6T, and 3T. Decreasing the values of these parameters improves the performance of the memory subsystem. During the tuning process, the following values were set: **Trp = 2T**, **Tras = 5T**, and **Trcd = 2T**. (The previously selected settings were retained: **Bank Interleave** was 4 Bank, **DRAM Command Rate** was 1T, and **CAS Latency** was 2T.)

Table 12.6. Performance Evaluation (Trp = 2T, Tras = 5T, Trcd = 2T)

Test	Rating
SiSoftware Sandra (integer)	2,039
SiSoftware Sandra (floating point)	1,906
Quake III (fastest)	245.0 frames per second

As follows from the test results, decreasing the values for the **Trp**, **Tras**, and **Trcd** parameters improved performance about 7.5% using the SiSoftware Sandra 2002 test, and more than 12% using the Quake III game test.

Diagrams illustrating performance gain are presented in Figs. 12.4–12.6.

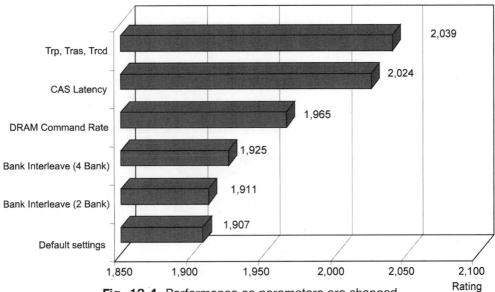

Fig. 12.4. Performance as parameters are changed
(SiSoftware Sandra, integer)

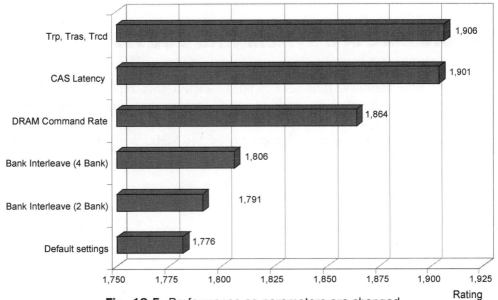

Fig. 12.5. Performance as parameters are changed
(SiSoftware Sandra, floating point)

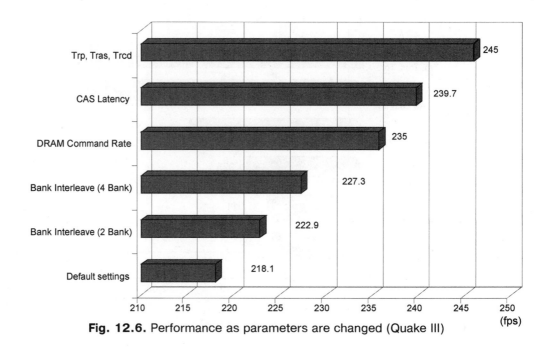

Fig. 12.6. Performance as parameters are changed (Quake III)

Performance of a System with DDR333

The previous test results were obtained on a computer equipped with DDR266 (PC2100) memory. It is reasonable to expect that replacing the memory with DDR333 (PC2700) will ensure further performance growth. However, the test memory module could operate on the nominal frequency (i.e., at an FSB frequency of 133 MHz and a memory frequency of 166 MHz) only when the following settings were chosen:

❑ **Bank Interleave** — 4 Bank
❑ **DRAM Command Rate** — 1T
❑ **DRAM CAS Latency** — 2T
❑ **Trp** — 3T
❑ **Tras** — 6T
❑ **Trcd** — 3T

Table 12.7. Performance Evaluation (FSB = 133 MHz)

Test	Rating
SiSoftware Sandra (integer)	2,052
SiSoftware Sandra (floating point)	1,932
Quake III (fastest)	255.1 frames per second

Increasing the FSB frequency from 133 MHz to 166 MHz with a DDR333 memory module ensured performance growth with the same parameters. The test results are provided in Table 12.8.

Table 12.8. Performance Evaluation (FSB = 166 MHz)

Test	Rating
SiSoftware Sandra (integer)	2,426
SiSoftware Sandra (floating point)	2,272
Quake III (fastest)	307.2 frames per second

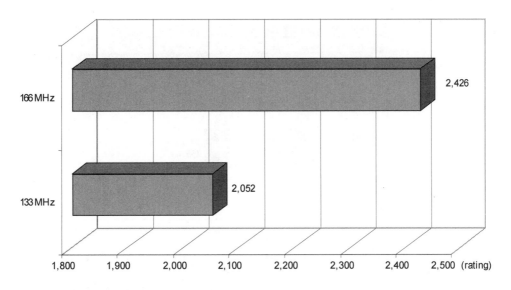

Fig. 12.7. Performance growth caused by increased frequency
(SiSoftware Sandra, integer)

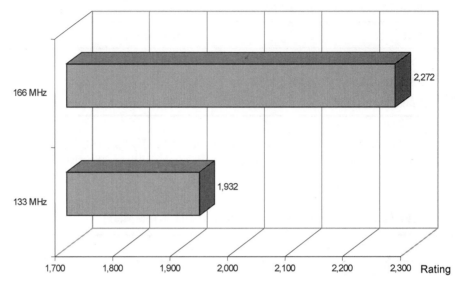

Fig. 12.8. Performance growth caused by increased frequency
(SiSoftware Sandra, floating point)

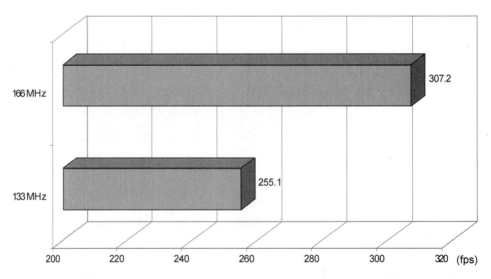

Fig. 12.9. Performance growth caused by increased frequency (Quake III)

To simplify the analysis of how the memory module settings influence overall system performance, all test data are summarized in Table 12.9. In the Timing column, the memory module parameters are specified as followed: **Bank Interleave, DRAM Command Rate, DRAM CAS Latency-Trp-Tras-Trcd.**

Table 12.9. Memory Module Parameters and Performance Evaluation

FSB/memory frequency (MHz)	Timing	SiSoftware Sandra integer/float	Quake III (frames per second)	Quake III, gain over default (%)
133/133	Disable, 2T, 2.5T-3T-6T-3T	1,907/1,776	218.1	default
133/133	2 Bank, 2T, 2.5T-3T-6T-3T	1,911/1,791	222.9	2.2
133/133	4 Bank, 2T, 2.5T-3T-6T-3T	1,925/1,806	227.3	4.2
133/133	4 Bank, 1T, 2.5T-3T-6T-3T	1,965/1,864	235.0	7.7
133/133	4 Bank, 1T, 2T-3T-6T-3T	2,024/1,901	239.7	9.9
133/133	4 Bank, 1T, 2T-2T-5T-2T	2,039/1,906	245.0	12.3
133/166	4 Bank, 1T, 2T-3T-6T-3T	2,052/1,932	255.1	16.9
166/166	4 Bank, 1T, 2T-3T-6T-3T	2,426/2,272	307.2	40.8

Note that if the memory parameters are set in a nonoptimal way, the computer performance drops significantly. The same is true if the user tries to economize and purchases poor-quality RAM; the performance can drop 5% to 10%. For example, the growth from 5 frames per second to 10 frames per second in the Quake III test corresponds to the difference between systems equipped with AMD Athlon XP 1700+ and 1600+.

When analyzing the results provided here, it is expedient to pay attention to the 166/166 MHz frequency mode. This ensures synchronous operation of the memory subsystem and processor bus. (In this frequency mode, the processor is overclocked from 1,400 MHz to 1,750 MHz.) In this mode, no delays are required for clock synchronization of the signals, which ensures high performance.

Starting from 166 MHz, the test motherboard (as well as many other motherboards) uses a factor of 1/5 for the PCI frequency (2/5 for the AGP). This guarantees operation of hard disk controllers and video adapters on standard PCI frequencies: PCI of 33 MHz, and AGP of 66 MHz.

Memory optimization is not limited to fine-tuning the parameters discussed here. This set of parameters is standard, and appropriate options are supported by most contemporary motherboards.

Choosing optimal parameters for memory modules ensures maximum performance. To achieve stable operation of the system at minimum values of the **DRAM Timing** parameter, it is expedient to increase the voltage supplied to memory modules (Vmem). The motherboard used in these experiments supported the following voltages: 2.55 V, 2.65 V, 2.75 V, and 2.85 V. However, this will increase heat generation, sometimes significantly. To avoid dangerous overheating of memory modules, it is expedient to use heatsinks for memory or organize other active cooling of the memory modules.

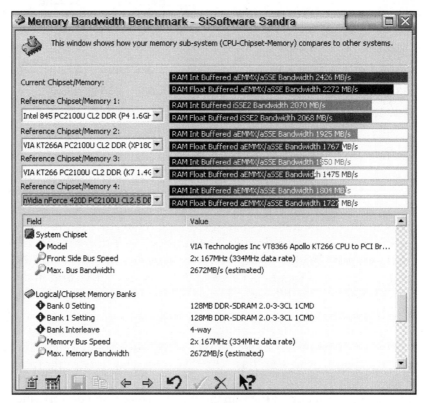

Fig. 12.10. Computer performance with FSB and memory frequencies of 166 MHz (SiSoftware Sandra)

Chapter 13

Video Subsystem Overclocking

A computer's performance can be increased significantly by overclocking its video subsystem based on the Accelerated Graphics Port (AGP) video adapter. This can be achieved by increasing the bus frequency or by programmatically raising the operating frequency of the video chip, the video memory, or both, using the latest versions of drivers.

Working with the Bus

Contemporary video adapters are connected to other computer subsystems via the AGP bus, through which all data exchange is accomplished. Thus, the performance of modern video adapters directly depends on the AGP bus frequency.

The AGP bus frequency, in turn, depends on the Front Side Bus (FSB) frequency (GTL+/AGTL+, Alpha EV6). Usually, the AGP bus frequency is specified by dividing the FSB frequency. The most common combinations of FSB and AGP frequencies, implemented in motherboards with the Intel 440BX chipset, are listed in Table 13.1.

Table 13.1. Combinations of FSB and AGP Frequencies

FSB frequency (MHz)	AGP frequency (MHz)
66	66
75	75
83	83*
100	66
103	69
112	75
124	83*
133	89*

* Unstable operation is probable

The architecture of most motherboards provides tools for correcting AGP and Peripheral Component Interconnect (PCI) bus frequencies, not only by changing the FSB frequency but also by setting the frequency divider values for the processor bus. This is accomplished via parameters in BIOS Setup or jumpers on the motherboard. By changing the bus frequency values, you can select optimal operating modes for the devices controlled by the buses.

Table 13.2. Standard Frequencies for Contemporary Motherboards

FSB frequency (MHz)	Divider	AGP frequency (MHz)
100	2/3	66
133	1/2	66
166	2/5	66
200	1/3	66

Contemporary high-performance video adapters, based on fast components, provide the ability to change the AGP bus frequency within a wide range. However, even they are not always stable at the high frequencies achieved by processor over-clocking. (See Table 13.1.)

Increasing the frequency of the AGP bus, to which the video adapter is connected, improves the throughput, which in turn improves the speed of video-data transmission. This improves the performance of the video subsystem in proportion to the growth of its bus frequency. Architectural features and frequency characteristics of electronic components that serve as a basis for modern video adapters also allow the AGP bus frequency to be increased significantly. Some devices created using fast components, manufactured with the most advanced technologies, retain usability at a frequency of 100 MHz. This is more than 50% higher than the standard AGP frequency (typically set to 66 MHz).

Table 13.3. Clock Frequency and Throughput of the AGP Bus

FSB (MHz)	Divider	AGP (MHz)	AGP 2X (MB/sec)	AGP 4X (MB/sec)	AGP 8X (MB/sec)
100	2/3	66	533	1,067	2,133
110	2/3	73	587	1,173	2,347
120	2/3	80	640	1,280	2,560
133	2/3	89	711	1,422	2,844
140	2/3	93	747	1,493	2,987
133	1/2	66	533	1,066	2,132
140	1/2	70	560	1,120	2,240
150	1/2	75	600	1,200	2,400
160	1/2	80	640	1,280	2,560
170	1/2	85	680	1,360	2,720
180	1/2	90	720	1,440	2,880
166	2/5	66	533	1,067	2,133
170	2/5	68	544	1,088	2,176
180	2/5	72	576	1,152	2,304
190	2/5	76	608	1,216	2,432
200	2/5	80	640	1,280	2,560
210	2/5	84	672	1,344	2,688
220	2/5	88	704	1,408	2,816
240	2/5	96	768	1,536	3,072
200	1/3	66	533	1,067	2,133
210	1/3	70	560	1,120	2,240
220	1/3	73	587	1,173	2,347

continues

Table 13.3 Continued

FSB (MHz)	Divider	AGP (MHz)	AGP 2X (MB/sec)	AGP 4X (MB/sec)	AGP 8X (MB/sec)
230	1/3	77	613	1,227	2,453
240	1/3	80	640	1,280	2,560
250	1/3	83	667	1,333	2,667

However, the potential of this overclocking method is limited. The maximum growth of the AGP bus frequency provided in Table 13.3 are characteristic of rare, high-quality models of video adapters. As a rule, the limits are lower. The growth of frequency and performance of video adapters also is limited by some components, whose characteristics do not allow them to work at higher frequencies. At the same time, the capabilities of other components are not implemented.

This statement can be illustrated by an example that overclocked the Matrox Millenium G200 video adapter. This overclocking was accomplished using the standard, built-in tools of the motherboard.

Configuration of the Test System

- ❏ Test — 3D WinBench 98 (800 × 600 × 32)
- ❏ Overclocking parameters — Increase the bus frequency 75/83/103 MHz
- ❏ Video adapter — Matrox Millennium G200, AGP, 250 MHz RAMDAC, 8 MB SGRAM, 128 MB graphics aperture
- ❏ Motherboard — Asus P2B-S
- ❏ Processor — Intel Celeron 300A
- ❏ RAM — 128 MB CAS2 SDRAM
- ❏ BIOS — Award Modular BIOS v4.51PG
- ❏ Operating system — Windows 98

Overclocking of the hardware components was accomplished by increasing the FSB frequency from 66 MHz (the nominal value) to 103 MHz. The growth of video subsystem performance achieved as a result of this overclocking is presented in Table 13.4 and Figs. 13.1–13.3.

Table 13.4. Test Results with a Matrox Video Adapter

3D WinBench 98 Test	300/66	340/75	375/83	466/103
3D processing	23.0	25.8	28.7	35.5
3D scene/user defined (frames per second)	12.5	14.1	15.6	18.8
3D WinMark rating	1,000	1,110	1,220	1,420

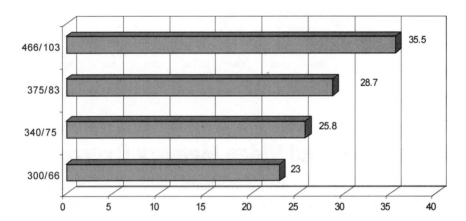

Fig. 13.1. Results of the 3D WinBench 98 (3D processing) test

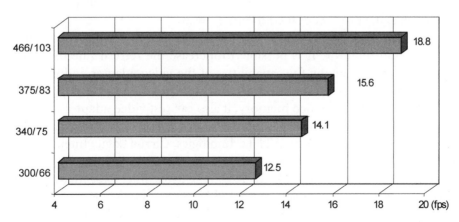

Fig. 13.2. Results of the 3D WinBench 98 (3D scene) test

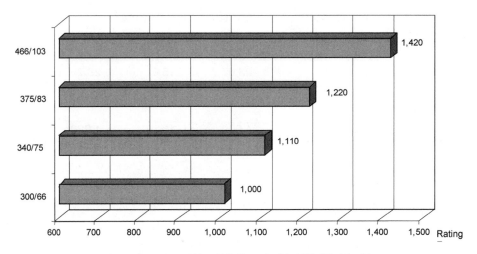

Fig. 13.3. Results of the WinBench 98 (3D WinMark) test

Video Processor and Video Memory Overclocking

The most significant and, more importantly, the most balanced increase of the video adapter speed can be achieved using specialized software tools. These tools, as a rule, allow you to selectively accelerate the video chip and the video memory, the basis for the video adapter. The capabilities of software tools can be complemented by increasing the AGP bus frequency.

The PowerStrip utility is a good example of such a universal program. This program is the product of the EnTech Taiwan.

This software tool allows you to change the operating mode of the video adapter and monitor. It is possible to increase the refresh rate of the monitor to 200 Hz, limited only by the capabilities of the video adapter and the monitor. Besides controlling the monitor refresh rate, this program can change the frequencies of video chipsets and video memory; it also can test video adapters.

The PowerStrip program supports video chipsets from manufacturers including 3dfx Interactive, 3Dlabs, ATI Technologies, Cirrus Logic, Intel, Nvidia, Matrox, S3, SIS, Trident Microsystems, and Tseng Labs. This long list of video chips includes ATI Rage II Pro, CL GD543x/544x/546x, Intel 740, Matrox G100, 3Dlabs Permedia, PowerVR, Nvidia Riva128/128ZX, S3 Vision86x/968, S3 Trio32/64/V+/3D, S3 Trio v2 DX/GX, S3 Virge/VX/DX/GX/GX2, SIS 6326, Trident Providia 9685, and Tseng Labs ET6000/ET6100.

This program works under Windows 9x and Windows NT/2000/XP/Server 2003. It provides the possibility of controlling almost all monitor models, including monitors from well-known companies such as Hitachi, MAG Innovision, Mitsubishi, NEC, Nokia, Panasonic, Philips, Sony, and ViewSonic.

One major drawback of this program is its excessive number of settings, which can be misleading and confusing.

An alternative program is Nvidia's RivaTuner. This program works via manufacturer-provided video-adapter drivers (named Detonator). These drivers allow you to implement the hidden potential of the video adapter. The program supports all video adapters based on Nvidia video chips starting from Riva TNT, and ATI R200/RV250/RV280/R300/R350. The program supports all versions of Detonator drivers from Detonator 2.08 for Windows 98 SE/ME to Detonator 5.08 for Windows 2000/XP. RivaTuner allows low-level settings far below those provided by standard drivers.

An illustration of RivaTuner operation is provided in Figs. 13.4–13.8.

To fine-tune video adapter operation, it is necessary to set the **Enable low level hardware overclocking** checkbox. (See Fig. 13.8.) You may have to reboot the system before the new settings are effective.

Fig. 13.4. Window of the RivaTuner program

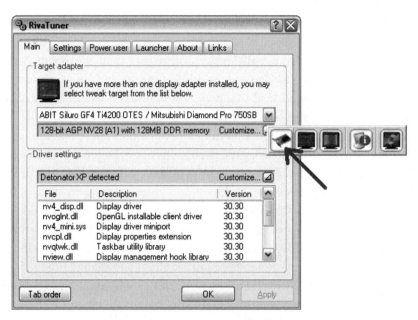

Fig. 13.5. Selecting low-level frequency settings

Fig. 13.6. Settings window for the video processor core and video memory

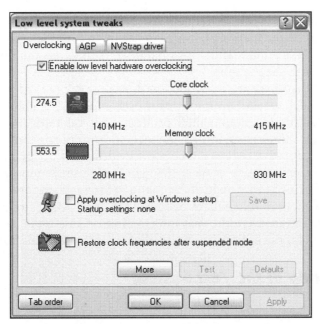

Fig. 13.7. Specifying frequencies (before change)

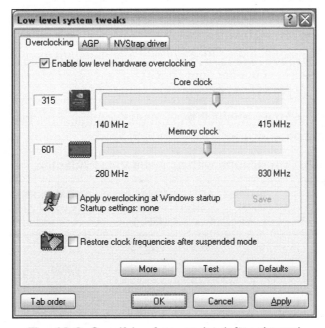

Fig. 13.8. Specifying frequencies (after change)

Having specified the frequencies (in this example, 315 MHz for the core, and 601 MHz for the memory), it is necessary to test the selected mode. To do so, just click the **Test** button. If the new parameters undergo the testing successfully, you can accept the new settings.

Note that there are other universal programs intended to support a wide range of video adapters and monitors. However, most video adapter manufacturers supply special programs with their products. Besides testing and optimizing the settings, these utilities usually provide tools for optimizing the video chipset and video memory. Such tools often can be downloaded from the manufacturer's Web site or obtained from companies specializing in the sale and support of video adapters.

Besides utilities provided by manufacturers, there are lots of shareware and freeware tools developed by overclocking fans. Many tools can be downloaded from the Internet. (Additional information on this topic, as well as the Web sites for some of these utilities, is provided in *Chapter 19* of this book.)

Configuration of the Test System

- ❒ Tests — 3DMark2000 (1,024 × 786 × 16 bits), 3D WinBench/WinMark 2000
- ❒ Overclocking parameters — Increase the video chip, video memory, and AGP bus frequencies
- ❒ Video adapter — Asus V3800, AGP, 32 MB SGRAM, 125 MHz video-chip frequency, 150 MHz video-memory frequency
- ❒ Motherboard — Abit BE-6 II
- ❒ Processor — Intel Pentium III 550 MHz
- ❒ RAM — 256 MB CAS2 SDRAM
- ❒ BIOS — Award Modular BIOS v4.51PG
- ❒ Operating system — Windows 2000, SP1

Table 13.5. Test Results with an Asus Video Adapter

CPU mode (MHz)	CPU bus (MHz)	AGP (MHz)	Video chip/ memory (MHz)	3DMark2000 (1,024 × 786 × 16)	3D WinBench/ WinMark 2000 (fps)
550 = 100 × 5.5	100	66	125/150	2,586	26.7
			160/150	2,750	27.4
			125/200	2,802	33.0
			160/200	3,051	34.7

continues

Table 13.5 Continued

CPU mode (MHz)	CPU bus (MHz)	AGP (MHz)	Video chip/ memory (MHz)	3DMark2000 (1,024 × 786 × 16)	3D WinBench/ WinMark 2000 (fps)
733 ≈ 133 × 5.5	133	89	125/150	2,740	27.2
			160/150	2,975	28.1
			125/200	3,052	34.4
			160/200	3,432	36.7

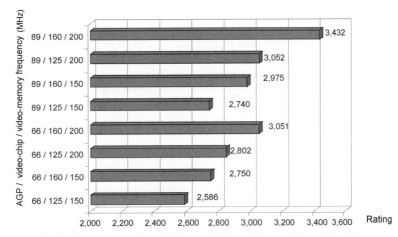

Fig. 13.9. Test results using 3DMark2000 (1,024 × 786 × 16 bit)

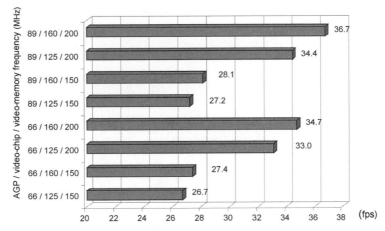

Fig. 13.10. Test results using 3D WinBench/WinMark 2000

Configuration of Another Test System

- ❏ Test — 3DMark2001 SE Pro (1,024 × 786 × 32 bits)
- ❏ Overclocking parameters — Increase video-chip and video-memory frequencies
- ❏ Video adapter — Abit Siluro OTES, GeForce4 Ti4200, AGP, 128 MB
- ❏ Motherboard — Abit IT7-MAX2 v.2.0
- ❏ Processor — Intel Pentium 4 3.06 GHz with hyperthreading
- ❏ RAM — 768 MB DDR400
- ❏ Operating system — Windows XP, SP2

Table 13.6. Test Results with an Abit Video Adapter

Video-chip/video-memory frequency (MHz)	3DMark2001 SE Pro rating
250/500	10,775
275/550	11,426
290/550	11,623
290/580	11,854

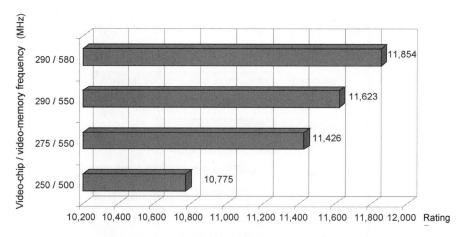

Fig. 13.11. Test results using 3DMark2001 SE Pro

New Driver, New Functionality

(Based on materials and with the permission of **http://www.fcenter.ru**, a Russian-language Web site.)

Computer hardware components are joined to operate as an integral system using not only standards and interfaces, but also appropriate software. The lead role in this process is delegated to drivers, specialized programs that ensure operation of computer hardware. The functional capabilities of hardware components, including performance, depend on the efficiency of the driver code.

This is especially true for such important components as video adapters, which have numerous drivers. The Nvidia Detonator family serves as a good example of such drivers.

When the 3DMark03 test was released, Detonator 42.86 was the newest version. Later, according to the user reviews, Detonator 42.68 was optimized for the 3DMark03 test. When these drivers are installed, video adapters based on GeForce FX chips show far better results in 3DMark03. However, these drivers do not always work correctly with GeForce4 Titanium products. For example, a wide horizontal line may appear across the screen.

Fig. 13.12. Incorrect operation of a driver

The screenshot in Fig. 13.12 is a good illustration of why you should select and test drivers carefully, even if the developers of those drivers guarantee high performance of the video subsystem. Some experts recommend using the Detonator 42.86 driver with the video adapters based on GeForce4 chips. This recommendation can be found on many popular Web sites dedicated to hardware topics. This driver ensures reliable operation and high performance for the previously mentioned family of video adapters. Still, for products of the GeForce FX series, the same experts recommended using the Detonator 42.68 driver.

After installing the Detonator 42.68 driver, the video adapter settings, as usual, are placed on the appropriate tab of the **Properties** window. Most driver settings are standard; therefore, they do not present any special interest. However, some of them contain settings only for GeForce FX. This includes specifying the video adapter clock frequencies using driver functionality.

For Nvidia GeForce FX 5800 Ultra, the clock frequencies of the graphic engine and video memory can be specified separately for 2D and 3D modes. By default, adapter clock frequencies are 300/600 MHz in 2D applications and 500/1,000 MHz in 3D applications.

Another interesting tab contains the settings for working with the adapter and applications that use 3D functions.

Fig. 13.13. GeForce FX 5800 Ultra video adapter

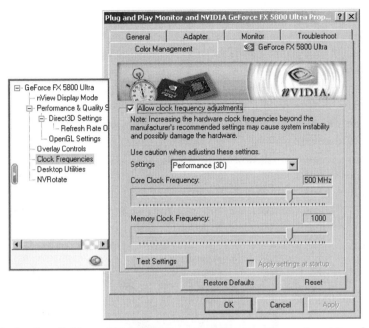

Fig. 13.14. Setting GeForce FX 5800 Ultra clock frequencies using driver functionality

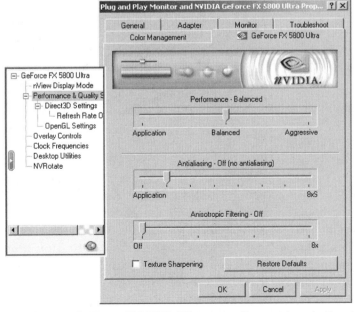

Fig. 13.15. Setting GeForce FX 5800 Ultra operating modes via the driver

Here, you can choose from the following modes responsible for the speed-to-quality ratio: **Application, Balanced,** and **Aggressive.**

The **Application** mode ensures maximum quality. However, the best quality is achieved at the expense of performance. The **Aggressive** mode, on the contrary, ensures the strongest performance at the expense of decreased image quality.

In addition to these modes, it is possible to set full-screen smoothing (**2x, Quincunx, 4x,** and several modes available only with Direct3D — **4xS, 6xS,** and **8xS**) and anisotropic filtering (**2x, 4x,** and **8x**).

The influence of these modes on the quality of the display can be seen in Figs. 3.16–3.18.

First, consider a small test program that displays a pyramid with a base coinciding to the screen surface and a distant vertex. The pyramid has numerous edges; therefore, it is perceived as a cone. The texture is applied to the side faces of the pyramid, MIP levels are colored, and trilinear filtering is used.

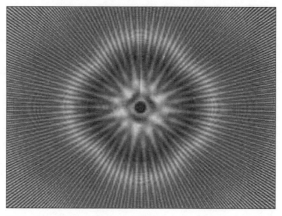

Fig. 13.16. On-screen display of the test image

Now, consider this test image in different GeForce FX modes. Unfortunately, this illustration (256 shades of gray) cannot adequately illustrate the color transitions. (For a color version, see **http://www.fcenter.ru/articles.shtml?videos/6101**.) Still, the boundaries are distinct in the **Aggressive** mode, in contrast to smooth transitions between MIP levels in the **Application** mode.

With trilinear filtering, transitions in the **Application** mode are smoothened. This happens because two values from adjacent MIP levels participate in color creation. These two values are added to weight coefficients that depend on the pixel distance. This means that with trilinear filtration, halftones on the resulting image must smoothly and continuously change.

Application

Balanced

Aggressive

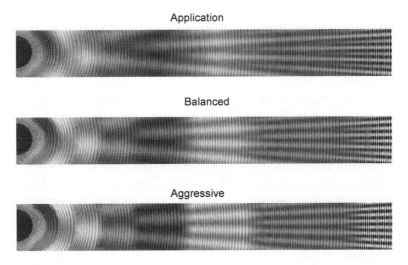

Fig. 13.17. Dependence of the image quality on the mode, with trilinear filtering

Application

Balanced

Aggressive

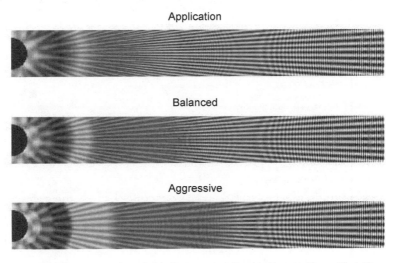

Fig. 13.18. Dependence of the image quality on the mode, with trilinear and anisotropic filtering

However, this behavior is only characteristic of the **Application** mode. When you choose the **Balanced** or **Aggressive** mode, smooth color transitions are no longer visible, and regions appear with boundaries between tones as well as with pure tones.

This means that in the **Balanced** and **Aggressive** modes, GeForce FX uses a combination of bilinear and trilinear filtering instead of the true trilinear filtering. In the **Balanced** mode, the portion of pixels that used true trilinear filtering is less than half; in the **Aggressive** mode, the portion is less than a quarter of the entire image area.

In addition to trilinear filtering, you can employ anisotropic filtering of the maximum level — **8x**.

Besides the effect of using the mix of bilinear and trilinear filtering, the chip has decreased the detail level of textures in the **Balanced** and **Aggressive** modes by displacing the MIP levels closer to the observer.

This series of examples demonstrating the decrease of the image quality when changing the **Application** mode to the **Balanced** or **Aggressive** mode can be continued. However, these details go beyond the scope of this discussion, which concentrates on the capabilities of specialized software and its influence on the video adapter functionality.

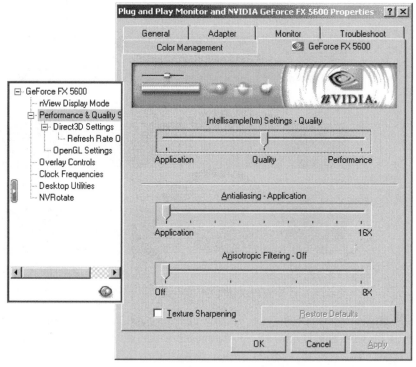

Fig. 13.19. Setting GeForce FX 5600 Ultra operating modes via the driver

By considering the entire range of video adapter drivers, it is necessary to point out that shortly after Detonator 42.68 became available, Detonator 43.45 was released. This new version of the driver has several differences from the 42.68 version.

First, new full-screen smoothing for Nvidia GeForce FX 5800 Ultra was introduced — **8cx** and **16x**. These modes employ super-sampling and also are available for Nvidia GeForce FX 5600 Ultra.

The second interesting aspect of Detonator 43.45 is the renaming of modes.

The best image quality that can be provided by the chips of the GeForce FX family is available in the **Application** mode, where all features aiming at performance optimization are disabled. The second position is held by the mode that provides lower quality but ensures higher performance. In pervious versions, it was named **Balanced**; it has been renamed **Quality**. Finally, there is the fastest mode, which provide the worst quality. This is the mode was previously known as **Aggressive**. In the newer version of the driver, the name of this mode has been changed to **Performance**.

It is not difficult to guess why Nvidia has renamed these modes without observing any logical rules. This approach is pure marketing. Most users of the driver, having seen the **Quality** mode in the settings window (the default setting), will believe this mode ensures the best quality. In reality, the video adapter won't ensure the best quality, which is only available in the **Application** mode. However, the video adapter will operate faster than if the **Application** mode was used.

Chapter 14

Hardware Acceleration of Video Adapters

It is possible to speed up the PC video subsystem, not only by increasing the clock frequencies of the AGP bus, video chip, and video memory, but also by modifying the hardware of your video adapter.

(Based on materials and with the permission of **http://www.fcenter.ru**, a Russian-language Web site.)

The performance of the video subsystem, represented by the video adapter, strongly depends on clock frequencies. Clock frequencies determine the operating modes of the graphical video core and the video memory.

The range of clock frequencies that can be set independently for the video core and video memory can be widened significantly by increasing the supply voltage.

Modifying and Overclocking GeForce3

Using the experience accumulated during the development and support of products based on GeForce2, Nvidia designed and released the GeForce3 chip, with several modifications. The standard GeForce3 chip supports core and memory frequencies of 200 MHz and 460 MHz, respectively. GeForce3 Ti500 supports frequencies of 240 MHz and 500 MHz, and GeForce3 Ti200 supports frequencies of 175 MHz and 400 MHz.

Modifying VisionTek GeForce3

The VisionTek GeForce3 video adapter is manufactured according to the Nvidia reference design (Fig. 14.1).

Fig. 14.1. VisionTek GeForce3 adapter

The VisionTek adapter has an AGP 2x/4x interface and is equipped with 64 MB of DDR SDRAM, represented by eight chips installed on the front side of the printed circuit board (PCB).

The adapter is equipped with memory chips from Elite Semiconductor Memory Technology (ESMT, sometimes referred to as EliteMT), with an access time of 3.8 nanoseconds. This corresponds approximately to a clock frequency of 263 MHz (and a data-transmission frequency of approximately 526 MHz). According to the specification, the memory operates at a frequency of 230 (460) MHz.

The adapter is equipped with SC1175CSW stabilizers from Semtech, which are duplicated pulse-duration controllers. These chips are intended mainly for memory power-supply stabilizers installed on video adapters and peripheral devices. Two independent controllers of these chips can operate in two modes: independently or with current sharing.

To obtain a stabilized core supply voltage of the GeForce3 adapter, the current sharing mode is used. In this mode, the output voltage of the first controller is specified by the resistor ratio (R1:R12 on a typical connection layout). The second controller uses the output voltage from the first one as a reference. Its output is connected to the output of the first controller, which means that two built-in stabilizers operate in parallel. Hence, the name of this mode is current sharing.

The typical method of connecting the stabilizers in this mode is shown in Fig. 14.2. The following formulas are applicable:

$$V_{out} = 1.25 \times (1 + R12/R1) \qquad \text{(Formula 14.1)}$$

$$V_{out}{}^* = 1.25 \times (1 + R12/R1^*) \qquad \text{(Formula 14.2)}$$

$$R1^* = (R1 \times R1')/(R1 + R1') \qquad \text{(Formula 14.3)}$$

$$V_{out}{}^* = 1.25 \times (1 + R12 \times (R1 + R1')/(R1 \times R1')) \qquad \text{(Formula 14.4)}$$

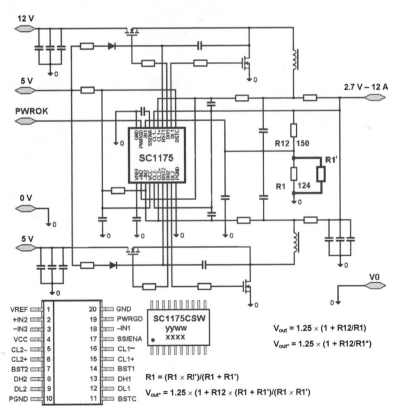

Fig. 14.2. Design of stabilizer connection

On VisionTek GeForce3, the resistance of R12 and R1 (R832 and R810 on the PCB) is 130 ohms and 770 ohms, respectively. Output voltage, calculated using Formula 14.1, is 1.45 V.

In the course of modification, the R1 resistor was shunted by a 510-ohm resistor, soldered to the contacts labeled 18 and 20 on the SC1175CSW chip (Fig. 14.3). As a result, the output voltage changed to 1.78 V.

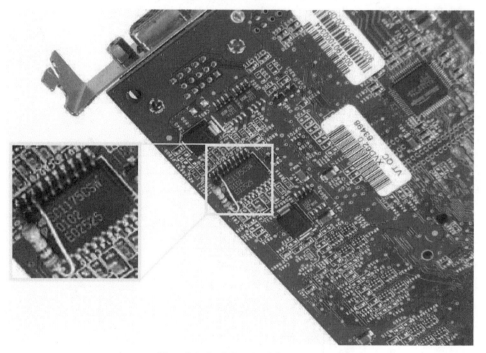

Fig. 14.3. SC1175CSW chip

Because another SC1175CSW chip was installed on the board to supply power to the video memory, it became possible to increase the video-memory power-supply voltage.

The chip channels operate independently, and the output voltage of each is set individually by the divider. A typical method of connecting a chip in the mode with two independent channels is shown in Fig. 14.4.

According to the specification, DDR SDRAM memory chips used with GeForce3 are supplied with two voltages: 3.3 V and 2.5 V. One channel of the SC1175CSW chip ensures power supply to the internal circuitry of the video memory chips; another supplies voltage for input/output buffers.

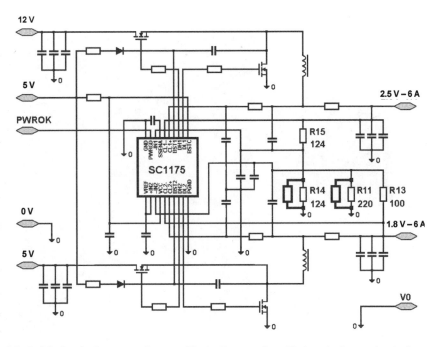

Fig. 14.4. Method of connecting a chip in the mode with two independent channels

Output voltages for the channels are set by the R15:R14 resistor ratio for the 3.3 V channel, and R13:R11 for the 2.5 V channel.

Resistors installed on the board (R822:R824 for 3.3 V, and R825:R829 for 2.5 V) have resistance values of 170 ohms, 100 ohms, 110 ohms, and 100 ohms, respectively. Coupled, they ensure output voltages of 3.37 V and 2.63 V, which means that the supply voltages for the video memory are already slightly higher than the nominal values. To increase these voltages further, R14 and R11 were shunted. To achieve this, 820-ohm resistors were soldered to the chip output contacts labeled 3, 18, and 20, as shown in Figs. 14.5 and 14.6.

As a result, the "new" resistance values for R14 and R11 were 89 ohms each, and the output voltages of the chip channels, calculated using the same formula, were 3.64 V and 2.8 V.

Increasing the core voltage and the video-memory supply voltage drastically increases the chip workloads and results in intense heat emission. Therefore, it is necessary to consider efficient cooling. To improve the temperature mode, specially designed heatsinks from Thermaltake were installed on the memory chips. To cool the video core, it was equipped with a heatsink taken from a standard ND3 processor cooler and an efficient fan from a Thermaltake Volcano cooler (Fig. 14.7).

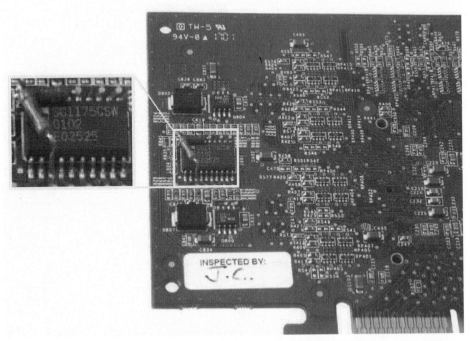

Fig. 14.5. Additional resistance (view of contact 3)

Fig. 14.6. Additional resistance (view of contacts 18 and 20)

Fig. 14.7. Cooling facilities

Fig. 14.8. Leveled and polished video chip

This cooling system seemed to be insufficient; therefore, a variant with a Peltier element also was tried. Because of the high efficiency of such a cooling system, the GeForce3 chip retained stability at frequencies of 280 MHz to 290 MHz. However, after a drop of the condensation trickled into the AGP, only luck kept the motherboard and video adapter from failing. Therefore, the Peltier element was abandoned. Without it, the video chip overheated at a frequency of 270 MHz, and the system hung up.

During experiments, it was discovered that the surface of the GeForce3 chip is curved inward. This made it difficult to ensure normal heat evacuation from the small, round metal surface bent inward. The solution to this problem requires leveling and polishing the chip surface (Fig. 14.8).

The surface of the GeForce3 chip and the base of the heatsink were polished, it became possible to achieve stable operation of the video adapter at high frequencies. As a result of this modification, the VisionTek adapter operated reliably at a 270 MHz core frequency and a 600 MHz (300 MHz DDR) video memory frequency. All video adapters based on Nvidia GeForce3 are equipped with DDR SDRAM chips with an access time of 3.8 nanoseconds; therefore, this value of the video memory frequency is a great result.

Modifying Asus V8200

The Asus V8200 video adapter is implemented on the PCB with a design different from the reference one. Nevertheless, the core and video-memory power-supply stabilizers are the same ones used for the previous adapter. The only difference lies in the positioning of their elements (Fig. 14.9).

Resistors specifying the core voltage (on the board, they are labeled R134 and R138) are on the underside of the board. Their resistance is 140 ohms and 780 ohms, respectively. The power supply voltage of the Nvidia GeForce3 chip on this adapter is 1.48 V. After installing an additional 820-ohm resistor connected in parallel to R1 (R138 on board), it became possible to obtain a "new" R1 value of 400 ohms (Fig. 14.10).

The voltage at the stabilizer output is 1.68 V. Because of the highly efficient cooling system, the core temperature on Asus V8200 didn't rise as significantly as that of the VisionTek adapter. Therefore, additional steps for cooling the core were not required.

The video-memory supply voltage was raised as it was for VisionTek GeForce3 (Figs. 14.11 and 14.12). Two 820-ohm resistors were used for this purpose.

After this modification, the video adapter from Asus operated at a 260 MHz core frequency and a 580 MHz (290 MHz DDR) video memory frequency.

Fig. 14.9. Asus V8200 adapter

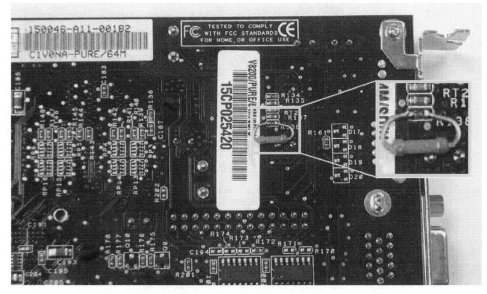

Fig. 14.10. Resistor correcting the video core voltage

Fig. 14.11. Raising the memory supply voltage

Fig. 14.12. Raising the memory supply voltage (continued)

Overclocking and Testing

The following hardware configuration was used to test the video adapters:

❒ Processor — AMD Athlon 1,200 MHz (133 MHz FSB frequency)
❒ Motherboard — Abit KT7A (VIA KT133A)
❒ RAM — 256 MB, NCP PC133
❒ Hard disk — Fujitsu MPE3084AE, 8.4 GB

The following software was used:

❒ Driver — DirectX8.1a
❒ Operating system — Windows 98 SE, build 4.10.2222 A
❒ Test — Quake III Arena v1.27g

Video adapters were tested with the Detonator 12.41 driver. To set the core and video memory clock frequencies, the RivaTuner utility was used.

To improve the temperature conditions of the hardware components, the test system was assembled without a case. Because of this, there were no problems with removing the hot air typical of systems assembled in closed cases. A standard 80 mm fan was placed in front of the video adapter, at a distance of 5 cm to 10 cm. This fan ensured forced air cooling of the heatsinks installed on the video memory chips. The temperature in the test room was between 20°C (68°F) and 23°C (73°F).

The tests were conducted using the VisionTek GeForce3 video adapter, which showed more stable operation than Asus V8200 did at a high frequency.

Using Quake III Arena as a game test, the VisionTek adapter was tested at the following settings: For the modes with a color depth of 16 bits, 16-bit textures were chosen. For 32-bit modes, 32-bit textures were used. The texture quality and geometry details were set at maximum. Trilinear texture filtering was enabled; compression was disabled.

Graphs illustrating performance growth as a percentage of the results achieved at nominal frequencies are provided in Figs. 14.13 and 14.14.

At screen resolutions set to 800 × 600 and 1,024 × 768, the performance was limited by the clock frequency of the processor and by overall system performance. As a result, performance growth under conditions of extreme overclocking did not exceed 10%. With higher screen resolutions, it increased more than 30%.

In 16-bit modes, core overclocking ensured more dramatic performance growth than overclocking of video memory.

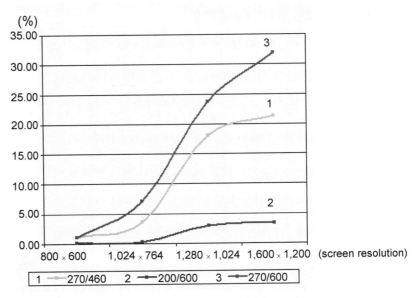

Fig. 14.13. Performance evaluation in 16-bit modes
(1–3 show the core/memory frequency in megahertz)

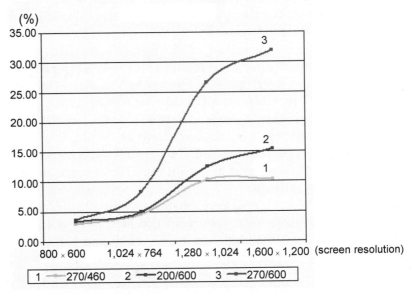

Fig. 14.14. Performance evaluation in 32-bit modes
(1–3 show the core/memory frequency in megahertz)

In 32-bit modes, the performance gain obtained by overclocking the video memory and the core was approximately the same. With an increased screen resolution, video memory overclocking became more efficient, but the performance gain obtained by core overclocking stabilized at 10%.

In 16-bit modes, core overclocking, as was expected, produced more impressive results. Changing the video memory frequency from 460 MHz to 600 MHz had a weak effect at the nominal core frequency, but it provided more significant growth when the core frequency was increased.

In 32-bit modes, video memory overclocking was more efficient. Core overclocking also ensured performance growth, especially when the video memory frequency operated at an increased frequency.

Conclusion

For those who are not satisfied with the performance ensured by GeForce3 video adapters and who are not discouraged by the difficulties and risk of failure encountered when implementing overclocked modes, there is another solution — extreme overclocking. By raising the supply voltage not only for the core, but also for the video memory, it becomes possible to increase the operating frequencies to values that are fantastic for GeForce3 — 270/600 MHz. This makes it possible to obtain a video adapter with excellent performance under the most challenging conditions.

Modifying and Overclocking GeForce3 Ti500/Ti200

After the GeForce3 chip, Nvidia released GeForce3 Ti500 and GeForce3 Ti200. These chips are similar to GeForce3. The main change is that they use different clock frequencies.

Increasing Supply Voltages

After announcing the release of the chips, Nvidia presented a new reference design for adapters based on Ti500/Ti200. However, because these chips differed from GeForce3 only in operating frequency, most manufacturers that released products based on Ti500/Ti200 didn't migrate to the new reference design. They simply installed the new chips on previously produced, standard GeForce3 video adapters.

Some manufacturers have released video adapters based on the new reference design from Nvidia. As a result, most video adapters based on Ti500/Ti200 have one of three reference-design variations: the design for GeForce3, Ti500, or Ti200.

Generally, the designs of all three variations are different. Nevertheless, the methods used to stabilize the core and video-memory supply voltages are almost identical. In all three variations, the same chips connect in the same manner. Usually, the differences lie only in the locations of the elements on the board.

As a rule, the SC1175CSW chips are the basis of designs implementing the power supply of the video adapter elements.

To stabilize the core supply voltage, the SC1175CSW chip is used in the current sharing mode. Its two independent channels serve the same workload — the graphical core. A typical connection plan implemented for a chip operating in this mode was presented in Fig. 14.2. A fragment is shown in Fig. 14.15.

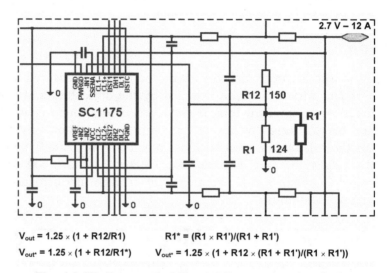

$V_{out} = 1.25 \times (1 + R12/R1)$ $R1^* = (R1 \times R1')/(R1 + R1')$

$V_{out^*} = 1.25 \times (1 + R12/R1^*)$ $V_{out^*} = 1.25 \times (1 + R12 \times (R1 + R1')/(R1 \times R1'))$

Fig. 14.15. Fragment of the stabilizer connection design

The output voltage is calculated from Formula 14.1. Formulas 14.2–14.4 show how it is possible to raise the input voltage using the shunting R1' resistor.

To supply voltage to the video memory, the same SC1175CSW chip is used. In this situation, both channels operate independently, supplying memory chips with 2.5 V for input/output buffers and 3.3 V for internal circuitry (Fig. 14.16).

The output voltages of the channels are set by the R15:R14 resistor ratio for the channel supplying 3.3 V, and by R13:R11 for the channel supplying 2.5 V. Channel output voltages are calculated using the following formulas:

$$V_{out1} = 1.25 \times (1 + R15/R14) \qquad \text{(Formula 14.5)}$$

$$V_{out2} = 1.25 \times (1 + R13/R11) \qquad \text{(Formula 14.6)}$$

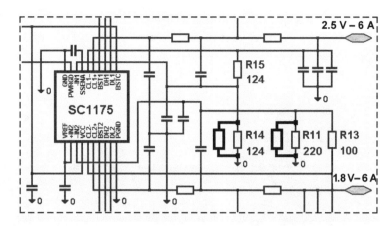

Fig. 14.16. Fragment of a connection design with two independent channels

By shunting R11 and R14, it is possible to increase the supply voltage of the video memory.

GeForce3/Ti500/Ti200 Reference Design

For implementations of the GeForce3/Ti500/Ti200 reference design, power supply stabilizers are on the underside of the board (Fig. 14.17).

Fig. 14.17. Voltage stabilizers of the video memory (*1*) and core (*2*)

Three variants of positioning stabilizers on boards, implemented according to the three versions of the reference design, are shown in Figs. 14.18–14.20.

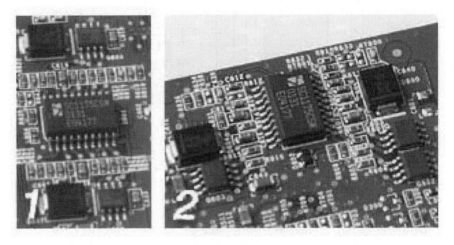

Fig. 14.18. Voltage stabilizers of the video memory (*1*) and core (*2*) (GeForce3 reference design)

Fig. 14.19. Voltage stabilizers of the video memory (*1*) and core (*2*) (Ti200 reference design)

Fig. 14.20. Voltage stabilizers of the video memory (*1*) and core (*2*)
(Ti500 reference design)

The layouts of the stabilizers are practically identical, and the wiring layout of each version is different only in the positions of the elements. Therefore, modification of all three versions will be almost the same.

Increasing the Video-Memory Supply Voltage

On boards implemented according to the GeForce3/Ti500/Ti200 reference design, the ratios of the resistors specifying the video-memory supply voltage usually are 110:100 ohm for the first channel (which produces an output voltage of 2.6 V), and 170:110 ohm for the second channel (which produces an output voltage of 3.4 V). After shunting each divider by additional 1-kilohm resistors, these ratios will be 110:91 ohm and 170:90 ohm. As a result, the output video-memory supply voltages will be raised to 2.8 V and 3.6 V, respectively.

For convenience, shunting resistors are soldered directly to the chip pins labeled 3, 10, 18, and 20, as shown in Fig. 14.21.

Fig. 14.21. Raising the video-memory supply voltage
(GeForce3/Ti200/Ti500 reference design)

Increasing the Video-Core Supply Voltage

Core supply voltage is different for Ti500 and Ti200 video adapters.

The ratio of the resistance that determines the core supply voltage for adapters based on Ti200 is 130:770 ohm. The core supply voltage at this ratio is 1.46 V.

For adapters based on Ti500, the resistance ratio is 130:580 ohm; the output voltage is 1.53 V.

Despite these differences, the core supply voltage can be raised in a manner similar to the one previously used. An additional shunting resistor is necessary. For convenience, it is soldered to the chip outputs labeled 18 and 20, as shown in Fig. 14.22.

When using an additional 1-kohm resistor, the new resistance ratios on Ti200 and Ti500 video adapters are 130:435 ohm and 130:367 ohm. Consequently, the video-core supply voltage rises to 1.62 V for Ti200 and 1.69 V for Ti500.

Before discussing the changes in the overclocking potential of these video adapters produced by this modification, consider Asus video adapters.

Fig. 14.22. Raising the video-core supply voltage
(GeForce3/Ti200/Ti500 reference design)

Asus V8200 T2/T5 Adapter

Two stabilizers are installed on the Asus V8200 T5 video adapter (Figs. 14.23 and 14.24). The first stabilizer is practically the same as the one installed on video adapters implemented according to the SC1175CSW reference design (labeled *A1*). The second one is the standard single-channel AMS1505 stabilizer from Advanced Monolithic Systems (labeled *A2*).

The first channel of the SC1175CSW chip ensures power supply for the core; the second one, 3.3 V, serves as the internal circuitry of the video memory chips. The AMS1505 chip ensures a voltage of 2.5 V for the input/output buffers of the video memory chips. This is an adjustable stabilizer; its typical connection design is shown in Fig. 14.25 and relates to the following formula:

$$V_{out} = V_{ref} \times (1 + R2/R1) + I_{adj} \times R2 \qquad \text{(Formula 14.7)}$$

Asus V8200 T2 has no stabilizer for 2.5 V supplied to video memory. All circuits of the memory chips are supplied with 3.3 V, even though the manufacturer's specifications say that video memory chips must be supplied with two signals: 3.3 V ± 0.3 V, and 2.5 V ± 0.2 V (Figs. 14.26 and 14.27).

The method of raising the video-memory supply voltage is illustrated in Fig. 14.28.

Fig. 14.23. Voltage stabilizers on an Asus V8200 T5 adapter
(Ti500 reference design)

Fig. 14.24. Detailed view of voltage stabilizers on an Asus V8200 T5 adapter

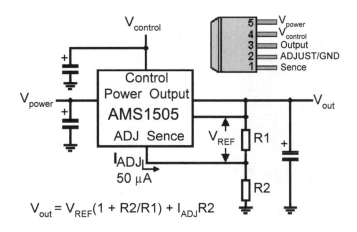

Fig. 14.25. Typical connection design of the AMS1505 chip

Fig. 14.26. Voltage stabilizers on an Asus V8200 T2 adapter
(Ti200 reference design)

Fig. 14.27. Detailed view of voltage stabilizers on an Asus V8200 T2 adapter

Fig. 14.28. Raising video-memory and video-core supply voltages
on Asus V8200 T2/T5

Resistance ratios for setting the core supply voltage on Asus V8200 T2 and V8200 T5 are 140:780 ohm and 140:590 ohm. Consequently, core supply voltages are 1.47 V for Asus V8200 T2 and 1.55 V for Asus V8200 T5.

The resistance ratio that determines the supply voltage for internal circuitry of the video memory chips on Asus V8200 T2/T5 is 220:120 ohm, which produces a supply voltage of 3.54 V.

When using 1-kohm shunting resistors, the core supply voltage on Asus V8200 T2 and V8200 T5 video adapters becomes 1.67 V and 1.72 V. The voltage supplied to video memory changes from 3.3 V to 3.81 V.

Because of the previously described lack of a stabilizer for the 2.5 V signal to the input/output buffers of the video memory chips, these Asus V8200 T2 chips are supplied with the same voltage: 3.81 V (Fig. 14.29).

Fig. 14.29. Voltage stabilizer for 2.5 V is missing on Asus V8200 T2

Perhaps 3.81 V is too much for the circuits intended for 2.5 V. Although the modified Asus V8200 T2 adapter completed all stability tests, this doesn't mean that there will be no problems during lengthy operation of the video memory chips, especially in an extremely overclocked mode.

Fig. 14.30. Raising the memory supply voltage on Asus V8200 T5

On Asus V8200 T5 (Fig. 14.30), this problem doesn't exist. After using the 1-kilohm shunting resistor, the output voltage at the AMS1505 stabilizer was 2.76 V.

Overclocking and Testing

The following hardware configuration was used to test the modified video adapters:

❏ Processor — AMD Athlon XP 1500+

❏ Motherboard — Gigabyte Technology GA-7VTX (VIA KT266A)

❏ RAM — 256 MB, DDR SDRAM, PC2100, Apacer CL2

❏ Hard disk — IBM DTLA 307020, 20 GB

The following software was used:

❏ Driver — Nvidia Detonator v. 22.80 for Windows XP

❏ Operating system — Windows XP

❏ Test — 3DMark2001

The performance of the video adapters was evaluated using 3DMark2001 (Figs. 14.31 and 14.32).

As is obvious from the data in Figs. 14.31 and 14.32, the results shown by Ti500 are not improved considerably by extreme overclocking. This relates to the standard operating frequencies of the core and video memory on Ti500, which already are close to the limit. Therefore, even with extreme overclocking, the frequency increases and the performance gain are insignificant. This does not apply to low resolutions, for which the result is determined by the CPU frequency and overall system performance, rather than by video adapter frequency.

Ti200 is ahead of Ti500 in extreme overclocking modes at standard frequencies. However, this result is achieved only because of the high frequency of video memory. In the nominal operating mode, Ti200 shows minor performance growth; at high resolutions, it is about 50%.

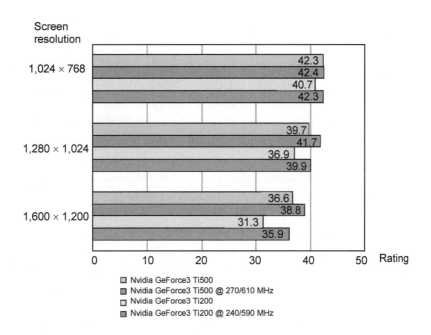

Fig. 14.31. Test results obtained using 3DMark2001 (Car Chase)

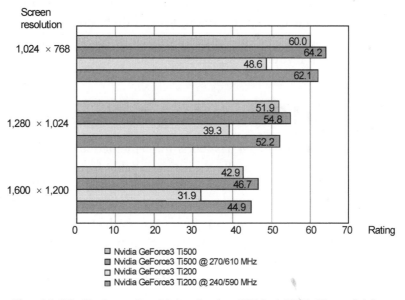

Fig. 14.32. Test results obtained using 3DMark2001 (Dragothic)

Conclusion

Thus, it is possible to draw an unambiguous conclusion: Modification and extreme overclocking of video adapters based on GeForce3 Ti500 are pointless. The performance growth doesn't justify the difficulties that arise from adapter modification. It is possible to raise the supply voltage on the core and video memory even higher, and to install on the core a powerful cooler, such as Dragon Orb 3 or Volcano 6. It is even possible to equip the video adapter with Peltier elements, but these would be too much, even for extreme overclocking. All these expenses wouldn't be justified by the performance growth.

The situation is somewhat different with video adapters based on GeForce3 Ti200. The frequency limits for Ti200 in overclocked modes are between 220 MHz and 230 MHz. Extreme overclocking achieves even higher values, between 240 MHz and 250 MHz. This is lower than the frequency limit of Ti500. However, extreme overclocking of Ti200 ensures a significant increase of the core frequency from the initial level (175 MHz), providing greater performance gain than Ti500.

When overclocking the video memory of Ti200-based adapters, everything depends on the quality of the memory chips installed by the adapter manufacturer. Consequently, the smaller the access time of the memory chips (compared to the standard variant of 5 nanoseconds), the greater the memory frequency growth provided by overclocking. Therefore, when purchasing a video adapter, always pay attention to the type of video memory installed on it by the manufacturer. This is important even if you do not plan to overclock the adapter.

Modifying and Overclocking GeForce4 Ti4400

VisionTek Xtasy GeForce4 Ti4400 is implemented according to the Nvidia reference design, and is practically undistinguishable from Nvidia products. The only indication of the manufacturer is the small sticker with VisionTek logo on the cooler (Fig. 14.33).

This video adapter is equipped with the Nvidia GeForce4 Ti4400 graphical chip and has 128 MB of DDR SDRAM from Samsung for video memory, with a clock time of 3.6 nanoseconds.

The maximum frequencies achieved when overclocking Xtasy GeForce4 Ti4400 are 300/660 MHz.

Fig. 14.33. VisionTek Xtasy GeForce4 Ti4400 adapter

Raising the Video-Core and Video-Memory Supply Voltages

The SC1175CSW chip is responsible for supplying voltage to the graphical core. The methods of increasing the supply voltage were described previously in this chapter.

To increase the supply voltage of the video core, it is possible to decrease the R1 resistor by shunting. (See the typical connection design in Fig. 14.35.) For this purpose, an additional resistor was soldered to the chip outputs labeled 18 and 20 (Fig. 14.34).

Fig. 14.34. Increasing the video-core supply voltage on VisionTek Xtasy GeForce4 Ti4400

The adapter uses 130-ohm and 390-ohm resistors as R1 and R12 (numeration according to the typical method). As a result, the video-core supply voltage is 1.66 V by default. When R1 was shunted with an additional 620-ohm resistor, the video-core supply voltage reached 1.92 V.

The adapter is equipped with video memory chips from Samsung. These chips have a supply voltage for internal circuitry and input/output buffers (Vdd/Vddq) of 2.8 V. This voltage is formed by the SC1102CS chip from Semtech.

This chip operates according to the same principles as the SC1175CSW chip. However, it has only one channel, instead of the two independent channels in SC1175CSW. Another important difference is that the reference voltage in SC1102CS is 1.265 V, rather than 1.25 V in SC1175CSW. Consequently, the output voltage of the stabilizer must be calculated according to the following formula:

$$V_{out} = 1.265 \times (1 + R8/R7) \qquad \text{(Formula 14.8)}$$

In this formula, the resistors are numbered according to the typical connection design (as shown in Fig. 14.35).

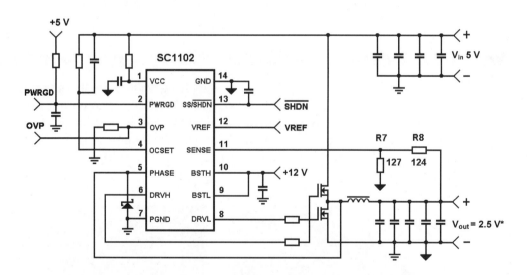

Fig. 14.35. Typical connection design for the SC1102CS chip

As previously mentioned, video adapters based on Nvidia GeForce3/ Ti200/Ti500 have video memory chips with independent supplies of internal circuitry and input/output buffers (3.3/2.5 V = Vdd/Vddq). In contrast, in video adapters based on Nvidia GeForce4, the Vdd and Vddq circuits of the video memory are connected electrically. The input/output buffers of the GeForce4 chip are supplied with the same voltage as the input/output buffers of the video memory chips. This significantly limits the possibilities of raising the supply voltage: For example, when Vdd/Vddq is raised to 3.0 V, "ripples" appear in text modes. This should not be allowed.

Fortunately, the reference design of the adapter allows an additional stabilizer to be installed that supplies the input/output buffers of the video memory chips when necessary (i.e., when the supply voltages of the internal circuitry and the input/output buffers of the video memory chips are different). Before installing an additional stabilizer, it is necessary to remove the connection between Vdd and Vddq by unsoldering the bridges on the front side of the video adapter (Fig. 14.36). The underside of the adapter is shown in Fig. 14.37.

Fig. 14.36. VisionTek Xtasy GeForce4 Ti4400 bridges (front side)

Fig. 14.37. VisionTek Xtasy GeForce4 Ti4400 bridges (underside)

Having accomplished this, it is necessary to unsolder the voltage stabilizer that supplies power to the input/output buffers of the video memory chips. (The positions for installing the components are visible in Figs. 14.36 and 14.37.) This task is not difficult, especially for an experienced specialist. However, using a normal diode is simpler. On directly connected silicon diodes, the voltage drop is normally 0.7 V to 0.8 V. Therefore, it is possible to increase the supply voltage of the internal circuitry of the video memory chips (Vdd) while supply power to the input/output buffers from Vdd via the diode.

This approach was chosen in this example. First, the output voltage at the stabilizer was raised to 3.51 V by soldering a 270-ohm resistor to pins 11 and 14 of the SC1102CS chip (Fig. 14.38).

Fig. 14.38. Increasing the video-memory supply voltage on VisionTek Xtasy GeForce4 Ti4400

Fig. 14.39. Additional diode

Thus, the supply voltage of the internal circuitry of the video memory chips was increased from 2.82 V to 3.51 V.

Next, the powerful silicon diode was chosen and soldered to the position that was previously occupied by the bridges (Fig. 14.39).

After that, the supply voltage of the input/output buffers of the video memory chips and graphical core was 2.77 V. This resulted from the 0.74 V drop on the diode.

After increasing the voltage, it was necessary to consider an efficient cooling system. Overclocking shortens the life of a video adapter. Overclocking combined with an increased supply voltage makes adapter components work overtime. By implementing an efficient cooling system, it is possible to achieve stable operation of the graphical core and video memory at increased frequencies and to prolong the adapter's life as well.

Improving the Cooling System

First, it was necessary to level the surface of the video chip (Fig. 14.40).

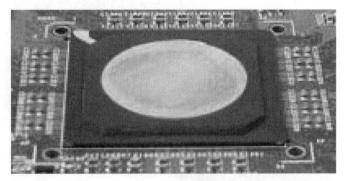

Fig. 14.40. Video chip after its surface has been leveled and polished

After that, a powerful cooler was installed on the video chip (Fig. 14.41).

The fins of the heatsink of the cooler were fastened to the video chip using nylon clips that were passed through the holes in the board.

The final step implies installing heatsinks on the video memory chips. For this purpose, heatsinks supplied in the Thermaltake Memory Cooling Kit were used. Heatsinks were fastened using adhesive thermal stickers from this kit.

After the cooling system was reinforced, the Xtasy GeForce4 Ti4400 adapter looked as shown in Fig. 14.42

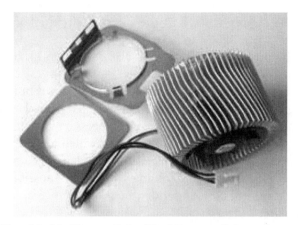

Fig. 14.41. Thermaltake Mimi Copper Orb cooler

Fig. 14.42. VisionTek Xtasy GeForce4 Ti4400 with a modified cooling system

Maximum frequencies at which the modified adapter operated reliably made 340/710 MHz (355 MHz DDR) for video adapter and video memory, respectively. For the moment, this is a record for the products based on Nvidia GeForce4 Ti4400. By achieved frequencies, this modified adapter is far ahead even GeForce4 Ti4600.

Overclocking and Testing

The following hardware configuration was used to test the modified video adapters:

- ❏ Processor — AMD Athlon XP 2000+
- ❏ Motherboard — MSI K7T266 Pro2 v2.0 (VIA KT266A)
- ❏ RAM — 2 × 256 MB, DDR SDRAM, PC 2700, Crucial CL2.5
- ❏ Hard disk — Fujitsu MPF3153AH

The following software was used:

- ❏ Driver — Nvidia Detonator v. 28.32 for Windows XP
- ❏ Operating system — Windows XP
- ❏ Tests — Codecult Codecreatures and 3DMark2001 SE

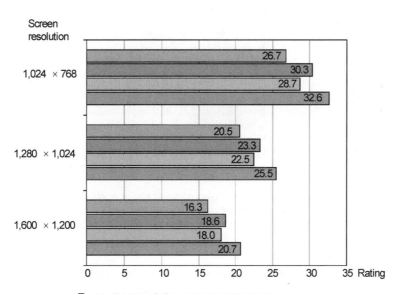

Fig. 14.43. Test results obtained using Codecult Codecreatures

In the Codecult Codecreatures test, the default settings were used.

The following parameters specified the 3DMark2001 operating mode: 32-bit frame buffer, 32-bit textures, 32(24)-bit Z-buffer, and D3D Pure Hardware T&L.

Codecreatures places a very heavy workload on the video adapter. This is visible even without measuring the number of frames per second.

The large number of polygons in the nature scene (500,000 and more) and stringent requirements of the fill rate manifested — overclocking the video core proved to be more fruitful that overclocking the video memory (Fig. 14.43).

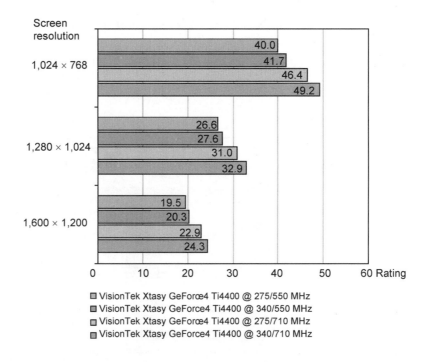

Fig. 14.44. Test results obtained using 3DMark2001 (Nature)

In the 3DMark 2001 Nature test (Fig. 14.44), the reverse occurred: Video-memory overclocking was more efficient than video-core overclocking. This can be easily explained: In the Nature test, the number of polygons in each scene is considerably smaller.

Conclusion

The percentage increase of the video core and video memory frequencies obtained by extreme overclocking with Nvidia GeForce4 was not as impressive as with Nvidia GeForce3. However, it is essential to remember that GeForce3 and GeForce4 are manufactured according the same technology — 0.15 micrometer. It's no wonder that video adapters of the GeForce4 generation, which have higher nominal frequencies, have lower overclocking potential. Overclocking potential increases only after migration to more advanced manufacturing technologies.

Although extreme overclocking of GeForce4 Ti4400 is a tedious and troublesome task, the performance increase of 20%–25% is impressive. By implementing this performance reserve, it is possible to enjoy full-screen smoothing, anisotropic filtering, and a high screen resolution.

Modifying and Overclocking GeForce4 Ti4600

Nvidia GeForce4 Ti4600 is the most powerful member of the Ti4*xxx* chip family.

An example of the products based on this chip is the VisionTek Xtasy GeForce4 Ti4600 video adapter (Figs. 14.45 and 14.46).

Fig. 14.45. VisionTek Xtasy GeForce4 Ti4600 adapter (front side)

The performance of this video adapter is relatively high. Nevertheless, even this high-performance product, like its predecessors, can be modified and overclocked. (Note that this might cause the adapter failure.)

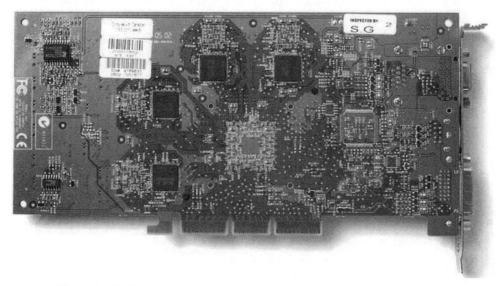

Fig. 14.46. VisionTek Xtasy GeForce4 Ti4600 adapter (underside)

Modifying the Adapter

Operations described for Xtasy GeForce4 Ti4400 were performed for this adapter.

Fig. 14.47. VisionTek Xtasy GeForce4 Ti4600 after modification

First, the video chip surface was leveled and polished to make it flat. Then, the standard cooler was replaced with the more powerful one tested in the previous experiment.

After modification, the video adapter looked as shown in Fig. 14.47.

Maximum frequencies at which Xtasy GeForce4 Ti4600 operation was stable without increasing the voltage (i.e., in the moderate overclocking modes) was 315/750 MHz (375 MHz DDR).

Increasing the Voltage and Extreme Overclocking

On VisionTek Xtasy GeForce4 Ti4600, like all products based on Nvidia GeForce4 Ti4600 and manufactured according to the reference design, the supply of the graphical core is ensured using the SC1102CS stabilizer from Semtech. This chip is a controller for the pulse power-supply units and DC/DC converters. Output voltage of the stabilizer is specified by the R8:R7 resistor ratio (marked as in the typical connection design) and is calculated according to the following formula:

$$V_{out} = V_{ref} \times (1 + R8/R7) \qquad \text{(Formula 14.9)}$$

Here, V_{ref} is the reference voltage; for SC1102CS, it is 1.265 V. The resistors in this formula are numbered according to the typical connection design shown in Fig.14.35. A fragment of this method is in Fig. 14.48.

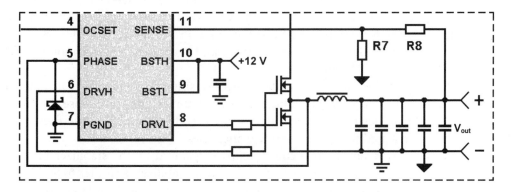

Fig. 14.48. Fragment of the SC1102CS connection design

The simplest way to increase the supply voltage of the graphical core is to reduce the resistance R7 (in the typical connection design) by shunting it with an additional resistor, connected in parallel. This task was accomplished by soldering a 1-kilohm resistor to pins 11 and 14 of the SC1102CS chip (Fig. 14.49).

Fig. 14.49. Voltage stabilizer for the SC1102CS chip

As a result, the R8:R7 ratio (according to the typical connection design) has changed, and output voltage of the stabilizer has been raised from 1.66 V to 1.81 V.

In the course of experiments, the supply voltage on the video chip was increased even higher — to 2.0 V. However, this didn't provide additional frequency growth during overclocking. The maximum frequency at which the graphical core was capable of operating under conditions of extreme overclocking was 340 MHz. The optimal frequency of the Nvidia GeForce4 Ti4400 chip under conditions of extreme overclocking proved to be the same. Presumably, 340 MHz to 350 MHz is the limit set by the internal architecture and manufacturing technology of Nvidia GeForce4 Ti4600/Ti4400.

Finally, a decision was made to stop raising the voltage after it has been increased only 9%. This was done because it is undesirable to expose the chip to the risk of being destroyed, especially after it was discovered that the frequency limit could be reached with a small voltage increase.

The power supply to memory chips is ensured by the stabilizer based on the SC1175CSW chip. This controller of the pulse stabilizer is similar to SC1102CS, but it has two independent channels. On adapters based on Nvidia GeForce4 Ti4600, one channel of this stabilizer ensures a power supply to internal circuitry and to the input/output buffers of the video memory chips (Vdd/Vddq). The other stabilizes the workload voltage (Vtt) for coordinating circuits by the impedance.

The supply voltages of the internal circuits and input/output buffers coincide for the chips used in Nvidia GeForce4 Ti4600; therefore, Vdd and Vddq are connected, and chips are supplied by one channel of the SC1175CSW stabilizer.

The output voltage on the stabilizer is set by the resistance ratio, according to the following formulas:

$$V_{out1} = V_{ref} \times (1 + R15/R14) \qquad \text{(Formula 14.10)}$$

$$V_{out2} = V_{ref} \times (1 + R13/R11) \qquad \text{(Formula 14.11)}$$

Here, the V_{ref} for SC1175CSW is 1.25 V, and the resistance numeration corresponds to the typical connection design (Fig. 14.50).

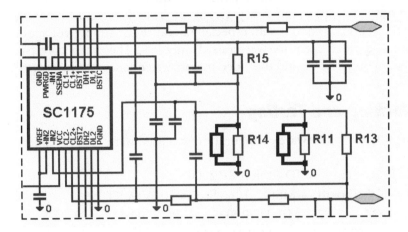

Fig. 14.50. Fragment of the SC1175CSW connection design

The default supply voltage of the video memory chips was 2.83 V.

The V_{out1} voltage was increased by shunting the R14 resistor with an additional 720-ohm resistor that was soldered to pins 18 and 20 of the controller chip (Fig. 14.51).

Fig. 14.51. Voltage stabilizer of the video core

At the same time, the supply voltage of the video memory was increased to 3.09 V. With such a voltage supplied to video memory, the video adapter operation was unstable; ripples and list pixels appeared. These problems arose when the test computer was booted. Because of this, a decision was made to stop increasing the voltage at 3.09 V. As a result, the video-memory supply voltage was increased only 9.2%.

The maximum video-memory frequency at which VisionTek Xtasy GeForce4 Ti4600 operated reliably was 800 MHz (400 MHz DDR).

After modification, the maximum frequencies of the graphical core and video memory on VisionTek Xtasy GeForce4 Ti4600 were 340/800 MHz (400 MHz DDR). This is a good result, especially because the supply voltages of the graphical core and video memory were raised only 9%. The video core frequency was increased only 13.3%, and the video memory frequency was increased 23.1%.

Overclocking and Testing

The following hardware configuration was used to test the modified video adapters:

- ❏ Processor — AMD Athlon XP 2000+
- ❏ Motherboard — MSI K7T266 Pro2 v2.0 (VIA KT266A)
- ❏ RAM — 2 × 256 MB, DDR SDRAM, PC 2700, Crucial CL2.5
- ❏ Hard disk — Fujitsu MPF3153AH

The following software was used:

- ❏ Driver — Nvidia Detonator v. 29.20 for Windows XP
- ❏ Operating system — Windows XP
- ❏ Tests — Codecult Codecreatures and 3DMark2001 SE

The default settings were used in the Codecult Codecreatures test.

The following parameters specified the operating modes in 3DMark2001: 32-bit frame buffer, 32-bit textures, 32(24)-bit Z-buffer, and D3D Pure Hardware T&L.

The performance growth under conditions of extreme overclocking was approximately 20% in the 3DMark2001 test (Fig. 14.52).

With the Codecreatures test, the performance gain was smaller. This is not surprising because this test is more sensitive to the growth of the graphical core frequency than to video memory overclocking. Extreme overclocking increased the core frequency only 13.3% (Fig. 14.53).

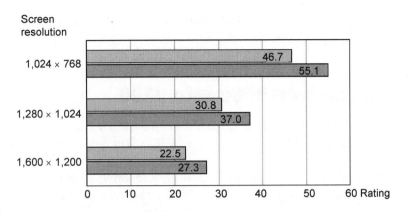

Fig. 14.52. Test results obtained using 3DMark2001 (Nature)

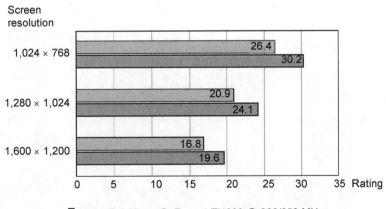

Fig. 14.53. Test results obtained using Codecult Codecreatures

Conclusion

The results of extreme overclocking of VisionTek Xtasy GeForce4 Ti4600 cannot be considered outstanding. The reason is that the nominal clock frequencies of the graphical core and video memory are close to the frequency limit set by the chip architecture and the manufacturing technology. In such a situation, it doesn't make sense to hope for good overclocking potential.

Turning ATI Radeon 9500 into 9700

Researchers from the test lab of **http://www.fcenter.ru** conducted an experiment that turned Radeon 9500 into Radeon 9700. The modification procedure is described here.

A video adapter from Sapphire, based on Radeon 9500 and equipped with 128 MB video memory (Figs. 14.54 and 14.55), was chosen for the experiment.

The sequence of modification was as follows:

1. The cooler was removed from the graphical chip. Using a soldering iron, the resistor on the chip mount was placed in a new location. Figs. 14.56 and 14.57 show this resistor in the new location.

Fig. 14.54. Sapphire adapter based on Radeon 9500 (front side)

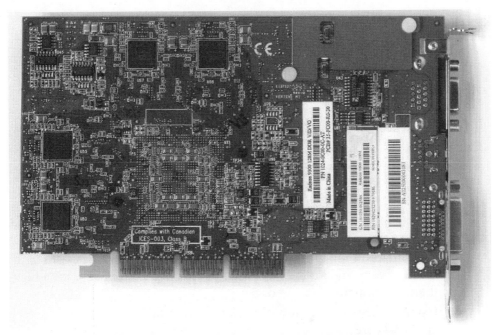

Fig. 14.55. Sapphire adapter based on Radeon 9500 (underside)

Fig. 14.56. Positions of resistors on the Radeon 9500 chip

Fig. 14.57. Detailed view of resistors on the Radeon 9500 chip

2. The surface of the graphical core and cooler base had to be cleansed of the remains of the standard thermal paste. Instead of the thermal paste, a high-quality thermal compound was used.

3. Using standard procedures, the cooler was installed and fastened on top of the graphical core.

4. An MS-DOS boot diskette was created. All files required by the flash utility to replace the video BIOS were copied to this diskette: atiflash.exe, dos4gw.exe, and atiflash.cfg. (These files can be downloaded from **www.3dchipset.com/ files/bios/ati/flash/atiflash.zip**.) The file containing the new BIOS version was copied to the same diskette. The experiments used the modified BIOS from the Hercules video adapter, based on Radeon 9700. It can be downloaded from **http://home.mindspring.com/~warp11/97npherc.bin**.

5. The video adapter was installed, then the system was booted from the diskette just created.

6. To be on the safe side, a backup copy was made of the old video BIOS and the file was named old.bin. This can be accomplished by issuing the following command: `atiflash -s 0 old.bin`.

7. The new BIOS code was loaded into the video adapter ROM chip by issuing the following command: `atiflash -u 0 -f 97npherc.bin`. The utility prompts you to confirm the action. If you decide to complete the update procedure, answer `Yes`.

8. The diskette was removed, and the computer was rebooted.

During this experiment, the Radeon 9500 128MB was modified successfully and turned into Radeon 9700. After this modification, the video adapter started to operate at the speed of Radeon 9700. The modified adapter operated smoothly; during testing, no problems were encountered. Maximum frequencies at which the adapter was stable were 390/620 MHz (310 MHz DDR).

Notes on Modifying and Testing Video Adapters

- ❏ Materials provided in this chapter are a report on experiments conducted by the authors, their colleagues, and their friends. This material should not be considered a recommendation for extreme overclocking or the unsoldering and resoldering video adapters.

- ❏ Modifications described in this chapter, as well as overclocking, reduce the lifetime of video adapters.

- ❏ Performing any of the modifications described here automatically revokes any warranties.

- ❏ If a video adapter or another component fails as a result of such a modification, the user holds all responsibility for this failure.

Chapter 15

Technology and Problems of Overclocking IDE Drives

Computer performance can be increased by speeding up the disk subsystem: hard disks and optical drives. Faster operating speed can be achieved by increasing the bus clock frequency or by using the hidden capabilities of the drive architecture.

The performance and stability of drives that use Integrated Drive Electronics (IDE), including most hard disks, greatly depends on the mode of operation.

Overclocking Hard Disks

The operating modes of hard disks strongly depend on the frequencies of buses to which these devices are connected via controllers. For current hard disks, frequency modes are determined by the PCI bus. Note that motherboards released ten years ago and oriented toward the 486 and 386 processor families usually employ VLB, MCA, ISA, or EISA buses.

The frequency of the PCI bus — and, often, the frequencies of its obsolete predecessors — depends on the FSB frequency (GTL+/AGTL+, Alpha EV6). PCI frequencies typically are set by dividing the FSB frequency. The most common values of FSB and PCI frequencies implemented in motherboards are listed in Table 15.1.

Table 15.1. Prevalent Frequencies in Motherboards Based on Intel 440BX

FSB (MHz)	PCI/IDE (MHz)
66	33
75	38
83	42*
100	33
103	34
112	37
124	41*
133	44*

* Unstable operation is probable

The architectures of most motherboards provide the possibility of correcting the PCI frequency, both by changing the FSB frequency and by setting the appropriate dividers of the FSB frequency. This can be accomplished using parameters in BIOS Setup or switches and jumpers on the motherboard. By changing the clock frequencies of the computer buses, it is possible to choose optimal frequency modes for devices controlled by those buses (Table. 15.2).

Table 15.2. Standard Frequencies for Contemporary Motherboards

FSB (MHz)	Divider	PCI (MHz)
100	1/3	33
133	1/4	33
166	1/5	33
200	1/6	33

Contemporary hard disks based on fast elements tolerate increases to the frequencies of their buses. However, even they cannot ensure stable operation at increased frequencies obtained by processor overclocking. (See Table 15.3.)

Some increase in the clock frequency of the PCI bus, to which the hard disk is connected, helps boost the data-transmission speed. Raising the frequency of this bus ensures the increase of its bandwidth.

Table 15.3. Clock Frequencies and Bandwidths of the PCI Bus

FSB (MHz)	Divider	PCI (MHz)	PCI (MB/sec)
100	1/3	33	133
110	1/3	37	147
120	1/3	40	160
133	1/3	44*	177
133	1/4	33	133
140	1/4	35	140
150	1/4	38	150
160	1/4	40	160
170	1/4	43*	170
166	1/5	33	133
170	1/5	34	136
180	1/5	36	144
190	1/5	38	152
200	1/5	40	160
210	1/5	42*	168
220	1/5	44*	176
200	1/6	33	133
210	1/6	35	140
220	1/6	37	147
230	1/6	38	153
240	1/6	40	160
250	1/6	42*	167

* Unstable operation is probable

Standard hardware and software rarely provide tools for overclocking hard drives. However, the operating speed of a hard disk depends on the frequency of the PCI bus to which it is connected via a special controller. To confirm this, test the PC in the overclocked mode using WinCheckIt 2.03 at different FSB frequencies. This bus determines the PCI clock frequency; via the PCI, it influences hard disk performance. Performance evaluations obtained by testing hard disks using the WinCheckIt and WinBench 99 programs at different PCI frequencies are provided in Table 15.4 and illustrated in Figs. 15.1–15.3.

Table 15.4. Hard Disk Performance

	PCI = 33 MHz	PCI = 38 MHz	PCI = 42 MHz
WinCheckIt rating	6,686	7,395	8,141
WinMark 99 rating (business disk)	1,700	1,770	1,850
WinMark 99 rating (high-end disk)	6,250	6,490	6,690

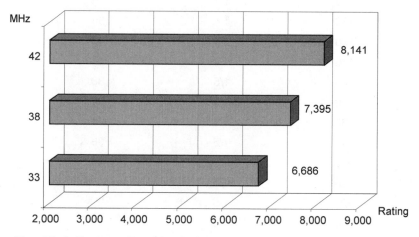

Fig. 15.1. Test results of hard disk performance using WinCheckIt

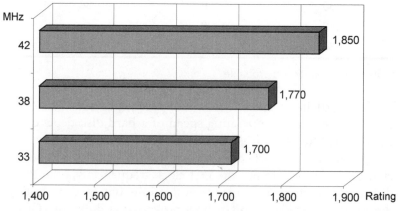

Fig. 15.2. Test results of hard disk performance using WinMark 99 (business disk)

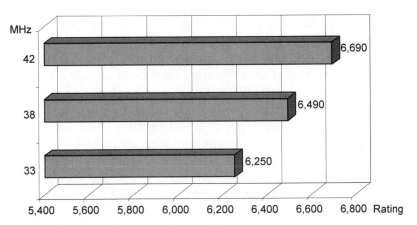

Fig. 15.3. Test results of hard disk performance using WinMark 99 (high-end disk)

Note that not all hard disks tolerate overclocking by increasing the bus frequency. For some disks, performance actually decreases. This behavior depends on the disk type and on the physical disk.

Most contemporary hard disks with a capacity larger than 10 GB operate well at increased frequencies (42 MHz or higher) if used with a high-quality motherboard. As a rule, such modes are impossible for disks smaller than 1 GB. For hard disks between 1 GB and 10 GB, such modes are undesirable because elements and technologies used in manufacturing such disks are less advanced.

Although high-capacity hard disks can operate at increased PCI frequencies, you should not set frequencies exceeding 40 MHz. Doing so would increase of the probability of failure and data loss when reading or writing data; it also would induce temperature far from optimal for the electronic and mechanical components of hard disks. Problematic temperatures are the consequence of increased heat emission from hard disk components, caused by increased clock frequencies.

At this point, it is expedient to recall the formula that determines the dependence of thermal power emitted by chips on their operating frequency. For chips used in the electronic components of the hard disk, this formula looks as follows:

$$P_0 = P \times (F_0/F)$$

Here, P_0 is the power in overclocked mode, P is the power in normal mode, F_0 is the operating frequency in overclocked mode, and F is the operating frequency in normal mode.

By adding the P_0 values of each chip, it is possible to obtain an approximate value of the heat emission in the overclocked mode, if the power supply voltage did not change.

From this formula, it follows that 30% frequency growth increases the thermal power emitted by the chips. Because of this, the temperature under conditions of extreme overclocking worsens dramatically.

Bear in mind that contemporary hard disks include a large amount of built-in cache memory (often 8 MB) and have a high rotation speed (7,200 rpm, and often 10,000 rpm). This typically requires these components to be cooled, even in standard operating modes. This is especially true when using several such devices mounted in a small system unit case with other high-performance components. Operation of these components frequently is accompanied by high heat emission. In such situations, it is recommended that you use adequate cooling devices not only for the processor and the video adapter, but for the hard disks as well. Unfortunately, this can't always be implemented. Thus, high temperatures and insufficient speed parameters of the electronic and mechanical components of hard disks are the main factors preventing overclocking of these devices.

If you have stringent requirements for hard disks reliability, increasing the speed of their operation by significantly raising the bus frequency cannot be a solution. Most motherboards provide the capability of fixing the PCI bus frequency. For such motherboards, the PCI bus frequency doesn't depend on the FSB frequency and can be set to a standard (33 MHz) or overclocked value. Usually, this is achieved by setting the appropriate parameter in BIOS Setup.

Overclocking Optical Drives

Most optical drives, including those for CD-ROM, CD-R, CD-RW, and numerous DVD models, are intended for use within the PCs. Generally, they are connected to the PCI bus via the ATA/33 interface.

Most problems caused by high PCI bus frequencies with these IDE devices are similar to the problems with hard disks. The list of such problems includes errors, violation of temperature modes, and even failure of the device.

However, these devices have overclocking methods different from the traditional increase of clock frequencies.

One such method, which ensures the employment of undocumented functionality, is modification of the microcode that controls the optical device. (Information on this topic is provided from materials and with the permission of Russian-language Web sites **http://www.ixbt.com** and **http://www.overclockers.ru**.)

The controlling microcode is written into the flash memory chip included in each optical drive. Replacing the microcode with a newer version typically increases the operating speed of the optical drive. For devices with writing capabilities, it widens the range of media and writing modes.

This method is not new. There are numerous online discussions and entire Web sites dedicated to this topic. Furthermore, vast libraries make available for downloading various microcode versions and utilities for the most popular drive types and models.

New versions of microcodes also are available at the official sites of optical drive manufacturers. Usually, these versions include useful additions and corrections of known bugs. As with motherboard BIOS versions, you must follow special procedures to obtain a newer version of software code, and you must update the contents of flash memory using specialized tools. This has the same advantages and drawbacks typical of BIOS updating.

Some optical drives include unique chips; therefore, the microcodes and updating utilities also might be unique. However, most manufacturers use base products and sell them under their respective trademarks.

As a result of such a business practice, most optical drives are based on a limited number of device types. Because of this, you may encounter "twins" among the devices that at first seem to be of different types and bear different names. For such products, the microcodes and software updating utilities are interchangeable. Furthermore, because such devices are sometimes positioned in different categories, replacing the microcode can improve the device rating by increasing its functionality and widening its functional parameters.

The Teac CD-W512EB CD-RW drive is an illustrative example of this statement. Replacing the 2.0A microcode with version 2.0B adds the possibility of writing disks in the DAO-RAW mode.

Another example that implements hidden device potential shifts the LG-8083B (4/4/32) CD-RW device to the LG-8080B (8/4/32) model. The procedures for performing this modification are described in detail at **http://www.cdrinfo.com**. The procedure is straightforward and only requires replacement of the microcode.

Pay attention to the following circumstances that accompany the procedure of replacing the microcode in optical drives:

❐ Unauthorized use of the microcode might violate someone's copyright.

❐ An error in code choice can result in partial or complete loss of device usability, as well as the device's warranty.

❐ As a rule, it is impossible to convert a low-end device into a high-end device. By updating the microcode, you usually can increase the device rating by one or two steps within the model row.

❐ Besides increasing speed, microcode modification can remove limitations for viewing DVD films. This may violate copyright law and rules regulating DVD devices and media sales.

One of the most popular utilities for changing the microcode of optical drives is MTK WinFlash. It performs this operation under Windows operating systems and under DOS.

This utility works with drives based on the MediaTek chip; therefore, it is suitable only for a limited number of drive models (Fig. 15.4).

When solving problems related to updating microcode, bear in mind that a device belonging to a group released by one manufacturer may not use the same chips as other devices in the group.

A good example of this is Teac. For some time, this manufacturer has used chips from Sanyo in its products. For example, the Sanyo LC898098 chip is a main chip in the Teac CD-W524E device. However, the Teac CD-W540E drive uses the Sanyo LC898094 chip (Fig. 15.5).

Fig. 15.4. MT1508E chip from MediaTek **Fig. 15.5.** LC898094 chip from Sanyo

Later, Teac started to use chips from MediaTek for its CD-RW drives, including CD-W548E (Fig. 15.6).

A similar situation exists for TDK products. The devices manufactured by this company rely on drives from different market segments: A drive manufactured by Ricoh is intended for low-end and intermediate TDK devices; a drive manufactured by Sanyo is oriented toward high-end TDK devices. With its CyClone 401248B optical drive, TDK changed its direction and used MediaTek chips (Fig. 15.7).

Fig. 15.6. Teac CD-W548E CD-RW drive (*a*) and MediaTek chipset (*b* and *c*)

Fig. 15.7. TDK CyClone 401248B CD-RW drive

The technical characteristics and outward appearance of the Asus CRW2410S design reproduce the Sanyo BP-1500 drive. The basis of the Asus CD-RW drive is Sanyo's LC898098Y UF8 1FK3G chip. The same is true for a similar product from TDK.

A more advanced Asus product — CRW4012A — is based on the MT1508E chip from MediaTek (Fig. 15.8).

Fig. 15.8. Asus CRW4012A CD-RW drive

These examples show that different chips frequently are used in optical drives from the same manufacturer. With any drive, it is necessary to make sure that the microcode-updating utility is compatible with the chip version.

When deciding to update an optical device, it is necessary to correctly evaluate the necessity of this step. It is hardly expedient to try to get the maximum performance from a drive only a few months old. The performance gain obtained during the writing of a standard 700 MB disk using a 48x device will be insignificant in comparison to that of the 40x device, whose warranty will be lost. In addition, contemporary drives tune their writing speed to the media quality. Users who want to economize often use cheap media, which cannot be written with the required quality at high speeds.

Nevertheless, in some cases, the replacement of the existing microcode and the use of updated drivers can boost performance, make new modes available, improve the operating stability, and increase the capacity of traditional media.

For example, in 2002, the Sanyo Electric division announced that it had developed a new technology for writing optical disks, known as HD-Burn (High-Density

Burn). This technology writes 1.4 GB — almost twice the typical amount of data on standard CD-R media.

Researchers from **http://www.fcenter.ru** attribute such a high writing density to two innovations. First, Sanyo decreased the size of the groove on the media surface from 0.83 micrometers (μm) to 0.62 μm. This allowed the company to increase the media capacity 1.34 times. The second innovation was a new technology for error correction, the Reed-Solomon (RS) product code. This new technology ensures a capacity increase of 1.49 times. As a result, the total increase nearly doubled the media capacity.

Table 15.5. Comparison of CD-R and HD-Burn

	CD-R	HD-Burn	Capacity increase
Minimum track width	0.83 μm	0.62 μm	1.343
Error correction algorithm	CIRC	RS product code	1.489
Media capacity	700 MB (type 80)	1,400 MB (type 80)	2.000

Using the HD-Burn technology, disks can be written at a speed of 36x and read at a speed of 80x. Protection against buffer underflow is supported. It is also possible to write to CD-RW media; the write speed would be 24x. This technology is incompatible with audio CD technology. Up to 30 minutes of video data can be written to such a compressed disc in the DVD-Video format (at a resolution of 720 × 576).

For now, manufacturers that supported this technology are few. (Among them are Lite-On and BenQ.) It may be used as a useful addition in DVD/CD-RW drives, but cannot replace DVD. However, if information won't fit on a single CD but would use little space on a DVD, HD-Burn is expected to be helpful. Sanyo also plans to create a technology for threefold data-write compression, which could make the following media capacities available: 700 MB, 1.4 GB, and 2.1 GB.

In conclusion, modification can give standard products new functional capabilities. Updating the software code stored in the flash memory chips of optical devices can make these devices faster, enable them to write media that requires a higher capacity, and improve performance. This can be considered correct and justified overclocking.

Chapter 16

Overclocking To Achieve Processor and Motherboard Compatibility

Motherboards cannot always work with newer processors, even if those processors correspond to the standards of those motherboards. In such cases, the recommendation is to update the BIOS code. It often is difficult to implement this advice because it requires a second processor manufactured with the earlier technology. Unfortunately, few end users have a second processor at their disposal. In most cases, however, this compatibility problem can be solved by unlocking the frequency multiplier.

(Materials provided with the permission of **http://www.overclockers.ru**, a Russian-language Web site.)

Physically, AMD's first Athlon XP processors based on the Thoroughbred core (0.13-micrometer technology) were no different than Athlon XP processors based on the Palomino core (0.18-micrometer technology). The technological process changed, and the core area, operating voltage, and heat generation decreased. Nevertheless, the first models were practically identical in the internal structure of the die, the number of transistors, the amount of cache memory, and the FSB frequency.

AMD Athlon XP 2200+ based on the Thoroughbred core is a good example. Nominal frequency of this model is 1,800 MHz, the bus frequency is 133 MHz, and the multiplier 13.5x. Operating voltage of the processor is 1.65 V.

Despite the similarities between the Thoroughbred and Palomino architectures, unexpected difficulties were encountered when testing AMD Athlon XP 2200+ (AIRGA 0224WPAW) processors. Testing revealed that processors based on the Thoroughbred core are not supported by all motherboards. When processors based on the Palomino core were used, problems were not encountered with those motherboards. Furthermore, those motherboards were recommended on the AMD Web site for Athlon XP processors.

For all such cases, AMD recommends that you update the BIOS code. However, in most cases, it is impossible to accomplish this task. Problematic motherboards don't even start with processors based on the Thoroughbred core, and most users have no second processor compatible with the motherboard.

From several available motherboards, the Asus A7V333 revision 1.01 was chosen. It showed stable operation even with BIOS version 1005. AMD recommends using BIOS starting from version 1007.

Configuration of the Test System

- ❑ Motherboard — Asus A7V333 (VIA KT333, revision 1.01, BIOS version 1008)
- ❑ Processor — AMD Athlon XP 2200+ (Thoroughbred)
- ❑ Hard disk — IBM DTLA 305020
- ❑ RAM — Samsung 512 MB PC2700 DDR SDRAM CL2.5
- ❑ Video adapter — Nvidia GeForce4 Ti4600
- ❑ Cooler — Thermaltake Volcano 7
- ❑ Operating system — Windows XP (Nvidia Detonator 29.42)

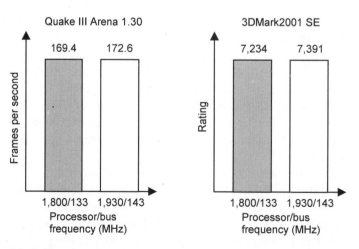

Fig. 16.1. Results of testing with a screen resolution of 1,600 × 1,200

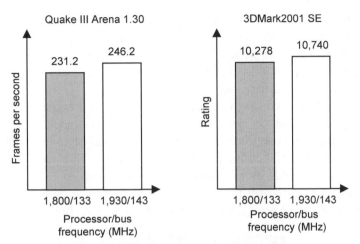

Fig. 16.2. Results of testing with a screen resolution of 1,024 × 768

The overclocking potential of the processors used proved to be rather low. However, this was not related to the motherboard used in testing. This motherboard, in contrast to the products of other manufacturers, worked not only with the latest BIOS version, but also with the initial one, which was not listed among the recommended versions. Nevertheless, the problem of incompatibility between motherboards and processors didn't lose its importance. If you decide to purchase a new processor, it is unlikely that you will have the opportunity to test a dozen of motherboards to find a suitable one. Furthermore, if the motherboard won't start, you may not have a spare processor to update the BIOS code.

In the course of testing motherboards for compatibility with processors based on the Thoroughbred core, it was revealed that most of them do not work. Those motherboards that worked prompted researchers to choose lower clock frequencies for the processor. One of the motherboards — Asus A7N266-C (Nvidia nForce415D chipset, revision 1.03), with BIOS version 1001e — chose the multiplier 5.5x (100 × 5.5 = 550 MHz, and 133 × 5.5 ≈ 733 MHz), the most suitable one from its point of view. It was impossible to update the BIOS code on this motherboard using a Thoroughbred processor because neither of the multiplier values supported by the motherboard was suitable for the processor, which meant the motherboard wouldn't start. At a new startup, there will be another transition to BIOS Setup, and you again will be prompted to choose the right frequency. You can't even reach the startup stage that allows you to boot from the diskette. The only solution in this situation is to update the BIOS code to version 1003e, using a processor based on the Palomino core. In a newer BIOS version, there were no problems with the Thoroughbred core, and the motherboard operated correctly. A similar situation existed for the Asus A7V266-E motherboard based on the VIA KT266A chipset revision 1.07 and BIOS version 1004b. Only after the BIOS was upgraded to version 1010e did it recognize processors based on the Thoroughbred core and operate without problems.

Taking into account the multiplier problem that existed for motherboards with unsuitable BIOS code, researchers decided to conduct experiments using a processor with an unlocked multiplier value. This was justified particularly for processors based on the Thoroughbred core, because this procedure is simpler for them than for their predecessors based on the Palomino core. To unlock the multiplier for processors based on the Thoroughbred core, it is necessary to restore only one bridge from the L3 group, rather than all L1 bridges as previously required (Fig. 16.3).

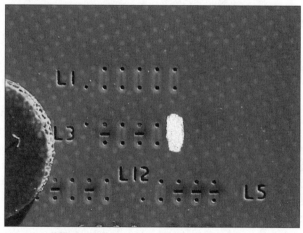

Fig. 16.3. Unlocking the multiplier for a processor based on the Thoroughbred core

Note that during the check, the Asus A7N266-C and A7V266-E motherboards started but didn't work. As a result, it was impossible to update the BIOS, because it was impossible to set the correct multiplier value.

When the AMD Athlon XP 2200+ (Thoroughbred) processor with an unlocked multiplier was installed, the motherboard with the old BIOS version displayed the standard prompt to choose a processor frequency of 550 MHz or 733 MHz. This time, a bus frequency of 133 MHz and a multiplier of 10x were set. As a result, the motherboard successfully recognized an Athlon XP 1500+ processor, and the system booted.

Thus, for a processor with an unlocked multiplier, there appeared the possibility of changing the CPU frequency, as well as the possibility of updating the BIOS code and working at nominal frequencies. There was no need to use a second processor created with earlier technology.

As a result, researchers hypothesized that motherboards that wouldn't start with newer processors were unable to do so because they couldn't set the correct multiplier value.

A check was conducted using an Abit KX7-333 motherboard. As with previous motherboards, the same situation arose: The motherboard allowed the multiplier to be set to 5.5x instead of 13.5x. Using a smaller multiplier value and a higher frequency of the processor bus, it was possible to improve the performance of the computer.

In the newer test system with the Abit KX7-333 motherboard (BIOS version 9k), the same test conditions were reproduced. However, in this case, the RAM power supply voltage was raised to 2.75 V. As a result, it became possible to achieve a processor frequency of 2 GHz.

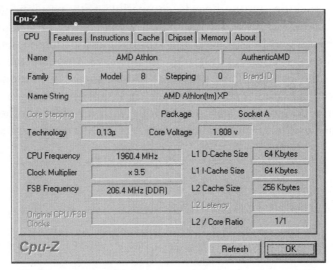

Fig. 16.4. Parameters of an overclocked processor based on the Thoroughbred core

The CPU bus frequency and memory-bus frequency were set to 206 MHz (412 MHz DDR). The multiplier was 9.5x, and the voltage was 1.8 V.

The operating system also could be booted at a frequency of 208 MHz; however, in this mode, the system was unstable. The required level of stability for the processor used was achieved at a clock frequency of 1,930 MHz (203 MHz × 9.5). At this frequency, tests were conducted using 3DMark2001 SE and Quake III Arena at screen resolutions of 1,600 × 1,200 and 1,024 × 768.

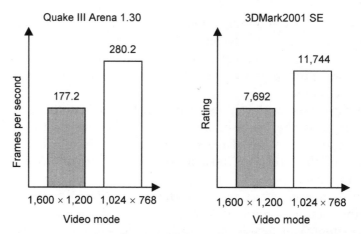

Fig. 16.5. Test results at a CPU frequency of 1,930 MHz (203 MHz × 9.5)

To conclude, motherboards compatible with previous-generation Socket A processors do not always work correctly with newer processors that comply with the same standard. However, the compatibility problem is the responsibility of motherboard manufacturers, who do not always update the BIOS code in time. Usually, the compatibility problem can be solved by unlocking the multiplier. Based on the results of experiments, it is possible to state that in most cases, a newer processor will start successfully with an older motherboard, which provides the possibility of changing the multiplier, bus frequency, and voltage levels.

Chapter 17

Solving Problems by Anti-Overclocking

In some cases, high performance affects software compatibility. Besides this, as hardware components become more technologically advanced and sophisticated, energy consumption, heat emission, and noise increase. These negative factors create problems with computer operation. One solution is to use modes with changeable clock frequencies, supplemented by technical tools.

In the last ten years, advances in semiconductor technology and processor architecture have increased clock frequency and performance dozens of times — even hundreds of times for some tasks. This rapid growth has extended the functional capabilities of contemporary computers, but it also has become a source of problems. A typical example is the loss of software compatibility.

Ensuring Software Compatibility

The high clock frequency and performance of contemporary hardware components might make it impossible to run software developed for earlier PC models. Examples can be found among games and business applications. This problem is important because some applications developed for the systems based on Intel's 486, 386, and even 286, 8088, or 8086 chips might be of great value to end users.

Contemporary computers prove to be too powerful for such applications. As a result, games impose steep demands on user response, and application software often fails to run altogether. Nevertheless, operating, maintaining, and supporting obsolete equipment only to run several applications is an expensive and troublesome solution.

One possible solution is to reduce the processor clock frequency. This can be achieved from the BIOS Setup by manually setting the FSB frequency to its low limit. By doing this, you perform anti-overclocking. The fragment of BIOS Setup responsible for setting the FSB frequency is shown in Fig. 17.1.

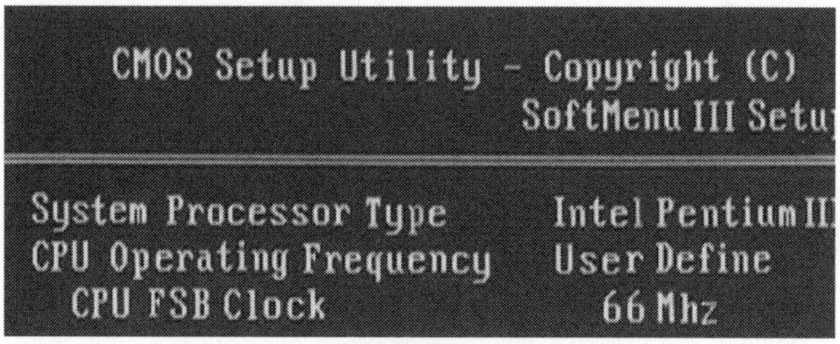

Fig. 17.1. Fragment of BIOS Setup responsible for setting the FSB frequency

As a result of this action, performance is decreased, and programs that were unable to run get the chance for a second life. If the performance decrease is insufficient, it is possible to disable cache memory in BIOS Setup. This can be done in addition to the frequency decrease or even instead of it. In extreme situations, it is possible to disable L2 and L1 cache memory simultaneously. The fragment of BIOS Setup used to enable or disable cache memory is shown in Fig. 17.2.

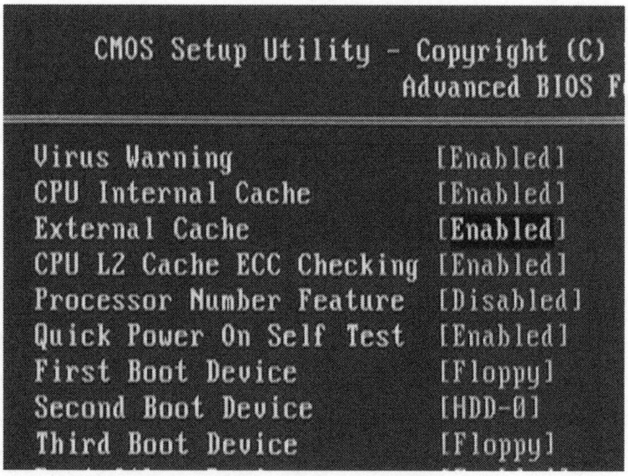

Fig. 17.2. Fragment of BIOS Setup responsible for enabling or disabling cache memory

The advantage of this method is its simplicity and availability, even for inexperienced users. The simplicity of returning to the nominal mode ensuring traditional (i.e., high) performance makes this approach even more attractive. The high performance will allow you to run contemporary applications and solve relatively difficult and complicated tasks.

The tasks being solved gradually are becoming more complicated. Even an optimally tuned computer eventually ceases to meet the demands placed on it.

Decreasing Power Consumption

To solve the problem of limited capabilities in a computer system, you can upgrade the existing system or purchase a new computer. The second approach can be expensive. Because of this, most experienced and thrifty PC users choose to upgrade.

As a rule, all manipulations related to an upgrade can be performed on your own or with the help of support specialists. Usually, you must purchase and install new adapters and a new processor. Most PC users choose a newer model of the same product line, which ensures higher performance. You often can return the previous processor to the vendor and get a rebate.

However, this approach can lead to unexpected problems. Most components are retained in the system during an upgrade. The list of such components is long and includes the power supply unit and the motherboard. This can become a source of trouble.

Powerful processors consume significant power. For the latest models, this parameter has approached 100 W. Rapid growth of power consumption has forced processor manufacturers to introduce changes into Voltage Regulator Module (VRM) specifications and motherboard architecture. In the past few years, such changes have been introduced several times. Recommendations have involved power supply units. Newer devices are released according to new specifications, but most devices released earlier fail to satisfy such requirements.

Adding new components and replacing the processor can increase energy consumption to such a degree that the supplied power might be insufficient.

The thermal power of the newest models of Intel Pentium 4 processors, with clock frequencies of 3 GHz or higher and 0.13-micrometer technology, is more than 80 W. AMD products keep pace with Intel processors in this area.

Powerful processors whose consumption current exceeds 60 amperes place a heavy load on transformers, rectifiers, and stabilizers.

The load on the computer's power-supply unit includes several factors typically overlooked not only by end users, but also by many specialists. The real efficiency coefficient is far from 100%, and the load reactive component, related to a parameter known as cosφ, is a factor. Including these, the power consumed by the processor from the power supply unit can be increased 1.5–2 times. This is a large share of the nominal power of the power supply unit. Still, other loads also consume considerable power, such as the video adapter and hard disks. When implementing RAID 0+1, the system must have no less than four physical hard disks.

These components and others require great power for their operation and have intensive heat emission. Like the processor, they are not exclusively active loads for all sources, including the power supply unit. When they are active, the consumed power increases significantly.

When relatively low power supply units or motherboards are used, whose transformers do not ensure the required values of electric power, the system might become unstable. Replacing a component with a more powerful model only worsens the situation. In some cases, this might result in total failure. This might occur only when performing specific kinds of operations, such as intense calculations or CD/DVD writing.

The powerful processor consumes the lion's share of the power; therefore, it is possible to overcome the problem of insufficient power by anti-overclocking the processor (i.e., by reducing its clock frequency).

As previously demonstrated, the thermal power of semiconductor circuits, including that of the CPU and graphic processor, depends on the supply voltage and on the clock frequency:

$$P_f = P_o \times (V_f / V_o)^2 \times (F_f / F_o)$$

Here, P_f is the thermal power at the f frequency, P_o is the thermal power at the nominal frequency, V_f is the supply voltage at the f frequency, V_o is the supply voltage at the nominal frequency, F_f is the value of the current frequency, and F_o is the value of the nominal frequency.

From this formula, it follows that power grows with the frequency and, conversely, decreases with the frequency. Furthermore, to retain stability of operation, it is necessary to increase the supply voltage with the frequency. If the frequency is decreased, it is possible to decrease the supply voltage. Taking into account this relationship greatly decreases thermal power and energy consumption.

This method is widely used in portable computers to reduce power consumption and prolong battery usage.

With desktop computers, the reduction of power consumption is not as urgent. Besides this, reducing the clock frequency also reduces system performance, which lowers the value of upgrade. Nevertheless, this approach can help you detect the causes of unstable operation. Furthermore, if the system becomes unstable only when performing specific tasks, related to operation of specific components with high power consumption, temporary anti-overclocking can help you circumvent the problem of insufficient power supply.

Finally, anti-overclocking reduces the load on the tools that support optimal temperature modes required for the operation of hardware components. This allows you to reduce the power of cooling fans, which reduces noise — frequently an urgent problem.

Reducing the Noise Level

(Based on materials from and with the permission of the Russian-language *ComputerPress* magazine and **http://www.ixbt.com** Web site.)

PCs are widely used not only in an office or production environment, but also in homes, where the elimination of undesirable sounds can be an urgent problem. However, the increased performance of processors, video adapters, hard disks, and CD/DVD drives can impose stringent requirements on temperature and require an additional cooling system. This inevitably increases the background noise.

Furthermore, as computers acquire additional consumer functions, such as multimedia centers, digital audio- and video-recorders, game stations, or Internet terminals, the intensity of their operation grows. Therefore, the problem of reducing background noise becomes even more important.

Contemporary ecological and ergonomic requirements limit the noise produced by any home appliance, and computers are no exception. Furthermore, turning a home PC into a home theater and audio center, the elimination of background noise turns into an economical problem. It doesn't make sense to spend money on high-quality video components or audio systems if sound will be accompanied by annoying background noise.

As a result, leading manufacturers of computer hardware have begun to pay attention to the acoustic characteristics of their products. Requirements become more stringent as computers move closer to home appliances.

Unfortunately, contemporary PCs are far behind audio and video systems in this parameter. Until the designers of hardware components change their approach to manufacturing computer equipment, PC users will have to improve existing equipment and choose appropriate components on their own.

Theoretical Background

The range of sounds that can be heard by humans generally is thought to span from 20 MHz to 20,000 Hz.

Noise levels are evaluated using sound pressure and acoustic intensity.

Sound pressure is a relative value characterized by an increase in air pressure on the eardrum, caused by sound oscillations (measured in pascals, with $1 Pa = 1 N/m^2$).

Acoustic intensity is the power of a sound wave per area unit (measured in W/m^2). This is the value proportional to the square of the sound pressure.

The range of acoustic intensities perceived by humans is limited from below by the sensitivity of the eardrum (the so-called audibility threshold) and from above by the threshold of pain.

The audibility threshold depends on frequency. It is generally thought that sound with a frequency of 1 kHz, producing sound pressure of about 20 micropascals (μPa) at an ambient temperature of 20°C (68°F), is perceivable. Sound intensity at this pressure is 1 picowatts (pW), much weaker than a mosquito's buzz. This threshold value is assumed to correspond to 0 decibels (dB). The threshold of pain at the same frequency corresponds to the sound pressure of 20 Pa. (Sound intensity is equal to $1 W/m^2$, which approximately corresponds to the roar of a supersonic engine if a fighter jet takes off nearby.) This sound level equals 120 dB.

Thus, the range of sound intensity distinguished by humans is sufficiently wide. When measuring this value, it is convenient to use relative units (i.e., the level relative to the audibility threshold).

Volume is measured in decibels and depends on the sound pressure, as shown in the following formula:

$$D = 20 \ lg \ (P/P_{min})$$

Here, P is the current value of the sound pressure, and P_{min} is the value of the sound pressure for the audibility threshold.

Volume and noise level, expressed in sound intensity, have half the proportionality coefficient, as shown in the following formula:

$$D = 10 \ lg \ (I/I_{min})$$

Here, I and I_{min} are the current and threshold values of the sound intensity.

The sound intensity is used most frequently as a characteristic of the noise level. The measurement results must be ranked depending on the sound frequency and the characteristics of human hearing. Curves of equal volumes are shown in Fig. 17.3.

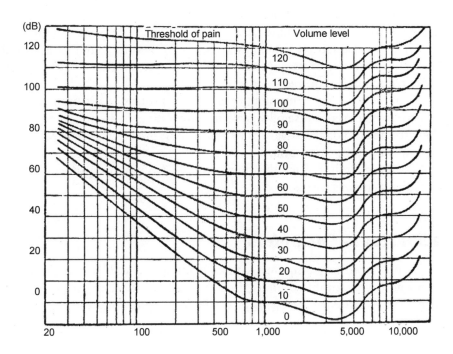

Fig. 17.3. Curves of equal volume

The dynamic range of a sound source is the difference between its minimum and maximum volume in decibels. For example, the minimum volume for speech perception is 25–30 dB (a whisper), low conversation corresponds to 35–45 dB, and so on.

Clear perception of sound is possible only when its intensity exceeds by at least 10 dB noise within the same frequency range.

Thus, unwanted sounds are injurious because they decrease the dynamic range of the desired sound sources. This decrease is often so significant that the desired sound can't be distinguished from background noise.

For example, the typical level of noise from a contemporary computer is 35–45 dB. This means that people can't perceive a whisper and have difficulties understanding soft voices near the computer. As a result, it is necessary to speak louder (for example, by raising the voice to 50–55 dB). You can forget about listening to high-quality recordings; this would require the volume to be increased to the threshold of pain.

Average background noise at home rarely exceeds 35 dB, and at night it usually decreases to 20 dB. This is the most important factor determining the requirements of a home computer. If the home user plans to work only during the day, noise from the computer must not exceed 30 dB. For comfortable work at night, greater noise reduction is required — to at least 20 dB.

Requirements for computers operating in professional sound-recording premises are stringent. Because of this, sound professionals do not try to keep pace with the latest technological advances in processors; they purchase expensive cases with high-quality noise insulation.

To successfully reduce the noise emitted from a computer, it is necessary to consider its main sources.

Noise Sources in Computers

Noise produced by computers comes from sound oscillations generated by mechanical drives, amplified many times by resonating elements of the construction. The main sources of mechanical oscillations and vibrations in a computer are the following:

❏ Power supply unit (its fan and transformers)
❏ Fan of the CPU cooler
❏ Fan of the cooler installed on a high-performance video adapter
❏ Additional cooling fans that might be installed in the case of the system unit (or in the cases of peripheral devices)
❏ Drives and media (hard disks, optical drives, and so on) as a result of spindle rotation (constant) and positioning the read/write heads (periodic)

Controlling Fans

The largest contribution to the noise produced by a contemporary computer comes from numerous coolers and fans. The average noise level from a single fan is approximately 35 dB. The difference from model to model might be considerable.

Although fans regularly are improved, their contribution to the noise pollution of the system tends to grow.

The design of the first PCs didn't include fans. Clock frequencies of the first processors were so low they didn't cause heat emission that would require additional cooling. To achieve adequate cooling, heat transmission via heatsinks and the computer case was sufficient; free airflow convection via ventilation holes dispersed heat from the case. In the first power supply units, only powerful transformers produced noise. Later, power supply units became the pulse-based, and transformers became small and relatively noiseless. However, a new, powerful noise source appeared — the fan in the power supply unit.

Starting with some Intel 486 models, heatsinks appeared with fans on tops of the processors. The noise problem became urgent for processors such as Intel Pentium 4 and AMD Athlon XP, which required intense cooling. Video adapters also appeared, equipped with a couple of fans. Fig. 17.4 shows coolers for Intel 486-100 and Intel Pentium 4 3.06 GHz processors.

Fig. 17.4. Coolers for Intel 486-100 and Intel Pentium 4 3.06 GHz processors

In addition to the fans installed in the power supply unit, processor, and other hardware components, it gradually became necessary to build fans into the system unit case. Currently, even motherboard chipsets are equipped with a separate heatsink, with a fan on top. Quite often, hard drives also require additional cooling. Thus, a contemporary computer typically contains five or more coolers.

The main source of noise in any fan is produced from the mechanics and airflow — air moved by the blades and blown through the fins of the heatsink, small holes in the sides of the case, and outlets in the rear or front panels of the case.

At first, it seems intolerable to decrease the performance of cooling facilities; this might violate the temperature modes required for operation of the hardware components. However, because the workload on each component is not constant, it is expedient to decrease the fan rotation speeds during periods of low workload. This will reduce the noise caused by their operation.

To decrease the rotation speed of the blades, it is necessary to use specialized fans or complement the cooling devices with specially designed circuits. The designs of these circuits can vary from simple, with manual control over the voltage, to complicated, with automatic control using a thermal sensor. It is necessary to warn against using too simplistic of an approach. Many models of 12 V fans are capable of stable operation at a supply voltage of 5 V. In this case, the fan rotation speed will be approximately half the nominal speed. However, not every model will start at such a voltage. Supplying a voltage of 7 V by taking +5 V as the "ground" and +12 V from another contact doesn't save the situation. In this case, the fan might stop after reboot.

It is possible to start fans at their nominal voltages and gradually decrease them to the required level — for example, to the half of the nominal voltage. One possible implementation of such a plan is shown in Fig. 17.5.

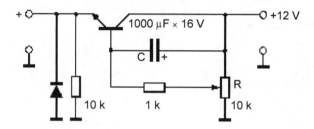

Fig. 17.5. Circuit design ensuring fan startup, with subsequent decrease of the supply voltage to the required level

This circuit design is based on a simple principle: At the moment the computer powers up, the base potential of the transistor (T) equals the potential on its collector. This ensures supply of the full power (12 V) to the fan connected to the transistor's emitter. As the capacitor (C) charges (this takes several seconds), the voltage is decreased to the level set by the variable resistor (R). By changing the position of this resistor, it is possible to control the fan rotation speed during operation.

To implement this device, it is possible to use a powerful n-p-n transistor that guarantees the current required for the collector-emitter voltage is no less than 12 V. A low-power diode can protect the transistor from breaking down during transient processes that take place in relatively powerful fans. It is expedient to choose a diode model intended for voltages greater than 100 V and currents greater than 50 mA.

The design is connected to the power supply wire of the cooling fan. Connection of the ground (GND) wire remains unchanged, except that the common wire of this regulator is connected to it.

This solution can be used to control the fans included in a processor cooler, a video adapter, and even a power supply unit.

The main drawback of this plan is the necessity of constant control over the temperature of the elements being cooled.

The heatsink temperature or even the air temperature within the computer case can be used as a parameter that determines the necessity of choosing a speed of fan rotation. Therefore, many manufacturers supply fans with built-in thermal sensors (Fig. 17.6).

Fig. 17.6. Thermal sensor built into the cooler

Until the temperature exceeds a predefined limit, the fans might operate at half of their nominal power or even stop. When the temperature increases to the predefined limit, the fans gradually speed up to their nominal power.

It is possible to produce efficient devices that ensure automatic control over the heatsink temperature and fan rotation speed on your own.

As an example, consider two plans for simple analogous regulators with thermal sensors fastened to the cooler heatsink. The first design is based on a chip; the second one employs transistors.

If the cooler has no output for a tachometer (or if this output is not used), the rotation speed regulator can based on the circuit containing minimal components (Fig. 17.7).

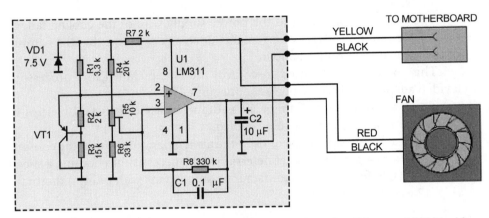

Fig. 17.7. Schematic circuit of a thermal regulator based on an LM311 chip

This regulator is based on an LM311 chip. Although this chip is a comparator, the device ensures linear regulation, rather than switching-type regulation. A comparator, instead of an operational amplifier, was chosen for the following reasons:

❑ The comparator has a relatively powerful output with an open collector, which allows the fan to be connected directly, without additional transistors.

❑ Because the input cascade is based on p-n-p transistors connected in a common collector design, even with a unidirectional power supply, it is possible to work with low input voltages at the ground level. For example, when using a diode as a thermal sensor, it may be necessary to work with a 0.7 V input, which is not supported by most contemporary operational amplifiers.

❑ The comparator can be enveloped in negative feedback, after which it will operate in a way similar to operational amplifiers.

Diodes are used frequently as thermal sensors. Silicone diodes have a p-n transition with a thermal voltage coefficient of approximately –2.3 mV/°C and a direct voltage drop of approximately 0.7 V. However, most diodes have a case unsuitable for fastening on a heatsink. Some transistors are more suitable for this.

Some transistors have cases designed for fastening on a heatsink using a screw. However, when using such transistors, remember that after fastening the transistor to the heatsink, its collector will be connected to it electrically. Because of the convenience of assembling and ensuring electric safety, the heatsink must be connected electrically to the common power supply wire. Therefore, it is most convenient to use a p-n-p transistor (VT1) in this device.

Note that it is possible to use one of the transistors simply as a diode in the thermal control circuit. However, the diode has a relatively low thermal coefficient, and measurements are performed under unfavorable conditions — the supply voltage is unstable and there are background noises and interference.

Using a transistor connected as a dipole, as shown in Fig 7.17, is a better approach. The temperature coefficient of such a sensor is determined by the ratio of the R2 and R3 resistance, based on the following formula:

$$K_t \times (R3/R2 + 1)$$

Here, K_t is the temperature coefficient of a single p-n transition. It is impossible to increase the value of the resistor ratio without limitations, because a direct-voltage drop grows with the increase of the thermal coefficient. It can even reach the supply voltage, meaning the system will cease to operate. In the regulator being described, the thermal coefficient of the sensor is approximately –20 mV/°C, ten times the similar parameter of the diode. The direct-voltage drop on the transistor is about 6 V.

The VT1R2R3 thermal sensor is included in the measuring bridge composed of the R1, R4, R5, and R6 resistors. The bridge is powered from the VD1R7 parametric voltage stabilizer, because the +12 V supply voltage within the computer isn't known for stability.

The misbalance voltage of the measuring bridge is applied to the comparator inputs. The comparator is used in linear mode because of the influence of the inverse feedback. The R5 correcting resistor allows the correcting characteristic curve to be displaced. Changing the nominal value of the R8 feedback resistor changes the angle of its slope. The C1 and C2 capacitors ensure stability of the regulator.

The regulator is mounted on a board made of single-sided, foil-clad fiberglass laminate (Fig. 17.8).

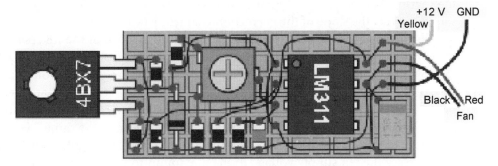

Fig. 17.8. Wiring diagram of a thermal regulator based on an LM311 chip

To decrease the external dimensions of the board, it is expedient to use surface-mountable elements. It is possible to use ordinary elements. The board is fastened at the cooler heatsink using the fastening screw of the VT1 transistor. It is best to drill a small hole into the heatsink and cut a thread for the M3 screw. It is possible to use a screw and nut. When choosing where to fasten the board on the heatsink, ensure an easy access to the correcting resistor after the heatsink is installed in the computer. Using this approach, it is not difficult to fasten the thermal regulator board to typical heatsinks. However, difficulties might arise when fastening it to a cylindrical heatsink, such as the popular Orb.

Note that only the transistor used as a thermal sensor must have good heat contact with the heatsink. If the entire board can't be placed on the heatsink, you can install only the transistor on it. It will be necessary to connect the transistor to the board using wires. The board itself can be placed anywhere near the sensor.

The transistor can be fastened onto the heatsink without metalwork. For example, it is possible to fit it tight between the fins and ensure good heat contact using thermal paste. Heat conductive glue also can be used to fasten the thermal sensor.

After installing the transistor that performs the functions of a thermal sensor on the heatsink, the latter is connected to the common wire. This doesn't cause problems. The transistor can be easily insulated from the heatsink, such as by using a lining made of mica or Mylar.

Electrically, the plate is connected sequentially into the cutoff of the fan wire. When necessary, it is possible to install cutoff points to avoid cutting the wire. A correctly assembled design requires little tuning; just use the R5 correction resistor to set the fan rotation speed corresponding to the current temperature. Each fan has a minimal voltage that must be supplied to make the fan rotate. By tuning the regulator, it is possible to make the fan rotate at the minimal rotation speed when the heatsink temperature is close to the ambient temperature. Nevertheless, the thermal resistance of different heatsinks can vary; therefore, it might be necessary to correct the slope of the correction characteristic curve.

The slope of the curve is specified by the nominal value of the R8 resistor. This value can range from 100 kilohm to 1,000 kilohm. The greater this nominal value, the lower the temperature at which the fan reaches its maximum rotation speed. The processor workload can be only several percent, a situation that often takes place when working in text editors. When using a software cooler, the fan might run at a much slower speed. This regulator is intended to do the same. However, as the processor workload increases, its temperature rises. The regulator must gradually increase the fan supply voltage to the maximum to prevent the processor from being overheated. The heatsink temperature must not rise too high when the fan starts to rotate at full speed. It must be 5°C–10°C (41°F–50°F) below the temperature at which the system starts to experience instability.

It is desirable to perform first power-on of this arrangement from an external power source. Otherwise, if the arrangement short-circuits, its link to the motherboard connector might damage the motherboard.

The second design is based on transistors.

If the fan is equipped with a tachometer, the regulating transistor cannot be connected to the ground wire of the fan. Because of this, the internal transistor of the comparator cannot be used here. An additional transistor is required to regulate the +12 V circuit of the fan. It might be possible to improve slightly the previous design based on the comparator. Nevertheless, this design, based on transistors, is more compact than the previous one. The principal circuit is shown in Fig. 17.9.

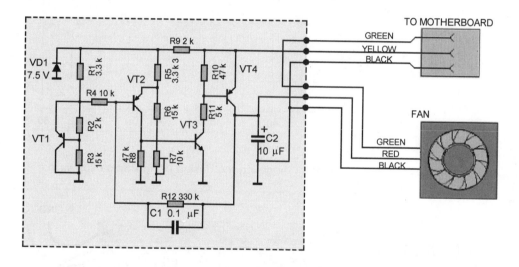

Fig. 17.9. Principal diagram of a thermal regulator based on transistors

Because the entire board is placed on the heatsink and is heated, it is hard to predict the behavior of the transistor design. Researchers investigated the design using the PSpice modeling software. The modeling result is shown in Fig. 17.10.

As can be seen from this illustration, the fan supply voltage grows linearly, from 4 V at 25°C (77°F) to 12 V at 58°C (136°F). The regulator's behavior generally meets the requirements.

The principal circuits of these two variants of the thermal regulator have much in common. The temperature sensors and measurement bridges are practically identical. The difference is only in the voltage amplifier of the bridge. In the second variant, this voltage is supplied to the cascade represented by the VT2 transistor. The transistor base is the inverting input of the amplifier; the emitter is the noninverting input. The signal is supplied to the next amplifying cascade based on the VT3 transistor, and, finally, to the output cascade based on the VT4 transistor. The aim of the capacitor is the same as in the first variant. The wiring scheme of the regulator is shown in Fig. 17.11.

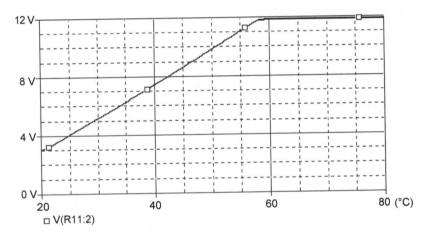

Fig. 17.10. Results of modeling the design using PSpice software

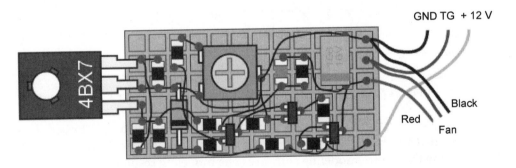

Fig. 17.11. Wiring plan of a thermal regulator based on transistors

This design is similar to the first variant, except the board has smaller dimensions. In this design, it is possible to employ any elements. Besides this, any silicone, low-powered transistors can be used, because the fans consume a current that rarely exceeds 100 mA.

This design can also be used to control fans consuming stronger currents. With such fans, the VT4 transistor must be replaced with more powerful one. The signal from the tachogenerator (TG) passes through the regulator board to the connector on the motherboard. The method of tuning the second variant is no different from the first variant. In the second variant, tuning is performed using the R7 tuning resistor, and the slope of the curve is specified by the nominal of the R12 resistor.

The usage of thermal regulators (with software coolers) has demonstrated their high efficiency as tools for reducing the noise from cooling fans. The devices described here can be used to control the speed of cooling fans installed on various computer components. The cooler used on each component must be powerful enough to ensure the required temperature mode at maximum workload.

Hardware facilities considerably reduce the average noise level produced by a computer. However, as the workload grows, noise increases. This might be acceptable in an office environment. However, it is not always tolerable at home, especially in evening or at night.

Temporary usage of the modes with reduced clock frequencies (anti-overclocking) can solve this problem. As previously mentioned, this can be achieved through the appropriate settings in BIOS Setup. Setting the appropriate performance level allows control over heat emission, which allows a reduction in the workload on the coolers. As a result, the temperature is reduced, and fans decrease their rotation speed. At the same time, anti-overclocking ensures a reduction in the upper level of performance; therefore, the maximum rotation speed is not reached even if the workload is at its maximum. Thus, anti-overclocking and appropriate thermal regulators make it possible to reduce or decrease the noise level in the evening and at night.

Chapter 18

Examples and Analysis of PC Overclocking

The implementation of the overclocking modes for PC components improves overall system performance. If several simple recommendations are observed, implementation of moderate overclocking modes for desktop PCs does not noticeably reduce stability and reliability. Evaluation of the performance growth achieved for various hardware configurations is possible by analyzing the results achieved during the experiments described in detail in this chapter.

Before reproducing the experiments described in this chapter, it is necessary to remind you once again that you must be very careful when using these overclocking methods. You should constantly bear in mind that the overclocking operations might produce irreversible results. Your processor might end its life in smoke, your video adapter or hard disk may fail, and so on. In other words, when trying to achieve the highest possible results, you are not protected against the loss of a usable computer.

The plan for increasing the performance of your system must be comprehensive. The following advice emphasizes several aspects directly related to the implementation of the overclocking modes:

1. Perform detailed physical diagnostics of the system and carefully read the documentation. This will help you understand the possible ways of optimizing and overclocking your system. The implementation of overclocking modes

sometimes requires you to open the system unit case. This allows you to identify the system components correctly. Besides this, it will help you make sure that all components are present, that there are no loose or unneeded wires, etc.

The following situation is an illustrative example: When inspecting the system unit components, it was detected that the fan connection to the motherboard was insecure. This could have caused the fan to stop, which would cause CPU overheating and failure. Besides this, it was necessary to correct the cable connection between the motherboard and hard disk. All loose cables and wires were carefully bound together. This improved the ventilation of all components within the system unit case.

2. Carefully test all functional capabilities of the computer to be overclocked. Make sure that all components operate normally in the nominal mode. To perform this check, it is recommended that you employ popular testing software, by doing the following:

   - Start popular tests (Winstone, WinBench, CheckIt, etc.) and run them several times
   - Try to work in popular applications (Word/Excel, CorelDraw, Photoshop, Xing, Winamp, etc.)
   - Perform sequential checks of your computer using popular games (Doom, Descent, Quake, etc.)

   If you are conducting tests, record the results obtained. (At least, write the results and preserve them as a hard copy.) You can proceed only after you make sure the computer is usable and its operation is stable.

3. Using either BIOS Setup or the appropriate jumpers on the motherboard, set the desired overclocking mode. Proceed step by step. For example, it makes sense to increase the system-bus frequency slightly (from 133 MHz to 145 MHz or in smaller increments, if they are supported by the motherboard.) It is not recommended to jump several steps (from 100 MHz to 150 MHz or from 133 MHz to 166 MHz). The best approach is to do everything gradually (remembering to record every step). If you keep track of each step that you have taken, then, if anything goes wrong, you'll be able to perform a smooth rollback to the previous mode.

4. Remember that the entire system, and especially the processor, requires adequate cooling. It often is necessary to install a massive heatsink and a powerful cooler on the processor, the video adapter, and possibly on other hardware components.

5. Repeat the testing described in Step 1, but as long as possible and under the hardest conditions. Some recommendations on testing computer systems were

provided in *Chapter 7*. If you discover any problems or instability, find the reason and take the steps necessary to eliminate the problem. Sometimes, you'll have to return to the previous step or even abandon the idea of overclocking this particular computer. If the system is usable and stable, proceed to the next step.

Suppose that not all tests were passed normally: There was a failure at the second stage of the testing process, related to playing video clips. When performing this test, the system hung up after 40 minutes of operation. This led to a conclusion that the system was unstable. In this situation, you can consider returning to the previous mode. However, there are other approaches to the problem: You could try to improve the cooling system of the processor and/or other components, replace the unstable component, and so on. After analyzing the situation and carefully investigating the operation of all hardware components of this particular system, the conclusion was drawn that the video adapter was causing the problem. This component became unstable because, in the course of overclocking, the Accelerated Graphics Port (AGP) bus frequency increased to 83 MHz. As a result, the heat emission of the graphical core grew accordingly, and the adapter became overheated. Replacing the cooler installed on the video adapter with a more powerful one returned stability to the system and enabled it to operate reliably in this particular overclocking mode.

6. Change the settings in BIOS Setup. This can be accomplished before, after, or even instead of overclocking. This usually relates to parameters of memory operation. Sometimes it is possible to significantly increase memory subsystem performance by changing several parameters in BIOS Setup. Extreme caution still is required, as well as testing.

Overclocking Computers with Intel Pentium II

This section describes the results of overclocking computers based on the following processors:

❏ Pentium II 300 MHz
❏ Pentium II 333 MHz

Computer with Pentium II 300 MHz

Pentium II processors with a clock frequency of 300 MHz operate well in overclocked modes. Overclocking will be particularly successful if such processors are used with motherboards that have built-in overclocking capabilities. The best motherboards include Abit BX6. This particular motherboard allows very high performance to be achieved.

The following results came from overclocking and testing a computer with a Pentium II 300 MHz processor and an Abit BX6 motherboard. Overclocking parameters were set using BIOS Setup in CPU SoftMenu II.

System Configuration

❏ Processor — Intel Pentium II 300 MHz (integrated coprocessor, 32 KB L1 cache, 512 KB L2 cache, recommended processor-bus frequency of 66 MHz, 2 V core supply)

❏ Motherboard — Abit BX6

❏ Hard disk — Western Digital 8.4 GB

❏ RAM — 64 MB, SDRAM

❏ Video adapter — Asus V3400TNT

❏ CD-ROM drive — Advanced Technology Attachment Packet Interface (ATAPI) 40x

❏ Operating system — Windows 98 (4/10/98)

Establishing Overclocking Modes

The following settings were specified in BIOS Setup (Award Modular BIOS v4.51PG):

❏ CPU operating speed — User defined

❏ Turbo frequency — Disabled

❏ External clock — 100 MHz

❏ Multiplier clock — 4.5x

❏ AGPCLK/CPUCLK — 2/3 (relative speeds of the AGP and CPU bus clocks)

❏ Speed error hold — Enabled

❏ CPU power supply — User defined

❏ Core voltage — 2.10 V

In the course of overclocking, the system-bus frequency was raised from 66 MHz to 100 MHz. As a result, the processor frequency was increased 1.5 times, from 300 MHz to 450 MHz. To ensure stable operation, the core voltage was raised from 2.00 V to 2.10 V. To retain control over the system, the system temperature was monitored constantly, using the **System Temperature** parameter in the

CHIPSET Features Setup menu. Before overclocking, the temperature was 41°C (106°F); after this procedure, it was 42°C (108°F).

Testing the System

The following WinBench 99 tests were conducted: FPU WinMark (Fig. 18.1)[i], business disk, and high-end disk. (See Figs. 18.2–18.4 and Tables 18.1 and 18.2.) Unfortunately, the CPUmark 99 test could not be loaded, presumably because of instability of the operating system used in the test (Windows 98).

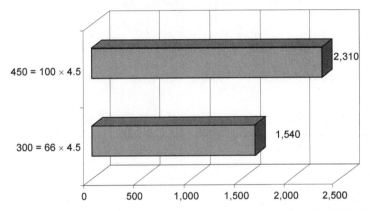

Fig. 18.1. Pentium II 300 MHz processor performance (FPU WinMark)

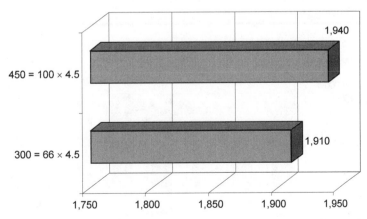

Fig. 18.2. Pentium II 300 MHz hard-disk performance (WinMark 99 business disk)

---

[i] In all figures of this chapter, except Figs. 18.4, 18.5, and 18.21, the vertical axis is in megahertz and the horizontal axis is the rating.

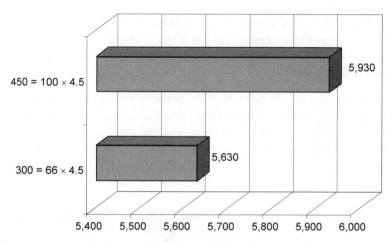

Fig. 18.3. Pentium II 300 MHz hard-disk performance (WinMark 99 high-end disk)

Table 18.1. Results of Overclocking Pentium II 300 MHz

WinBench 99 test	300 MHz ≈ 66 × 4.5	450 MHz = 100 × 4.5
FPU WinMark	1,540	2,310
WinMark 99 business disk (1,000 bytes/sec)	1,910	1,940
WinMark 99 high-end disk (1,000 bytes/sec)	5,630	5,930

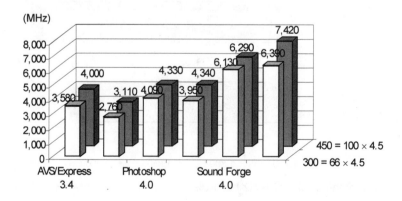

Fig. 18.4. Pentium II 300 MHz test results (WinMark 99 high-end disk)

Table 18.2. Results for Pentium II 300 MHz (high-end disk, 1,000 bytes/sec)

WinMark 99 high-end disk	300 MHz ≈ 66 × 4.5	450 MHz = 100 × 4.5
AVS/Express 3.4	3,800	4,000
FrontPage 98	27,600	31,100
Photoshop 4.0	4,090	4,330
Premiere 4.2	3,950	4,340
Sound Forge 4.0	6,130	6,290
Visual C++ 5.0	6,390	7,420

Computer with Pentium II 333 MHz

Pentium II 333 MHz is one of the most popular processor models. It shows good results in tests and is one of the best representatives of the Pentium II product line.

Pentium II 333 MHz shows high overclocking results. It is possible to overclock this processor to 416 MHz (5 × 83 MHz).

With some motherboards that support higher frequencies of the host bus (such as 92 MHz or 95 MHz), it was possible to overclock this processor to 460 MHz. However, at these frequencies, additional cooling of the processor and other hardware components is required.

Processor overclocking was accomplished by raising the system-bus frequency from 66 MHz to 95 MHz. At system-bus frequencies of 83 MHz, 92 MHz, and 95 MHz (relatively high for products of this class), computer operation was unstable. At frequencies of 92 MHz and 95 MHz, the system often hung up during the tests, even with an improved cooling system. It was possible to ensure stable operation of the system only by increasing the CPU core voltage 0.1 V.

WinBench 98 was used for testing.

Table 18.3. Results of Overclocking Pentium II 333 MHz

Parameters (MHz)	CPUmark 32 rating	FPU WinMark rating
333 = 5 × 66	850	1,700
375 = 5 × 75	950	1,950
416 = 5 × 83	1,050	2,150
460 = 5 × 92	1,200	2,400
475 = 5 × 95	1,250	2,500

Test results (Table 18.3 and Fig. 18.5) show significant growth of overall system performance, achieved by processor overclocking. However, as previously mentioned, system operation was unstable at high system-bus frequencies of 83 MHz, 92 MHz, and 95 MHz (416 MHz, 460 MHz, and 475 MHz processor frequencies) without an appropriate increase in CPU core voltage.

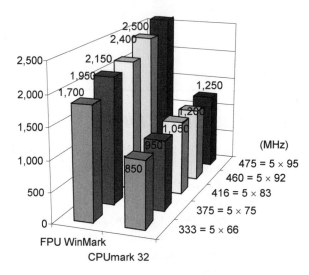

Fig. 18.5. Pentium II 333 MHz test results

Without increasing the CPU core voltage, the optimal and most recommended mode is 375 MHz (5 × 75 MHz). With increased CPU core voltage, the optimal mode is 416 MHz (5 × 83 MHz).

As usual, when overclocking the processor, it is necessary to carefully consider efficient cooling.

Overclocking Computers with Intel Pentium III (Coppermine)

Intel Pentium III with the Coppermine core, manufactured according to 0.18-micrometer technology, is characterized by relatively strong performance and overclocking capabilities.

The existing technological reserve allows a comparatively large increase of the Front Side Bus (FSB) frequency, which determines the internal and external processor frequencies. Such frequency growth is accompanied by an equivalent increase in CPU performance and, consequently, by improvement in overall system performance.

The best overclocking potential is found in the earliest representatives of the Coppermine line. Technological reserve allowed Intel to release processors based on this core with a clock frequency of 1 GHz or higher.

The following sections provide the results of overclocking this high-performance Pentium III processor and an analysis of its operation in the overclocked mode.

Computer with Pentium III 500E

System Configuration

❏ Processor — Intel Pentium III 500E (Coppermine core, 256 KB L2 cache, processor frequency operation, recommended processor-bus frequency of 100 MHz, 1.6 V core supply, FC-PGA installed on the motherboard via Slot 1, Socket 370 adapter)

❏ Motherboard — Abit BE6-II (Intel 440BX AGPset chipset)

❏ Hard disk — IBM DPTA-372050 (20 GB, 2 MB cache memory, Ultra DMA/66)

❏ RAM — 128 MB, PC100

❏ Video adapter: Asus AGP-V3800 TV (TNT2 video chip and 32 MB video memory)

❏ CD-ROM drive — Asus CD-S400/A (40x)

❏ Operating system — Windows 98 with installed drivers for an Ultra DMA/66 controller

Establishing Overclocking Modes

The overclocking modes were established in BIOS Setup by increasing the processor-bus frequency. The core supply voltage for all frequencies was standard (1.6 V). The sequence of selecting and setting parameters is illustrated in Figs. 18.6–18.8.

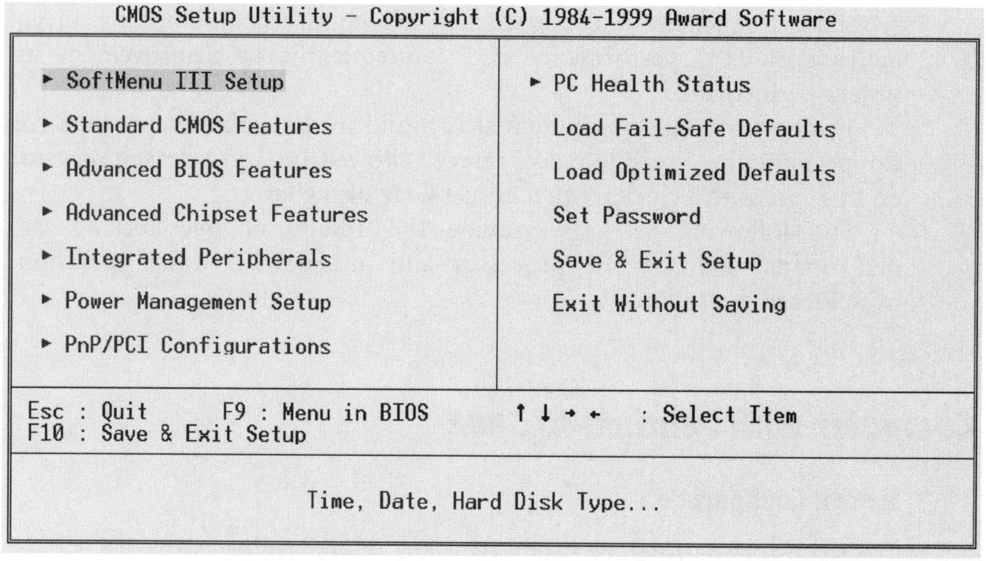

```
CMOS Setup Utility - Copyright (C) 1984-1999 Award Software
┌─────────────────────────────────────┬─────────────────────────────────┐
│  ▶ SoftMenu III Setup               │  ▶ PC Health Status             │
│                                      │                                 │
│  ▶ Standard CMOS Features           │    Load Fail-Safe Defaults      │
│                                      │                                 │
│  ▶ Advanced BIOS Features           │    Load Optimized Defaults      │
│                                      │                                 │
│  ▶ Advanced Chipset Features        │    Set Password                 │
│                                      │                                 │
│  ▶ Integrated Peripherals           │    Save & Exit Setup            │
│                                      │                                 │
│  ▶ Power Management Setup           │    Exit Without Saving          │
│                                      │                                 │
│  ▶ PnP/PCI Configurations           │                                 │
├─────────────────────────────────────┴─────────────────────────────────┤
│  Esc : Quit       F9 : Menu in BIOS      ↑ ↓ → ←   : Select Item       │
│  F10 : Save & Exit Setup                                                │
├─────────────────────────────────────────────────────────────────────────┤
│                    Time, Date, Hard Disk Type...                        │
└─────────────────────────────────────────────────────────────────────────┘
```

Fig. 18.6. Opening the **SoftMenu III Setup** menu in BIOS Setup
(Pentium III 500E)

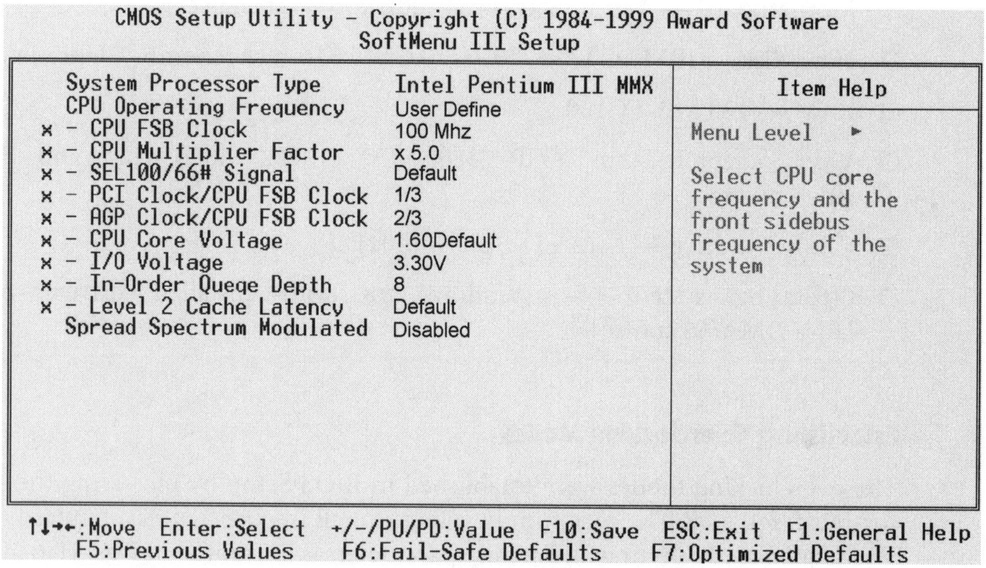

```
CMOS Setup Utility - Copyright (C) 1984-1999 Award Software
                        SoftMenu III Setup
┌──────────────────────────────────────────────────┬─────────────────────┐
│  System Processor Type      Intel Pentium III MMX │    Item Help        │
│  CPU Operating Frequency    User Define           ├─────────────────────┤
│  x - CPU FSB Clock          100 Mhz               │ Menu Level   ▶      │
│  x - CPU Multiplier Factor  x 5.0                 │                     │
│  x - SEL100/66# Signal      Default               │ Select CPU core     │
│  x - PCI Clock/CPU FSB Clock 1/3                  │ frequency and the   │
│  x - AGP Clock/CPU FSB Clock 2/3                  │ front sidebus       │
│  x - CPU Core Voltage       1.60Default           │ frequency of the    │
│  x - I/O Voltage            3.30V                 │ system              │
│  x - In-Order Quege Depth   8                     │                     │
│  x - Level 2 Cache Latency  Default               │                     │
│      Spread Spectrum Modulated  Disabled          │                     │
│                                                    │                     │
├──────────────────────────────────────────────────┴─────────────────────┤
│ ↑↓→←:Move  Enter:Select  +/-/PU/PD:Value  F10:Save  ESC:Exit  F1:General Help │
│      F5:Previous Values     F6:Fail-Safe Defaults    F7:Optimized Defaults │
└─────────────────────────────────────────────────────────────────────────┘
```

Fig. 18.7. Setting the recommended parameters in **SoftMenu III Setup**
(Pentium III 500E)

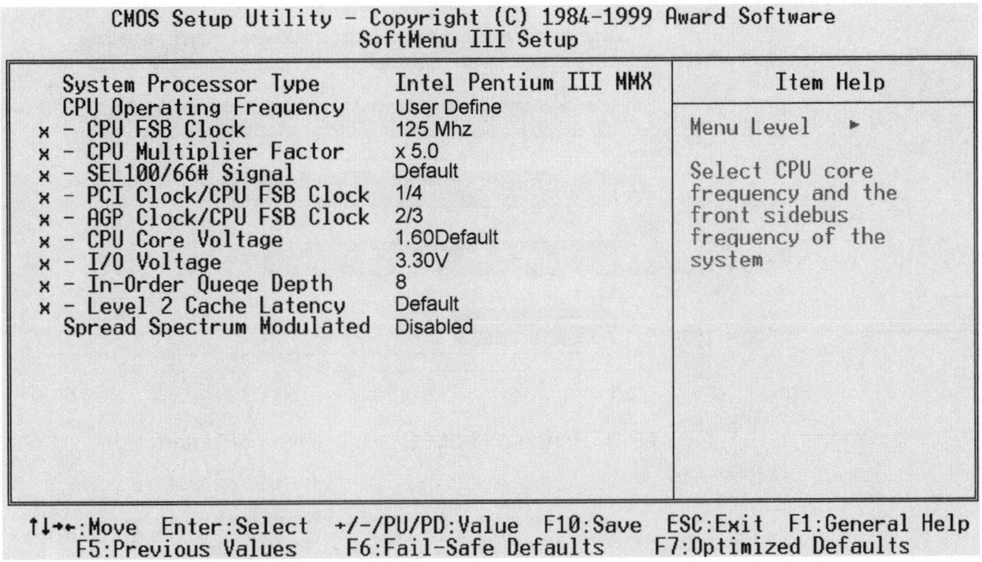

```
       CMOS Setup Utility - Copyright (C) 1984-1999 Award Software
                          SoftMenu III Setup
    ┌─────────────────────────────────────────────┬──────────────────────┐
    │  System Processor Type      Intel Pentium III MMX │     Item Help    │
    │  CPU Operating Frequency    User Define       │                      │
    │ x - CPU FSB Clock           125 Mhz           │ Menu Level    ►      │
    │ x - CPU Multiplier Factor   x 5.0             │                      │
    │ x - SEL100/66# Signal       Default           │ Select CPU core      │
    │ x - PCI Clock/CPU FSB Clock 1/4               │ frequency and the    │
    │ x - AGP Clock/CPU FSB Clock 2/3               │ front sidebus        │
    │ x - CPU Core Voltage        1.60Default       │ frequency of the     │
    │ x - I/O Voltage             3.30V             │ system               │
    │ x - In-Order Quege Depth    8                 │                      │
    │ x - Level 2 Cache Latency   Default           │                      │
    │     Spread Spectrum Modulated  Disabled       │                      │
    │                                               │                      │
    └─────────────────────────────────────────────┴──────────────────────┘
    ↑↓◄►:Move  Enter:Select  +/-/PU/PD:Value  F10:Save  ESC:Exit  F1:General Help
        F5:Previous Values       F6:Fail-Safe Defaults   F7:Optimized Defaults
```

Fig. 18.8. Establishing the overclocking mode in **SoftMenu III Setup**
(Pentium III 500E)

Testing the System

WinBench 99 v1.1 tests (CPUmark 99 and FPU WinMark) were used. Test results are provided in Table 18.4 and in Figs. 18.9 and 18.10.

Table 18.4. Results of Overclocking Pentium III 500E

FSB frequency (MHz)	CPU frequency (MHz)	CPUmark 99 rating	FPU WinMark rating
100	$500 = 100 \times 5.0$	41.9	2,700
120	$600 = 120 \times 5.0$	50.2	3,255
125	$625 = 125 \times 5.0$	52.1	3,373
135	$675 = 135 \times 5.0$	56.1	3,636
140	$700 = 140 \times 5.0$	58.5	3,781

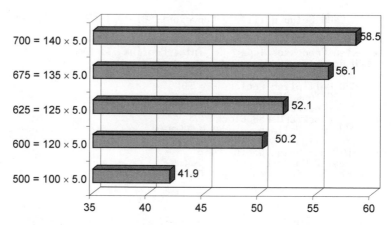

Fig. 18.9. Pentium III 500E test results (CPUmark 99)

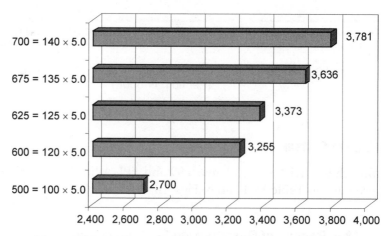

Fig. 18.10. Pentium III 500E test results (FPU WinMark)

Computer with Pentium III 550E

System Configuration

❏ Processor — Intel Pentium III 550E (Coppermine core, 256 KB L2 cache, processor frequency operation, recommended processor-bus frequency of 100 MHz, 1.65 V core supply, in box, 1/28/00 pack date, version A13433-001, made in Malaysia, SL3V5 S-Spec)

- ❏ Motherboard — Abit BE6-II (Intel 440BX AGPset chipset)

- ❏ Hard disk — IBM DPTA-372050 (20 GB, 2 MB cache memory, Ultra DMA/66)

- ❏ RAM — 128 MB, PC100

- ❏ Video adapter — Asus AGP-V3800 TV (TNT2 video chipset, 32 MB SGRAM video memory)

- ❏ CD-ROM drive — Asus CD-S400/A (40x)
- ❏ Operating system — Windows 98 with installed drivers for an Ultra DMA/66 hard disk controller

Establishing Overclocking Modes

The overclocking modes were established in BIOS Setup by increasing the processor-bus frequency. The core voltage was standard for all frequencies (1.65 V). The order of choosing and setting parameters is illustrated in Figs. 18.11–18.13.

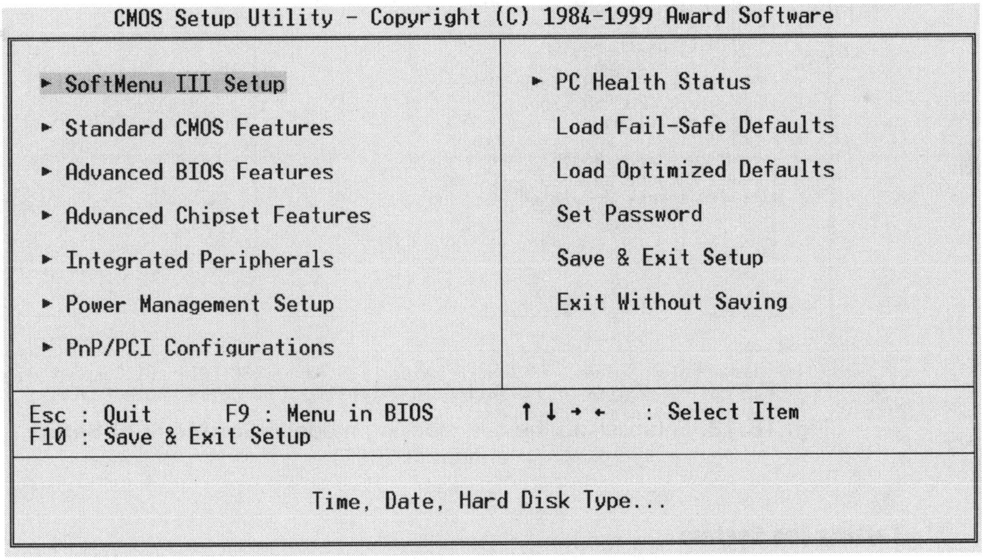

```
          CMOS Setup Utility - Copyright (C) 1984-1999 Award Software
 ┌──────────────────────────────────────────────────────────────────────┐
 │  ► SoftMenu III Setup          ► PC Health Status                      │
 │                                                                        │
 │  ► Standard CMOS Features         Load Fail-Safe Defaults              │
 │                                                                        │
 │  ► Advanced BIOS Features          Load Optimized Defaults             │
 │                                                                        │
 │  ► Advanced Chipset Features       Set Password                        │
 │                                                                        │
 │  ► Integrated Peripherals          Save & Exit Setup                   │
 │                                                                        │
 │  ► Power Management Setup          Exit Without Saving                 │
 │                                                                        │
 │  ► PnP/PCI Configurations                                              │
 ├──────────────────────────────────────────────────────────────────────┤
 │  Esc : Quit      F9 : Menu in BIOS      ↑ ↓ → ←   : Select Item        │
 │  F10 : Save & Exit Setup                                               │
 ├──────────────────────────────────────────────────────────────────────┤
 │               Time, Date, Hard Disk Type...                            │
 └──────────────────────────────────────────────────────────────────────┘
```

Fig. 18.11. Opening the **SoftMenu III Setup** menu in BIOS Setup
(Pentium III 550E)

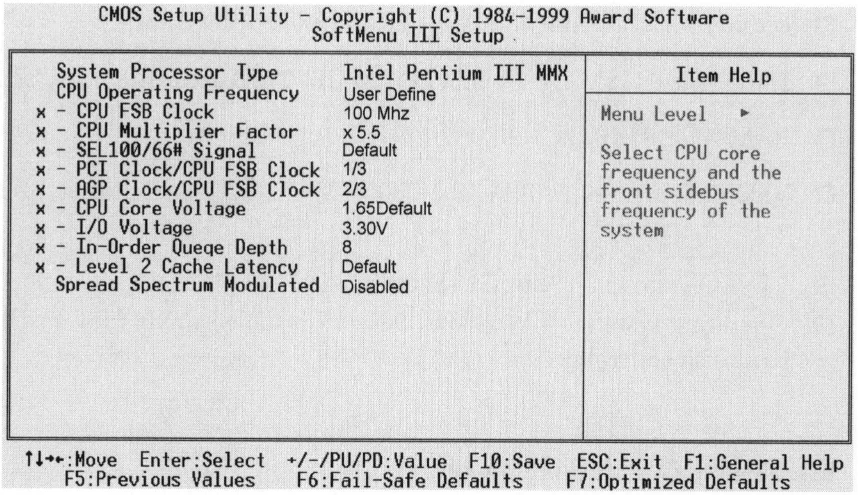

```
      CMOS Setup Utility - Copyright (C) 1984-1999 Award Software
                         SoftMenu III Setup

    System Processor Type      Intel Pentium III MMX    ┃    Item Help
    CPU Operating Frequency    User Define              ┃
  x - CPU FSB Clock            100 Mhz                  ┃  Menu Level    ►
  x - CPU Multiplier Factor    x 5.5                    ┃
  x - SEL100/66# Signal        Default                  ┃  Select CPU core
  x - PCI Clock/CPU FSB Clock  1/3                      ┃  frequency and the
  x - AGP Clock/CPU FSB Clock  2/3                      ┃  front sidebus
  x - CPU Core Voltage         1.65Default              ┃  frequency of the
  x - I/O Voltage              3.30V                    ┃  system
  x - In-Order Quege Depth     8                        ┃
  x - Level 2 Cache Latency    Default                  ┃
    Spread Spectrum Modulated  Disabled                 ┃


  ↑↓→←:Move  Enter:Select  +/-/PU/PD:Value  F10:Save  ESC:Exit  F1:General Help
         F5:Previous Values    F6:Fail-Safe Defaults    F7:Optimized Defaults
```

Fig. 18.12. Setting the recommended parameters in **SoftMenu III Setup**
(Pentium III 550E)

```
      CMOS Setup Utility - Copyright (C) 1984-1999 Award Software
                         SoftMenu III Setup

    System Processor Type      Intel Pentium III MMX    ┃    Item Help
    CPU Operating Frequency    User Define              ┃
  x - CPU FSB Clock            125 Mhz                  ┃  Menu Level    ►
  x - CPU Multiplier Factor    x 5.5                    ┃
  x - SEL100/66# Signal        Default                  ┃  Select CPU core
  x - PCI Clock/CPU FSB Clock  1/4                      ┃  frequency and the
  x - AGP Clock/CPU FSB Clock  2/3                      ┃  front sidebus
  x - CPU Core Voltage         1.65Default              ┃  frequency of the
  x - I/O Voltage              3.30V                    ┃  system
  x - In-Order Quege Depth     8                        ┃
  x - Level 2 Cache Latency    Default                  ┃
    Spread Spectrum Modulated  Disabled                 ┃


  ↑↓→←:Move  Enter:Select  +/-/PU/PD:Value  F10:Save  ESC:Exit  F1:General Help
         F5:Previous Values    F6:Fail-Safe Defaults    F7:Optimized Defaults
```

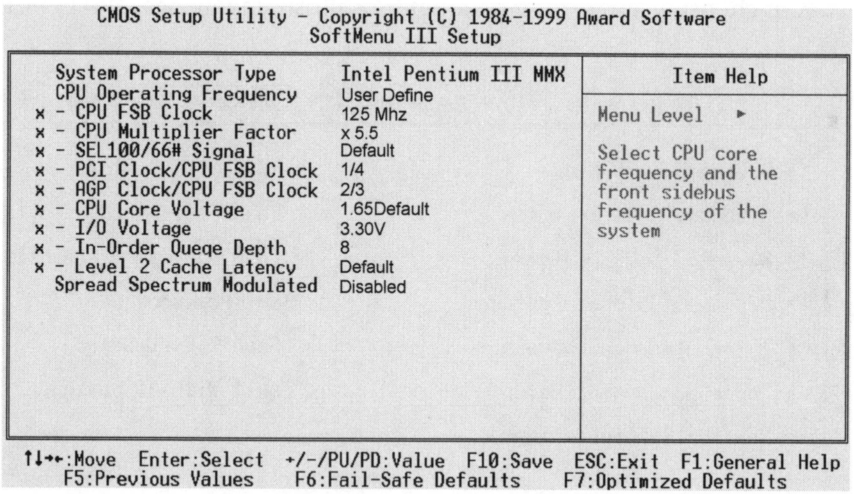

Fig. 18.13. Establishing the overclocking mode in **SoftMenu III Setup**
(Pentium III 550E)

Testing the System

WinBench 99 v1.1 (CPUmark 99 and FPU WinMark), 3DMark2000, and Video 2000 were used for testing. The results are provided in Tables 18.5–18.7 and in Figs. 18.14 and 18.15.

Table 18.5. Results for Pentium III 550E (WinBench 99)

FSB frequency (MHz)	CPU frequency (MHz)	CPUmark 99 rating	FPU WinMark rating
100	$550 = 100 \times 5.5$	46.1	2,970
120	$660 = 120 \times 5.5$	55.2	3,580
125	$688 = 125 \times 5.5$	57.3	3,710
135	$743 = 135 \times 5.5$	61.7	4,000
140	$770 = 140 \times 5.5$	64.3	4,160

Table 18.6. Results for Pentium III 550E (3DMark2000, Video 2000)

FSB frequency (MHz)	CPU frequency (MHz)	3DMark2000 rating	Video 2000 rating
100	$550 = 100 \times 5.5$	5,013	335
133	$733 = 133 \times 5.5$	6,299	393

Table 18.7. Analysis of the Results for Pentium III 550E (Video 2000)

CPU frequency (MHz)		$550 = 100 \times 5.5$	$733 = 133 \times 5.5$
Video 2000 rating ($800 \times 600 \times 32$)		335	393
Data transfer rate (MB/sec)	Non-local → local video memory	332.8	447.2
	Local → non-local video memory	15.6	17.0
	Video memory → system memory	75.0	89.4
	System memory → video memory	169.6	213.6
MPEG2 encoding (frames per second)		18.32	24.67
MPEG2 decoding (% of processor workload)	3 Mbits/sec	98	98
	6 Mbits/sec	98	98
	9 Mbits/sec	98	100

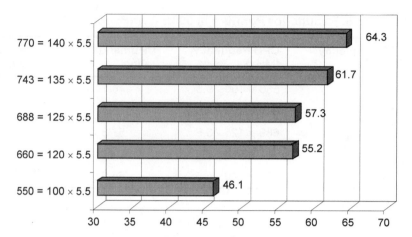

Fig. 18.14. Pentium III 550E test results (CPUmark 99)

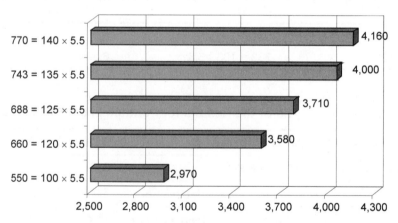

Fig. 18.15. Pentium III 550E test results (FPU WinMark)

The results in Tables 18.5–18.7 and in Figs. 18.14 and 18.15 show that Pentium III 500E and 550E have significant technological reserve. Their architecture, based on the Coppermine core, uses cache memory that operates at the full core frequency and has an improved operating algorithm (256-bit Advanced Transfer Cache).

Computer with Pentium III 700E

System Configuration

☐ Processor — Intel Pentium III 700E (Coppermine core, 256 KB L2 cache, full core frequency operation, recommended processor-bus frequency of 100 MHz, 1.65 V core supply, in box, FC-PGA (connected via adapter), 4/27/00 pack date, version A15753-001, SL45Y S-Spec)

☐ Motherboard — Abit BE6-II (Intel 440BX AGPset chipset)

☐ Hard disk — IBM DPTA-372050 (20 GB, 2 MB cache memory, Ultra DMA/66)

☐ RAM — 128 MB, PC100

☐ Video adapter — Asus AGP-V3800 TV (TNT2 video chipset, 32 MB video memory)

☐ CD-ROM drive — Asus CD-S400/A (40x)

☐ Operating system — Windows 98 with installed drivers for an Ultra DMA/66 hard disk controller

Establishing Overclocking Modes

The overclocking parameters were set in BIOS Setup by increasing the processor-bus frequency in **SoftMenu III Setup**. At frequencies of 700 MHz, 770 MHz, and 840 MHz, the core supply voltage was standard (1.65 V). At 910 MHz, it was increased to 1.7 V. Parameter selection is illustrated in Fig. 18.16.

```
        CMOS Setup Utility - Copyright (C) 1984-1999 Award Software
                          SoftMenu III Setup
  ┌────────────────────────────────────────┬─────────────────────────┐
  │  System Processor Type    Intel Pentium III MMX │   Item Help       │
  │  CPU Operating Frequency  User Define           │                   │
  │ x - CPU FSB Clock         130 Mhz               │ Menu Level   ▶     │
  │ x - CPU Multiplier Factor x 7.0                 │                   │
  │ x - SEL100/66# Signal     Default               │ Select CPU core   │
  │ x - PCI Clock/CPU FSB Clock  1/4                │ frequency and the │
  │ x - AGP Clock/CPU FSB Clock  2/3                │ front sidebus     │
  │ x - CPU Core Voltage      1.70                  │ frequency of the  │
  │ x - I/O Voltage           3.30V                 │ system            │
  │ x - In-Order Queqe Depth  8                     │                   │
  │ x - Level 2 Cache Latency Default               │                   │
  │   Spread Spectrum Modulated  Disabled           │                   │
  │                                                 │                   │
  └────────────────────────────────────────┴─────────────────────────┘
   ↑↓→←:Move  Enter:Select  +/-/PU/PD:Value  F10:Save  ESC:Exit  F1:General Help
        F5:Previous Values   F6:Fail-Safe Defaults   F7:Optimized Defaults
```

Fig. 18.16. Establishing the overclocking mode in **SoftMenu III Setup** (Pentium III 700E)

Testing the System

WinBench 99 v1.1 was used as the main testing package (CPUmark 99 and FPU WinMark). Test results are in Table 18.8 and in Figs. 18.17 and 18.18.

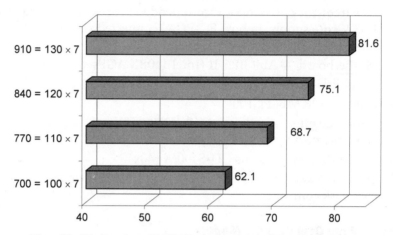

Fig. 18.17. Pentium III 700E test results (CPUmark 99)

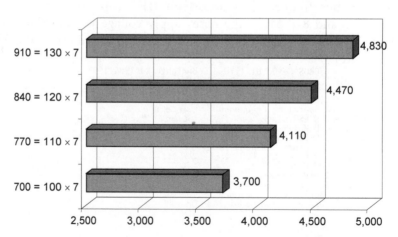

Fig. 18.18. Pentium III 700E test results (FPU WinMark)

Table 18.8. Results of Overclocking Pentium III 700E

FSB frequency (MHz)	CPU frequency (MHz)	CPUmark 99 rating	FPU WinMark rating
100	$700 = 100 \times 7$	62.1	3,700
110	$770 = 110 \times 7$	68.7	4,110
120	$840 = 120 \times 7$	75.1	4,470
130	$910 = 130 \times 7$	81.6	4,830

Computer with Pentium III 800EB

System Configuration

❏ Processor — Intel Pentium III 800EB (Coppermine core, 256 KB L2 cache, full core frequency operation, recommended processor-bus frequency of 133 MHz, 1.65 V core supply, in box, FC-PGA2)
❏ Motherboard — Asus TUSL2-C (Intel 815E B-Step chipset)
❏ Hard disk — IBM DPTA-372050 (20 GB, 2 MB cache memory, Ultra DMA/66).
❏ RAM — 256 MB, PC133
❏ Video adapter — Asus GeForce2, 64 MB
❏ CD-ROM drive — Asus CD-S500/A (50x)
❏ Operating system — Windows 2000, Service Pack 2

Establishing Overclocking Modes

The overclocking mode parameters were set in BIOS Setup by increasing the processor-bus frequency in SoftMenu III Setup. The following frequencies were set: 133 MHz (nominal), 160 MHz, and 177 MHz. At these frequencies, memory operated in asynchronous mode at frequencies of 133 MHz, 120 MHz, and 133 MHz. Such modes were chosen because the memory used in this system didn't support operation at increased frequencies. Its operation was accompanied by failures at 140 MHz.

Because the processor multiplier is small (6x), increasing the processor frequency 44 MHz allowed the CPU frequency to be raised only 200 MHz. The resulting frequency was 177 MHz; therefore, overall system performance increased significantly.

Testing the System

The WinBench 99 v1.1 test package (CPUmark 99 and FPU WinMark) was used. Test results are provided in Table 18.9 and in Figs. 18.19 and 18.20.

Table 18.9. Results of Overclocking Pentium III 800EB

FSB frequency/ RAM (MHz)	CPU frequency (MHz)	CPUmark 99 rating	FPU WinMark rating
133/133	$800 = 133 \times 6$	73.6	4,250
160/120	$960 = 160 \times 6$	84.4	5,090
177/133	$1,062 = 177 \times 6$	93.5	5,640

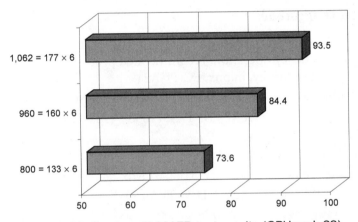

Fig. 18.19. Pentium III 800EB test results (CPUmark 99)

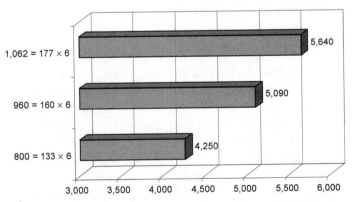

Fig. 18.20. Pentium III 800EB test results (FPU WinMark)

Overclocking Computers with Intel Celeron (Coppermine)

Celeron processors based on the Coppermine core and manufactured with 0.18-micrometer technology have architecture similar to Pentium III processors based on the same core.

However, because of the smaller amount of L2 cache memory and the lower FSB frequency, these Celeron processors have lower performance than their more powerful prototypes. Nevertheless, like their Pentium III counterparts, they are characterized by high performance and wide possibilities of operating in overclocked modes.

As with Coppermine-based Pentium III, the processor multiplier, specifying the internal CPU frequency via the external frequency, is fixed for Coppermine-based Celeron. It is impossible to change the multiplier value. However, the existing technological reserve of Celeron allows significant increases of the FSB frequency, which determines external and internal processor frequencies. The process of increasing this value results in equivalent growth of processor performance and, consequently, overall system performance.

Overclocking potential is the highest for the first models of the Celeron line based on the Coppermine core.

The results of investigating such Celeron processors in overclocked modes are in the following sections.

Computer with Celeron 533 MHz

System Configuration

- ❏ Processor — Intel Celeron 533 MHz (Coppermine core, 128 KB L2 cache, processor frequency operation, 66 MHz nominal FSB frequency, SL46S, made in Malaysia, Slot 1 — Socket 370 adapter)
- ❏ Motherboard — Abit BE6-II (Intel 440BX AGPset chipset)
- ❏ Temperature control — Massive heatsink and powerful fan for the processor
- ❏ Hard disk — Western Digital 6.4 GB
- ❏ RAM — 128 MB, DIMM, PC133, SDRAM
- ❏ Video adapter — MSI MS-8809 GeForce
- ❏ CD-ROM drive — Asus CD-S400/A (40x)
- ❏ Operating system — Windows 98

Establishing Overclocking Modes

During overclocking, the system-bus frequency was increased from 66 MHz to 100 MHz. The built-in capabilities of the motherboard, based on the Intel 440BX chipset, allowed the hard disk, the video adapters, and other devices to operate in the nominal mode. The AGP bus coefficient was 2/3; the Peripheral Component Interconnect (PCI) bus coefficient was 1/3.

According to the previously listed parameters, the CPU clock frequency was set to 800 MHz. The video-adapter clock frequency was 66 MHz. For the hard disk and other PCI devices, the frequency was 33 MHz.

Later, the FSB frequency was increased to 104 MHz and the CPU frequency to 832 MHz.

Testing the System

The following programs were used for testing: SiSoftware Sandra 2000 Professional, 3DMark2000, and Quake III (demo1). Test results are presented in Tables 18.10–18.12 and in Figs. 18.21–18.23.

Table 18.10. Results for Celeron 533 MHz (SiSoftware Sandra)

FSB frequency (MHz)	CPU frequency (MHz)	CPU rating	FPU rating	MMX Integer rating	MMX FPU rating
66	$533 = 66 \times 8$	1,389	658	1,547	2,131
100	$800 = 100 \times 8$	2,093	1,023	2,419	3,269
104	$832 = 104 \times 8$	2,227	1,069	2,522	3,407

Table 18.11. Results for Celeron 533 MHz (3DMark2000)

FSB frequency (MHz)	CPU frequency (MHz)	3DMark2000 rating
66	$533 = 66 \times 8$	3,166
100	$800 = 100 \times 8$	3,987
104	$832 = 104 \times 8$	4,037

Table 18.12. Results for Celeron 533 MHz (Quake III)

FSB frequency (MHz)	CPU frequency (MHz)	Frames per second
66	$533 = 66 \times 8$	62.6
100	$800 = 100 \times 8$	94.8
104	$832 = 104 \times 8$	100.6

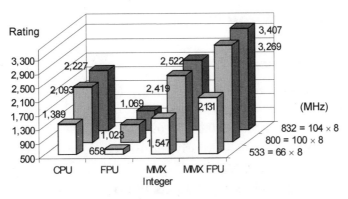

Fig. 18.21. Celeron 533 MHz test results (SiSoftware Sandra)

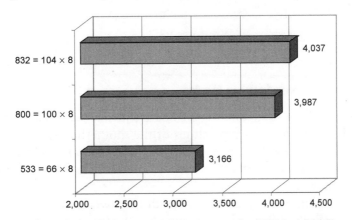

Fig. 18.22. Celeron 533 MHz test results (3DMark2000)

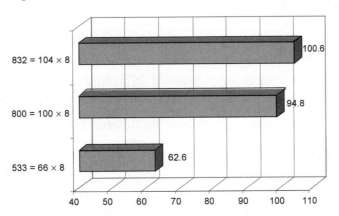

Fig. 18.23. Celeron 533 MHz test results (Quake III)

Computer with Celeron 600 MHz

System Configuration

- ❏ Processor — Intel Celeron 600 MHz (Coppermine core, 128 KB L2 cache, processor frequency operation, 66 MHz nominal FSB frequency, Socket 370)
- ❏ Motherboard — MSI-6309 (VIA 694X, VT82C686B chipset)
- ❏ Temperature control — Massive heatsink and powerful cooler for the CPU
- ❏ Hard disk — Seagate 20 GB
- ❏ RAM — 192 MB DIMM, PC133, SDRAM
- ❏ Video adapter — Noname TNT2 Vanta (8 MB)
- ❏ CD-ROM drive — Asus CD-S400/A (40x)
- ❏ Operating system — Windows 98

Establishing Overclocking Modes

During overclocking, the system-bus frequency was increased from 66 MHz to 100 MHz. The built-in capabilities of the motherboard based on a Via Technologies chipset, allowed the hard disk, the video adapter, and other devices to operate at the nominal frequency. The AGP bus coefficient was set to 2/3; the PCI bus coefficient was 1/3.

According to the parameters set during overclocking, the CPU operating frequency was 900 MHz. For video adapter, the frequency was 66 MHz. For the hard disk and other PCI devices, it was 33 MHz.

Testing the System

For testing, the following WinBench 99 programs were used: CPUmark 99 and FPU WinMark. Test results are presented in Table 18.13 and in Figs. 18.24 and 18.25.

Table 18.13. Results of Overclocking Celeron 600 MHz

FSB frequency (MHz)	CPU frequency (MHz)	CPUmark 99 rating	FPU WinMark rating
66	600 = 66 × 9	41.2	3,190
100	900 = 100 × 9	56.1	4,690

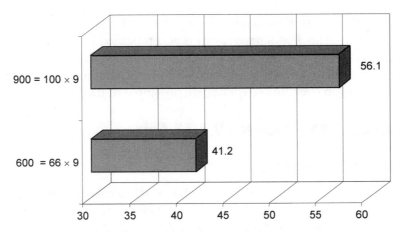

Fig. 18.24. Celeron 600 MHz test results (CPUmark 99)

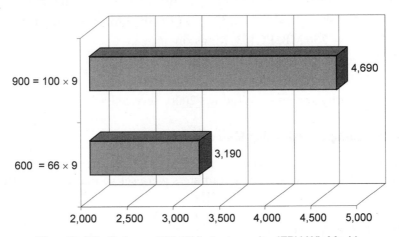

Fig. 18.25. Celeron 600 MHz test results (FPU WinMark)

Overclocking Computers with Intel Pentium III (Tualatin)

Intel Pentium III based on the Tualatin core and manufactured according to 0.13-micrometer technology is characterized not only by relatively high performance in nominal modes, but also by broad capabilities of running in overclocked modes.

The existing technological reserve ensures the possibility of increasing the FSB frequency, which controls both internal and external processor frequencies. Because the processor multiplier is relatively high, increasing FSB frequency

10 MHz — 20 MHz allows the CPU core frequency to be raised 120 MHz — 240 MHz. This frequency growth is accompanied by an increase in CPU performance and, consequently, overall system performance.

The results of performance analysis for Tualatin-based Pentium III processors operating in overclocked modes are presented in the following sections.

Computer with Pentium III 1.13 GHz

System Configuration

❐ Processor — Intel Pentium III 1.13 GHz (Tualatin core, 512 KB L2 cache, CPU core frequency operation, recommended processor-bus frequency of 133 MHz, 8.5x multiplier, 1.45 V core supply, FC-PGA2)

❐ Motherboard — Asus TUSL2-C (Intel 815E B-Step chipset)

❐ Hard disk — IBM DPTA-372050 (20 GB, 2 MB cache memory, Ultra DMA/66)

❐ RAM — 256 MB, PC133, Kingston

❐ Video adapter — Asus GeForce2, 64 MB

❐ CD-ROM drive — Asus CD-S500/A (50x)

❐ Operating system — Windows 2000, Service Pack 2

Establishing Overclocking Modes

In the course of overclocking, the system-bus frequency was increased from 133 MHz to 165 MHz. The parameters were set so that the CPU frequency was increased from 1.13 GHz to 1.40 GHz.

Testing the System

WinBench 99 was used as the main testing package (CPUmark 99 and FPU WinMark). The results of testing the overclocked system are presented in Table 18.14 and in Figs. 18.26 and 18.27.

Table 18.14. Results of Overclocking Pentium III 1.13 GHz

FSB frequency (MHz)	CPU frequency (MHz)	CPUmark 99 rating	FPU WinMark rating
133	$1{,}133 = 133 \times 8.5$	99.1	6,210
140	$1{,}190 = 140 \times 8.5$	104.0	6,480

continues

Table 18.14 Continued

FSB frequency (MHz)	CPU frequency (MHz)	CPUmark 99 rating	FPU WinMark rating
150	1,275 = 150 × 8.5	107.0	6,960
160	1,360 = 160 × 8.5	112.0	7,430
165	1,403 = 165 × 8.5	115.0	7,650

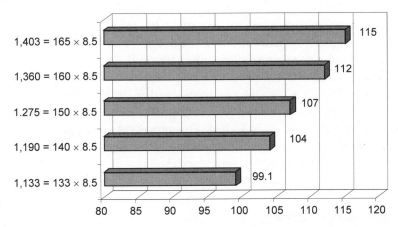

Fig. 18.26. Pentium III 1.13 GHz test results (CPUmark 99)

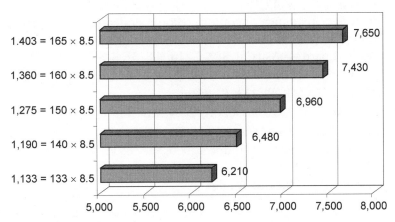

Fig. 18.27. Pentium III 1.13 GHz test results (FPU WinMark)

Overclocking Computers with Intel Celeron (Tualatin)

Intel Celeron processors based on the Tualatin core and manufactured according to 0.13-micrometer technology have practically the same architecture as Pentium III processors based on the same core. However, a smaller amount of L2 cache memory gives them lower performance than their more powerful prototypes. Still, Tualatin-based Pentium III processors are powerful and have a high overclocking potential. The processor-bus frequency is 100 MHz.

The multiplier that sets the internal CPU frequency via external FSB frequency is a fixed value for Tualatin-based processors. However, the existing technological reserve of these processors allows increases in the FSB frequency, which determines the external and internal processor frequencies.

The multiplier is high for a processor with a 100 MHz bus frequency; therefore, increasing the FSB frequency 10 MHz — 20 MHz allows the internal processor frequency to be raised 120 MHz — 240 MHz. This process is accompanied by equivalent growth in processor performance and, consequently, overall system performance.

The following sections show the results of investigating overclocked Celeron processors with the Tualatin core.

Computer with Celeron 1.3 GHz

System Configuration

☐ Processor — Intel Celeron 1.3 GHz (Tualatin core, 256 KB L2 cache memory, processor frequency operation, recommended processor-bus frequency of 100 MHz, 13x multiplier, 1.5 V core supply, FC-PGA2)
☐ Motherboard — Asus TUSL2-C (Intel 815E B-Step chipset)
☐ Hard disk — IBM DPTA-372050 (20 GB, 2 MB cache memory, Ultra DMA/66)
☐ RAM — 256 MB, PC133, Kingston
☐ Video adapter — Asus GeForce2, 64 MB
☐ CD-ROM drive — Asus CD-S500/A (50x)
☐ Operating system — Windows 2000, Service Pack 2

Establishing Overclocking Modes

In the course of overclocking, the system-bus frequency was increased from 100 MHz to 123 MHz. Note that this result was achieved without increasing the processor core voltage.

Testing the System

The following WinBench 99 tests were conducted: CPUmark 99, FPU WinMark, and WinMark 99 business disk. Test results are in Table 18.15 and in Figs. 18.28–18.30.

Table 18.15. Results of Overclocking Celeron 1.3 GHz

FSB frequency (MHz)	CPU frequency (MHz)	CPUmark 99 rating	FPU WinMark rating	WinMark 99 business disk rating
100	1,300 = 100 × 13	105	7,160	7,480
110	1,430 = 110 × 13	112	7,780	7,580
120	1,560 = 120 × 13	121	8,500	7,650
123	1,600 = 123 × 13	125	8,720	7,760

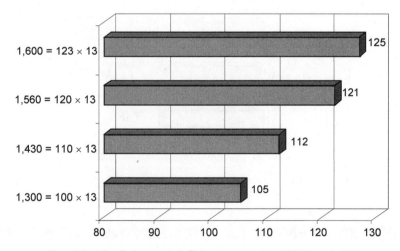

Fig. 18.28. Celeron 1.3 GHz test results (CPUmark 99)

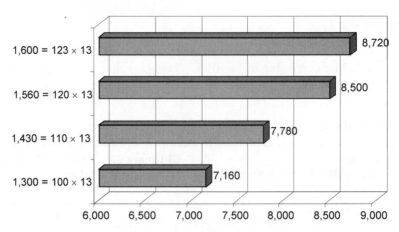

Fig. 18.29. Celeron 1.3 GHz test results (FPU WinMark)

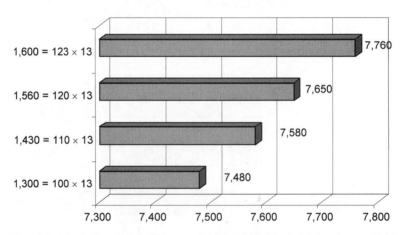

Fig. 18.30. Celeron 1.3 GHz test results (WinMark 99 business disk)

Computer with Celeron 1.3 GHz (Hardware Acceleration)

System Configuration

☐ Processor — Intel Celeron 1.3 GHz (Tualatin core, 256 KB L2 cache memory, processor frequency operation, recommended processor-bus frequency of 100 MHz, 13x multiplier, 1.5 V core supply, FC-PGA2, SL6VR, made in the Philippines)

❏ Motherboard — FIC FR33E (VIA Apollo PLE133T chipset)
❏ Hard disk — IBM DPTA-372050 (20 GB, 2 MB cache memory, Ultra DMA/66)
❏ RAM — 256 MB, PC133, Kingston
❏ Video adapter — Built-in, Trident Blade3D
❏ CD-ROM drive — Asus CD-S400/A (40x)
❏ Operating system — Windows 2000 Server, Service Pack 2

Establishing Overclocking Modes

During overclocking, the system-bus frequency was increased from 100 MHz to 112 MHz. This result was achieved without increasing the processor core voltage; the FR33E motherboard used in this configuration simply didn't provide the appropriate settings.

After that, the voltage was raised by implementing a hardware modification: Insulating some processor contacts and connecting other ones. This technology was covered in detail in *Chapter 8.*

By changing the state of specific processor contacts, it was possible to control the processor-bus clock frequency. For example, by insulating one processor contact, it was possible to make the processor operate at a bus frequency of 133 MHz. The internal frequency for this mode was 1.73 GHz (Fig. 18.31). After raising the core voltage from 1.5 V to 1.75 V, the computer could be booted successfully only once. Unfortunately, some time later, the system hung up. After restarting, it couldn't accomplish the POST routine and never started again.

Fig. 18.31. Implementing the 133 MHz FSB frequency and 1.75 V core supply

Finally, the following mode was implemented: 1.6 V supply voltage, 124 MHz bus frequency, and 1.61 GHz CPU core frequency.

Testing the System

WinBench 99 was used as the main testing package (CPUmark 99 and FPU WinMark). Test results are presented in Table 18.16 and in Figs. 18.32 and 18.33.

Table 18.16. Results of Overclocking the Modified Celeron 1.3 GHz

FSB frequency (MHz)	CPU frequency (MHz)	CPUmark 99 rating	FPU WinMark rating
100	1,300 = 100 × 13	96	7,080
112	1,460 = 112 × 13	108	7,930
124	1,612 = 124 × 13	120	8,750

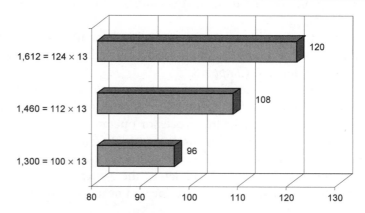

Fig. 18.32. Modified Celeron 1.3 GHz test results (CPUmark 99)

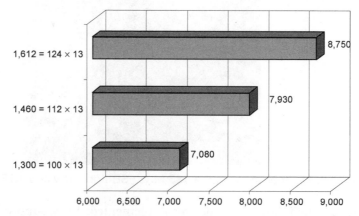

Fig. 18.33. Modified Celeron 1.3 GHz test results (FPU WinMark)

Overclocking Computers with Intel Pentium 4 (Willamette)

Intel Pentium 4 processors based on the Willamette core are manufactured with 0.18-micrometer technology. They are based on the Intel NetBurst microarchitecture, which uses the Quad Pumped Bus as the FSB.

Willamette-based Pentium 4 processors are manufactured with two variations of the Flip-Chip Pin Grid Array (FCPGA) form factor, providing for Socket 423 and Socket 478 slots. The voltage supplied to the core (Vcore) for Socket 423 processors is 1.7 V and 1.75 V; for Socket 478 processors, it is 1.75 V.

High performance of Pentium 4 processors is the product of the core architecture and technology, which was refined on the previous generation of processors with the Coppermine core. Furthermore, these processors have significant technological reserve that can be implemented by carefully performing moderate overclocking. Special chipsets designed for Pentium 4 processors and serving as a basis for appropriate motherboards allow the capabilities of the core architecture and high technological potential to be implemented.

When planning overclocking operations (with analysis of advantages and drawbacks), note that as in case of previous models, Pentium 4 processors have fixed multipliers. Because of this, processor overclocking is accomplished exclusively by increasing the FSB clock frequency and, consequently, changing the frequency modes of other computer components.

To successfully accomplish overclocking procedures, it is recommended that you use a motherboard that ensures the required functional capabilities, including hardware monitoring. The chosen motherboard must be compatible with the chosen processor line (Socket 423 or Socket 478). High-quality motherboards allow considerable performance gain when overclocking Pentium 4 processors. For 1.7 GHz (Socket 478) models, correct overclocking procedures often provide performance growth of 20% or more. For some models with a clock frequency of 1.4 GHz (Socket 478), the performance gain is 25%–30%. Remember that overclocking potential depends not only on the operating modes and processor model, but also on the specific processor.

Tables 18.17 and 18.18 outline the results of overclocking for several Pentium 4 1.4 GHz and Pentium 4 1.7 GHz processors. (These materials were obtained from **http://www.overclockers.ru**, a Russian-language Web site.)

Table 18.17. Results of Overclocking Pentium 4 1.4 GHz (http://www.overclockers.ru)

Processor marking	Maximum stable frequency (GHz)
SL59U-MALAY-L130A673-0772	1.67
SL59U-MALAY-L130A673-1037	1.67
SL59U-MALAY-L130A673-1056	1.91
SL59U-MALAY-L130A673-0774	1.75
SL59U-MALAY-L130A673-0780	1.68
SL59U-MALAY-L130A673-1034	1.61
SL59U-MALAY-L130A673-0840	1.79
SL59U-MALAY-L130A673-0771	1.68
SL59U-MALAY-L130A673-0777	1.75

Table 18.18. Results of Overclocking Pentium 4 1.7 GHz (http://www.overclockers.ru)

CPU marking	Maximum stable frequency (GHz)
SLSTG-L129B272-0226-MALAY	2.10
SLSTG-L129B272-0223-MALAY	2.10
SLSTG-L129B272-0222-MALAY	2.10
SL59X-MALAY-L132A473-0683	2.09
SL59X-MALAY-L132A473-0105	1.95
SL59X-MALAY-L132A473-0686	1.95
SL5TK-COSTAR-3141A265-1341	2.04
SL5TK-COSTAR-3141A265-1344	2.04

Computer with Pentium 4 1.5 GHz

System Configuration

❏ Processor — Intel Pentium 4 1.5 GHz (Willamette core, 8 KB L1 cache, 256 KB L2 cache, core frequency operation, nominal processor-bus frequency of 100 MHz that ensures a data-transfer frequency of 400 MHz, 1.75 V core supply, Socket 478)

❏ Motherboard — Shuttle AV40 (VIA P4X266 chipset)

❏ Hard disk — IBM DPTA-372050 (20 GB, 2 MB cache memory, Ultra DMA/66)
❏ RAM — 256 MB, DDR266
❏ Video adapter — Asus GeForce2
❏ CD-ROM drive — Asus CD-S400/A (40x)
❏ Operating system — Windows 2000 Server, Service Pack 2

Establishing Overclocking Modes

Overclocking was achieved by increasing the processor-bus frequency.

Testing the System

The following tests were used to investigate the overclocking results: CPUmark 99, FPU WinMark, 3DMark2000, and Video 2000. Testing results are presented in Tables 18.19 and 18.20 and in Figs. 18.34–18.36.

Table 18.19. Results of Overclocking Pentium 4 1.5 GHz

FSB frequency (MHz)	CPU frequency (MHz)	CPUmark 99 rating	FPU WinMark rating	3DMark2000 rating
100	1,500 = 100 × 15	89.1	5,200	7,626
119	1,785 = 119 × 15	105.0	6,170	8,643

Table 18.20. Analysis of the Results for Pentium 4 1.5 GHz (Video 2000)

CPU frequency (MHz)		1,500 = 100 × 15	1,785 = 119 × 15
Video 2000 (800 × 600 × 32)		879	990
Data-transfer rate (MB/sec)	Non-local → local video memory	554.6	661.0
	Local → non-local video memory	14.8	15.0
	Video memory → system memory	49.0	58.4
	System memory → video memory	498.6	638.6
MPEG2 encoding (frames per second)		36.06	42.65
MPEG2 decoding (% of processor workload)	3 Mbits/sec	29.18	22.04
	6 Mbits/sec	38.54	29.38
	9 Mbits/sec	54.10	40.34

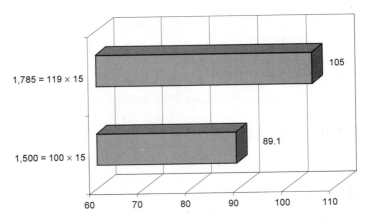

Fig. 18.34. Pentium 4 1.5 GHz test results (CPUmark 99)

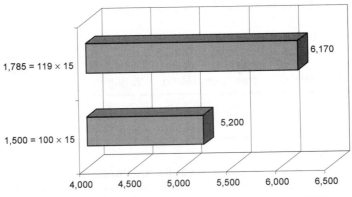

Fig. 18.35. Pentium 4 1.5 GHz test results (FPU WinMark)

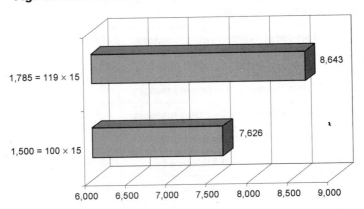

Fig. 18.36. Pentium 4 1.5 GHz test results (3DMark2000)

Computer with Pentium 4 1.7 GHz

System Configuration

❑ Processor — Intel Pentium 4 1.7 GHz (Willamette core, 8 KB L1 cache, 256 KB L2 cache, processor core frequency operation, nominal processor-bus frequency of 100 MHz that ensures a data-transfer rate of 400 MHz, 1.75 V core supply, Socket 423)

❑ Motherboard — Asus P4T (Intel 850 chipset, BIOS 1004 Final, 3/30/01)

❑ Hard disk — IBM Deskstar 75GXP (45 GB, 2 MB cache memory, 7,200 rpm, Ultra ATA/100)

❑ RAM — Buffalo PC800, 2x128 MB, ECC RDRAM

❑ Video adapter — Nvidia GeForce3 64 MB (200 MHz core, 230 MHz memory, DDR)

❑ CD-ROM drive — Asus CD-S400/A (40x)

❑ Operating system — Windows 2000 Professional (SP1)

Establishing Overclocking Modes

The overclocking modes were set by increasing the processor-bus frequency.

Testing the System

The following tests were used: Business Winstone 2001, SYSmark 2000, and 3DMark2001. Testing results are presented in Table 18.21 and in Figs. 18.37–18.39.

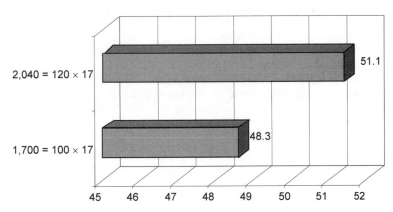

Fig. 18.37. Pentium 4 1.7 GHz test results (Business Winstone 2001)

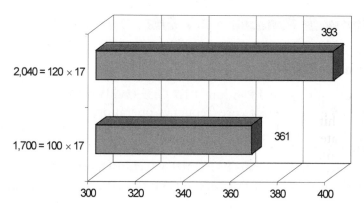

Fig. 18.38. Pentium 4 1.7 GHz test results (SYSmark 2000)

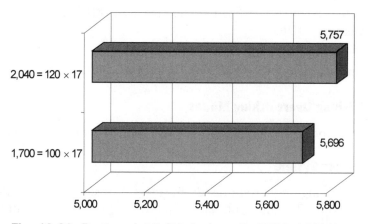

Fig. 18.39. Pentium 4 1.7 GHz test results (3DMark2001)

Table 18.21. Results of Overclocking Pentium 4 1.7 GHz

FSB frequency (MHz)	CPU frequency (MHz)	Business Winstone 2001 rating	SYSmark 2000 (Windows Media Encoder 4) rating	3DMark2001 rating
100	1,700 = 100 × 17	48.3	361	5,696
120	2,040 = 120 × 17	51.1	393	5,757

The results in Table 18.21 and in Figs. 18.37–18.39 demonstrate that Pentium 4 processors have significant technological reserve.

Overclocking Computers with Intel Pentium 4 (Northwood)

Intel Pentium 4 processors based on the Northwood core are manufactured according to 0.13-micrometer technology. They are based on the Intel NetBurst microarchitecture, which uses the Quad Pumped Bus as the FSB. The system bus can operate at 400 MHz, 533 MHz, and 800 MHz. These processors have 512 KB of L2 cache memory.

Northwood-based Pentium 4 processors are implemented according to the FC-PGA form factor, providing for Socket 478 slots.

Computer with Pentium 4 2.2 GHz

System Configuration

- ❏ Processor — Intel Pentium 4 2.2 GHz (Northwood core, 512 KB L2 cache, CPU core frequency operation, nominal processor-bus frequency of 100 MHz that ensures a data-transfer rate of 400 MHz, 1.5 V core supply, Socket 478, SL5YS, made in Malaysia)
- ❏ Motherboard — Shuttle AV40 (VIA P4X266 chipset)
- ❏ Hard disk — IBM DPTA-372050 (20 GB, 2 MB cache memory, Ultra DMA/66)
- ❏ RAM — 256 MB, DDR266
- ❏ Video adapter — Asus GeForce2
- ❏ CD-ROM drive — Asus CD-S400/A (40x)
- ❏ Operating system — Windows 2000 Server, Service Pack 2

Fig. 18.40. Pentium 4 2.2 GHz processor

Establishing Overclocking Modes

The overclocking modes were set by increasing the processor-bus frequency.

Testing the System

The WinBench 99 v1.1 test package (CPUmark 99) and the 3DMark2000 and Video 2000 tests were used. Test results are presented in Tables 18.22 and 18.23 and in Figs. 18.41–18.43.

Table 18.22. Results of Overclocking Pentium 4 2.2 GHz

FSB frequency (MHz)	CPU frequency (MHz)	3DMark2000 rating	CPUmark 99 rating
100	$2,200 = 100 \times 22$	9,346	145
110	$2,618 = 110 \times 22$	9,568	156

Table 18.23. Analysis of the Results for Pentium 4 2.2 GHz (Video 2000)

CPU frequency (MHz)		$2,200 = 100 \times 22$	$2,618 = 110 \times 22$
Video 2000 (800 × 600 × 32)		1,078	1,120
Date-transfer rate (MB/sec)	Non-local → local video memory	610.4	662.2
	Local → non-local video memory	14.0	15.0
	Video memory → system memory	57.0	61.6
	System memory → video memory	474.0	528.4
MPEG2 encoding (frames per second)		52.73	56.72
MPEG2 decoding (% of processor workload)	3 Mbits/sec	15.42	12.70
	6 Mbits/sec	20.88	18.80
	9 Mbits/sec	28.88	22.56

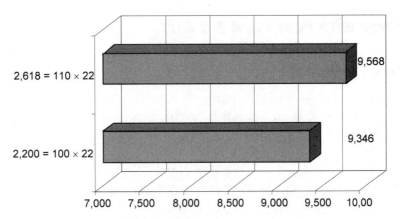

Fig. 18.41. Pentium 4 2.2 GHz test results (3DMark2000)

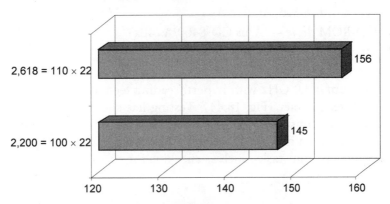

Fig. 18.42. Pentium 4 2.2 GHz test results (CPUmark 99)

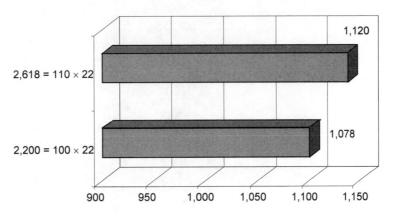

Fig. 18.43. Pentium 4 2.2 GHz test results (Video 2000)

Computer with Pentium 4 3.0 GHz

System Configuration

❑ Processor — Intel Pentium 4 3.0 GHz with hyperthreading technology (Northwood core, 512 KB L2 cache, processor frequency operation, nominal processor-bus frequency of 100 MHz that ensures a data-transfer rate of 400 MHz, 1.55 V core supply, Socket 478)

❑ Motherboard — Intel D875PBZ (Intel 875 chipset)

❑ Hard disk — IBM 180GXP (120 GB, 2 MB cache memory, Ultra DMA/100)

❑ RAM — 2x256 MB, DDR400, Kingmax

❑ Video adapter — Abit GeForce4 Ti4200, Outside Thermal Exhaust System (OTES), 128 MB, AGP 8x

❑ CD-ROM drive — Asus CD-S400/A (40x)

❑ Operating system — Windows XP, Service Pack 1

Pentium 4 3.0 GHz with hyperthreading technology is supplied with a powerful, high-tech cooler (Fig. 18.44). Testing has showed that for office applications, which do not consume much resources, it is possible to use the standard cooler of earlier Pentium 4 models. However, the processor will heat significantly even when performing routine tasks, such as checking for viruses.

Fig. 18.44. Cooler for Pentium 4 3.0 GHz with hyperthreading technology (underside view)

Establishing Overclocking Modes

For a long time, Intel did not provide motherboard functionality that would allow PC users to set the overclocking modes for processors. By now, the manufacturer has released motherboards that allow the processor frequency to be raised 4% and the frequencies of the PCI and AGP buses to be increased.

The overclocking mode was set in BIOS Setup by increasing the processor-bus frequency 4%. Parameters of the overclocked processor are shown in Fig. 18.45.

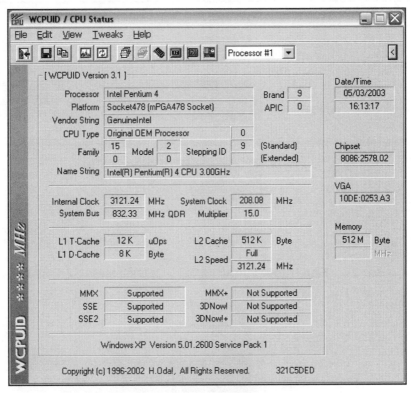

Fig. 18.45. Parameters for Pentium 4 3.0 GHz with hyperthreading technology (WCPUID)

Testing the System

The following programs were used for testing: CPUmark 99, 3DMark2001 SE Pro, and the SiSoftware Sandra 2003 memory bandwidth benchmark. Test results are presented in Table 18.24 and in Figs. 18.46–18.48.

Table 18.24. Results of Overclocking Pentium 4 3.0 GHz

FSB frequency (MHz)	CPU frequency (MHz)	CPUmark 99 rating	3DMark2001 SE Pro rating	SiSoftware Sandra benchmark
100	$3,000 = 200 \times 15$	202	12,454	4,774
104	$3,120 = 208 \times 15$	211	12,839	5,004

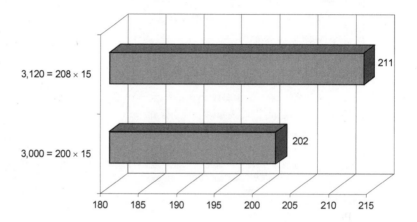

Fig. 18.46. Pentium 4 3.0 GHz test results (CPUmark 99)

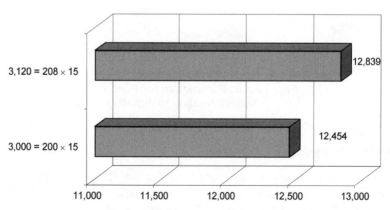

Fig. 18.47. Pentium 4 3.0 GHz test results (3DMark2001 SE Pro)

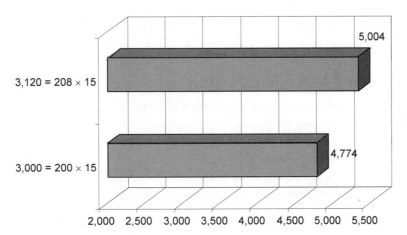

Fig. 18.48. Pentium 4 3.0 GHz test results
(SiSoftware Sandra memory bandwidth benchmark)

Overclocking Computers with Intel Celeron (Northwood)

Intel Celeron processors based on the Northwood core are manufactured according to 0.13-micrometer technology. They have a smaller amount of L2 cache memory than Pentium 4 processors based on the same core. These processors have significant technological reserve and, consequently, high overclocking potential. Testing has shown that most models can be overclocked to frequencies exceeding the nominal 50%.

Computer with Celeron 2.0 GHz

System Configuration

- ❏ Processor — Intel Celeron 2.0 GHz (Northwood core, 128 KB L2 cache, processor core frequency operation, recommended processor-bus frequency of 100 MHz, data-bus frequency of 400 MHz, 1.55 V core supply, Socket 478)
- ❏ Motherboard — Abit IT7-MAX2 v.2.0 (Intel 845EB chipset)
- ❏ Hard disk — IBM 180GXP (120 GB, 2 MB cache memory, Ultra DMA/100)
- ❏ RAM — 512 MB, DDR266, Kingston
- ❏ Video adapter — Abit GeForce4 Ti4200, OTES, 64 MB video memory, AGP 4x

❑ CD-ROM drive — Asus CD-S400/A (40x)

❑ Operating system — Windows XP, Service Pack 1

Establishing Overclocking Modes

The overclocking mode was set in BIOS Setup using the SoftMenu III technology. The processor-bus frequency was increased 50% to 150 MHz. The data-transfer rate via the processor bus reached 600 MHz (4 × 150 MHz). The processor frequency was increased from 2 GHz to 3 GHz (Fig. 18.49). No steps for additional cooling of the processor were taken. An additional fan was installed in the system unit case, which blew out the hot air. Because DDR266 memory was used in this configuration, to ensure stable operation at 150 MHz, it was necessary to increase the voltage supplied to the memory 0.5 V.

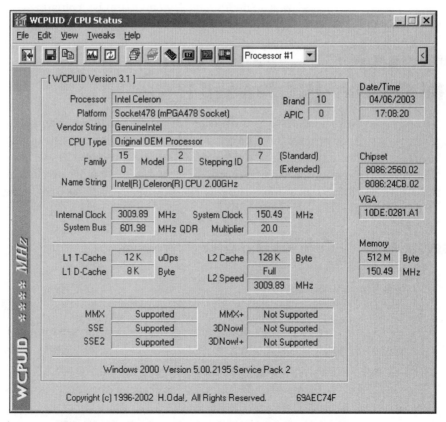

Fig. 18.49. Parameters for Celeron 2.0 GHz (WCPUID)

Testing the System

As tests, the following software were used: CPUmark 99, 3DMark2001 SE Pro, SiSoftware Sandra 2003, and SYSmark 2002 Internet Content Creation (ICC). The time required to encode a music file with a duration of 14 minutes and 5 seconds into MP3 format also was found. Test results are presented in Table 18.25 and in Figs. 18.50–18.53.

When operating in a nominal mode, the processor temperature was 48°C (188°F). After overclocking the processor to 3 GHz, the temperature reached 56°C (133°F).

Table 18.25. Results of Overclocking Celeron 2.0 GHz

FSB frequency (MHz)	CPU frequency (MHz)	CPUmark 99 rating	3DMark2001 SE Pro rating	SiSoftware Sandra memory bandwidth benchmark	SYSmark 2002 ICC rating	MP3 encoding (sec)
100	2,000 = 100 × 20	75	6,966	1,400	183	51
133	2,666 = 133 × 20	100	8,893	1,611	246	37
150	3,000 = 150 × 20	114	9,656	1,859	279	33

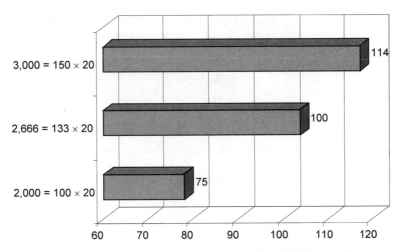

Fig. 18.50. Celeron 2.0 GHz test results (CPUmark 99)

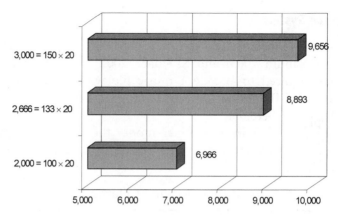

Fig. 18.51. Celeron 2.0 GHz test results (3DMark2001 SE Pro)

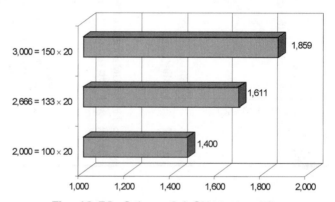

Fig. 18.52. Celeron 2.0 GHz test results
(SiSoftware Sandra memory bandwidth benchmark)

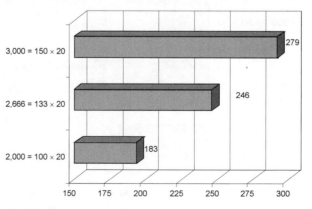

Fig. 18.53. Celeron 2.0 GHz test results (SYSmark 2002 ICC)

Overclocking Computers with AMD Athlon (Thunderbird)

Contemporary processors, including AMD Athlon, usually have fixed a multiplier that relates internal and external frequencies. Because of this, overclocking of Athlon typically is achieved by increasing external frequency.

Athlon has significant technological reserve that provides the possibility of using overclocking modes. Overclocking generally is accomplished by increasing FSB (EV6 bus) frequency. The limit of this frequency — and, consequently, the limit of performance growth for the entire computer system — depends on the motherboard used in the hardware configuration.

Athlon requires a specialized motherboard with chipsets that support the processor. Such a motherboard ensures stable operation of operation of Athlon if 235 W or higher power supply units are used.

The results of performance investigations conducted for overclocked computers based on Athlon processors are provided in the following sections.

Computer with Athlon 700

System Configuration

❏ Processor — AMD Athlon 700 (128 KB L1 cache, 256 KB L2 cache, on-die, CPU core frequency operation, standard FSB EV6 frequency of 100 MHz and a data-transfer rate of 200 MHz, 1.7 V core supply, Socket A with 462 pins)

❏ Motherboard — Abit KT7 (VIA Apollo KT133, VT8363+VT82C686A chipset)

❏ RAM —128 MB, SDRAM, PC100

❏ Hard disk — IBM DPTA-372050 (20 GB, 2 MB cache memory, Ultra DMA/66)

❏ Video adapter — Asus AGP-V3800 TV (TNT2 video chipset, 32 MB video memory)

❏ Power supply unit — 250 W

❏ Operating system — Windows 98 Second Edition

Testing was performed using the WinBench 99 package (CPUmark 99 and FPU WinMark).

Fig. 18.54. Athlon (Thunderbird) processor

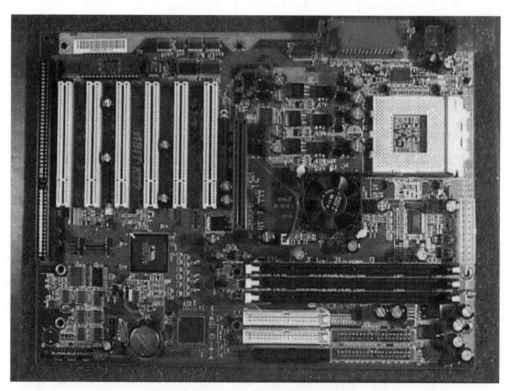

Fig. 18.55. Abit KT7 motherboard

Main Parameters of the Abit KT7 Motherboard

❑ Supported processors — AMD Athlon (Thunderbird) and AMD Duron (Socket A processor slot with 462 contacts, nominal FSB frequency of 100 MHz)

❑ Overclocking — 100/101/103/105/107/110/112/115/117/120/122/124/127/133/136/140/145/150/155 MHz via BIOS Setup

❑ Core voltage — 1.1 V–1.85 V, with an increment of 0.25 V

❑ Sets the multiplier —BIOS Setup

❑ Chipset — VIA Apollo KT133 (VT8363+VT82C686A)

❑ RAM — Up to 1.5 GB in three DIMM modules (168 pins, 3.3 V), PC100/133 SDRAM, 100/133 MHz frequency

❑ BIOS — Award Plug-and-Play BIOS

Cooling Devices

The Titan TTC-D2T cooler (Fig. 18.56) was used in the test configuration. This cooler ensures efficient cooling of Thunderbird-based Athlon and Duron. Control over the fan is ensured by the built-in hardware-monitoring tools of the VT82C686A chip.

Fig. 18.56. Titan TTC-D2T cooler

The processor temperature was controlled using the hard thermal sensor on the motherboard (Fig. 18.57) and hardware-monitoring tools.

Fig. 18.57. Hard thermal sensor on the Abit KT7 motherboard

Overclocking by Increasing the FSB Frequency

The processor-bus frequency is selected in BIOS Setup. The processor-bus frequency was increased up to 115 MHz. The results of overclocking the processor by increasing the processor-bus frequency are summarized in Table 18.26 and in Figs. 18.58 and 18.59.

Table 18.26. Results of Increasing the FSB Frequency for Athlon 700

Processor frequency = bus frequency × multiplier	CPUmark 99 rating	FPU WinMark rating
700 MHz = 100 × 7	64.7	3,810
770 MHz = 110 × 7	71.2	4,190
784 MHz = 112 × 7	72.5	4,270

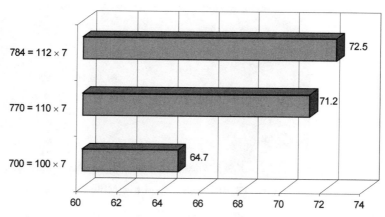

Fig. 18.58. Athlon 700 results after increasing the bus frequency (CPUmark 99)

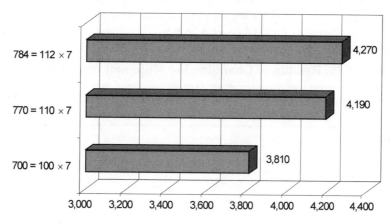

Fig. 18.59. Athlon 700 results after increasing the bus frequency (FPU WinMark)

Overclocking by Changing the Multiplier

Thunderbird-based Athlon has a fixed multiplier. The Abit KT7 motherboard used in this test belongs to a group of motherboards that provide the possibility of changing the multiplier. Although AMD has limited this capability by cutting the L1 bridges on the surface of the processor case, the processor used in this experiment had closed L1 bridges.

Thus, this specific processor did not require restoration of the L1 bridges (Fig. 18.60).

Fig. 18.60. Bridges on the Athlon processor

The overclocking parameters were chosen and set in BIOS Setup using SoftMenu. The overclocking results, as well as the chosen modes, are presented in Table 18.27 and in Figs. 18.61 and 18.62.

Table 18.27. Results of Changing the Multiplier for Athlon 700

Processor frequency = bus frequency × multiplier	CPUmark 99 rating	FPU WinMark rating
700 MHz = 100 × 7	64.7	3,810
800 MHz = 100 × 8	71.8	4,350

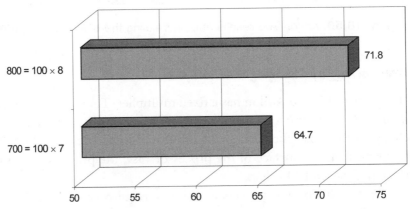

Fig. 18.61. Athlon 700 results after changing the multiplier (CPUmark 99)

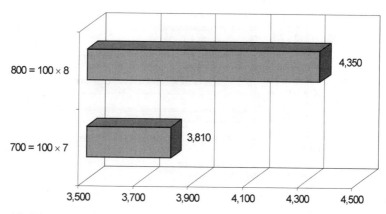

Fig. 18.62. Athlon 700 results after changing the multiplier (FPU WinMark)

Overclocking via the Bus and Multiplier

Maximum performance levels are achieved by choosing the optimal processor frequency at the best multiplier value.

The results of overclocking Athlon using this approach are in Tables 18.28–18.30 and in Figs. 18.63 and 18.64. Although Athlon could be overclocked only to 825 MHz, a significant improvement in system performance was achieved.

Table 18.28. Results of Combined Overclocking of Athlon 700

Processor frequency = bus frequency × multiplier	CPUmark 99 rating	FPU WinMark rating
700 MHz = 100 × 7.0	64.7	3,810
770 MHz = 110 × 7.0	71.2	4,190
784 MHz = 112 × 7.0	72.5	4,270
800 MHz = 100 × 8.0	71.8	4,350
824 MHz = 103 × 8.0	74.5	4,490
825 MHz = 110 × 7.5	75.4	4,490

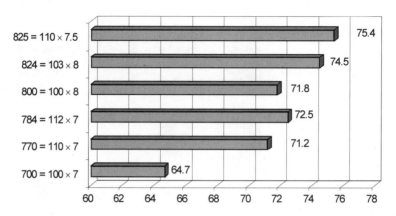

Fig. 18.63. Athlon 700 results after combined overclocking (CPUmark 99)

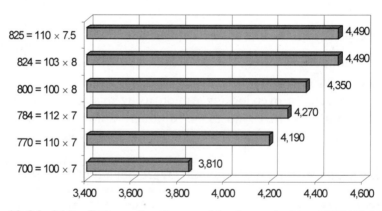

Fig. 18.64. Athlon 700 results after combined overclocking (FPU WinMark)

Table 18.29. Parameters When Overclocking Athlon 700

Processor frequency = bus frequency × multiplier	Voltage (V)	Temperature (°C)
700 MHz = 100 × 7.0	1.70	44
800 MHz = 100 × 8.0	1.75	45
824 MHz = 103 × 8.0	1.80	49
825 MHz = 110 × 7.5	1.80	49

Table 18.30. Test Stages While Overclocking Athlon 700

Parameters	Voltage (V)	POST routine	Windows	WinBench test
800 MHz = 100 × 8.0	1.700	Passed	Didn't boot	–
800 MHz = 100 × 8.0	1.725	Passed	Booted	Failed
800 MHz = 100 × 8.0	1.750	Passed	Booted	Failed
840 MHz = 105 × 8.0	1.800	Failed	–	–
840 MHz = 112 × 7.5	1.800	Failed	–	–

Overclocking Computers with AMD Duron (Thunderbird)

AMD Duron processors manufactured according to 0.18-micrometer technology have similar architecture to Athlon processors based on the same core, with the same operating frequencies of the EV6 bus. However, because of a smaller amount of the L2 cache memory, Duron processors are less powerful than their prototypes.

Duron manufactured according to the Socket A form factor has a fixed multiplier, which can be changed only by using specialized hardware and software. Not all motherboards support these functions. Therefore, Duron typically is overclocked by increasing the processor-bus frequency.

Features of the EV6 processor bus and motherboard architecture sometimes prevent large increases in clock frequency, even though Duron has significant technological reserve.

The results of analyzing Duron operation in overclocked modes are provided in the following sections.

Computer with Duron 650

System Configuration

❑ Processor — AMD Duron 650 (128 KB L1 cache, 64 KB L2 cache, full CPU core frequency operation, standard FSB frequency of 100 MHz, 1.5 V core supply, Socket A)

❑ Motherboard — Gigabyte GA-7ZM (VIA Apollo KT133 chipset)

❑ RAM — 128 MB, DIMM, PC133, SDRAM

❏ Hard disk — IBM DJNA 372200
❏ Video adapter — Creative 3DBlaster Annihilator Pro
❏ Sound card — Creative Sound Blaster Live!
❏ Operating system — Windows 98

Establishing Overclocking Modes

During overclocking, the system-bus frequency was increased from 100 MHz to 110 MHz. A further increase of the bus frequency resulted in system instability, which, presumably, was related to features of the EV6 processor bus and VIA Apollo KT133 chipset, used as the basis of the motherboard in these experiments.

Testing the System

Test results are provided in Table 18.31 and in Figs. 18.65 and 18.66.

Table 18.31. Results of Overclocking Duron 650

FSB frequency (MHz)	CPU frequency (MHz)	CPUmark 99 rating	FPU WinMark rating
100	650 = 100 × 6.5	55	3,520
105	683 = 105 × 6.5	58	3,695
110	715 = 110 × 6.5	61	3,870

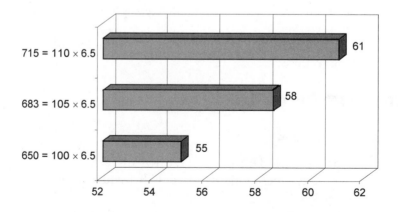

Fig. 18.65. Duron 650 test results (CPUmark 99)

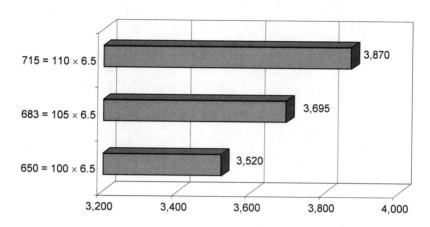

Fig. 18.66. Duron 650 test results (FPU WinMark)

Computer with Duron 600

System Configuration

❑ Processor — AMD Duron 600 (128 KB L1 cache, 64 KB on-die L2 cache, core frequency operation, standard FSB EV6 frequency of 100 MHz and a data-transfer rate of 200 MHz, 1.5 V core supply, Socket A with 462 pins)

❑ Motherboard 1 — Abit KT7 (VIA Apollo KT133, VT8363+VT82C686A chipset)

❑ Motherboard 2 — Soltek SL-75KV+ (VIA Apollo KT133, VT8363 +VT82C686A chipset)

❑ RAM — 128 MB, SDRAM, PC100

❑ Hard disk — IBM DPTA-372050 (20 GB, 2 MB cache memory, Ultra DMA/66)

❑ Video adapter — Asus AGP-V3800 TV (TNT2 video chipset, 32 MB video memory)

❑ Sound card — Creative Sound Blaster Live!

❑ Power supply unit — 250 W

❑ Operating system — Windows 98 Second Edition

Tests were conducted using CPUmark 99 and FPU WinMark from the WinBench 99 package.

Fig. 18.67. Duron 600 processor

Main Motherboard Parameters

The motherboards that were investigated are shown in Figs. 18.68 and 18.69.

Fig. 18.68. Soltek SL-75KV+ motherboard

- ❏ Supported processors — AMD Athlon (Thunderbird) and AMD Duron (Socket A processor slot with 462 pins, standard FSB frequency of 100 MHz)
- ❏ Overclocking — 100/103/105/110/112/115/120/124/133.3/140/150 MHz via Dual In-line Package (DIP) switches, 100/103/105/112/115/120/124 MHz via BIOS Setup
- ❏ Core voltage — 1.5 V–1.85 V, with an increment of 0.25 V
- ❏ Multiplier setup — DIP switches
- ❏ Chipset — VIA Apollo KT133 (VT8363+VT82C686A)
- ❏ RAM — Up to 768 MB in three DIMM modules (168 pin, 3.3 V), 100/133 MHz frequency
- ❏ BIOS — Award Plug-and-Play BIOS

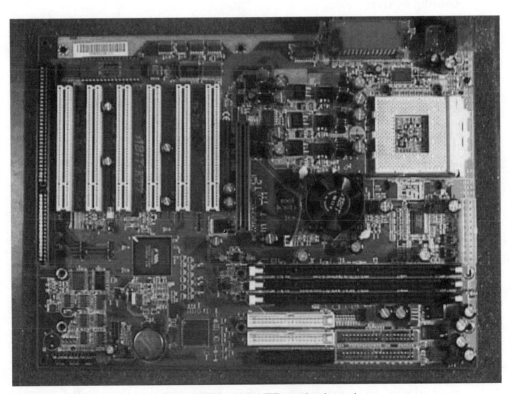

Fig. 18.69. Abit KT7 motherboard

- Supported processors — AMD Athlon (Thunderbird) and AMD Duron (Socket A processor slot with 462 pins, standard FSB frequency of 100 MHz)
- Overclocking — 100/101/103/105/107/110/112/115/117/120/122/124/127/133/ 136/140/145/150/155 MHz via BIOS Setup
- Core voltage — 1.1 V–1.85 V, with an increment of 0.25 V
- Multiplier setup — BIOS Setup
- Chipset — VIA Apollo KT133 (VT8363+VT82C686A)
- RAM — Up to 1.5 GB in three DIMM (168 pins, 3.3 V), PC100/133 SDRAM, 100/133 MHz frequency
- BIOS — Award Plug-and-Play BIOS

Cooling Devices

Titan TTC-D2T was used as a processor cooler (Fig. 18.70). This cooler ensures efficient cooling of Thunderbird-based Athlon and Duron. The fan is controlled by the built-in hardware-monitoring tools of the VT82C686A chip.

Fig. 18.70. Titan TTC-D2T cooler

The processor temperature is controlled using thermal sensors built into the motherboard and hardware-monitoring tools. The sensors in Soltek SL-75KV+ are flexible (Fig. 18.71); those in Abit KT7 are rigid (Fig. 18.72).

Fig. 18.71. Flexible thermal sensor on the Soltek SL-75KV+ motherboard

Fig. 18.72. Rigid thermal sensor on the Abit KT7 motherboard

Overclocking by Increasing the FSB Frequency

When using the Soltek SL-75KV+ motherboard, the clock frequency of the processor bus is set via one of the two DIP switches (SW1, marked in Fig. 18.73) and via BIOS Setup.

Fig. 18.73. DIP switches on the Soltek SL-75KV+ motherboard (SW1 is marked)

For Abit KT7, the frequency is selected in BIOS Setup via SoftMenu. When working with this motherboard, better results were obtained: The FSB clock frequency was increased to 115 MHz, as shown in Tables 18.32 and 18.33 and in Figs. 18.74–18.77.

Table 18.32. Results of Increasing the FSB Frequency for Duron 600 (Abit KT7)

Processor frequency = bus frequency × multiplier	CPUmark 99 rating	FPU WinMark rating
600 MHz = 100 × 6	51.4	3,260
672 MHz = 112 × 6	57.8	3,660
690 MHz = 115 × 6	59.4	3,760

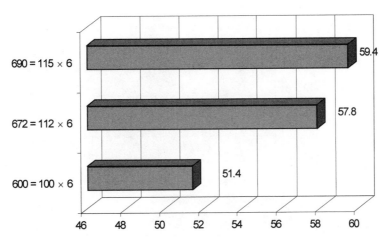

Fig. 18.74. Duron 600 (Abit KT7) after increasing the bus frequency (CPUmark 99)

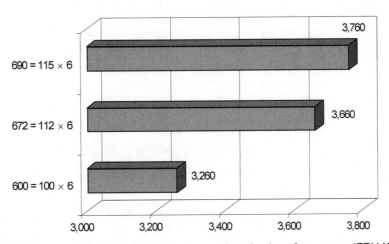

Fig. 18.75. Duron 600 (Abit KT7) after increasing the bus frequency (FPU WinMark)

Table 18.33. Results of Increasing the FSB Frequency for Duron 600 (Soltek SL-75KV+)

Processor frequency = bus frequency × multiplier	CPUmark 99 rating	FPU WinMark rating
600 MHz = 100 × 6	52.7	3,260
630 MHz = 105 × 6	55.4	3,430
672 MHz = 112 × 6	59.1	3,660

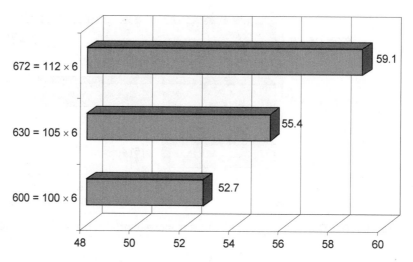

Fig. 18.76. Duron 600 (Soltek SL-75KV+) after increasing
the bus frequency (CPUmark 99)

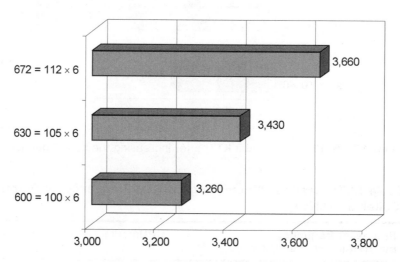

Fig. 18.77. Duron 600 (Soltek SL-75KV+) after increasing
the bus frequency (FPU WinMark)

Overclocking by Changing the Multiplier

Almost all contemporary processors are manufactured with fixed frequency multipliers. Nevertheless, with AMD processors, motherboards such as Soltek SL-75KV+ and Abit KT7 allow the multiplier to be changed. This is possible only with processors that have intact L1 bridges, located on the surface of the processor case.

If the L1 bridges on the processor case are cut, it is possible to restore the capability of changing the multiplier by closing the contacts. This operation can be accomplished easily, using a soft sharpened pencil with graphite, which has high conductivity. To restore disabled overclocking capabilities, rub the cut L1 bridges on the processor, pressing the pencil tight into the gaps to make small "hills." When performing this operation, avoid closing contacts between adjacent bridges. To control this operation visually, use a powerful magnifying glass and adequate lighting. Also, make sure that you observe all measures necessary to protect the processor from static electricity.

The results of restoring the conductivity of the L1 bridges are shown in Figs. 18.78 and 18.79, which illustrate fragments of the Duron surface.

After restoring the cut bridges on Duron, it becomes possible to change the frequency multiplier using the built-in functionality of the motherboards.

For Soltek SL-75KV+, the multiplier was chosen using the appropriate DIP switch (SW2, marked in Fig. 18.80).

Overclocking results, as well as the chosen modes, are presented in Tables 18.34 and 18.35 and in Figs. 18.81–18.84.

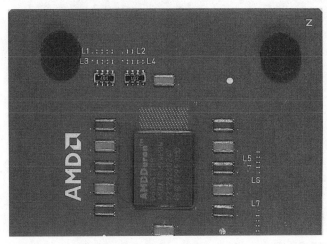

Fig. 18.78. Initial state of the L1 bridges on the Duron surface

Fig. 18.79. L1 bridges with restored contacts on Duron

Fig. 18.80. DIP switches on the Soltek SL-75KV+ motherboard (SW2 is marked)

Table 18.34. Results of Changing the Multiplier for Duron 600 (Abit KT7)

Processor frequency = bus frequency × multiplier	CPUmark 99 rating	FPU WinMark rating
600 MHz = 100 × 6.0	51.4	3,260
650 MHz = 100 × 6.5	55.0	3,550
700 MHz = 100 × 7.0	57.6	3,810
800 MHz = 100 × 8.0	63.2	4,350
850 MHz = 100 × 8.5	65.8	4,640
900 MHz = 100 × 9.0	68.3	4,900

Table 18.35. Results of Changing the Multiplier for Duron 600 (Soltek SL-75KV+)

Processor frequency = bus frequency × multiplier	CPUmark 99 rating	FPU WinMark rating
600 MHz = 100 × 6.0	52.7	3,260
650 MHz = 100 × 6.5	55.9	3,530
800 MHz = 100 × 8.0	65.0	4,350

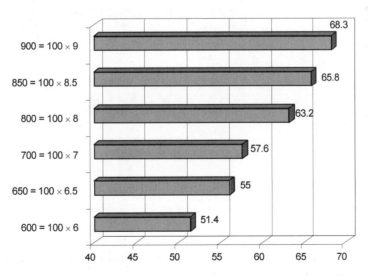

Fig. 18.81. Duron 600 (Abit KT7) after changing the multiplier (CPUmark 99)

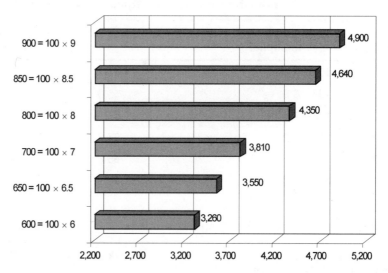

Fig. 18.82. Duron 600 (Abit KT7) after changing
the multiplier (FPU WinMark)

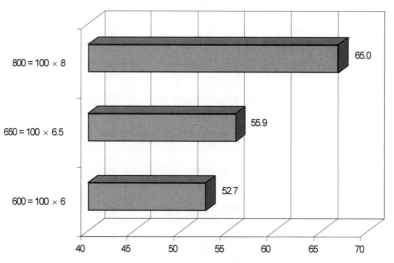

Fig. 18.83. Duron 600 (Soltek SL-75KV+) after changing
the multiplier (CPUmark 99)

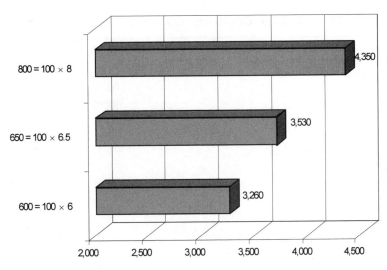

Fig. 18.84. Duron 600 (Soltek SL-75KV+) after changing
the multiplier (FPU WinMark)

Overclocking via the Bus and Multiplier

Maximum performance levels are achieved by choosing the optimal processor-bus frequency at the best value of the frequency multiplier.

Test results obtained when overclocking the processors on both motherboards are provided in Tables 18.36 and 18.37 and in Figs. 18.85–18.88.

Table 18.36. Results of Combined Overclocking of Duron 600 (Soltek SL-75KV+)

Processor frequency = bus frequency × multiplier	CPUmark 99 rating	FPU WinMark rating
600 MHz = 100 × 6.0	52.7	3,260
630 MHz = 105 × 6.0	55.4	3,430
650 MHz = 100 × 6.5	55.9	3,530
672 MHz = 112 × 6.0	59.1	3,660
683 MHz = 105 × 6.5	58.8	3,720
715 MHz = 110 × 6.5	61.6	3,890
800 MHz = 100 × 8.0	65.0	4,350
840 MHz = 105 × 8.0	68.4	4,580

Table 18.37. Results of Combined Overclocking of Duron 600 (Abit KT7)

Processor frequency = bus frequency × multiplier	CPUmark 99 rating	FPU WinMark rating
600 MHz = 100 × 6.0	51.4	3,260
650 MHz = 100 × 6.5	55.0	3,550
672 MHz = 112 × 6.0	57.8	3,660
683 MHz = 105 × 6.5	57.4	3,720
690 MHz = 115 × 6.0	59.4	3,760
700 MHz = 100 × 7.0	57.6	3,810
715 MHz = 110 × 6.5	60.2	3,890
748 MHz = 115 × 6.5	63.2	4,080
770 MHz = 110 × 7.0	63.5	4,190
800 MHz = 100 × 8.0	63.2	4,350
840 MHz = 105 × 8.0	66.7	4,580
850 MHz = 100 × 8.5	65.8	4,640
880 MHz = 110 × 8.0	69.9	4,790
893 MHz = 105 × 8.5	69.4	4,860
896 MHz = 112 × 8.0	71.2	4,880
900 MHz = 100 × 9.0	68.3	4,900
910 MHz = 107 × 8.5	70.9	4,980

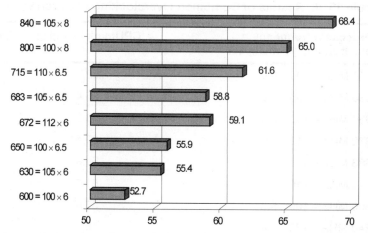

Fig. 18.85. Duron 600 (Soltek SL-75KV+) after combined overclocking (CPUmark 99)

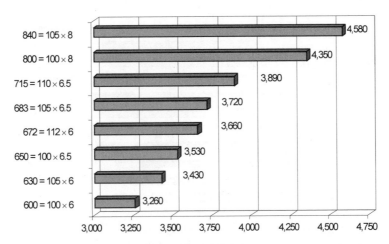

Fig. 18.86. Duron 600 (Soltek SL-75KV+) after combined
overclocking (FPU WinMark)

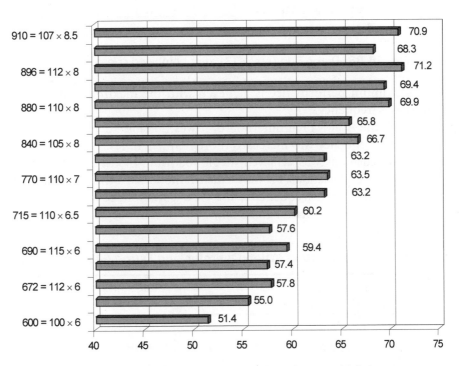

Fig. 18.87. Duron 600 (Abit KT7) after combined
overclocking (CPUmark 99)

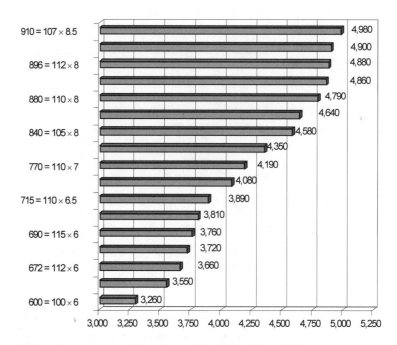

Fig. 18.88. Duron 600 (Abit KT7) after combined overclocking (FPU WinMark)

Maximum performance is achieved with the maximum multiplier and maximum bus frequency.

With the Abit KT7 motherboard, it was possible to achieve better results: The processor frequency was increased more than 1.5 times. Maximum performance of integer calculations was achieved in the following mode: 896 MHz = 112 × 8. For floating-point calculations, the most efficient mode had a CPU frequency of 910 MHz.

To achieve high frequencies, the CPU core voltage and input/output circuits had to be increased. Tables 18.38 and 18.39 specify the modes in which the voltage was raised.

Table 18.38. Parameters When Overclocking Duron 600 (Abit KT7)

Processor frequency = bus frequency × multiplier	Core voltage / I/O (V)	Temperature (°C)
600 MHz = 100 × 6.0	1.50/3.30	37
770 MHz = 110 × 7.0	1.60/3.40	41
850 MHz = 100 × 8.5	1.65/3.40	44

continues

Table 18.38 Continued

Processor frequency = bus frequency × multiplier	Core voltage/ I/O (V)	Temperature (°C)
880 MHz = 110 × 8.0	1.70/3.40	47
893 MHz = 105 × 8.5	1.70/3.40	48
900 MHz = 100 × 9.0	1.75/3.40	50
910 MHz = 107 × 8.5	1.75/3.40	50

Table 18.39. Parameters When Overclocking Duron 600 (Soltek SL-75KV+)

Processor frequency = bus frequency × multiplier	Core voltage/ I/O (V)	Temperature (°C)
600 MHz = 100 × 6	1.5/3.3	37
840 MHz = 105 × 8	1.6/3.4	43

Some overclocking attempts resulted in failures: The POST routine couldn't be accomplished successfully, the operating system wouldn't boot, or the computer hung up during the test. Variants in which at least the POST routine could be accomplished successfully are described in Table 18.40. From these data, it follows that, in most cases, the problem of unstable operation could be solved by increasing the core supply voltage. This increase would ensure a higher operating frequency of the processor. However, this seriously increases the risk of damaging the processor.

Table 18.40. Test Stages While Overclocking Duron 600 (Abit KT7)

Processor frequency = bus frequency × multiplier	Voltage (V)	POST routine	Windows	WinBench test
893 MHz = 110 × 8.5	1.650	Passed	Didn't boot (IOS error)	Not performed
893 MHz = 110 × 8.5	1.675	Passed	Didn't boot	Not performed
893 MHz = 110 × 8.5	1.700	Passed	Booted	Passed
800 MHz = 100 × 9.0	1.700	Passed	Booted	Failed
800 MHz = 100 × 9.0	1.750	Passed	Booted	Passed
927 MHz = 103 × 9.0	1.750	Passed	Didn't boot	Not performed
935 MHz = 110 × 8.5	1.750	Passed	Didn't boot	Not performed

Overclocking Computers with AMD Athlon XP

AMD Athlon XP represents further development of the Athlon line.

The architectures of these processors are based on Palomino (0.18 μm), Thoroughbred (0.13 μm), and Barton (0.13 μm) cores.

For the processor marking, a rating is used whose numeric value is different from the operating frequency.

Like its predecessors, Athlon XP has significant technological reserve that provides the possibility of improving performance with overclocking modes.

The results of investigations conducted for Athlon XP processors, analyzing performance gain obtained by overclocking, are provided in the following sections.

Computer with Athlon XP 1500+ (Palomino)

System Configuration

❏ Processor — AMD Athlon XP 1500+ (1.33 GHz CPU frequency, 128 KB L1 cache, 256 KB L2 cache, on-die, CPU core frequency operation, standard FSB EV6 frequency of 133 MHz, data-transfer rate of 266 MHz, 1.75 V core supply, Socket A with 462 pins)

❏ Motherboard — Abit AT7-MAX2 (VIA Apollo KT400 chipset)

❏ Hard disk — IBM 180GXP (120 GB, 2 MB cache memory, Ultra DMA/100)

❏ RAM — 512 MB, DDR266, Kingston

❏ Video adapter — Abit GeForce4 Ti4200, OTES, 128 MB, AGP 8x

❏ CD-ROM drive — Asus CD-S400/A (40x)

❏ Power supply unit — 300 W

❏ Operating system — Windows XP, Service Pack 1

Testing the System

The following tests were used: CPUmark 99, 3DMark2001 SE Pro, SiSoftware Sandra 2003, and SYSmark 2002 ICC. Besides this, the time required to encode a 14-minute-5-second music file into the MP3 format was measured. The test results are presented in Figs. 18.90–18.93.

Cooling Devices

Thermaltake Volcano 7 (Fig. 18.89) was used as a CPU cooler. This cooler ensures efficient cooling of Athlon and Duron. Furthermore, this cooler has built-in tools that control the fan rotation speed, depending on the temperature.

Fig. 18.89. Thermaltake Volcano 7 cooler

Establishing Overclocking Modes

The overclocking modes were set in BIOS Setup using SoftMenu III. The processor-bus frequency was increased to 145 MHz, which corresponds to a data-transfer rate of 290 MHz (2 × 145 MHz). As a result, the processor core started to operate like that of Athlon XP 1700+. (See Table 18.41 and Figs. 18.90–18.93.)

Table 18.41. Results of Overclocking Athlon XP 1500+

FSB frequency (MHz)	CPU frequency (MHz)	CPUmark 99 rating	3DMark2001 SE Pro rating	SiSoftware Sandra memory bandwidth benchmark	SYSmark 2002 ICC rating	MP3 encoding (sec)
133	1,333 = 133 × 10	124	9,073	1,971	175	39
145	1,450 = 145 × 10	134	9,597	2,151	195	34

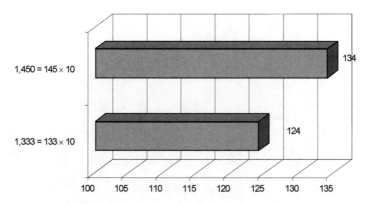

Fig. 18.90. Athlon XP 1500+ test results (CPUmark 99)

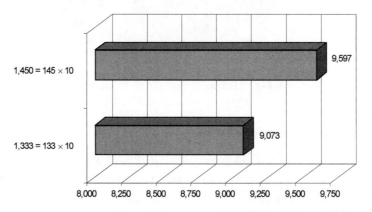

Fig. 18.91. Athlon XP 1500+ test results (3DMark2001 SE Pro)

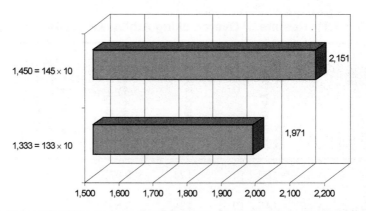

Fig. 18.92. Athlon XP 1500+ test results (SiSoftware Sandra memory bandwidth benchmark)

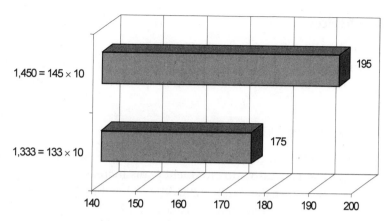

1,450 = 145 × 10   195

1,333 = 133 × 10   175

140   150   160   170   180   190   200

Fig. 18.93. Athlon XP 1500+ test results (SYSmark 2002 ICC)

Computer with Athlon XP 2200+ (Thoroughbred)

System Configuration

- ❏ Processor — AMD Athlon XP 2200+ (1.8 GHz CPU frequency, 128 KB L1 cache, 256 KB on-die L2 cache, core frequency operation, standard FSB EV6 frequency of 133 MHz, data-transfer rate of 266 MHz, 1.65 V core supply, Socket A with 462 pins)
- ❏ Motherboard — Abit AT7-MAX2 (VIA Apollo KT400 chipset)
- ❏ Hard disk — IBM 180GXP (120 GB, 2 MB cache memory, Ultra DMA/100)
- ❏ RAM — 512 MB, DDR266, Kingston
- ❏ Video adapter — Abit GeForce4 Ti4200, OTES, 128 MB, AGP, 8x
- ❏ CD-ROM drive — Asus CD-S400/A (40x)
- ❏ Power supply unit — 300 W
- ❏ Operating system — Windows XP, Service Pack 1

Testing the System

The following testing software was used in performance analysis: CPUmark 99, 3DMark2001 SE Pro, and SYSmark 2002 ICC. Besides this, the time required to encode a 14-minute-5-second music file into the MP3 format was determined. Test results are presented in Figs. 18.94–18.96.

Cooling Devices

Thermaltake Volcano 7 (shown in Fig. 18.89) was used to cool the processor. This cooler ensures efficient cooling of Athlon and Duron. Furthermore, this cooler has built-in tools that control the fan rotation speed, depending on the temperature.

Establishing Overclocking Modes

The overclocking modes were established in BIOS Setup using the SoftMenu III technology. The processor-bus frequency was increased to 145 MHz, which corresponds to a data-transfer rate of 290 MHz (2 × 145 MHz). As a result, the CPU core began to operate like that of Athlon XP 2400+. The internal CPU frequency was increased from 1.8 GHz to 1.96 GHz. (See Table 18.42 and Figs. 18.94–18.96.)

Table 18.42. Results of Overclocking Athlon XP 2200+

FSB frequency (MHz)	CPU frequency (MHz)	CPUmark 99 rating	3DMark2001 SE Pro rating	SYSmark 2002 ICC rating	MP3 encoding (sec)
133	1,800 = 133 × 13.5	156	9,883	218	29
145	1,960 = 145 × 13.5	170	10,467	237	27

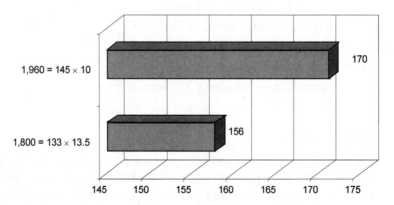

Fig. 18.94. Athlon XP 2200+ test results (CPUmark 99)

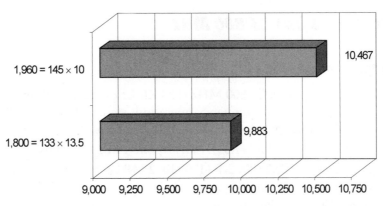

Fig. 18.95. Athlon XP 2200+ test results (3DMark2001 SE Pro)

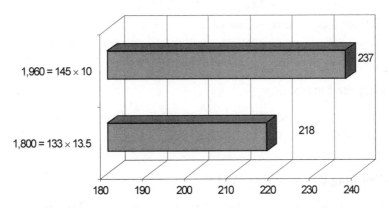

Fig. 18.96. Athlon XP 2200+ test results (SYSmark 2002 ICC)

Overclocking Computers with VIA C3

VIA C3 saw the development of the VIA Cyrix III line. The bases of VIA C3 processors are cores such as Samuel2, Ezra, Ezra-T, and Nehemiah. Because of their 0.13-micrometer technology, the development of these processors is characterized by increased operating frequency, low heat emission, and reduced supply voltage. For example, the Ezra core's supply voltage is 1.35 V, lower than this parameter for Samuel2 (1.6 V). VIA C3 processors are characterized by low power consumption, which allows them to use coolers without fans.

VIA C3 processors have significant technological reserve that allows increases in performance through overclocking modes.

Computer with VIA C3 800 MHz

System Configuration

- ❑ Processor — VIA C3 800 MHz (128 KB L1 cache, 64 KB on-die L2 cache memory, processor core frequency operation, standard FSB frequency of 133 MHz, 1.35 V core supply, Socket 370, 0.13-micrometer technology)
- ❑ Motherboard — FIC FR33E (VIA Apollo PLE133T chipset)
- ❑ Hard disk — IBM 180GXP (120 GB, 2 MB cache memory, Ultra DMA/100)
- ❑ RAM — 256 MB, PC133, SDRAM
- ❑ Video adapter — Trident Blade3D
- ❑ CD-ROM drive — Asus CD-S400/A (40x)
- ❑ Power supply unit — 250 W
- ❑ Operating system — Windows 2000 Server, Service Pack 2

Testing the System

The tests from the WinBench 99 v2.0 package were used for testing and performance analysis.

Establishing Overclocking Modes

The overclocking modes were set using BIOS Setup. The processor-bus frequency was increased to 150 MHz. The frequency increase was 100 MHz.

Test results are presented in Tables 18.43 and 18.44 and in Figs. 18.97–18.99.

Table 18.43. Results of Overclocking VIA C3 800 MHz (specialized programs)

Frequency (MHz)	$800 = 133 \times 6$	$840 = 140 \times 6$	$900 = 150 \times 6$
CPUmark 99 rating	45.1	47.5	51.2
FPU WinMark rating	1,550	1,630	1,750
Disk access time	9.46	9.48	9.44
Disk CPU utilization	13.8	13.1	12.3
WinMark 99 high-end disk rating	10,100	11,200	11,400
WinMark 99 business disk rating	2,520	2,590	2,900

Table 18.44. Results of Overclocking VIA C3 800 MHz (standard programs)

Frequency (MHz)	$800 = 133 \times 6$	$840 = 140 \times 6$	$900 = 150 \times 6$
AVS/Express 3.4	11,600	11,800	12,500
FrontPage 98	13,300	15,400	19,200
MicroStation SE	9,340	10,900	10,600
Overall	10,100	11,200	11,400
Photoshop 4.0	8,140	8,240	8,170
Premiere 4.2	9,830	12,800	9,720
Sound Forge 4.0	16,500	17,400	17,100
Visual C++ 5.0	7,060	7,850	9,660

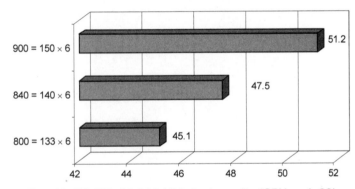

Fig. 18.97. VIA C3 800 MHz test results (CPUmark 99)

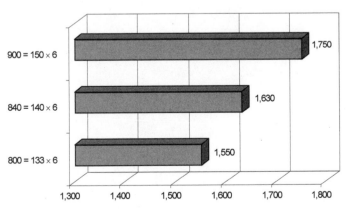

Fig. 18.98. VIA C3 800 MHz test results (FPU WinMark)

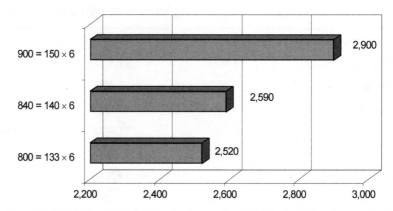

Fig. 18.99. VIA C3 800 MHz test results (WinMark 99 business disk)

Chapter 19

Recommended Web Sites

When fine-tuning and optimizing a computer by planning and accomplishing over-clocking and anti-overclocking, you must consult the documentation supplied with your computer system and with its components, such as the processor and mother-board. It also may be useful to visit some of the Web sites listed here.

Optimization and Overclocking

rudteam.narod.ru/english/index.html
www.anandtech.com
www.digit-life.com
www.digital-daily.com
www.gamers.com
www.hwupgrade.com *(archived articles in English)*
www.kryotech.com
www.phoenix.com/en/home/
www.sysopt.com
www.tomshardware.com
www.xbitlabs.com

Cooling Methods and Facilities

rudteam.narod.ru/english/index.html

www.aptekus.com

www.avc.com.tw

www.bergquistcompany.com

www.computernerd.com

www.coolermaster.com

www.digit-life.com

www.digital-daily.com

www.dynatron-corp.com

www.etrinet.com

www.globalwin.com.tw

www.heatsink-guide.com

www.indek.com

www.kryotech.com

www.melcor.com

www.sanyodenki.co.jp/index_e.html

www.sunon.com/english/index.htm

www.supercool.se

www.tennmax.com

www.thermalloy.com

www.titan-cd.com

www.tomshardware.com

www.wakefield.com

www.xbitlabs.com

Technical Characteristics of Components

Processors and Chipsets

rudteam.narod.ru/english/index.html

www.ali.com.tw

www.amd.com

www.anandtech.com

www.digit-life.com

www.digital-daily.com

www.ibm.com *and*

www-3.ibm.com/chips/index.html

www.idt.com

www.intel.com *and* developer.intel.com

www.opti-inc.com

www.sis.com

www.tomshardware.com

www.viatech.com

www.xbitlabs.com

Motherboards

rudteam.narod.ru/english/index.html

www.abit.com.tw

www.acer.com

www.achme.com.tw

www.acorp.com.tw

www.anandtech.com

www.aopen.com.tw

www.asus.com

www.bcmcom.com

www.biostar.com.tw

www.chaintech.com.tw

www.dfi.com

www.dfiusa.com

www.digit-life.com

www.digital-daily.com

www.dtk.com.tw

www.ecsusa.com

www.epox.com

www.fic.com.tw

www.freetech.com

www.giga-byte.com

www.intel.com

www.iwillusa.com

www.j-mark.com

www.jetway.com.tw

www.mitac.com

www.mpl.ch

www.msi.com.tw

www.mtiusa.com

www.opti-inc.com

www.pcchips.com

www.pcpartner.com.hk

www.pcware.com

www.pinegroup.com

www.premiopc.com

www.qdigrp.com *and* www.qdi.nl

www.shuttle.com

www.soyo.com

www.supermicro.com

www.tomshardware.com

www.tyan.com

www.xbitlabs.com

www.zida.com

Video Adapters and Video Chipsets

rudteam.narod.ru/english/index.html

www.aceshardware.com

www.anandtech.com

www.asus.com

www.atitech.ca

www.chaintech.com.tw

www.cirrus.com

www.digit-life.com

www.digital-daily.com

www.hercules.com

www.intel.com

www.matrox.com

www.nvidia.com

www.tomshardware.com

www.tridentmicro.com

www.xbitlabs.com

Hard Disks

rudteam.narod.ru/english/index.html

www.digit-life.com

www.digital-daily.com

www.fujitsu.com

www.maxtor.com/en/index.htm

www.quantum.com

www.seagate.com

www.storage.ibm.com

www.wdc.com

www.xbitlabs.com

Index

T